M000159538

Choose Your WoW!

A Disciplined Agile Delivery Handbook for Optimizing
Your Way of Working

Scott W. Ambler and Mark Lines

Dedication

To Beverley and Olivia, the best family I could have hoped for.
To Mark and Louise Lines, who have been fantastic partners to work with.

- Scott

First and foremost, Louise, Brian, and Katherine, thank you for everything, for your love, support, and understanding. To Scott for being my partner on this journey. I am humbled and proud to work with you. And last but not least for the "early adopters" of Disciplined Agile. Your feedback and sharing of your successes and challenges have been instrumental in helping us to advance DA in the interests of all.

- Mark

Copyright © 2019 Disciplined Agile Consortium
All rights reserved.
ISBN: 978-1790447848

Version: 1.1

FOREWORD

"All models are wrong but some are useful"
George Box, 1978

You are special, you are a beautiful and unique snowflake. So are your family, your friends, your communities, your team, your peers, your colleagues, your business area, your organisation. No other organisation has the same collections of people, the same behavioural norms, the same processes, the same current state, the same impediments, the same customers, the same brand, the same values, the same history, the same folklore, the same identity, the same 'this is the way we do things round here', as yours does.

Your organisation's behaviour is emergent. The whole is greater than the sum of the parts, the whole has unique properties that the individuals don't have. Acting in the space, changes the space. Individual and collective behaviours mutate and self-organise on a change-initiating event. Interventions are irreversible, like adding milk to coffee. The system changes. People don't forget what happened and what the outcome was. The system learns. Next time, the response to the change event will be different, either for the better or for the worse, reflecting what happened last time and based on incentivisation. Not only are your contexts unique, they are constantly changing and changing how they change.

With this uniqueness, emergence and adaptation, it is not possible to have one set of practices which will optimise outcomes for every context. One set of practices might improve outcomes for one context at one point in time. Over time as the system changes with new impediments and new enablers, it will no longer be optimal. One size does not fit all. There is no snake oil to cure all ills. Your organisation has tens, hundreds or thousands of contexts within contexts, each one unique. Applying one-size-fits-all across many contexts may raise some boats, however it will sink other boats and hold back many more boats from rising.

How practices are adopted is also important not only what the practices are. For lasting improvement and to apply an agile mindset to agility, the locus of control needs to be internal. People need to have autonomy and empowerment within guardrails to be able to experiment in order to improve on desired outcomes. High alignment and high autonomy are both needed. Not an imposition top down, which is disempowering, with the locus of control being external. With imposition people will not take responsibility for what happens, and will knowingly do things which are detrimental, a behaviour known as Agentic State.

Disciplined Agile is designed to cater to these realities, the characteristics of uniqueness, emergence and adaption. Disciplined Agile provides guardrails, guidance and enterprise awareness. It is unique in this regard. It provides a common vocabulary, minimal viable guardrails, which in turn enables empowerment and autonomy for teams and teams of teams to improve on their outcomes how they see fit, with an internal locus of control. Not everyone should follow a mandated synchronised iteration based approach, for example. In my experience, in a large organisation with more than one context, synchronised iterations suit one context (e.g. many teams on one product with a low level of mastery and with dependencies which have not been removed or alleviated) and do not suit 99 other contexts. It is not applying an agile mindset to agility. Some business areas are better off adopting a Kanban Method approach from the beginning, especially if there is a pathological culture where messengers are shot. Evolution over revolution stands a chance of progress.

Revolution will struggle, with a lack of psychological safety, the antibodies will be strong. Some business areas, with people who have been working this way in islands of agility for 20+ years and with psychological safety, may choose to take a more revolutionary approach as the soil is more fertile, people are more willing, failed experiments are viewed positively.

Disciplined Agile enables a heterogeneous, not homogeneous, approach across diverse, complex, organisations. It includes Principles "Choice is Good", "Context Counts", "Pragmatism" and "Enterprise Awareness". It enables the discipline that organisations need, whilst not forcing round pegs into square holes. It provides a common vocabulary and with the process goals it provides options to consider in your unique context with varying levels of mastery. This requires people to think rather than follow orders, to take ownership and experiment to achieve specific outcomes, not pursue agile for agile's sake. This is harder than following prescription or following a diktat, it requires servant leadership and coaching, in the same way as learning to drive, ski, play a musical instrument, play in an orchestra or in a team sport. As one size does not fit all, as there is no prescription (for example it is a fallacy to copy 'the Spotify Model' firm-wide, which even Spotify say is not the Spotify Model), this context sensitive, invitation over imposition, approach leads to better outcomes and is more likely to stick as it has come from within, the locus of control is internal, it is owned. There is no one else to blame and no one artificially keeping the elastic band stretched. It starts to build a muscle of continuous improvement.

Within Disciplined Agile, if teams choose to adopt Scrum, a Scrum scaled pattern such as LeSS, SAFe, Nexus, Scrum at Scale or adopt an evolutionary pull based limited work in progress approach, with a view that it will optimise outcomes in their unique context, they are free to do so. #allframeworks, not #noframeworks or #oneframework. Across an organisation DA provides the minimal viable commonality as well as guidance, which is needed for anything other than the simplest of firms.

The job you are hiring Disciplined Agile to do is to enable context-sensitive heterogeneous approaches to agility, which will maximise outcomes, organisation-wide. As with everything, treat it as a departure point, not a destination. As your organisation-wide level of mastery increases, keep on inspecting and adapting. This book is an indispensable guide for those looking to optimise ways of working in heterogeneous organisations.

Jonathan Smart @jonsmart
Enterprise Agility Lead, Deloitte
Former Head of Ways of Working, Barclays

PREFACE

Software development is incredibly straightforward, and if we may be so bold, it is very likely the simplest endeavor in modern organizations. It requires very little technical skill at all, requires little to no collaboration on the part of developers, and is so mundane and repetitive that anyone can create software by following a simple, repeatable process. The handful of software development techniques were established and agreed to decades ago, are easily learned in only a few days, and are both well-accepted and well-known by all software practitioners. Our stakeholders can clearly communicate their needs early in the lifecycle, are readily available and eager to work with us, and never change their minds. The software and data sources created in the past are high quality, easy to understand and to evolve, and come with fully automated regression test suites and high-quality supporting documentation. Software development teams always have complete control of their destiny, and are supported by effective corporate governance, procurement, and financing practices that reflect and enable the realities we face. And of course it is easy to hire and retain talented software developers.

Sadly, very little if anything in the previous paragraph is even remotely similar to the situation faced by your organization today. Software development is complex, the environments in which software developers work is complex, the technologies that we work with are complex and constantly changing, and the problems that we are asked to solve are complex and evolving. It is time to embrace this complexity, to accept the situation that we face, and to choose to deal with it head on.

Why You Need to Read This Book

One of the agile principles is that a team should regularly reflect and strive to improve their strategy. One way to do that is the sailboat retrospective game, where we ask what are the anchors holding us back, what rocks or storms should we watch out for, and what is the wind in our sails that will propel us to success. So let's play this game for current state of agile product development in the context of someone, presumably you, who is hoping to help their team choose and evolve their way of working (WoW).

First, there are several things that are potentially holding us back:

- **Product development is complex**. As IT professionals we get paid a lot of money because what we do is complex. Our WoW must address how to approach requirements, architecture, testing, design, programming, management, deployment, governance, and many other aspects of software/product development in a myriad of ways. And it must describe how to do this throughout the entire lifecycle from beginning to end, and it must address the unique situation that our team faces. In many ways this book holds up a mirror to the complexities faced by software developers and provides a flexible, context sensitive toolkit to deal with it.

- **Agile industrial complex (AIC)**. Martin Fowler, in a conference keynote in Melbourne in August 2018, coined the phrase "agile industrial complex" [Fowler]. He argued that we are now in the era of the AIC, with prescriptive frameworks being routinely imposed upon teams as well as upon the entire organization, presumably to provide management with a modicum of control over this crazy agile stuff. In such environments a set of processes defined by the chosen framework will now be "deployed" – whether it makes sense for your team or not. We are

iv

deploying this, you will like it, you will own it – but don't dream of trying to change or improve it because management is hoping to "limit the variability of team processes." As Cynefin advises, you can't solve a complex problem by applying a simple solution [Cynefin].

- **Agile growth greatly exceeded the supply of experienced coaches**. Although there are some great agile coaches out there, unfortunately their numbers are insufficient to address the demand. Effective coaches have great people skills and years of experience, not days of training, in the topic that they are coaching you in. In many organizations we find coaches who are effectively learning on the jobs, in many ways similar to college professors who are reading one chapter ahead of their students – They can address the straightforward problems but struggle with anything too far beyond what the AIC processes inflicted upon them deign to address.

There are also several things to watch out for that could cause us to run aground:

- **False promises**. You may have heard agile coaches claim to achieve 10x productivity increases through adoption of agile, yet are unable to provide any metrics to back up these claims. Or perhaps you've read a book that claims in it's title that Scrum enables you to do twice the work in half the time [Sutherland]? Yet the reality is that organizations are seeing on average closer to 7 to 12 percent improvements on small teams and 3 to 5 percent improvements on teams working at scale [Reifer].

- **More silver bullets**. How do you kill a werewolf? A single shot with a silver bullet. In the mid-1980s Fred Brook taught us that there is no single change that you can make in the software development space, no technology that you can buy, no process you can adopt, no tool you can install, that will give you the order of magnitude productivity improvement that you're likely hoping for [Brooks]. In other words, there's no silver bullet for software development, regardless of the promises of the schemes where you become a "Certified Master" after two days of training, a Program Consultant after four days of training, or any other quick fix promises. What you do need are skilled, knowledgeable, and hopefully experienced people working together effectively.

- **Process populism**. We often run into organizations where leadership's decision making process when it comes to software process boils down to "ask Gartner what's popular" or "what are my competitors adopting?" rather than what is the best fit for our situation. Process populism is fed by false promises and leadership's hope to find a silver bullet to the very significant challenges that they face around improving their organization's processes. Most agile methods and frameworks are prescriptive, regardless of their marketing claims – when you're given a handful of techniques out of the thousands that exist, and not given explicit options for tailoring those techniques, that's pretty much as prescriptive as it gets. We appreciate that many people just want to be told what to do, but unless that method/framework actually addresses the real problem that you face then adopting it likely isn't going to do much to help the situation.

Luckily there are several things that are the "winds in our sails" that propel you to read this book:

- **It embraces your uniqueness**. This book recognizes that your team is unique and faces a unique situation. No more false promises of a "one size fits all" process that requires significant, and risky, disruption to adopt.

v

- **It embraces the complexity you face**. This book effectively holds up a mirror to the inherent complexities of solution delivery, and presents an accesible representation to help guide your process improvement efforts. No more simplistic, silver bullet methods or process frameworks that gloss over the myriad of challenges your organizations faces because to do so wouldn't fit in well with the certification training they're hoping to sell you.
- **It provides explicit choices**. This book provides the tools you need to make better process decisions that in turn will lead to better outcomes. In short, it enables your team to own their own process, to choose their way of working (WoW), that reflects the overall direction of your organization. This book presents a proven strategy for guided continuous improvement (GCI), a team-based process improvement strategy rather than naïve adoption of a "populist process."
- **It provides agnostic advice**. This book isn't limited to the advice of a single framework or method, nor is it limited to agile and lean. Our philosophy is to look for great ideas regardless of their source and to recognize that there are no best practices (nor worst practices). When we learn a new technique we strive to understand what it's strengths and weaknesses are and in what situations to (not) apply it.

In our training we often get comments like "I wish I knew this five years ago", "I wish my Scrum coaches knew this now", "Going into this workshop I thought I knew everything about agile development, boy was I wrong." We suspect you're going to feel the exact same way about this book.

How This Book is Organized

This book is organized into six sections:

1. **Disciplined Agile Delivery in a Nutshell**. This section works through fundamental strategies to choose and evolve your WoW, the Disciplined Agile mindset, overviews DAD, describes typical roles and responsibilities of people on DAD teams, describes process goal/outcome-driven approach that makes your process choices explicit, and shows how DAD supports several lifecycles that share a common governance strategy.
2. **Successfully initiating your team**. This section is a reference lookup for agile, lean, and sometimes traditional techniques for initiating a solution delivery team/project in a streamlined manner. The tradeoffs of each technique are summarized so that your team can choose the most appropriate techniques that you can handle given the situation that you face. Better decisions lead to better outcomes.
3. **Producing business value**. Similar to Section 2, this is also a reference lookup describing a large collection of techniques available to you that are focused on Construction of a software-based product solution.
4. **Releasing into production**. You guessed it, this is a reference lookup for techniques for successfully releasing your solution into production or the marketplace.
5. **Sustaining and enhancing your team**. This section is a reference lookup for techniques that are applicable throughout the entire lifecycle, such as strategies to support the personal growth of team members, strategies to coordinate both within

your team and with other teams, and strategies to evolve your WoW as you learn over time.

6. **Summary and back matter**. A few parting thoughts, an appendix describing the rest of the DA toolkit, an appendix describing a respectable certification strategy for DA practitioners, a list of abbreviations, references, and an index.

How to Read This Book

Read the first section in it's entirety as it describes the fundamental concepts of guided continuous improvement (GCI) and the DAD portion of the Disciplined Agile (DA) toolkit. Then use the rest of the book as a reference handbook to help to inform your efforts in choosing and evolving your WoW. Sections Two through Five overview hundreds of techniques, and more importantly describe when you should consider using them, and thereby will prove to be an invaluable reference for your improvement efforts.

Who This Book is For

This book is for people who want to improve their team's WoW. It's for people who are willing to think outside of the "agile box" and experiment with new WoWs regardless of their agile purity. It's for people who realize that context counts, that everyone faces a unique situation and will work in their own unique way, that one process does not fit all. It's for people who realize that, although they are in a unique situation, others have faced similar situations before and have figured out a variety of strategies that you can adopt and tailor – you can reuse the process learnings of others and thereby invest your energies into adding critical business value to your organization.

Our aim in writing this book is to provide a comprehensive reference for Disciplined Agile Delivery (DAD). It is a replacement for our first DAD book, Disciplined *Agile Delivery: A Practitioner's Guide to Agile Software Delivery in the Enterprise* which was published in 2012. DAD has evolved considerably since then so it's time for an update. Here it is.

Acknowledgements

We would like to thank Beverley Ambler, Joshua Barnes, Klaus Boedker, Kiron Bondale, Tom Boulet, Paul Carvalho, Chris Celsie, Daniel Gagnon, Drennan Govender, Bjorn Gustafsson, Michelle Harrison, Michael Kogan, Katherine Lines, Louise Lines, Glen Little, Valentin Tudor Mocanu, Maciej Mordaka, Charlie Mott, Jerry Nicholas, Edson Portilho, Simon Powers, Aldo Rall, Frank Schophuizen, David Shapiro, Paul Sims, Jonathan Smart, Roly Stimson, Klaas van Gend, Abhishek Vernal, and Jaco Viljoen for all of their input and hard work that they invested to help us write this book. We couldn't have done it without you.

CONTENTS

SECTION 1: DISCIPLINED AGILE DELIVERY IN A NUTSHELL

This section is organized into the following chapters:

- **Chapter 1: Choosing Your WoW!** Overview of how to apply this book.
- **Chapter 2: Being Disciplined.** Values, principles, and philosophies for Disciplined Agilists.
- **Chapter 3: Disciplined Agile Delivery in a Nutshell.** An overview of DAD.
- **Chapter 4: Roles, Rights, and Responsibilities**. Individuals and interactions.
- **Chapter 5: The Process Goals.** How to focus on process outcomes rather than conform to process prescriptions.
- **Chapter 6: Choosing the Right Lifecycle.** How teams can work in unique ways, yet still be governed consistently.

1 CHOOSING YOUR WOW!

A man's pride can be his downfall, and he needs to learn when to turn to others for support and guidance. - Bear Grylls

Welcome to *Choose Your WoW!*, the book about how agile software development teams, or more accurately agile/lean solution delivery teams, can choose their way of working (WoW). This chapter describes some fundamental concepts around why choosing your WoW is important, fundamental strategies for how to do so, and how this book can help you to become effective at it.

Why Should Teams Choose Their WoW?

Agile teams are commonly told to own their process, to choose their WoW. This is very good advice for several reasons:

- **Context counts.** People and teams will work differently depending on the context of their situation. Every person is unique, every team is unique, and every team finds itself in a unique situation. A team of five people will work differently than a team of twenty, than a team of fifty. A team in a life-critical regulatory situation will work

> **Key Points in this Chapter**
> - Disciplined Agile Delivery (DAD) teams have the autonomy to choose their way of working (WoW).
> - You need to both "be agile" and know how to "do agile."
> - Software development is complicated, there's no easy answer for how to do it.
> - Disciplined Agile (DA) provides the scaffolding – a toolkit of agnostic advice – to choose your WoW.
> - Other people have faced, and overcome, similar challenges to yours. DA enables you to leverage their learnings.
> - You can use this book to guide how to initially choose your WoW and then evolve it over time.
> - The real goal is to effectively achieve desired organizational outcomes, not to be/do agile.
> - Better decisions lead to better outcomes.

differently than a team in a non-regulatory situation. Our team will work differently than your team because we're different people with our own unique skillsets, preferences, and backgrounds.

- **Choice is good.** To be effective a team must be able to choose the practices and strategies to address the situation that they face. The implication is that they need to know what these choices are, what the trade-offs are of each, and when (not) to apply each one. In other words, they either need to have a deep background in software process, something that few people have, or have a good guide to help them make these process-related choices. Luckily this book is a very good guide.

- **We should optimize flow.** We want to be effective in the way that we work, and ideally to delight our customers/Stakeholders in doing so. To do this we need to optimize the workflow within our team and in how we collaborate with other teams across the organization.

- **We want to be awesome.** Who wouldn't want to be awesome at what they do? Who wouldn't want to work on an awesome team or for an awesome organization? A significant part of being awesome is to enable teams to choose their WoW and to allow them to constantly experiment to identify even better ways they can work.

3

In short, we believe that it's time to take back agile. Martin Fowler recently coined the term "agile industrial complex" to refer to the observation that many teams are following a "faux agile" strategy, sometimes called "agile in name only" (AINO). This is often the result of organizations adopting a prescriptive framework, such as SAFe, and then forcing teams to adopt it regardless of whether it actually makes sense to do so (and it rarely does). Or forcing teams to follow an organizational standard application of Scrum. Yet canonical agile is very clear, it's individuals and interactions over processes and tools – teams should be allowed, and better yet supported, to choose and then evolve their WoW.

You Need to "Be Agile" AND Know How To "Do Agile"

Scott's daughter Olivia is eight years old. She and her friends are some of the most agile people we've ever met. They're respectful (as much as eight year olds can be), they're open minded, they're collaborative, they're eager to learn, and they're always experimenting. They clearly embrace an agile mindset, yet if we were to ask them to develop software it would be a disaster. Why? Because they don't have the skills. They could gain these skills in time, but right now they just don't know what they're doing when it comes to software development. We've also seen teams made up of millennials who collaborate very naturally and have the skills to develop solutions, although perhaps are not yet sufficiently experienced to understand the enterprise-class implications of their work. And of course we've seen teams of developers with decades of IT experience but very little experience doing so collaboratively. None of these situations are ideal. Our point is that it's absolutely critical to have an agile mindset, to "be agile," but you also need to have the requisite skills to "do agile" and the experience to "do enterprise agile." An important aspect of this book is that it comprehensively addresses the potential skills required by agile/lean teams to succeed.

The real goal is to effectively achieve desired organizational outcomes, not to be/do agile. What good is it to be working in an agile manner if you're producing the wrong thing, or producing something you already have, or are producing something that doesn't fit into the overall direction of your organization? Our real focus must be on achieving the outcomes that will make our organization successful, and becoming more effective in our WoW will help us to do that.

Accept That There's No Easy Answer

Software development, or more accurately solution delivery, is complex. You need to be able to initiate a team, produce a solution that meets the needs of your Stakeholders, then successfully release it to them. You need to know how to explore their needs, architect and design a solution, develop that solution, validate it, and deploy it. This must be done within the context of your organization, using a collection of technologies that are evolving, and for a wide variety of business needs. And you're doing this with teams of people with different backgrounds, different preferences, different experiences, different career goals, and they may report to a different group or even a different organization than you do.

We believe in embracing this complexity because it's the only way to be effective, and better yet, to be awesome. When we ignore important aspects of our WoW, say architecture for example, we tend to make painful mistakes in that area. When we denigrate aspects of our WoW, such as governance, perhaps because we've had bad experiences in the past with not-so-agile governance, then we risk people outside of our team taking responsibility for that aspect and inflicting their non-agile practices upon us. In this way, rather than enabling our agility, they act as impediments.

4

We Can Benefit from the Learnings of Others

A common mistake that teams make is that they believe that just because they face a unique situation that they need to figure out their WoW from scratch. Nothing could be further from the truth. When you develop a new application do you develop a new language, a new compiler, new code libraries, and so on from scratch? Of course not, you adopt the existing things that are out there, combine them in a unique way, and then modify them as needed. Development teams, regardless of technology, utilize proven frameworks and libraries to improve productivity and quality. It should be the same thing with process. As you can see in this book, there are hundreds if not thousands of practices and strategies out there that have been proven in practice by thousands of teams before you. You don't need to start from scratch, but instead can develop your WoW by combining existing practices and strategies and then modifying them appropriately to address the situation at hand. DA provides the toolkit to guide you through this in a streamlined and accessible manner. Since our first book on DAD [AmblerLines2012], we have received feedback that while it is seen as an extremely rich collection of strategies and practices, practitioners sometimes struggle to understand how to reference the strategies and apply them. One of the goals of this book is to make DAD more accessible so that you can easily find what you need to customize your WoW.

One thing that you'll notice throughout the book is that we provide a lot of references. We do this for three reasons: First, to give credit where credit is due. Second, to let you know where you can go for further details. Third, to enable us to focus on summarizing the various techniques and to put them into context, rather than going into the details of every single one. The goal is to make you aware of what techniques are available, and the tradeoffs of each based on context. You can then find other detailed information on how to apply a technique elsewhere. For example, we will identify and compare test-driven development (TDD) to test-after development as potential techniques to experiment with, and then you can do further research into your chosen option. Here is our approach to references:

- **[W]**. This indicates that there is a Wikipedia page for the concept at wikipedia.org. Having said that, many of these pages could use some work. Our hope is that readers such as yourself will step up and help to evolve these pages so as to share our expertise with the rest of the world.

- **[MeaningfulName]**. There is a corresponding entry in the references at the back of the book. This is an indication that either we couldn't find an appropriate Wikipedia page or that we had a detailed article on the subject already. Either way, we'd really like to see Wikipedia pages developed for these topics so please consider starting one if you're knowledgeable about that topic. Also feel free to reach out to us as we'd be happy to donate appropriate material to help seed the effort.

- **[W, MeaningfulNames]**. This indicates Wikipedia has a good page, plus there are a few more resources that we recommend. Please consider updating the Wikipedia page though.

- **No reference**. When a technique is a practice, such as TDD, we can often find a solid reference for it. When the technique is a strategy, such as testless programming, then it's difficult to find a reference for it. So please consider writing a blog about that strategy that we could refer to in the future.

5

DA Knowledge Makes You a Far More Valuable Team Member

We have heard from many DA organizations and they permit us to quote them, that Team Members who have invested in learning DA (and proving it through challenging certifications) become more valuable contributors. The reason to us is quite clear. Understanding a larger library of proven strategies means that teams will make better

decisions and "fail fast" less, and rather "learn and succeed earlier". A lack of collective self-awareness of the available options is a common source of teams struggling to meet their agility expectations – and that is exactly what happens when you adopt prescriptive methods/frameworks that don't provide you with choices. Every Team Member, especially consultants, are expected to bring a toolkit of ideas to customize the team's process as part of self-organization. A larger toolkit, and commonly understood terminology is a good thing.

The Disciplined Agile (DA) Toolkit Provides Accessible Guidance

One thing that we have learned over time is that some people, while they understand the concepts of DA by either reading the books or attending a workshop, struggle with how to actually apply DA. DA is an extremely rich body of knowledge that is presented in a accessible manner.

The good news is that the content of this book is organized by the goals, and that by using the goal-driven approach it is easy to find the guidance that you need for the situation at hand. Here's how you can apply this toolkit in your daily work to be more effective achieving your desired outcomes:

- Contextualized process reference
- Guided continuous improvement (GCI)
- Process tailoring workshops
- Enhance retrospectives
- Enhance coaching

Contextualized Process Reference

As we described earlier, this book is meant to be a reference. You will find it handy to keep this book nearby to quickly reference available strategies when you face particular challenges. This book presents you with process choices and more importantly puts those choices into context. DA provides three levels of scaffolding to do this:

1. **Lifecycles**. At the highest level of WoW guidance are lifecycles, the closest that

DAD gets to methodology. DAD supports six different lifecycles, as you can see in Figure 1.1, to provide teams with the flexibility of choosing an approach that makes the most sense for them. Chapter 6 explores the lifecycles, and how to choose between them, in greater detail. It also describes how teams can still be governed consistently even though they're working in different ways.

2. **Process goals**. Figure 1.2 presents the goal diagram for the *Improve Quality* process goal, which is described in detail in Chapter 18, and Figure 1.3 overviews the notation of goal diagrams. DAD is described as a collection of twenty-one process goals, or process outcomes if you like. Each goal is described as a collection of decision points, issues that your team needs to determine whether they need to address and if so how they will do so. Potential practices/strategies for addressing a decision point, which can be combined in many cases, are presented as lists. Goal diagrams are similar conceptually to mind maps, albeit with the extension of the arrow to represent relative effectiveness of options in some cases. Goal diagrams are, in effect, straightforward guides to help a team to choose the best strategies that they are capable of doing right now given their skills, culture, and situation. Chapter 5 explores the goal-driven approach in greater detail.

3. **Practices/strategies**. At the most granular level of WoW guidance are practices and strategies, depicted on goal diagrams in the lists on the right-hand side. Sections 2 through 4 of this book explore each process goal in detail, one per chapter. Each of these chapters overviews the process goal and key concepts behind the goal, describes each decision point for the goal, and then overviews each practice/strategy and the trade-offs associated with it in an agnostic manner.

7

Figure 1.1. The DAD lifecycles.

Figure 1.2. The Improve Quality process goal.

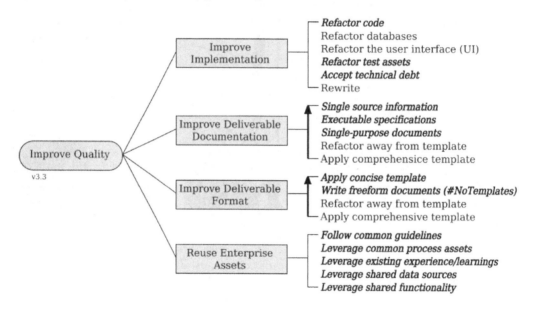

An important implication of goal diagrams, such as the one in Figure 1.2, is that you need less process expertise to identify potential practices/strategies to try out. What you do need is an understanding of the fundamentals of DAD, the focus of Section 1 of this book, and familiarity with the goal diagrams so that you can quickly locate potential options. You do not need to memorize all of your available options because you can look them up, and you don't need to have deep knowledge of each option because they're overviewed and put into context in the individual goal chapters. Rather, you can use this book to refer to DA when you need guidance to solve particular challenges that you face.

Figure 1.3. Goal diagram notation.

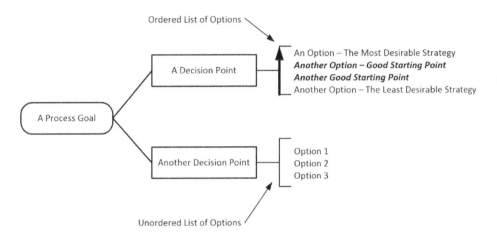

Improvement Occurs At Many Levels

Process improvement, or WoW evolution, occurs across your organization. Organizations are a collection of interacting teams and groups, each of which evolves continuously. As teams evolve their WoWs they motivate changes in the teams they interact with. Because of this constant process evolution, hopefully for the better, and because people are unique it becomes unpredictable how people are going to work together or what the results of that work will be. In short, your organization is a complex adaptive system (CAS) [W]. This concept is overviewed in Figure 1.4, which depicts teams, organization areas (such as divisions, lines of business (LoB), or value streams), and enterprise teams. Figure 1.4 is a simplification – there are far more interactions between teams and across organizational boundaries and in large enterprises an organizational area may have its own "enterprise" groups such as enterprise architecture or finance – the diagram is complicated enough as it is. There are several interesting implications for choosing your WoW:

1. **Every team will have a different WoW**. We really can't say this enough.
2. **We will evolve our WoW to reflect learnings whenever we work with other teams**. Not only do we accomplish whatever outcome we set to achieve by working with another team we very often learn new techniques from them or new ways of collaborating with them (that they may have picked up from working with other teams).
3. **We can purposefully choose to learn from other teams**. There are many strategies that we can choose to adopt within our organization to share learnings across teams, including practitioner presentations, Communities of Practice (CoPs)/guilds, coaching, and many others. Team-level strategies are captured in the *Evolve WoW* process goal (Chapter 24) and organizational-level strategies in the *Continuous Improvement* process blade[1] [AmblerLines2017]. In short, the DA toolkit is a generative resource that you can apply in agnostically choosing your WoW.
4. **We can benefit from organizational transformation/improvement efforts**.

---

[1] A process blade addresses a cohesive process area – such as Reuse Engineering, Finance, or Procurement – in other layers of Disciplined Agile.

Improvement can, and should, happen at the team level. It can also happen at the organizational area level, for example we can work to optimize flow between the teams within an area. Improvement also needs to occur outside of DAD teams, for example we can help the enterprise architecture, finance, and people management groups to collaborate with the rest of the organization more effectively.

Figure 1.4. Your organization is a complex adaptive system (CAS).

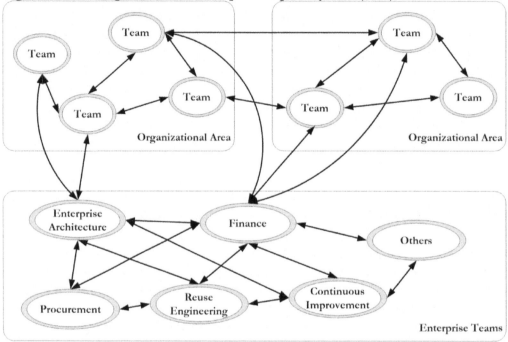

As Figures 1.5 and 1.6 depict, the Disciplined Agile (DA) toolkit is organized into four levels: Disciplined Agile Delivery (DAD), Disciplined DevOps, Disciplined Agile IT (DAIT), and Disciplined Agile Enterprise (DAE). Teams operating at all four of these levels can and should choose their WoW. Our focus in this book is on DAD teams, although at times we will delve into cross-team and organizational issues where appropriate.

Figure 1.5. The scope of this book.

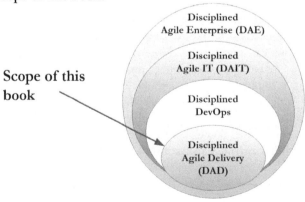

Figure 1.6. The scope of Disciplined Agile.

Guided Continuous Improvement (GCI)

Many teams start their agile journey by adopting agile methods such as Scrum [W], Extreme Programming (XP) [W], or Dynamic Systems Development Method (DSDM)-Atern [W]. Large teams dealing with "scale," we'll discuss what scaling really means in Chapter 2, may choose to adopt SAFe [W], LeSS [W], or Nexus [Nexus] to name a few. These methods/frameworks each address a specific class of problem(s) that agile teams face, and from our point of view they're rather prescriptive in that they don't provide you with many choices. Sometimes, particularly when frameworks are applied to contexts where they aren't an ideal fit, teams often find that they need to invest significant time "descaling" them to remove techniques that don't apply to their situation, then add back in other techniques that do. Having said that, when frameworks are applied in the appropriate context they can work quite well in practice. When you successfully adopt one of these prescriptive methods/frameworks your team productivity tends to follow the curve shown in Figure 1.7. At first there is a drop in productivity because the team is learning a new way of working, it's investing time in training, and people are often learning new techniques. In time productivity rises, going above what it originally was, but eventually plateaus as the team falls into its new WoW. Things have gotten better, but without concerted effort to improve you discover that team productivity plateaus.

Figure 1.7. Team productivity when adopting a prescriptive method or framework.

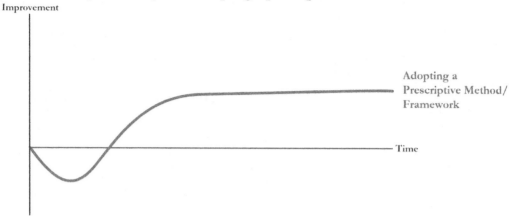

Some of the feedback that we get about Figure 1.7 is that this can't be, that Scrum promises that you can do twice the work in half the time [Sutherland]. Sadly this claim of 4X productivity improvement doesn't seem to hold water in practice. A recent study covering 155 organizations, 1,500 waterfall and 1,500 agile teams found actual productivity increases of agile teams, mostly following Scrum, to be closer to 7 to 12 percent [Reifer]. At scale, where the majority of organizations have adopted SAFe, the improvement goes down to 3 to 5 percent.

There are many ways that a team can adopt to help them improve their WoW, strategies that are captured by the *Evolve WoW* process goal described in Chapter 24. Many people recommend an experimental approach to improvement, and we've found guided experiments to be even more effective. The agile community provides a lots of advice around retrospectives, a working session where a team reflects on how they get better, and the lean community great advice for how to act on the reflections [Kerth]. Figure 1.8 summarizes W. Edward Deming's Plan Do Study Act (PDSA) improvement loop [W], sometimes called a kaizen loop. This was Deming's first approach to continuous improvement, which he later evolved to Plan Do Check Act (PDCA) which became popular within the business community in the 1990s and the agile community in the early 2000s. But, what many people don't realize is that after experimenting with PDCA for several years Deming realized that it wasn't as effective as PDSA and went back to it. The primary difference being that the Study activity motivated people to measure and think more deeply about whether a change worked well for them in practice. So we've decided to respect Deming's wishes and recommend PDSA rather than PDCA, as we found critical thinking such as this results in improvements that stick. Some people gravitate towards US Air Force Colonel John Boyd's OODA (Observe Orient Decide Act) loop to guide their continuous improvement efforts – as always, our advice is to do what works for you [W]. Regardless of which improvement loop you adopt, remember that your team can and perhaps should run multiple experiments in parallel, particularly when they potential improvements are on different areas of your process and therefore won't affect each other (if they effect each other it makes it difficult to determine the effectiveness of each experiment).

Figure 1.8. The PDSA continuous improvement loop.

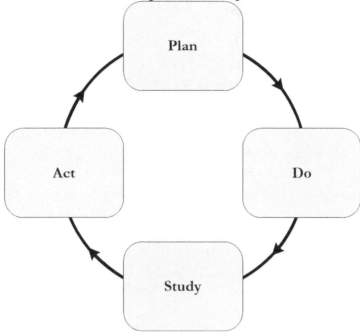

The basic idea with the PDSA/PDCA/OODA continuous improvement loop strategy is that you improve your WoW as a series of small changes, a strategy the lean community calls kaizen, which is Japanese for improvement. In Figure 1.10 you see the workflow for running an experiment. The first step is to identify a potential improvement, such as a new practice or strategy, that you want to experiment with to see how well it works for you in the context of your situation. Effectiveness of a potential improvement is determined by measuring against clear outcomes, perhaps identified via a Goal Question Metric (GQM) or Objectives and Key Results (OKRs) strategy as described in Chapter 27. Measuring the effectiveness of applying the new WoW is called validated learning [W] . It's important to note that Figure 1.9 provides a detailed description of a single pass through a team's continuous improvement loop.

The value of DA is that it can guide you through this identification step by helping you to agnostically identify a new practice/strategy that is likely to address the challenge you're hoping to address. By doing so you increase your chance of identifying a potential improvement that works for you, thereby speeding up your efforts to improve your WoW – we call this guided continuous improvement (GCI). In short, at this level the DA toolkit enables you to become a high-performing team quicker. In the original, 2012 DAD book we described a strategy called "measured improvement" that worked in a very similar manner.

Figure 1.9. An experimental approach to evolve our WoW.

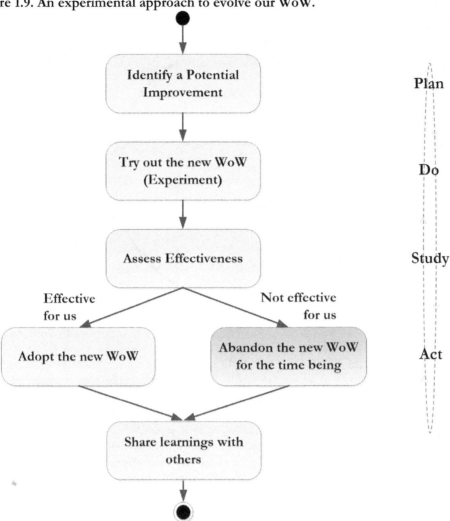

A similar strategy that we've found very effective in practice is Lean Change[2] [LeanChange1, LeanChange2], particularly at the organizational level. The Lean Change management cycle, overviewed in Figure 1.10, applies ideas from Lean Startup [Ries] in that you have insights (hypothesis), identify potential options to address your insights, and then you run experiments in the form of minimum viable changes (MVCs). These MVCs are introduced, allowed to run for awhile, and then the results are measured to determine how effective they are in practice. Teams than can choose to stick with the changes that work well for them in the situation that they face, and abandon changes that don't work well. Where GGI enables teams to become high performing, Lean Change enables high-performing organizations.

---

[2] In Chapter 7 of *An Executive's Guide to Disciplined Agile* we show how to apply Lean Change at the organizational level.

Figure 1.10. The Lean Change management cycle.

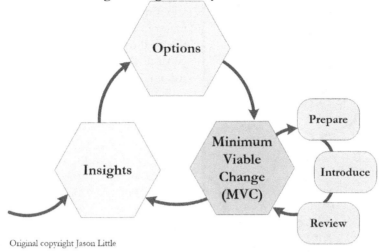

Original copyright Jason Little

The improvement curve for (unguided) continuous improvement strategies is shown in Figure 1.11 as a dashed line. You can see that there is still a bit of a productivity dip at first as teams learn how to identify MVCs and then run the experiments, but this is small and short-lived. The full line depicts the curve for GCI in context, teams are more likely to identify options that will work for them, resulting in a higher rate of positive experiments and thereby a faster rate of improvement. In short, better decisions lead to better outcomes.

Figure 1.11. Guided continuous improvement (GCI) enables teams to improve faster.

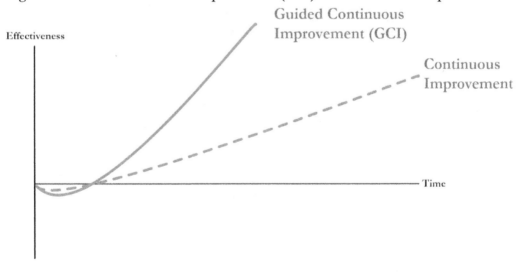

Of course, neither of the lines in Figure 1.11 are perfectly smooth. A team will have ups and downs, with some failed experiments (downs) where they learn what doesn't work in their situation and some successful experiences (ups) where they discover a technique that improves their effectiveness as a team. The full line, representing GCI, will be smoother than the dashed line because teams will have a higher percentage of ups.

The good news is that these two strategies, adopting a prescriptive method/framework, then improving your WoW through GCI, can be combined as you see in Figure 1.12. We are constantly running into teams that have adopted a prescriptive agile method, very often Scrum or SAFe, that have plateaued because they've run into one or more issues not directly addressed by their chosen framework/method. Because the method doesn't address the problem(s) they face, and because they don't have expertise in that area, they tend to flounder – Ivar Jacobson has coined the term "they're stuck in method prison" [Prison]. By applying a continuous improvement strategy, or better yet GCI, their process improvement efforts soon get back on track. Furthermore, because the underlying business situation that you face is constantly shifting it tells you that you cannot sit on your "process laurels" but instead must adjust your WoW to reflect the evolving situation.

Figure 1.12. Evolving away from a prescriptive agile method.

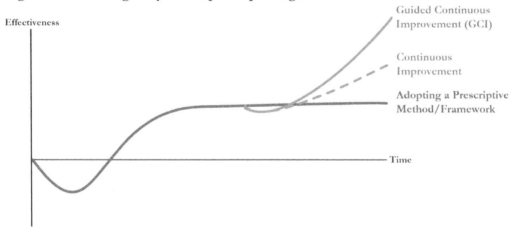

To be clear, GCI at the team level tends to be a simplified version of what you would do at the organizational level. At the team, level teams may choose to maintain an improvement backlog of things they hope to improve. At the organizational area or enterprise levels we may have a group of people guiding a large transformation or improvement effort that is focused on enabling teams to choose their WoWs and to address larger, organizational issues that teams cannot easily address on their own.

Process Tailoring Workshops

Another common strategy to apply DA to choose your WoW is a process tailoring workshop [Tailoring]. In a process tailoring workshop, a coach or Team Lead walks the team through important aspects of DAD and the team discusses how they're going to work together. This typically includes choosing a lifecycle, walking through the process goals one at a time and addressing the decision points of each one, and discussing roles and responsibilities.

A process tailoring workshop, or several short workshops, can be run at any time. As we show in Figure 1.13 they are typically performed when a team is initially formed to determine how they will streamline their initiation efforts (what we call Inception, described in detail in Section 2), and just before Construction begins to agree on how that effort will be approached. Any process decisions made in process tailoring workshops are not carved in stone but instead evolve over time as the team learns. You always want to be learning and improving your process as you go, and in fact most agile teams will regularly reflect on how to do so via holding retrospectives. In short, the purpose of process tailoring workshops is to get your team going in the right direction, whereas the purpose of retrospectives are to identify potential adjustments to that process.

Figure 1.13. Choosing and evolving Your WoW over time.

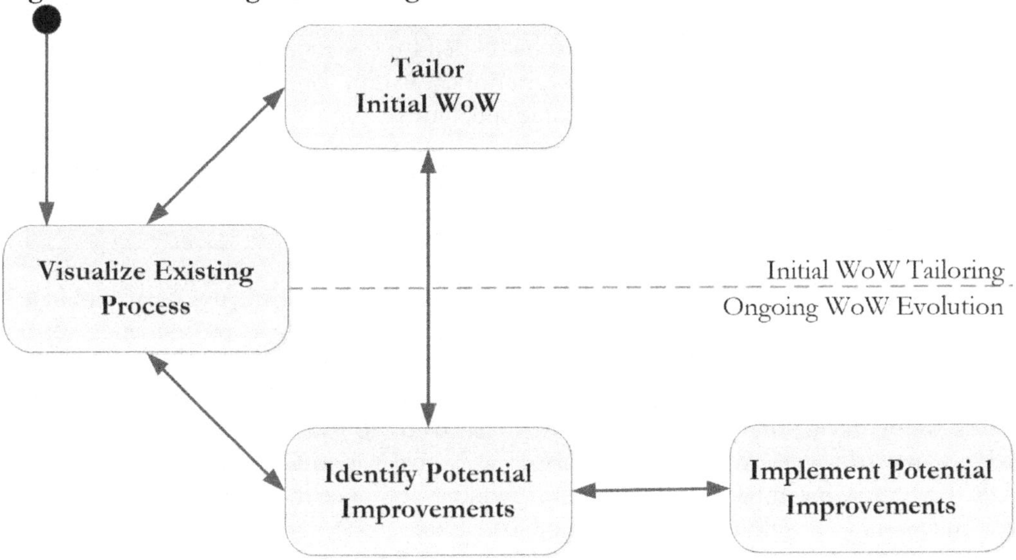

17

Sidebar: Process Tailoring Workshops In a Large Financial Institution by Daniel Gagnon

In my experience in running dozens of process tailoring workshops, over several years, with teams of every shape size and experience level and in different organizations [Gagnon]. Interestingly, the most recurring comment is that the workshops "revealed all kinds of options we didn't even realize were options!" Although almost always a bit of a hard sell at the outset, I have yet to work with a team unable to quickly grasp and appreciate the value of these activities.

Here are my lessons learned:

1. A Team Lead, Architecture Owner or senior developer can actually stand in for most of the developers in the early stages.
2. Tools help – We developed a simple spreadsheet to capture WoW choices.
3. Teams can make immediate WoW decisions and identify future, more "mature" aspirational choices that they set as improvement goals.
4. We defined a small handful of enterprise-level choices to promote consistency across teams, including some "infrastructure as code" choices.
5. Teams don't have to start from a blank slate, but instead can start with the choices made by a similar team and then tailor it from there.

Here's an important note on determining participation - Ultimately, the teams themselves are the best arbiters of who should attend the sessions at varying stages of advancement. The support will become easier and easier to obtain as the benefits of allowing teams to choose their WoW become apparent.

Daniel Gagnon, has coached the adoption of Disciplined Agile in two large Canadian financial institutions and is now a senior agile coach with Levio in Quebec.

A valid question to ask is what does the timeline look like for evolving the WoW within a team? Jonathan Smart, who guided the transformation at Barclays, recommends Dan North's visualize, stabilize, and optimize timeline as depicted in Figure 1.14. You start by visualizing your existing WoW and then identifying a new potential WoW that the team believes will work for them (this is what the initial tailoring is all about). Then the team needs to apply that new WoW and to learn how to make it work in their context. This stabilization phase could take several weeks or months, and once the team has stabilized its WoW then it is in a position to evolve it via a GCI strategy.

Figure 1.14. A timeline for process tailoring and improvement on a team.

Visualize	Stabilize	Optimize
• Explore existing WoW • Identify new WoW	• Apply your new WoW • Get training and coaching • Give yourself time to learn the new WoW	• Guided continuous improvement

The good news is that with effective facilitation you can keep process tailoring workshops streamlined. To do this we suggest that you:

- Schedule several short sessions (you may not need all of them)
- Have a clear agenda (set expectations)
- Invite the entire team (it's their process)
- Have an experienced facilitator (this can get contentious)
- Arrange a flexible work space (this enables collaboration)

A process tailoring workshop is likely to address several important aspects surrounding our way of working (WoW):

- The rights and responsibilities of Team Members, discussed in detail in Chapter 4.
- How do we intend to organize/structure the team?
- What lifecycle will the team follow? See Chapter 6 for more on this.
- What practices/strategies will we follow?
- Do we have a definition of ready (DoR) [Rubin], and if so what is it?
- Do we have a definition of done (DoD) [Rubin], and if so what is it?
- What tools will we use?

Process tailoring workshops require an investment in time, but they're an effective way to ensure that Team Members are well aligned in how they intend to work together. Having said that, you want to keep these workshops as streamlined as possible as they can easily take on a life of their own – the aim is to get going in the right "process direction," you can always evolve your WoW later as you learn what works and what doesn't work for you. Finally, you still need to involve some people experienced with agile delivery. DA provides a straightforward toolkit for choosing and evolving your WoW, but you still need the skills and knowledge to apply this toolkit effectively.

While DA provides a library or toolkit of great ideas, in your organization you may wish to apply some limits to the degree of self-organization your teams can apply. In DAD we recommend self-organization within appropriate governance. As such, what we have seen with organizations that adopt DA is that they sometimes help steer the choices so that teams self-organize within commonly understood organizational "guard rails".

Enhance Retrospectives Through Guided Improvement Options

A retrospective is a technique that teams use to reflect on how effective they are and hopefully to identify potential process improvements to experiment with [W, Kerth]. As you would guess, DA can be used to help you to identify improvements that would have a good chance of working for you. As an example perhaps you are having a discussion regarding excessive requirements churn due to ambiguous user stories and acceptance criteria. The observation may be that you need additional requirements models to clarify the requirements. But which models to choose? Referring to the *Explore Scope* process goal, described in Chapter 9, you could choose to create a domain diagram to clarify the relationships between entities, or perhaps a low-fidelity UI prototype to clarify user experience. We have observed that by using DA as a reference that teams are exposed to strategies and practices that they hadn't even heard of before.

19

Enhance Coaching By Extending the Coach's Process Toolkit

DA is particularly valuable for agile coaches. First of all, an understanding of DA means that you have a larger toolkit of strategies that you can bring to bear to help solve your team's problems. Second, we often see coaches refer to DA to explain that some of the things that the teams or the organization itself sees as "best practices" are actually very poor choices, and that there are better alternatives to consider. Third, coaches use DA to help fill in the gaps in their own experience and knowledge.

Documenting Your WoW

Sigh, we wish we could say that you don't need to document your WoW. But the reality is that you very often do, and for one or more very good reasons:

1. **Regulatory**. Your team works in a regulatory environment where by law you need to capture your process, your WoW, somehow.
2. **It's too complicated to remember**. There are a lot of moving parts in your WoW. Consider the goal diagram of Figure 1.2. Your team will choose to adopt several of the strategies called out in it, and that's only one of twenty-one goals. As we said earlier, solution delivery is complex. We've done our best in DA to reduce this complexity so as to help you to choose your WoW, but we can't remove it completely.
3. **It provides comfort**. Many people are uncomfortable with the idea of not having a "defined process" to follow, particularly when they are new to that process. They like to have something to refer to from time to time to aid their learning. As they become more experienced in the team's WoW they will refer to the documentation less until finally they never use it at all.

Because few people like to read process material, we suggest you keep it as straightforward as possible. Follow agile documentation [AgileDocumentation] practices such as keeping it concise and working closely with the audience (in this case the team itself) to ensure it meets their actual needs. Here are some options for capturing your WoW:

- Use a simple spreadsheet to capture goal diagram choices [Resources].
- Create an A3 (single sheet) overview of the process.
- Put up posters on the wall.
- Capture the process concisely in a wiki.

As we show in the *Evolve WoW* process goal (Chapter 24) there are several strategies that you can choose from to capture your WoW. A common approach is for a team to develop and commit to a working agreement. Working agreements will describe the roles and responsibilities that people will take on the team, the general rights and responsibilities of Team Members, and very often the team's process (their WoW). As we show in Figure 1.15 we like to distinguish between two important aspects of a team working agreement – the internal portion of it that describes how the team will work together and the external portion of it that describes how others should interact with the team. The external portion of a team's working agreement in some ways is a service level agreement (SLA), or application programming interface (API), for the team. It may include a schedule of common meetings that others may attend (for example daily coordination meetings and upcoming demos), an indication of how to access the team's automated dashboard, how to contact the team, and what the purpose of the team is. The team's working agreement, both the internal and external aspects of it, will of course be affected by the organization environment and culture in which it operates.

Figure 1.15. Team working agreements.

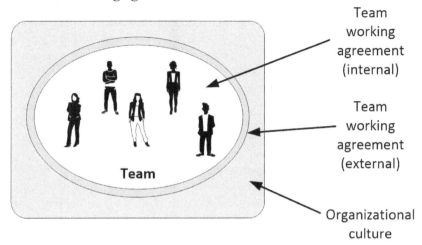

In Summary

We've worked through several critical concepts in this chapter:

- Disciplined Agile Delivery (DAD) teams choose their way of working (WoW).
- You need to both "be agile" and know how to "do agile."
- Solution delivery is complicated, there's no easy answer for how to do it.
- Disciplined Agile (DA) provides the agnostic scaffolding to support a team in choosing their WoW to deliver software-based solutions.
- Other people have faced, and overcome, similar challenges to yours. DA enables you to leverage their learnings.
- You can use this book to guide how to initially choose your WoW and then evolve it over time.
- A guided continuous improvement (GCI) approach will help your teams to break out of "method prison" and thereby improve their effectiveness.
- The real goal is to effectively achieve desired organizational outcomes, not to be/do agile.
- Better decisions lead to better outcomes.

2 BEING DISCIPLINED
Better decisions lead to better outcomes

What does it mean to be disciplined? To be disciplined is to do the things that you know are good for you, things that usually require hard work and perseverance. It requires discipline to regularly delight your customers. It takes discipline for teams to become awesome. It requires discipline for leaders to ensure that their people have a safe environment to work in. It takes discipline to recognize that you need to tailor your way of working (WoW) for the context that you face, and to evolve your WoW as the situation evolves. It takes discipline to recognize that you are part of a larger organization, that you should do what's best for the enterprise and not just what's convenient for you. It requires discipline to evolve and optimize your overall workflow, and it requires discipline to realize that you have many choices regarding how you work and organize yourselves, so you should choose accordingly.

Key Points in this Chapter

- There are seven principles – Delight Customers, Be Awesome, Pragmatism, Context Counts, Choice is Good, Optimize Flow, and Enterprise Awareness - that provide a foundation for the DA toolkit
- The Disciplined Agile Manifesto extends the original Agile Manifesto to capture learnings since 2001.
- Lean principles are critical to the success for agile solution delivery teams in the enterprise.
- There are several "hashtag rebellions" that we can learn from.

The Principles of Disciplined Agile

Let's start with the seven primary principles behind the Disciplined Agile (DA) toolkit. These ideas aren't new – there is a plethora of sources from which we can adopt ideas, including Alistair Cockburn's work around Heart of Agile [CockburnHeart], Joshua Kerievsky's Modern Agile [Kerievsky], and of course the Agile Manifesto for Software Development [Manifesto]. In fact, the DA toolkit has always been a hybrid of great strategies from the very beginning, with the focus being on how all of these strategies fit together in practice. DA has a foundation of seven fundamental principles – Delight Customers, Be Awesome, Pragmatism, Context Counts, Choice is Good, Optimize Flow, and Enterprise Awareness. These principles are captured in Figure 2.1. Let's explore each one.

Figure 2.1. The primary principles of Disciplined Agile.

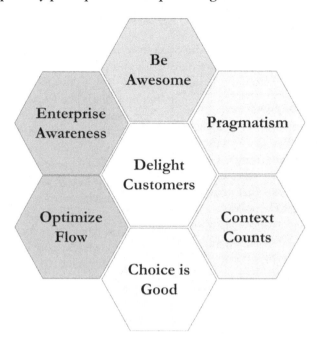

Principle: Delight Customers

We delight our customers when our products and services not only fulfill their needs and expectations but surpass them. Consider the last time you checked into a hotel. If you're lucky there was no line, your room was available, and there was nothing wrong with it when you got there. You were likely satisfied with the service but that's about it. Now imagine that you were greeted by name by the concierge when you arrived, that your favorite snack was waiting for you in the room, and that you received a complimentary upgrade to a room with a magnificent view – all without asking. This would be more than satisfying and would very likely delight you. Although the upgrade won't happen every time you check in, it's a nice touch when it does and you're likely to stick with that hotel chain because they treat you so well.

Successful organizations offer great products and services that delight their customers. Systems design tells us to build with the customer in mind, to work with them closely, to build in small increments and then seek feedback, so that we better understand what will actually delight them. As disciplined agilists we embrace change because we know that our Stakeholders will change their minds as they learn what they truly want as the solution evolves. We also strive to discover what our customers want and to care for our customers – it's much easier to take care of an existing customer than it is to get a new one.

Jeff Gothelf and Josh Seiden say it best in *Sense & Respond* – "If you can make a product easier to use, reduce the time it takes a customer to complete a task, or provide the right information at the exact moment, you win" [SenseRespond].

Principle: Be Awesome

Who doesn't want to be awesome? Who doesn't want to be part of an awesome team doing awesome things while working for an awesome organization? We all want these things. Recently Joshua Kerievsky has popularized the concept that modern agile teams make people awesome, and of course it isn't much of a leap that we want awesome teams and awesome organizations too. Similarly, Mary and Tom Poppendieck observe that sustainable advantage is gained from engaged, thinking people [Poppendieck]. Helping people to be awesome is important because, as Richard Branson of the Virgin Group says, "Take care of your employees and they'll take care of your business."

There are several things that you as an individual can do to be awesome. First and foremost, act in such a way that you earn the respect and trust of your colleagues – be reliable, be honest, be open, and treat them with respect. Second, willingly collaborate with others. Share information with them when asked, even if it is a work in progress. Offer help when it's needed and just as important reach out for help yourself. Third, be an active learner. Seek to master your craft, always being on the lookout for opportunities to experiment and learn. Go beyond your specialty and learn about the broader software process and business environment. By becoming a T-skilled "generalizing specialist" you will be able to better appreciate where others are coming from and thereby interact with them more effectively [GenSpec]. Fourth, seek to never let the team down. Yes, it will happen sometimes, and good teams understand and forgive that. Fifth, Simon Powers points out that you need to be willing to improve and manage your emotional responses to difficult situations. Innovation requires diversity, and by their very nature diverse opinions may cause emotional reactions. We must all work on making our workplace psychologically safe.

Awesome teams are built around motivated individuals who are given the environment and support required to fulfill their objectives. A 2015 study at Google found that successful teams provide psychological safety for Team Members, that Team Members are able to depend on one another, there is structure and clarity around roles and responsibilities, and people are doing work that is both meaningful and impactful to them [Google]. Awesome teams have a very good working relationship with their Stakeholders, collaborating with them to ensure that what they do is what the Stakeholders actually need. Finally, awesome teams are whole – they are cross functional, having the skills, resources, and authority required to be successful and Team Members themselves tend to be cross-functional generalizing specialists.

Awesome teams also choose to build quality in from the very beginning. Lean tells us that your process should not allow defects to occur in the first place, but when this isn't possible (yet) you should work in such a way that you do a bit of work, validate it, fix any issues that you find, and then iterate. The Agile Manifesto is clear that continuous attention to technical excellence and good design enhances agility [Manifesto].

Senior leadership within your organization can enable staff to be awesome individuals working on awesome teams through providing them with the authority and resources required for them to do their jobs, by building a safe culture and environment (see next principle), and by motivating them to excel. People are motivated by being provided with the autonomy to do their work, having opportunities to master their craft, and to do something that has purpose [Pink]. What would you rather have, staff who are motivated or demotivated[3]?

---

[3] If you think happy employees are expensive, wait till you try unhappy ones!

25

Principle: Pragmatism (Over Purism)

People are often surprised when we suggest that mainstream methods such as Scrum and Extreme Programming (XP) are prescriptive. But they are indeed. Scrum mandates a daily stand-up meeting (a Scrum) no longer than fifteen minutes to which all Team Members must attend, that teams must have a retrospective at the end of each iteration (Sprint), and that team size should not be more than nine people. Extreme Programming prescribes pair programming (two people sharing one keyboard) and Test-Driven Development (TDD) – granted, both of these are great practices in the right context. We are not suggesting that prescription is a bad thing, we're merely stating that it does exist. Many agilists are quite fanatical about following specific methods strictly. In fact, we have met many who say that to "do agile right" you need to have 5-9 people in a room, with the business (Product Owner) present at all times. The team should not be disturbed by people outside the team, and should be 100% dedicated to the project. However, in many established enterprises such ideal conditions rarely exist. The reality is that we have to deal with many suboptimal situations, such as distributed teams, large team sizes, outsourcing, multiple team coordination, and part-time availability of Stakeholders.

DA recognizes these realities and rather than saying "we can't be agile" in these situations we instead say "let's be as effective as we can be." Instead of prescribing "best practices" DA instead provides strategies for maximizing the benefits of agile despite certain necessary compromises being made. As such, DA is pragmatic, not purist in its guidance – DA provides guardrails helping you to make better process choices, not strict rules that may not even be applicable given the context that you face.

Principle: Context Counts

Every person is unique, with their own set of skills, preferences for workstyle, career goals, and learning styles. Every team is unique not only because it is composed of unique people but also because it faces a unique situation. Your organization is also unique, even when there are other organizations that operate in the same marketplace that you do. For example, automobile manufacturers such as Ford, Audi, and Tesla all build the same category of product yet it isn't much of a stretch to claim that they are very different companies. These observations – that people, teams, and organizations are all unique – lead us to a critical idea that your process and organization structure must be tailored for the situation that you currently face. In other words, context counts.

Figure 2.2, adapted from the Software Development Context Framework (SDCF) [SDCF], shows that there are several context factors that affect how a team chooses its WoW. The factors are organized into two categories: factors which have a significant impact on your choice of lifecycle (more on this in Chapter 6) and factors that motivate your choice of practices/strategies. As you can see the practice/strategy selection factors are a superset of the lifecycle selection factors. For example, a team of eight people working in a common team room on a very complex domain problem in a life-critical regulatory situation will organize themselves differently, and will choose to follow different practices, than a team of fifty people spread out across a corporate campus on a complex problem in a non-regulatory situation. Although these two teams could be working for the same company they could choose to work in very different ways.

26

Figure 2.2. Context factors that affect WoW choices.

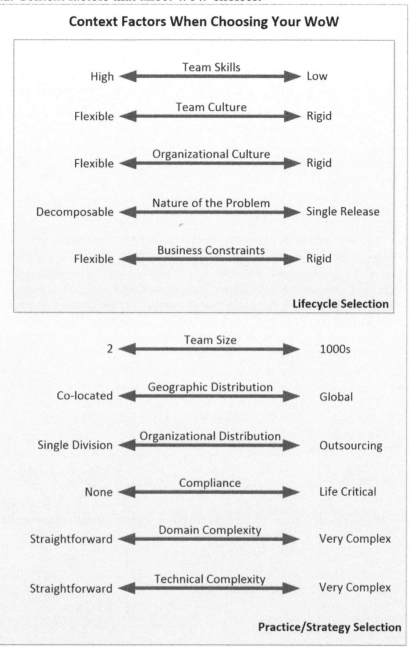

There are several interesting implications of Figure 2.2. First, the further to the right on each selection factor the greater the risk faced by a team. For example, it's much riskier to outsource than it is to build your own internal team. A team with a lower set of skills is a riskier proposition than a highly skilled team. A large team is a much riskier proposition than a small team. A life-critical regulatory situation is much riskier than a financial-critical situation, which in turn is riskier than facing no regulations at all. Second, because teams in different situations will need to choose to work in a manner that is appropriate for the

27

situation that they face, to help them tailor their approach effectively you need to give them choices. Third, anyone interacting with multiple teams needs to be flexible enough to work with each of those teams appropriately. For example, you will govern that small, co-located, life-critical team differently than the medium-sized team spread across the campus. Similarly, an Enterprise Architect who is supporting both teams will collaborate differently with each.

Scrum provides what used to be solid guidance for delivering value in an agile manner but it is officially described by only an eighteen-page guide [ScrumGuide]. Disciplined Agile recognizes that enterprise complexities require far more guidance and thus provides a comprehensive reference toolkit for adapting your agile approach for your unique context in a straightforward manner. Being able to adapt your approach for your context with a variety of choices rather than standardizing on one method or framework is a good thing and we explore this further below.

Principle: Choice is Good

Let's assume for a minute that your organization has multiple teams working in a range of situations, which in fact is the norm for all but the smallest of companies. How do you define a process that applies to each and every situation that covers the range of issues faced by each team? How do you keep it up to date as each team learns and evolves their approach? The answer is that you can't, documenting such a process is exponentially expensive. But does that mean you need to inflict the same, prescriptive process on everyone? When you do that you'll inflict process dissonance on your teams, decreasing their ability to be effective and increasing the chance that they invest resources in making it look as if they're following the process when in reality they're not. Or, does this mean that you just have a "process free-for-all" and tell all your teams to figure it out on their own? Although this can work, it tends to be very expensive and time consuming in practice. Even with coaching, each team is forced to invent or discover the practices and strategies that have been around for years, sometimes decades.

Organizations are complex adaptive systems (CASs) where a prescriptive, "one size fits all" process will not work for you. The Cynefin framework [Cynefin], see Figure 2.3, shows that in a complex domain we are dealing with "unknown unknowns" and there are no right answers, just approaches that work within a given context. The key is understanding what strategies are most appropriate for a given situation in the context of your unique and complex situation.

28

Figure 2.3. The Cynefin framework.

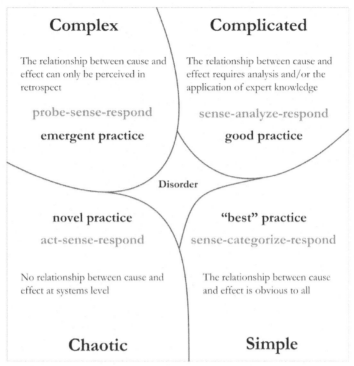

Original Copyright Dave Snowden

Let's discuss Disciplined Agile in relationship to the Cynefin framework, and in particular let's focus on IT for now. Let's explore each of the five Cynefin domains:

1. **Are you experiencing disorder?** This is when you don't know which of the other four domains that you're in. If so, gather information to determine what is happening and then start moving into one of the other domains quickly.

2. **Are you in a chaotic situation?** If your teams don't know why they are succeeding or failing you are likely in the "chaotic" domain. This is a bad place to be and you want to work your way out of that.

3. **Are you in a simple situation?** Product/solution development is rarely "simple", and certainly not in all situations. The only exception to this is the rare circumstances where your teams are consistently building the same sort of solution in the same sort of environments on a regular basis (likely because you're a specialized services company focused on this one thing). We've never seen this in practice, and if we did our recommendation would be to automate this work as much as possible.

4. **Are you in a complicated situation?** This is what traditional IT organizations often assume. Yes, IT is difficult but if all we needed to do is codify our processes in a detailed manner, train people to follow them, then everything would work out. If this was indeed true we would have more deterministic approaches and have predictable outcomes. But this was never the case, and at best resulted in onerous processes that proved to be expensive and slow only to produce solutions that Stakeholders don't really want. To be clear, "complicated" is not a bad thing. Aerospace is complicated, but understanding all the sophisticated and complicated yet predictable factors leads to predictable results. Alas, we live in a world of both

29

complication and unpredictability hence it is complex. Cynefin advises that the best we can do is sense, probe, and rely on patterns to predict a path that leads to success.

5. **Are you in a complex situation?** Very likely yes, although that might not be what you want to hear. In such situations there are a large number of interacting elements (in this case people or teams) and their interactions are non-linear – minor changes in behavior can have disproportionately major consequences. These consequences emerge and evolve as the situation evolves. Luckily we *can* get more dependable results if we provide proven, situational guidance. Cynefin recommends that in these situations we probe-sense-respond, often referred to "inspect and adapt". But how to adapt? Few people have a deep understanding of the vast array of potential options available. Disciplined Agile is a very rich toolkit of process decision strategies. Yes, one could suggest that this is "complicated", but the unfortunate truth that to try to make it "simple" is naïve. While there is a lot of content in Disciplined Agile, one does not need to understand it in its entirety. Understanding the basic structure of the DA toolkit and then referencing it to address complexity makes it quite consumable in practice. Of course, investing in learning as much as possible about DA reaps dividends in efficiency.

Different contexts require different strategies – teams need to be able to own their own process and to experiment to discover what works in practice for them given the situation that they face. As you learned in Chapter 1, DAD provides six lifecycles for teams to choose from and twenty-one process goals that guide you towards choosing the right practices/strategies for your team given the situation that you face. Yes, it seems a bit complicated at first, but this approach proves to be a straightforward strategy to address the complexities faced by solution delivery teams. Think of DAD, and DA in general, as the scaffolding that supports your efforts in choosing and evolving your WoW.

This choice-driven strategy is a middle way. At one extreme you have prescriptive methods, which have their place, such as Scrum, Extreme Programming (XP), and SAFe which tell you the one way to do things. Regardless of what the detractors of these methods will tell you these prescriptive strategies do in fact work quite well in some situations, and as long as you find yourself in that situation they'll work well for you. However, if you're not in the situation where a prescriptive method fits then it will likely do more harm than good. At the other extreme are experimental methods such as those used at Spotify[4] that tell you to experiment and learn as you go. This works well in practice but can be very expensive and time consuming and can lead to significant inconsistencies between teams which hampers your overall organizational process. Spotify had the luxury of evolving their process within the context of a product company, common architecture, no technical debt, and a culture that they could grow rather than change. DA sits between these two extremes – by taking this process goal driven approach it provides process commonality between teams that is required at the organizational level yet provides teams with flexible and straightforward guidance that is required to tailor and evolve their internal processes to address the context of the situation that they face. Teams can choose from known strategies the likely options to

---

[4] Spotify, like other methods, is a great source of potential ideas which we've mined in DA. We've particularly found their experimental approach to process improvement, which we've evolved into guided experiments (Chapter 1), to be useful. Unfortunately many organizations try to adopt the Spotify method verbatim, which is what the Spotify people tell you not to do. The Spotify method was great for them in their context several years ago. They are clear that if you are copying what they did then, that is not Spotify now. Your context, even if you happen to be a Swedish online music company, is different.

then experiment with, increasing the chance that they find something that works for them in practice. At a minimum, it at least makes it clear that they have choices, that there is more than the one way described by the prescriptive methods.

There is a catchy phrase in the agile world called "fail fast" or better yet "learn fast." As described earlier leadership should encourage experimentation early in the interest of learning and improving as quickly as possible. However, we would suggest that by referencing the proven strategies in Disciplined Agile you will make better choices for your context, speeding up process improvement through failing less. Better choices lead to better outcomes, earlier.

Principle: Optimize Flow

Your organization is a complex adaptive system (CAS) of interacting teams and groups that individually evolve continuously and affect each other as they do. The challenge that we face is how do we ensure that these collaborating teams do so in such a way as to effectively implement our organization's value streams? How do we ensure that these teams are well aligned, remain well aligned, and better yet improve their alignment over time?

The implication is that as an organization we need to optimize our overall workflow. DAD supports a large number of strategies to do so:

1. **Deliver continuously at a sustainable pace**. The Disciplined Agile Manifesto, described later in this chapter, advises teams to deliver consumable solutions frequently, from a few weeks to a couple of months, although more often is better.

2. **Optimize the whole**. Disciplined agilists work in an "enterprise aware" manner – they realize that their team is one of many teams within their organization and as a result they should work in such a way as to do what is best for the overall organization and not just what is convenient for them. More importantly they strive to streamline the overall process, to optimize the whole as the lean canon advises us to do. This includes finding ways to reduce the overall cycle time, the total time from the beginning to the end of the process to provide value to a customer [Reinertson].

3. **Make work flow**. The 14th principle of the DA Manifesto is to visualize work to produce a smooth delivery flow and keep work-in-progress (WIP) to a minimum. This strategy enables teams to identify and then remove bottlenecks quickly and is adopted straight out of Kanban [Anderson].

4. **Eliminate waste**. The 10th principle behind the Agile Manifesto, and the Disciplined Agile Manifesto, suggests that "Simplicity – the art of maximizing the amount of work not done - is essential".

5. **Improve continuously**. The process goal *Evolve WoW* (Chapter 24) captures strategies to improve your team's work environment, your process, and your tooling infrastructure over time.

6. **Experiment to learn**. Probably the most significant impact of Eric Ries' work in Lean Startup is the popularization of the experimentation mindset, the application of fundamental concepts of the scientific method to business. This mindset can be applied to process improvement following a Guided Continuous Improvement (GCI) strategy that we described in Chapter 1.

7. **Measure what counts**. When it comes to measurement, context counts. What are you hoping to improve? Quality? Time to market? Staff morale? Customer satisfaction? Combinations thereof? Every person, team, and organization has their own improvement priorities, and their own ways of working, so they will have their own set of measures that they gather to provide insight into how they're doing and

31

more importantly how to proceed. And these measures evolve over time as their situation and priorities evolve. The implication is that your measurement strategy must be flexible and fit for purpose, and it will vary across teams. The *Govern Delivery Team* process goal (Chapter 27) provides several strategies, including Goal Question Metric (GQM) [W] and Objectives and Key Results (OKRs) [W], that promote context-driven metrics.

8. **Prefer long-lived stable teams**. A very common trend in the agile community is the movement away from projects, and the project management mindset in general[5], to long-lived teams. This is referred to as the #NoProjects movement, described later in this chapter. DAD supports both project-based lifecycles and lifecycles for long-lived teams, described in more detail in Chapter 6.

Principle: Enterprise Awareness

When people are enterprise aware they are motivated to consider the overall needs of their organization, to ensure that what they're doing contributes positively to the goals of the organization and not just to the suboptimal goals of their team. This is an example of the lean principle of optimizing the whole, in this case "the whole" is the organization, over local optimization at the team level.

Enterprise awareness positively changes people's behaviors in several important ways. First, they're more likely to work closely with enterprise professionals to seek their guidance. These people – such as Enterprise Architects, Product Managers, Finance professionals, Auditors, and Senior Executives – are responsible for your organization's business and

technical strategies and for evolving your organization's overall vision. Second, enterprise aware people are more likely to leverage and evolve existing assets within your organization, collaborating with the people responsible for those assets (such as data, code, and proven patterns or techniques) to do so (one of the principles of the Disciplined Agile Manifesto, described below). Third, they're more likely to adopt and follow common guidance, tailoring it where need be, thereby increasing overall consistency and quality. Fourth, they're more likely to share their learnings across teams, thereby speeding up your organization's overall improvement efforts. In fact one of the process blades of DA, Continuous Improvement, is focused on helping people to share learnings. Fifth, enterprise aware people are more likely to be willing to work in a transparent manner although they expect reciprocity from others.

There is the potential for negative consequences as well. Some people believe that enterprise awareness demands absolute consistency and process adherence by teams, not realizing that context counts and that every

---

[5] It's important to note that this move away from project management in the agile community is not a move away from management but instead from the inherent risks and overhead of projects.

team needs to make their own process decisions (within bounds). Enterprise awareness can lead some people into a state of "analysis paralysis" – unable to make a decision because they're overwhelmed by the complexity of the organization.

The Seven Principles...And Beyond!

If there's one thing that our discussion about the seven principles should make clear it is that there's a lot more to it than seven principles. Figure 2.4 expands upon the seven Disciplined Agile principles to depict a collection of supporting ideas, or sub principles if you will. Of course, we could choose to explore even more detailed concepts, described in a fractal drilling down even further.

Figure 2.4 Principles for being disciplined.

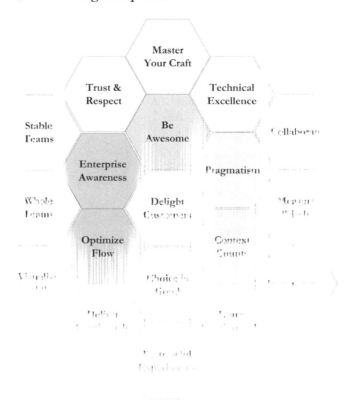

The Disciplined Agile Manifesto

Since 2001 we've applied the ideas captured in the Agile Manifesto [Manifesto] and have learned from our experiences doing so. What we've learned has motivated us to suggest changes to the manifesto to reflect the enterprise situations in which we have applied agile and lean strategies. Because the original authors of the Agile Manifesto have decided not to evolve the Manifesto, a decision that we fully respect, we have decided to move forward on our own. Others have of course done this too [BeyondManifesto].

The Disciplined Agile Manifesto is an evolution of the original Manifesto for Agile Software written in 2001. We believe that the changes we're suggesting, which are highlighted using underlining, are straightforward:

33

1. Where the original manifesto focused on software development, a term which too many people have understood to mean *only* software development, DA suggests that we should focus on solution delivery. In short, we prefer solutions (software + hardware + supporting documentation + business process + organization structure) over just software. We also believe those solutions should be consumable (provide valuable working functionality + be usable + be desirable) rather than just be working.

2. Where the original manifesto focused on customers, a word that for too many people appears to imply *only* end users, DA suggests that we focus on the full range of Stakeholders instead. We prefer Stakeholders – end users, operations people, sustainment people, audit, finance, and many more – over just customers. See Chapter 4 for a more detailed discussion of this.

3. Where the original manifesto talked about *projects*, we believe it is more accurate to talk about *teams*.

4. Where the original manifesto focused on development teams, DA suggests that the overall organization and its improvement be explicitly taken into consideration.

5. The original manifesto focused on the understanding of, and observations about, software development at the time. But we've learned a lot since then, particularly around continuous delivery and testing strategies that are embraced by DAD.

6. As Neil Killick and Dan North both point out, being agile is more about responding to feedback than it is to responding to change. This is an important nuance because it underlines the importance of working closely with our Stakeholders. Additionally, it is more accurate to say that requirements *emerge* rather than requirements change as we develop a better understanding of the true needs.

7. We have learned from the lean community. The Disciplined Agile Manifesto incorporates lean principles, in particular considering the whole, visualizing workflow, and minimizing work in progress (WIP).

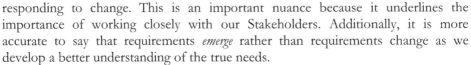

The Disciplined Agile Manifesto

We value:

1. *Individuals and interactions* over processes and tools
2. *Consumable solutions* over comprehensive documentation
3. *Stakeholder collaboration* over contract negotiation
4. *Responding to feedback* over following a plan
5. *Transparency* over (false) predictability

That is, while there is value in the items on the right, disciplined agilists value the items on the left more.

Supporting the five values of the Disciplined Agile Manifesto are seventeen principles:
1. Our highest priority is to satisfy the stakeholder through early and continuous delivery of valuable solutions.
2. Welcome emerging requirements, even late in the solution delivery lifecycle. Agile processes harness change for the stakeholder's competitive advantage.
3. Deliver valuable solutions continuously, from many times a day to every few weeks, with the aim to increase the frequency over time.
4. Stakeholders and developers must actively collaborate daily to deliver outcomes that will delight our organization's customers.
5. Build teams around motivated individuals. Give them the environment and support they need, and trust them to get the job done.
6. The most efficient and effective method of conveying information to and within a delivery team is face-to-face conversation, ideally around a whiteboard.
7. Continuous delivery of value is the primary measure of progress.
8. Agile processes promote sustainable delivery. The sponsors, developers, and users should be able to maintain a constant pace indefinitely.
9. Continuous attention to technical excellence and good design enhances agility.
10. Simplicity – the art of maximizing the amount of work not done – is essential.
11. The best architectures, requirements, and designs emerge from self-organizing teams enabled by organizational roadmaps and support.
12. The team continuously reflects on how to become more effective, then experiments, learns, and adjusts its behavior accordingly.
13. Leverage and evolve the assets within your enterprise, collaborating with the people responsible for those assets to do so.
14. Visualize work to produce a smooth delivery flow and keep work-in-progress (WIP) to a minimum.
15. Evolve the entire enterprise, not just individuals and teams, to support agile, non-agile, and hybrid teams.
16. We measure our work and its outcomes, preferring automated measures over manually gathered ones, to make data-led decisions.
17. We provide complete transparency to our stakeholders in everything we do and produce, to enable open and honest conversations and effective governance of our team.

The original manifesto principles were crafted to reflect the environment in the '90s when it was an accomplishment to have a demonstrable increment of a solution even every month. In modern times the bar is significantly higher. As such, if you compare the wording of the updated principles as we describe them to the original, you will observe that they reflect a lean philosophy of a continuous, just-in-time, experimental, and emergent approach to everything we do. What we have written may be perceived as heresy to some agile religious purists but we believe it is time to move on to reflect modern realities and capabilities.

Lean Software Development

In *The Lean Mindset*, Mary and Tom Poppendieck show how the seven principles of lean manufacturing can be applied to optimize the whole IT value stream [Poppendieck]. These principles are:
1. **Eliminate waste**. Lean thinking advocates regard any activity that does not directly add value to the finished product as waste. The three biggest sources of waste in software

35

development are the addition of unrequired features, project churn and crossing organizational boundaries (particularly between Stakeholders and development teams). To reduce waste it is critical that development teams be allowed to self-organize and operate in a manner that reflects the work they're trying to accomplish.

2. **Build quality in**. Your process should not allow defects to occur in the first place, but when this isn't possible you should work in such a way that you do a bit of work, validate it, fix any issues that you find, and then iterate. Inspecting after the fact, and queuing up defects to be fixed at some time in the future, isn't as effective. Agile practices which build quality into your process include test-driven development (TDD) and non-solo development practices such as pair programming, mob programming, and modeling with others (mob modeling).

3. **Create knowledge**. Planning is useful, but learning is essential. You want to promote strategies, such as iterative development, that help teams discover what Stakeholders really want and act on that knowledge. It's also important for a team to regularly reflect on what they're doing and then act to improve their approach through experimentation.

4. **Defer commitment**. It's not necessary to start solution development by defining a complete specification, and in fact that appears to be a questionable strategy at best. You can support the business effectively through flexible architectures that are change tolerant and by scheduling irreversible decisions to the last possible moment. Frequently, deferring commitment to the last most responsible moment requires the ability to closely couple end-to-end business scenarios to capabilities developed in multiple applications by multiple projects.

5. **Deliver quickly**. It is possible to deliver high-quality systems quickly. By limiting the work of a team to its capacity, you can establish a reliable and repeatable flow of work. An effective organization doesn't demand teams do more than they are capable of, but instead asks them to self-organize and determine what outcomes that they can accomplish. Constraining these teams to delivering potentially shippable solutions on a regular basis motivates them to stay focused on continuously adding value.

6. **Respect people**. The Poppendiecks also observe that sustainable advantage is gained from engaged, thinking people. The implication is that you need a lean approach to governance (see *Govern Delivery Team* in Chapter 27) that focuses on motivating and enabling teams—not on controlling them.

7. **Optimize the whole**. If you want to be effective at a solution you must look at the bigger picture. You need to understand the high-level business processes that individual projects support—processes that often cross multiple systems. You need to manage programs of interrelated systems so you can deliver a complete product to your Stakeholders. Measurements should address how well you're delivering business value and the team should be focused on delivering valuable outcomes to its Stakeholders.

#JoinTheRebellions!

Agile itself is a rebellion against traditional strategies which for the most part was based on theory, most of which has been shown to be false. But like all rebellions the agile thinking of the 1990s has become stale. Predictably a new generation of rabble rousers has come along with their ideas and in some cases movements.

Woody Zuill and Neil Killick started what we call the "hashtag rebellions" with their #NoEstimates movement. Since then #NoProjects [NoProjects], along with other movements described in Table 2.1, have appeared. We believe there are some very interesting and practical strategies coming out of these movements, many of which are captured in DA.

Are these hashtag rebellions good or bad? We think both. Our premise is that it depends because #ContextCounts. We also feel that it's unfortunate that these hashtags are negative in the sense that they're

Book IV A NEW HOPE

It is a period of civil war. Rebel developers, tweeting from a hidden base, have won their first victory against the Agile Industrial Complex (AIC). During the tweeting, Rebel developers have abandoned needless bureaucracy and avoided a DEATH MARCH, a hopeless project with enough soul-crushing power to destroy an entire team. Pursued by the AIC's sinister agents, the Agile Coach races back to her team to help them deliver value to their Stakeholders and restore freedom to their organization…

Our apologies to George Lucas.

against something rather than for something, but we also recognize that they've have been very effective in drawing attention to significant problems in the software process space. Most importantly, they represent a key agile philosophy to question the status quo, to always ask if that's really the way it needs to be.

Table 2.1. Common hashtag rebellions and their visions.

Hashtag	The Vision
#NoEstimates	Estimates are a source of waste because they don't add real value for Stakeholders, they're rarely accurate to begin with, and when we deploy regularly people stop asking for them anyway. See the process goals *Plan the Release* in Chapter 11 and *Accelerate Value Delivery* in Chapter 19 for options.
#NoFrameworks	This is pushback against the prescriptive agile scaling frameworks that experienced agilists find too restrictive and ineffective. More accurately this should be #NoPrescriptiveFrameworks but that's just too long to tweet. While DA is arguably a framework, being a collection of good options to consider experimenting with, it is very different than the prescriptive scaling frameworks that many organizations are struggling to succeed with. Instead we call DA a toolkit.
#NoProjects	This is based on the observation that it is better to flow constant value delivery to our Stakeholders, rather than batch up blobs of value that may or not be worthwhile. It's important to note that this move away from project management in the agile community is not a move away from management but instead from the inherent risks and overhead of projects.
#NoTemplates	Following a template blindly is wrong, as the applicability may be wrong. But selecting templates that suit context can both accelerate delivery and improve quality. See the process goal *Accelerate Value Delivery* in Chapter 19.

And a Few More Great Philosophies

Here are a few philosophies that we've seen work well in practice for disciplined agilists:

- **If it's hard, do it more often**. You believe system integration testing (SIT) is hard? Instead of pushing it to the end of the lifecycle, like traditionalists do, find a way to do it every single iteration. Then find a way to do it single day. Doing hard things more often forces you to find ways, often through automation, to make them easy.

- **If it's scary, do it more often**. You're afraid to evolve a certain piece of code? You're afraid to get feedback from Stakeholders because they may change their minds? Then do it more often. Find ways to overcome what you fear. Find ways to avoid the negative outcomes, or to turn them positive. Fix that code. Make it easier to evolve your solution. Help those Stakeholders understand the implications of the decisions they're making.

- **Keep asking why**. To truly understand something, you need to ask why it happened, or why it works that way, or why it's important to others. Then ask why again, and again, and again. Toyota calls this practice "5 whys" but don't treat 5 as a magic number – keep asking why until you get to the root cause.

- **Learn something every day**. Disciplined agilists strive to learn something every day. Perhaps its something about the domain they're working in. Perhaps it's something about the technologies, or something about their tools. Perhaps it's a new practice, or a new way to perform a practice. There's a lot of learning opportunities before you. Take them.

- **Be respectful**. Everyone is different, with different experiences and different preferences.

- **Be diverse**. The more diverse your team the better your ideas will be, the better your work will be, and the more you'll learn from each other.

- **Be humble**. In many ways this is key to having a learning mindset and to being respectful.

- **Be willing to experiment**. Experiments are opportunities to learn about what works, and what doesn't work, for you in your current context. Being willing and able to experiment is critical to your process improvement efforts.

- **Get comfortable with transparency**. Being agile and doing agile pull back the covers on what you and your team are really doing. Not everyone is comfortable with this. Organizations with traditional methods have a lot of water melon projects – green on the outside and red on the inside. The only way to become awesome is to experiment with new ways of working. Validated learning that an experiment did not work (fail) is good, and sharing that so others learn from your experience is great.

- **Focus on outcomes, not artifacts**. We need to understand what our customers need, what outcomes we can provide, that would delight them. This is why consumable solutions are so important – we need to deliver on the full picture, not just software, and we must provide real value to our customers that is both usable and desirable.

- **Have fun**. Done right, work is play.

In Summary

How can we summarize the Disciplined Agile mindset? Simon Powers sums up the mindset in terms of three core beliefs[Powers]. These beliefs are:

1. **The complexity belief.** Many of the problems that we face are complex adaptive problems, meaning by trying to solve these problems we change the nature of the problem itself.
2. **The people belief.** Individuals are both independent from and dependent on their teams and organisations. Human beings are interdependent. Given the right environment (safety, respect, diversity and inclusion) and a motivating purpose, it is possible for trust and self-organisation to arise. For this to happen, it is necessary to treat everyone with unconditional positive regard.
3. **The proactive belief.** Proactivity in the relentless pursuit of improvement.

We find these beliefs compelling. In many ways they summarize the fundamental motivations behind why you need to choose your WoW. Because we face a unique context we need to tailor our WoW, and in doing so we change the situation that we face which requires us to learn and evolve our WoW. The people belief motivates us to find a WoW that enables us to work together effectively and safely, and the proactive belief reflects the idea that we should continuously learn and improve.

Mindset is Only the Beginning

The Disciplined Agile mindset provides a solid foundation from which your organization can become agile, but it is only a foundation. Our fear is that too many inexperienced coaches are dumbing down agile, hoping to focus on the concepts overviewed in this chapter. It's a good start, but it doesn't get the job done in practice. It isn't sufficient to "be agile", you also need to know how to "do agile" as well. It's wonderful when someone wants to work in a collaborative, respectful manner but if they don't actually know how to do the work they're not going to get much done. Software development, and more importantly solution delivery, is complex – we need to know what we're doing.

3 DISCIPLINED AGILE DELIVERY (DAD) IN A NUTSHELL

Discipline is doing what you know needs to be done, even if you don't want to do it.
- Unknown

Many organizations start their agile journey by adopting Scrum because it describes a good strategy for leading agile software teams. However, Scrum is a very small part of what is required to deliver sophisticated solutions to your Stakeholders. Invariably, teams need to look to other methods to fill in the process gaps that Scrum purposely ignores, and Scrum is very clear about this. When looking at other methods, there is considerable overlap and conflicting terminology that can be confusing to practitioners as well as outside Stakeholders. Worse yet, people don't always know where to look for advice or even know what issues they need to consider.

To address these challenges, Disciplined Agile Delivery (DAD) provides a more cohesive approach to agile solution delivery. DAD is a people-first, learning-oriented, hybrid agile approach to IT solution delivery. These are the critical aspects of DAD:

> **Key Points in this Chapter**
> - DAD is the delivery portion of the Disciplined Agile (DA) toolkit – it is not just another methodology
> - If you are using Scrum, XP, or Kanban, you are already using variations of a subset of DAD
> - DAD provides six lifecycles to choose from, it doesn't prescribe a single way of working – choice is good
> - DAD addresses key enterprise concerns
> - DAD does the process heavy lifting so that you don't have to
> - DAD shows how agile development works from beginning-to-end
> - DAD provides a flexible foundation from which to tactically scale mainstream methods
> - It is easy to get started with DAD
> - You can start with your existing WoW and then apply DAD to improve it gradually – you don't need to make a risky "big bang" change

1. **People first**. People, and the way we work together, are the primary determinant of success for a solution delivery team. DAD supports a robust set of roles, rights, and responsibilities that you can tailor to meet the needs of your situation.
2. **Hybrid**. DAD is a hybrid toolkit that puts great ideas from Scrum, SAFe, Spotify, Agile Modeling (AM), Extreme Programming (XP), Unified Process (UP), Kanban, Lean Software Development, and several other methods into context.
3. **Full delivery lifecycle**. DAD addresses the full delivery lifecycle, from team initiation all the way to delivering a solution to your end users.
4. **Support for multiple lifecycles**. DAD supports agile, lean, continuous delivery, exploratory, and large-team versions of the lifecycle. DAD doesn't prescribe a single lifecycle because it recognizes that one process approach does not fit all. Chapter 6 explores lifecycles in greater detail, providing advice for selecting the right one to start with and then how to evolve from one to another over time.
5. **Complete**. DAD shows how development, modeling, architecture, management, requirements/outcomes, documentation, governance and other strategies fit together in a streamlined whole. DAD does the "process heavy lifting" that other

methods leave up to you.

6. **Context-sensitive**. DAD promotes what we call a goal-driven or outcome-driven approach. In doing so, DAD provides contextual advice regarding viable alternatives and their trade-offs, enabling you to tailor DAD to effectively address the situation in which you find yourself. By describing what works, what doesn't work, and more importantly why, DAD helps you to increase your chance of adopting strategies that will work for you and do so in a streamlined manner. Remember the DA principle – Context Counts.

7. **Consumable solutions over working software.** Potentially shippable software is a good start but what we really need are consumable solutions that delight our customers.

8. **Self-organization with appropriate governance**. Agile and lean teams are self-organizing, which means that the people who do the work are the ones who plan and estimate it. But that doesn't mean they can do whatever they want. They must still work in an enterprise aware manner that reflects the priorities of their organization, and to do that they will need to be governed appropriately by senior leadership. The *Govern Delivery Team* process goal of Chapter 27 describes options for doing exactly that.

This chapter provides a brief overview of DAD, with the details coming in later chapters.

What's New With DAD?

For existing DAD practitioners there are several exciting changes that you'll see in this book compared to Disciplined Agile Delivery [AmblerLines2012]. We've made these changes based on our work at dozens of organizations worldwide and more importantly from the input we've received from a myriad of practitioners. These changes are:

1. **The process goals have been refactored.** Over the past six years we've renamed several goals, introduced a new goal, and combined two pairs of goals. We believe it will make the goals more understandable.

2. **Every goal has been updated.** We've learned a lot over the last six years, a lot of great techniques have appeared, and we've applied older techniques in new situations. We've been posting updates to the goals online at DisciplinedAgileDelivery.com, and in our courseware, but this is the first time we've captured all of the updates in print.

3. **All of the goals are captured visually.** This is the first book to capture all of DAD's goal diagrams. We introduced the goal diagrams after the 2012 book came out, although have published some of them in our short book Introduction to Disciplined Agile Delivery 2nd Ed. [LinesAmbler2018] and An Executive Guide to Disciplined Agile [AmblerLines2017].

4. **New and updated lifecycles.** We've explicitly introduced the Program lifecycle (we had described it in terms of team structure before) and the Exploratory lifecycle. We've also introduced both agile and lean versions of what we used to call the Continuous Delivery lifecycle.

5. **Advice for applying the toolkit in practice.** A big difference you'll see in this book is much more advice for how to apply DA in practice. This advice reflects an additional six years of working with organizations around the world to adopt Disciplined Agile strategies.

Figure 3.1 shows the potential roles that people will fill on DAD teams, and Chapter 4 describes them in detail. The roles are organized into two categories: Primary roles that we find are critical to the success of any agile team and supporting roles that appear as needed.

Figure 3.1. Potential roles on DAD teams.

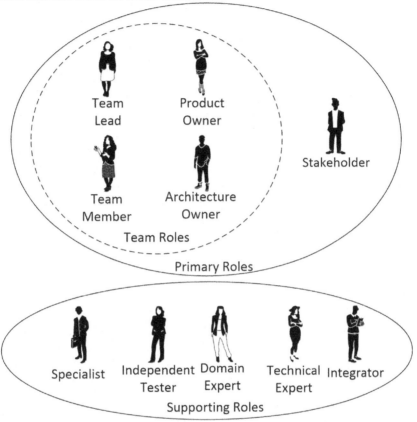

The primary roles are:
- **Team Lead**. This person leads the team, helping the team to be successful. This is similar to the Scrum Master role in Scrum [ScrumGuide].
- **Product Owner (PO)**. A PO is responsible for working with Stakeholders to identify the work to be done, to prioritize that work, to help the team to understand the Stakeholder needs, and to help the team interact effectively with Stakeholders [ScrumGuide].
- **Architecture Owner (AO)**. An AO guides the team through architecture and design decisions, working closely with the Team Lead and PO when doing so [AgileModeling].
- **Team Member**. Team Members work together to produce the solution. Ideally Team Members are generalizing specialists, or working on becoming so, who are often referred to as cross-skilled people. A generalizing specialist is someone with one or more specialities (such as testing, analysis, programming, …) and a broad knowledge of solution delivery and the domain they are working in [GenSpec].

43

- **Stakeholder**. A Stakeholder is someone who will be affected by the work of the team, including but not limited to end users, support engineers, operations staff, financial people, auditors, enterprise architects, and senior leadership. Some agile methods call this role Customer.

The supporting roles are:

- **Specialist**. Although most Team Members will be generalizing specialists, or at least striving to be so, we sometimes have specialists on teams when called for. User experience (UX) and security experts are specialists who may be on a team when there is significant user interface (UI) development or security concerns respectively. Sometimes Business Analysts are needed to support POs dealing with a complex domain or geographically distributed Stakeholders. Furthermore, roles from other parts of the DA toolkit such as Enterprise Architects, Portfolio Managers, Reuse Engineers, Operations Engineers, and others are considered specialists from a DAD point of view.

- **Independent Tester**. Although the majority of testing, if not all of it, should be performed by the team there can be a need for an independent test team at scale. Common scenarios requiring Independent Testers include: regulatory compliance that requires that some testing occur outside of the team; and a large program (a team of teams) working on a complex solution that has significant integration challenges.

- **Domain Expert**. A Domain Expert, sometimes called a subject matter expert (SME), is someone with deep knowledge in a given domain or problem space. They often work with the team, or POs, to share their knowledge and experience.

- **Technical Expert**. This is someone with deep technical expertise who works with the team for a short time to help them overcome a specific technical challenge. For example an operational database administrator (DBA) may work with the team to help them setup, configure, and learn the fundamentals of a database.

- **Integrator**. Also called a system integrator, they will often support Independent Testers who need to perform system integration testing (SIT) of a complex solution or collection of solutions.

Everyone on agile teams have rights and responsibilities. Everyone. For example everyone has the right to be given respect but they also have the responsibility to give respect to others. Furthermore, each role on an agile team has specific additional responsibilities that they must fulfill. Rights and responsibilities are also covered in detail in Chapter 4.

A Hybrid of Great Ideas

We like to say that DAD does the heavy process lifting so that you don't have to. What we mean by that is that is we've mined the various methods, frameworks, and other sources to identify potential practices and strategies that your team may want to experiment with and adopt. We put these techniques into context, exploring fundamental concepts such as what are the advantages and disadvantages of the technique, when would you apply the technique, when wouldn't you apply the technique, and to what extent would you apply it? Answers to these questions are critical when a team is choosing its WoW.

Figure 3.2 indicates some of the methodologies and frameworks that we've mined for techniques. For example, XP is the source of technical practices such as test-driven development (TDD), refactoring, and pair programming to name a few. Scrum is the source

44

of strategies such as product backlogs, sprint/iteration planning, daily coordination meetings, and more. Agile Modeling gives us model storming, initial architecture envisioning, continuous documentation, and active Stakeholder participation. Where these methods go into detail about these individual techniques, the focus of DAD, and DA in general, is to put them into context and to help you choose the right strategy at the right time.

Figure 3.2. DAD is a hybrid of great ideas.

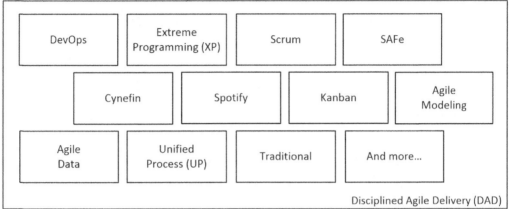

Choice is Good: Process Goals

DAD includes a collection of twenty-one process goals, or process outcomes if you like, as Figure 3.3 shows. Each goal is described as a collection of decision points, issues that your team needs to determine whether they need to address and if so how they will do so. Potential practices/strategies for addressing a decision point, which can be combined in many cases, are presented as lists. Goal diagrams, an example is shown in Figure 3.4, are similar conceptually to mind maps, albeit with the extension of the arrow to represent relative effectiveness of options in some cases. Goal diagrams are, in effect, guides to help a team to choose the best strategies that they are capable of doing right now given their skills, culture, and situation. Chapter 5 explores DAD's goal-driven approach and Sections 2 through 5 describe each goal in detail.

Figure 3.3. The process goals of DAD.

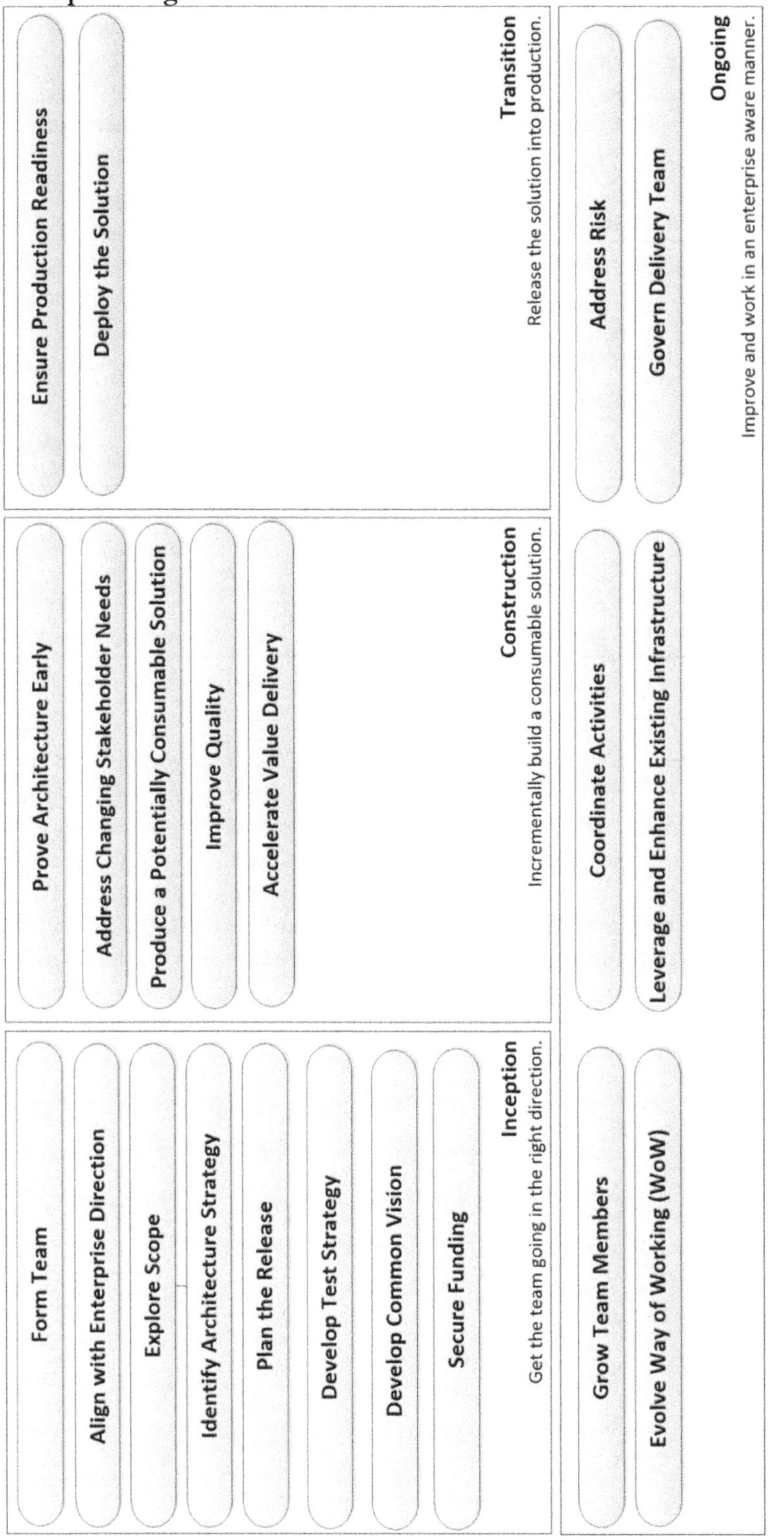

Inception
Get the team going in the right direction.

- Form Team
- Align with Enterprise Direction
- Explore Scope
- Identify Architecture Strategy
- Plan the Release
- Develop Test Strategy
- Develop Common Vision
- Secure Funding

Construction
Incrementally build a consumable solution.

- Prove Architecture Early
- Address Changing Stakeholder Needs
- Produce a Potentially Consumable Solution
- Improve Quality
- Accelerate Value Delivery

Transition
Release the solution into production.

- Ensure Production Readiness
- Deploy the Solution

Ongoing
Improve and work in an enterprise aware manner.

- Grow Team Members
- Evolve Way of Working (WoW)
- Coordinate Activities
- Leverage and Enhance Existing Infrastructure
- Address Risk
- Govern Delivery Team

46

Figure 3.4 The Improve Quality process goal diagram.

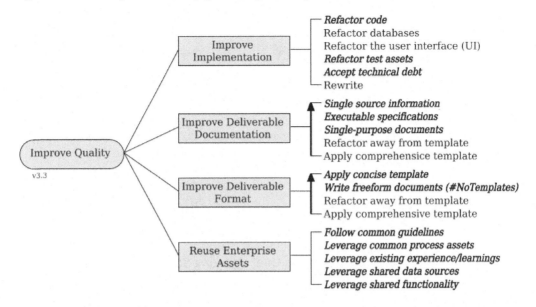

Choice is Good: Multiple Lifecycle Support

Lifecycles put an order to the activities that a team performs to build a solution, in effect they organize the techniques that we apply to get the work done. Because solution delivery teams find themselves in a range of different situations, they need to be able to choose a lifecycle that best fits the context that they face. You can see in Figure 3.5 that DAD supports six lifecycles:

1. **Agile**. This is a Scrum-based lifecycle for solution delivery projects.
2. **Lean**. This is a Kanban-based lifecycle for solution delivery projects.
3. **Continuous Delivery: Agile**. This is a Scrum-based lifecycle for long-standing teams.
4. **Continuous Delivery: Lean**. This is a Kanban-based lifecycle for long-standing teams.
5. **Exploratory**. This is a Lean-Startup-based lifecycle for running experiments with potential customers to discover what they actually want.
6. **Program**. This is a lifecycle for a team of agile or lean teams.

Chapter 6 describes the six DAD lifecycles in detail, as well as the Traditional lifecycle, and provides advice for when to choose each one.

Figure 3.5. DAD supports six lifecycles.

Agile   Continuous Delivery: Agile   Exploratory

Lean   Continuous Delivery: Lean   Program

Consumable Solutions Over Working Software

The Agile Manifesto suggests that we measure progress based upon "working software". But what good is that if the customer doesn't want to use it? What if they don't like using it? From a design thinking point of view it is clear that "working" isn't sufficient, instead we need to deliver is something that is consumable:

- **It works**. What we produce must be functional and provide the outcomes that our Stakeholders expect.
- **It's usable**. Our solution should work well, with a well-designed user experience (UX).
- **It's desirable**. People should want to work with our solution, and better yet feel a need to work with it, and where appropriate to pay us for it. As the first principle of Disciplined Agile recommends, our solution should delight our customers, not just satisfy them.

Additionally, what we produce isn't just software but instead is a full-fledged solution that may include improvements to:

- **Software**. Software is an important part, but just a part, of our overall solution.
- **Hardware**. Our solutions run on hardware, and sometimes we need to evolve or improve that hardware.
- **Business processes**. We often improve the business processes around the usage of the system that we produce.
- **Organizational structure**. Sometimes the organization structure of the end users of our systems evolves to reflect changes in the functionality supported by it.
- **Supporting documentation**. Deliverable documentation, such as technical overviews and user manuals/help are often a key aspect of our solutions.

DAD Terminology

Table 3.1 maps common DAD terms to the equivalent terms in other approaches. There are several important observations that we'd like to make about the terminology:

1. **There is no standard agile terminology**. There isn't an ISO industry standard for agile and even if there was it very likely would be ignored by agile practitioners.
2. **Scrum terminology is questionable at best**. When Scrum was first developed in the 1990s its creators purposefully decided to choose unusual terminology, some adopted from the game of rugby, to indicate to people that it was different. That's perfectly fine, but given that DA is a hybrid we cannot limit it to apply goofy terms from the mid-1990s.
3. **Terms are important**. We believe terms should be clear. You need to explain what a scrum meeting is, and that it isn't a status meeting, whereas it's pretty clear what a coordination meeting is. Nobody sprints through a marathon. And Scrum Master? Misogynistic and kinky all at once.
4. **Choose whatever terms you like**. Having said all this, DAD doesn't prescribe terminology, so if you want to use terms like sprint, scrum meeting, or Scrum Master then go ahead.
5. **Some mappings are tenuous**. An important thing to point out is that the terms don't map perfectly. For example, we know that there are differences between Team Leads, Scrum Masters, and Project Managers but those differences aren't pertinent for this discussion.

Table 3.1. Mapping some of the varying terminology in the agile community.

DAD	Scrum	Spotify	XP	SAFe	Traditional
Architecture Owner	-	-	Coach	Solution Architect	Solution Architect
Coordination meeting	Daily Standup	Huddle	-	Daily Standup	Status Meeting
Domain Expert	-	Customer	Customer	Product Owner	Subject Matter Expert (SME)
Iteration	Sprint	Sprint	Iteration	Iteration	Timebox
Product Owner	Product Owner	Product Owner	Customer Representative	Product Owner	Change Control Board (CCB)
Stakeholder	-	Customer	Customer	Customer	Stakeholder
Team	Team	Squad, Tribe	Team	Team	Team
Team Lead	Scrum Master	Agile Coach	Coach	Scrum Master	Project Manager

Context Counts: DAD Provides The Foundation for Scaling Agile Tactically

Disciplined Agile (DA) distinguishes between two types of "agility at scale":

1. **Tactical agility at scale.** This is the application of agile and lean strategies on individual DAD teams. The goal is to apply agile deeply to address all of the complexities, what we call scaling factors, appropriately.

2. **Strategic agility at scale.** This is the application of agile and lean strategies broadly across your entire organization. From an IT point of view this includes Disciplined DevOps and Disciplined Agile IT in general. From an enterprise point of view this includes all divisions and teams within your organization, not just your IT department.

Let's examine what it means to tactically scale agile solution delivery. When many people hear "scaling" they often think about large teams that may be geographically distributed in some way. This clearly happens, and people are clearly succeeding at applying agile in these sorts of situations, but there's often more to scaling than this. Organizations are also applying agile in compliance situations, either regulatory compliance that is imposed upon them (such as HIPAA, PIPEDA, or GDPR) or self-selected compliance (such as CMMI, ISO, and ITIL). They are also applying agile to a range of domain and technical complexities, and even when multiple organizations are involved (as in outsourcing). Figure 3.6 summarizes the potential tactical scaling factors that you need to consider when tailoring your agile strategy. These scaling factors are a subset of the factors described in the Software Development Context Framework (SDCF) in Chapter 2. The further out on each scale you are the greater the risk that you face.

Figure 3.6. Tactical scaling factors.

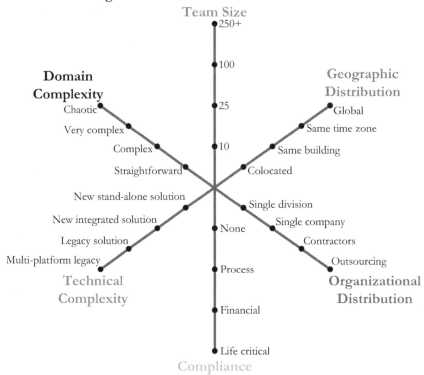

50

DAD provides a solid foundation for tactically scaling agile in several ways:
- DAD promotes a risk-value lifecycle where teams attack the riskier work early to help eliminate some or all of the risk, thereby increasing the chance of success. Some people like to refer to this as an aspect of "failing fast" although we like to put it in terms of learning fast or better yet succeeding early.
- DAD promotes self-organization enhanced with effective governance based on the observation that agile teams work within the scope and constraints of a larger, organizational ecosystem. As a result, DAD recommends that you adopt an effective governance strategy that guides and enables agile teams.
- DAD promotes the delivery of consumable solutions over just the construction of working software.
- DAD promotes *Enterprise Awareness* over team awareness (this is a fundamental principle of DA as you learned in Chapter 2). What we mean by this is that the team should do what's right for your organization – work to a common vision, leverage existing legacy systems and data sources, follow common guidelines – and not just do what's convenient or fun for them.
- DAD is context-sensitive and goal driven, not prescriptive (another DA principle is that *Choice is Good*). One process approach does not fit all, and DAD teams have the autonomy to choose and evolve their WoW.

It's Easy to Get Started with DAD

We'd like to share several strategies that we've seen applied to get people, teams, and organizations started with DAD:
1. **Read this book**. A good way for individuals to get started is to read this book, particularly Section 1. Sections 2 through 5 are reference material that you will use to choose your WoW.
2. **Take training**. Even after reading this book you're likely to benefit from training as it will help to round out your knowledge. At some point we hope that you choose to get certified in Disciplined Agile (see Appendix A).
3. **Start with a prescribed method/framework, then work your way out of "method prison."** Teams might choose to start with an existing method such as Scrum or SAFe and then apply the strategies described in this book to evolve their WoW from there.
4. Start with DAD. We believe that it's easier to start with DAD to begin with and thereby avoid running into the limitations of prescriptive methods.
5. **Work with an experienced agile coach**. We highly suggest you bring in a Certified Disciplined Agile Coach (CDAC) to help guide you through applying the DA toolkit.

Organizational adoption of Disciplined Agile will take time, potentially years when you decide to support agile WoWs across all aspects of your organization. Agile transformations such as this, which evolve into continuous improvement efforts at the organizational level, are the topics of Chapters 7 and 8 in our book *An Executive Guide to Disciplined Agile* [AmblerLines2017].

51

In Summary

Disciplined Agile Delivery (DAD) provides a pragmatic approach for addressing the unique situations in which solution delivery teams find themselves. DAD explicitly addresses the issues faced by enterprise agile teams that many agile methodologies prefer to gloss over. This includes how to successfully initiate agile teams in a streamlined manner, how architecture fits into the agile lifecycle, how to address documentation effectively, how to address quality issues in an enterprise environment, how agile analysis techniques are applied to address the myriad of Stakeholder concerns, how to govern agile and lean teams, and many more critical issues. We'll explore strategies to do this in Sections 2 through 5 of this book.

In this chapter you learned that:

- DAD is the delivery portion of Disciplined Agile (DA).
- If you are using Scrum, XP, or Kanban, you are already using variations of a subset of DAD.
- You can start with your existing WoW and then apply DAD to improve it gradually – you don't need to make a risky "big bang" change.
- DAD provides six lifecycles to choose from, it doesn't prescribe a single approach, providing you with solid choices on which to base your WoW.
- DAD addresses key enterprise concerns and shows how to do so in a context-sensitive manner.
- DAD does the heavy process lifting so that you don't have to.
- DAD shows how agile development works from beginning-to-end.
- DAD provides a flexible foundation from which to tactically scale mainstream methods.
- It is easy to get started with DAD, and there are multiple paths to do so.

4 ROLES, RIGHTS, AND RESPONSIBILITIES

Alone we can do so little, together we can do so much. Helen Keller

This chapter explores the potential rights and responsibilities of people involved with Disciplined Agile Delivery (DAD) teams, and the roles that they may choose to take on. We say potential because you may discover that you need to tailor these ideas to fit into your organization's cultural environment. However, our experience is that the further you stray from the advice we provide below the greater the risk you will take on. As always, do the best you can do in the situation that you face and strive to improve over time. Let's start with general rights and responsibilities.

> **Key Points in this Chapter**
> - DAD suggests there are five primary roles – Team Lead, Product Owner, Team Member, Architecture Owner, and Stakeholder.
> - An Architecture Owner is the technical leader of the team and represents the architecture interests of the organization.
> - DAD's Stakeholder role recognizes that we need to delight all Stakeholders, not just our customers.
> - In many situations teams will rely on people in supporting roles – specialists, Domain Experts, technical experts, Independent Testers, or integrators – as appropriate and as needed.
> - DAD's roles are meant to be, like everything else, a suggested starting point. You may have valid reasons for tailoring the roles in your organization.

Rights and Responsibilities

Becoming agile requires a culture change within your organization, and all cultures have rules, some explicit and some implicit, so that everyone understands their expected behavior. One way to define expected behavior is to negotiate the rights and responsibilities that people have. Interestingly, a lot of very good thinking on this topic was done in the Extreme Programming (XP) method, ideas which we've evolved for Disciplined Agile (DA) [RightsResponsibilities]. The following lists of potential rights and responsibilities are meant to act as a potential starting point for your team.

As an agile Team Member, we have the right to:
- Be treated with respect.
- Work in a "safe environment."
- Produce and receive quality work based upon agreed standards.
- Choose and evolve our way of working (WoW).
- Self-organize and plan our work, signing up for tasks that we will work on.
- Own the estimation process – the people who do the work are the ones who estimate the work.
- Determine how the team will work together – the people who do the work are the ones who plan the work.
- Be provided good-faith information and decisions in a timely manner.

To misquote Uncle Ben Parker, with great rights come great responsibilities. Agile Team Members have the responsibility to:

- Optimize their WoW.
- Be willing to collaborate extensively within your team.
- Share all information including "work in progress."
- Coach others in your skills and experience.
- Expand your knowledge and skills outside your specialty.
- Validate your work as early as possible, working with others to do so.
- Attend co-ordination meetings in person or through other means if not collocated.
- Proactively look for ways to improve team performance.
- For teams following an agile lifecycle, see Chapter 6, avoid accepting work outside of the current iteration without consent from the team.
- Make all work visible at all times, typically via a taskboard, so that current team work and capacity is transparent.

Potential Roles

DAD provides a set of five primary roles "out of the box" three of which are similar to those of Scrum. As you see in Figure 4.1 DAD has a Team Lead (similar to ScrumMaster), Product Owner, and Team Member. DAD adds Stakeholder (an extension of customer), and a role that we have seen to be extremely valuable in enterprise settings, that of Architecture Owner. Ideally we have a "whole team" wherein we have all the skills on the team required to get the job done. However, while not ideal, in non-trivial situations it is common to require skills from outside the team and as such DAD includes a set of supporting roles that may join the team as needed.

Figure 4.1. Potential DAD roles.

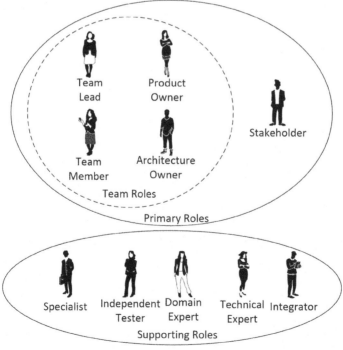

54

To start, let's explore the primary roles.

Stakeholder

A Stakeholder is someone who is materially impacted by the outcome of the solution. In this regard, the Stakeholder is clearly more than an end-user or customer: A Stakeholder could be a:

- Direct user
- Indirect user
- Manager of users
- Senior leader
- Operations staff member
- The "gold owner" who funds the team,
- Support (help desk) staff member
- Auditors
- A program/portfolio manager
- Developers working on other solutions that integrate or interact with ours
- Maintenance professionals potentially affected by the development and/or deployment of a software-bases solution.
- And many more.

Product Owner

The Product Owner (PO) is the person on the team who speaks as the "one voice of the Stakeholder" [ScrumGuide]. As you see in Figure 4.2, he or she represents the needs and desires of the Stakeholder community to the agile delivery team. As such, the PO clarifies any details regarding Stakeholder desires or requirements for the solution and is also responsible for prioritizing the work that the team performs to deliver the solution. While the PO may not be able to answer all questions, it is their responsibility to track down the answer in a timely manner so that the team can stay focused on their tasks.

Each DAD team, or subteam in the case of large programs organized as a team of teams, has a single PO. A secondary goal for a PO is to represent the work of the agile team to the Stakeholder community. This includes arranging demonstrations of the solution as it evolves and communicating team status to key Stakeholders.

As a Stakeholder proxy, the Product Owner:

- Is the "go to" person for domain information.
- Provides information and makes decisions in a timely manner.
- Prioritizes all work for the team, including but not limited to requirements (perhaps captured as user stories); defects to be fixed; technical debt to be paid down; and more. The PO takes both Stakeholder and team needs into account when doing so.
- Continually reprioritizes and adjusts scope based on evolving stakeholder needs.
- Is an active participant in modeling and acceptance testing.
- Helps the team gain access to expert Stakeholders.
- Accepts the work of the team as either done or not done.
- Facilitates requirements modeling sessions, including requirements envisioning and

look-ahead modeling.
- Educates the team in the business domain.
- Is the gateway to funding.

When representing the agile team to the Stakeholder community, the Product Owner:
- Is the public face of the team to Stakeholders.
- Demos the solution to key Stakeholders, which may include coaching Team Members to run the demo.
- Announces releases.
- Monitors and communicates team status to interested Stakeholders, which may include educating Stakeholders on how to access and understand the team's automated dashboard.
- Organizes milestone reviews, which should be kept as simple as possible (see *Govern Delivery Team* in Chapter 27).
- Educates Stakeholders in the delivery team's way of working (WoW).
- Negotiates priorities, scope, funding, and schedule.

It is important to note that Product Owner tends to be a full time job, and may even require help at scale in complex domains. A common challenge that we see in organizations new to agile is that they try to staff this role with someone on a part-time basis, basically tacking the PO role onto an already busy person.

Figure 4.2. The Product Owner as a bridge between the team and Stakeholders.

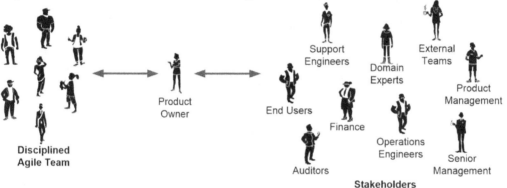

Team Member

Team Members focus on producing the solution for Stakeholders. Team Members will perform testing, analysis, architecture, design, programming, planning, estimation, and many more activities as appropriate. Note that not every Team Member will have every single one of these skills, at least not yet, but they will have a subset of them and they will strive to gain more skills over time. Ideally Team Members are generalizing specialists, someone with one or more specialties (such as analysis, programming, testing, …), a general knowledge of the delivery process, at least a general knowledge of the domain that they're working in, and the willingness to pick up new skills and knowledge from others [GenSpec]. Figure 4.3 compares four categories of skill levels – Specialists who are narrowly focused on a single specialty, generalists with a broad knowledge who are often good at organizing and coordinating others but who do not have the detailed skills required to do the work, experts who have deep knowledge and skills in many specialties, and generalizing specialists who are a happy medium between generalists and specialists.

In practice requiring people to be generalizing specialists can be daunting at first, particularly for people who are new to agile, because this is very different than the traditional approach of having generalists manage teams of specialists. The traditional approach is problematic because of the overhead required to make it work – specialists do their jobs, producing something for the next group of specialists downstream from them. To move the work along they need to write and maintain documentation, often containing new versions of information that has already been documented upstream from them in the process. In short, specialists inject a lot of waste into the process with interim artifacts, reviews of these artifacts, and wait time to do the reviews. Generalizing specialists, on the other hand, have a wider range of skills enabling them to collaborate more effectively with others, to do a wider range of work and thereby avoid creation of interim artifacts. They work smarter, not harder.

Figure 4.3. The skill levels of Team Members.

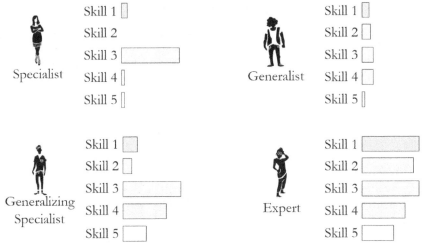

The challenge is that if you're new to agile then you very likely have staff who are either generalists or specialists, but very few generalizing specialists. As Donald Rumsfeld once said, you go to war with the army that you have, not the army that you want. The implication is that if you currently have people who are either specialists or generalists then you put your teams together with these people. Because you want to improve your team's productivity, you help your Team Members become generalizing specialists through non-solo work techniques such as pair programming, mob programming, and modeling with others (see *Grow Team Members* in Chapter 22). By doing so, over several months specialists will pick up a wider range of skills and become more effective generalizing specialists as a result.

In addition to the general rights and responsibilities described earlier, Team Members have several additional responsibilities. They will:

- **Self-organize**. Team Members will identify tasks, estimate tasks, "sign-up" for tasks, perform the tasks, and track their status towards completion.
- **Go to the Product Owner (PO) for domain information and decisions**. Although Team Members will provide input to the PO, in the end the PO is responsible for providing the requirements and prioritizing the work, not the Team

Members. It requires significant discipline on the part of Team Members to respect this, and to not add new features (known as "scope creep") or to guess at the details.

- **Work with the Architecture Owner (AO) to evolve the architecture**. The AO is responsible for guiding the team through architecture and design work. Team Members will work closely and collaboratively with the AO to identify and evolve the architectural strategy. When the team isn't able to come to an agreement around the direction to take the AO may need to be the tie breaker and choose what they feel to be the best option, which Team Members are expected to support. More on this below.

- **Follow enterprise conventions and leverage and enhance the existing infrastructure**. One of the DA principles, see Chapter 2, is to be enterprise aware. An implication of this is that DAD Team Members will adopt and have the discipline to tailor where appropriate, any enterprise/corporate coding standards, user interface design conventions, database guidelines, and so on. They should also try to reuse and enhance existing, reusable assets such as common web services, frameworks, and yes, even existing legacy data sources. The *Leverage and Enhance Existing Infrastructure* process goal is described in Chapter 26.

- **Lead meetings**. Although other agile methods will assign this responsibility to the Team Lead, the fact is that anyone on the team can lead or facilitate meetings. The Team Lead is merely responsible for ensuring that this happens.

Team Lead

An important aspect of self-organizing teams is that the Team Lead facilitates or guides the team in performing technical management activities instead of taking on these responsibilities him or herself. The Team Lead is a servant-leader to the team, or better yet a host leader, creating and maintaining the conditions that allow the team to be successful. This can be a hard role to fill – attitude is key to their success.

The Team Lead is also an agile coach, helping to keep the team focused on delivering work items and fulfilling their iteration goals and commitments that they have made to the Product Owner. He or she acts as a true leader, facilitating communication, empowering them to choose their way of working (WoW), ensuring that the team has the resources that it needs, and removes any impediments to the team (issue resolution) in a timely manner. When teams are self-organizing, effective leadership is crucial to your success.

A Team Lead's leadership responsibilities can be summarized as:

- Guides the team through choosing and evolving their WoW.
- Facilitates close collaboration across all roles and functions.
- Ensures that the team is fully functional and productive.

> **Why not call a Team Lead a ScrumMaster?**
> Since DAD supports several lifecycle approaches, not every team in your organization is likely to use Scrum. Lean teams will have Team Leads. So why confuse your organization with two different terms for Team Lead, depending on the approaches that they use? And, what if a Scrum team moves to a lean approach, and then back to Scrum. Would role names have to change accordingly? Clearly this would be silly.

58

- Keeps team focused within the context of their vision and goals.
- Is responsible for removal of team-based impediments and for the escalation of organization-wide impediments, collaborating with organizational leadership to do so.
- Protects the team from interruptions and external interferences.
- Maintains open honest communication between everyone involved.
- Coaches others in the use and application of agile practices.
- Prompts the team to discuss and think through issues when they're identified.
- Facilitates decision making, but does not make decisions or mandate internal team activity.
- Ensures that the team keeps their focus on producing a potentially consumable solution.

When there are no project managers (PMs) or resource/functional managers Team Leads may be asked to take on the responsibilities that people in these roles would have fulfilled. The optional responsibilities that a Team Lead may be required to fulfill, and the challenges associated in doing so, include:

- **Assessing Team Members**. There are several strategies for assessing or providing feedback to people, described by the *Grow Team Members* process goal in Chapter 22, that you may apply. Doing so is often the responsibility of a resource manager, but sometimes people in these roles are not available. When a Team Lead is responsible for assessing their fellow Team Members it puts them in a position of authority over the people they're supposed to lead and collaborate with. This in turn can significantly alter the dynamics of the relationship that Team Members have with the Team Lead, reducing their psychological safety when working with the Team Lead because they don't know how doing so will affect their assessment.
- **Managing the team's budget**. Although the PO is typically the gateway to funding, somebody may be required to track and report how the funds are spent. If the PO does not do this then the Team Lead typically becomes responsible for doing so.
- **Management reporting**. Ensures that someone on the team, perhaps themselves, captures relevant team metrics and reports team progress to organizational leadership. Hopefully this type of reporting is automated via dashboard technology, but if not the Team Lead is often responsible for manually generating any required reports. See the *Govern Delivery Team* process goal in Chapter 27 for more on metrics.
- **Obtains resources**. The Team Lead is often responsible for ensuring that collaborative tools, such as task boards for team coordination and white boards for modeling, are available to the team.
- **Meeting facilitation**. Ensures that someone on the team, sometimes themselves, facilitates the various meetings (coordination meetings, iteration planning meetings, demos, modeling sessions, and retrospectives).

The Team Lead role is often a part-time effort, particularly on smaller teams. The implication is that a Team Lead either needs to have the skills to also be a Team Member or perhaps in some cases an Architecture Owner (more on this below). However, on a team new to agile the coaching aspects of being a Team Lead are critical to your success at adopting agile. This is something that organizations new to agile can struggle with conceptually, because they've never had to make a similar investment in their staff's growth.

Another alternative is to have someone be the Team Lead on two or three teams, although that requires the teams to stagger their ceremonies such as coordination meetings, demos, and retrospectives so that the Team Lead can be involved. This can work with teams that are experienced with agile thinking and techniques because they don't require as much coaching. Furthermore, as teams gel and become adept at self-organization there is less need for someone to be in the Team Lead role and it may be sufficient for someone to step up from time to time to address Team Lead responsibilities.

Architecture Owner

The Architecture Owner (AO) is the person who guides the team through architecture and design decisions, facilitating the identification and evolution of the overall solution design [AgileModeling]. On small teams the person in the role of Team Lead will often also be in the role of AO, assuming they have the skills for both roles. Having said that, our experience is that it is hard enough to find someone qualified to fill either of these roles, let alone both.

Although the Architecture Owner is typically the senior developer on the team – and sometimes may be known as the technical architect, software architect, or solution architect – it should be noted that this is not a hierarchical position into which other Team Members report. He or she is just like any other Team Member and is expected to sign-up and deliver work related to tasks like any other Team Member. Architecture Owners should have a technical background and a solid understanding of the business domain.

The responsibilities of the Architecture Owner include:

- Guiding the creation and evolution of the architecture of the solution that the team is working on. Note that the Architecture Owner is not solely responsible for the architecture, instead they lead the architecture and design discussions.

- Mentoring and coaching other Team Members in architecture practices and issues.

- Understanding the architectural direction and standards of your organization and helping to ensure that the team adheres to them appropriately.

- The AO will work closely with the Enterprise Architects, if they exist, and may even be an Enterprise Architect. Note that this can be an interesting change for larger organizations where their Enterprise Architects are not currently actively involved with teams. For smaller organizations this is quite common.

- The AO will work closely with the Product Owner (PO) to help them to understand the needs of technical stakeholders, to help them understand the implications of technical debt and the need to invest in paying it down, and in some cases to understand and interact with Team Members more effectively.

- Understanding existing enterprise assets such as frameworks, patterns, subsystems and ensuring that the team uses them where appropriate.

- Ensuring that the solution will be easy to support by encouraging good design and refactoring to minimize technical debt. See the *Improve Quality* process goal in Chapter 18 for details.

- Ensuring that the solution is integrated and tested on a regular basis, ideally via a continuous integration (CI) strategy.

- Having the final say regarding technical decisions, but they try to avoid dictating the architectural direction in favor of a collaborative, team-based approach. The Architecture Owner should work very closely with the team to identify and determine strategies to mitigate key technical risks (see the *Prove Architecture Early*

60

process goal in Chapter 15).

- Leads the initial architecture envisioning effort at the beginning of a release and supports the initial requirements envisioning effort (particularly when it comes to understanding and evolving the non-functional requirements for the solution).

Potential Supporting Roles

We would like to be able to say that all you need are the five primary roles described above to succeed. The fact is the primary roles don't cover the entire gamut – it's unlikely your team will have all of the technical expertise that it needs, your Product Owner couldn't possibly have expert knowledge in all aspects of the domain, and even if your organization had experts at all aspects of solution delivery it couldn't possibly staff every single team with the full range of expertise required. Your team may include the need to add some or all of the following roles:

1. **Domain Expert (subject matter expert).** The PO represents a wide range of Stakeholders, not just end users, so it isn't reasonable to expect them to be experts in every nuance of the domain, something that is particularly true in complex domains. The PO will sometimes bring in Domain Experts to work with the team, for example, a tax expert to explain the details of a requirement or the sponsoring executive to explain the vision.

2. **Specialist.** Although most agile Team Members are generalizing specialists, sometimes, particularly at scale, specialists are required. For example, on large teams or in complex domains one or more agile business analysts may join the team to help you to explore the requirements for what you're building. On very large teams a program manager may be required to coordinate the Team Leads on various squads/subteams. You will also see specialists on teams when generalizing specialists aren't yet available – when your organization is new to agile it may be staffed with specialists who haven't yet made the transition to generalizing specialists.

3. **Technical expert.** Sometimes the team needs the help of technical experts, such as a build master to set up their build scripts, an agile database administrator to help design and test their database, or a security expert to provide advice around writing a secure solution. Technical experts are brought in on an as-needed, temporary basis to help the team overcome a difficult problem and to transfer their skills to one or more developers on the team. Technical experts are often working on other teams that are responsible for enterprise-level technical concerns or are simply specialists on loan to your team from other delivery teams.

4. **Independent Tester.** Although the majority of the testing is done by the people on the DAD team themselves, some teams are supported by an independent test team working in parallel to them who validates their work throughout the lifecycle. This independent test team is typically needed for scaling situations within complex domains, using complex technology, or addressing regulatory compliance issues

5. **Integrator.** For large DAD teams that have been organized into a team of subteams/squads, the subteams are typically responsible for one or more subsystems or features. The larger the overall team, generally the larger and more complicated the solution being built. In these situations, the overall team may require one or more people in the role of integrator responsible for building the entire solution from its various subsystems. On smaller teams or in simpler situations the Architecture Owner is typically responsible for insuring integration, a

61

responsibility that is picked up by the integrator(s) for more complex environments. Integrators often work closely with the independent test team, if there is one, to perform system integration testing regularly throughout the release. This integrator role is typically only needed at scale for complex technical solutions.

An interesting implication for organizations that are new to agile is that the agile teams may need access to people in these supporting roles earlier in the lifecycle than they are accustomed to with traditional teams. And the timing of the access is often a bit less predictable, due to the evolutionary nature of agile, than with traditional development. We've found that people in these supporting roles will need to be flexible.

The Three Leadership Roles

We often refer to the Team Lead, PO, and AO as the leadership triumvirate of the team. As you see in Figure 4.4 the PO is focused on getting the right product built, the AO on building the product right, and the Team Lead on building it fast. All three of these priorities must be balanced through close collaboration by the people in these roles – Figure 4.4 also indicates what happens when one of these priorities is ignored. When teams are new to agile the center spot may prove to be quite small at first, but that over time the people in these three leadership roles, and more importantly the entire team itself, will help to grow it.

Figure 4.4. Viewpoints of the three leadership roles.

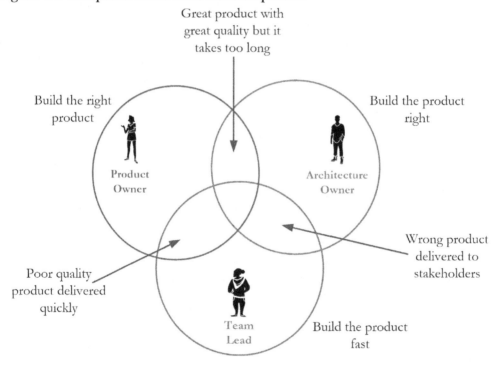

Do We Need the Scrum Roles At All?

We recently were intrigued to hear Dan North speak at a conference in the UK, making a case that Scrum is past its expiry date and we really need to move on. To sum up his message, the Agile Manifesto, written by a bunch of middle-aged white male programmers is almost irrelevant because it reflects the context faced by software developers of the 1990s. Scrum is a batch system inconsistent with rapid delivery, wasteful, and retrospectives are mechanical and too infrequent for continuous process improvement. Afterward he said he might slip out the back lest a bunch of Scrum Alliance people were waiting outside with torches to burn the heretic!

Dan's message is well thought out and coherent. In the 90's when Scrum was created, it was a different world. We were used to working in specialist silos, building software from documents and didn't really know how and when to collaborate hence the need for a ScrumMaster to forcibly bring Team Members together, unifying them behind a team goal. These days, anyone who is young enough not to be around pre-Internet has never worked in a silo. They don't need an designated role within the team to ensure collaboration happens effectively. Similarly, why do we need a formal PO between the team and the rest of our Stakeholders? This degree of separation increases chances of miscommunications and limits opportunities of the teams to develop empathy for the people they are building the solution for. In Scrum's early days it was difficult to gain access to Stakeholders so the "mandatory" PO was created. It is more commonly accepted practice these days to have direct access to all Stakeholders, and hopefully active stakeholder participation.

These interesting and admittedly controversial views have merit in our opinion, and in fact Dan's thinking influenced the evolution of the DA Manifesto (Chapter 3). In Disciplined Agile we constantly need to remind teams that context counts, and choice is good. Like everything in DA, the roles we outline are "good ideas" which may or may not make sense for you. In the *Form Team* process goal (Chapter 7), we encourage you to consider the roles that make sense for your team. If you are new to agile, and there is little organizational resistance to change then you probably want to adopt the DAD classic roles. If your agile maturity and capability is more advanced, or, if adopting new roles would be too disruptive, then you may wish to adapt roles accordingly.

Tailoring DAD Team Roles for Your Organization

As we mentioned earlier, we believe in the philosophy of "you go to war with the army that you have," or in other words, you build your teams from the people that you have. Many organizations find that they cannot staff some of the roles, or that some of the DAD roles simply don't fit well in their existing culture. As a result they find they need to tailor the roles to reflect the situation that they find themselves in. Tailoring the roles can be a very slippery slope as we've found the DAD roles work very well in practice, so any tailoring that you do likely increases the risk faced by the team. Table 4.1 captures tailoring options for the primary roles, and the risks associated with doing so.

Table 4.1 Potential tailoring options for the primary roles.

Role	Tailoring Options and Risks
Architecture Owner	• **Application/solution architect**. A traditional architect does not work as collaboratively as an AO, so runs the risk of having their vision misunderstood or ignored by the team. • **No AO**. Without someone in the AO role the team must actively collaborate to identify an architectural strategy on their own, which tends to lead to the team missing architectural concerns and paying the price later in the lifecycle with increased rework.
Product Owner	• **Business analyst (BA)**. BAs typically don't have the decision making authority that a PO does, so they become a bottleneck when the team needs a decision quickly. BAs also tend to favor production of requirements documentation rather than direct collaboration with Team Members. • **Active Stakeholder participation**. Team Members work directly with Stakeholders to understand their needs and to gain feedback on their work. The team will need a way to identify and work to a consistent vision, otherwise they risk getting pulled in multiple directions.
Stakeholder	• **Personas**. Although there are always Stakeholders you might not have access to them, or more accurately access to the full range of them. Personas are fictional characters that represent classes of Stakeholders. Personas enable the team to talk in terms of these fictional people and to explore how these people would interact with the solution.
Team Lead	• **ScrumMaster**. We've had mixed results with Scrum Masters on teams, mostly because the Certified ScrumMaster (CSM) designation requires very little effort to gain. Few Scrum Masters seem to have the experience, knowledge, or organizational knowledge to be effective leaders. • **Project manager (PM)**. By assigning work to people and then monitoring them a PM will negate a team's ability to benefit from self-organization and will very likely decrease psychological safety on the team. Having said that, a significant percentage of PMs are willing, and able, to drop command and control strategies in favor of a leadership approach. • **No Team Lead**. We have seen teams that are truly self-organizing who do not need a Team Lead. There have always been teams that have been working together for a long time where people choose to address what would normally be Team Lead responsibilities as needed, just like any other type of work.
Team Member	• **Specialists**. As we said earlier, if all you have available are specialists then that's what you build your team from.

DAD and Traditional Roles

Many agile purists will insist that traditional roles such as project manager (PM), business analyst (BA), resource manager, and many others go away with agile. Although that MAY happen in the long run, it isn't practical in the short term. The elimination of traditional roles at the beginning of your agile transformation is revolutionary and often results in resistance to, and the undermining of, agile adoption. We prefer a more evolutionary, less disruptive approach that respects people and their career aspirations. While agile requires different ways of working, the skills and rigour of traditional specialties still are extremely valuable. PMs understand risk management, estimating strategies, and release planning. Classically trained or certified business analysts bring a rich toolkit of modeling options (many of which are described in the *Explore Scope* goal in Chapter 9). To say that we don't need PMs or BAs is short-sighted, naïve and disrespectful to these professions.

Having said that, the primary DAD roles are extremely effective in practice. When we work with organizations to improve their WoW we help as many people as we can to transition out of their existing traditional roles into the DAD roles, which they often find more fulfilling in practice. Figure 4.5 depicts common options for several traditional roles. What we show are generalizations and it's important to recognize that people will choose their own career paths based on their own preferences and desires. The important thing is to recognize that everyone can find a place for themselves in an agile organization if they're willing to learn new WoW and move into new roles.

Figure 4.5. Common transitions from traditional to DAD roles.

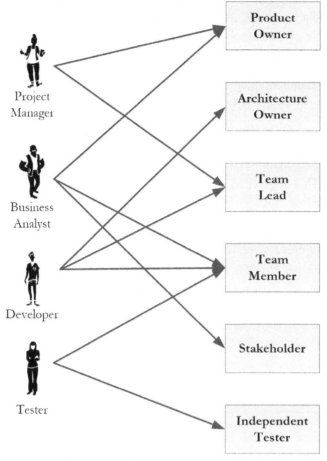

In Summary

This chapter explored the potential rights and responsibilities of people involved with DAD teams, and the roles that they may choose to take on. We say potential because you need to tailor these ideas to fit into your organization's cultural environment. However, we showed that the further you stray from the DAD roles and responsibilities the greater the risk you will take on. You learned:

- DAD defines five primary roles – Team Lead, Product Owner, Team Member, Architecture Owner, and Stakeholder – that appear on all teams.
- In many situations teams will rely on people in supporting roles – specialists, Domain Experts, technical experts, Independent Testers, or integrators – as appropriate and as needed.
- DAD's roles are meant to be, like everything else, a suggested starting point. You may have valid reasons for tailoring the roles for your organization.
- With roles, as with everything else, do the best you can do in the situation that you face and strive to improve over time.

66

5 PROCESS GOALS

We must learn not just to accept differences between ourselves and our ideas, but to enthusiastically welcome and enjoy them. Gene Roddenberry

Disciplined Agile Delivery (DAD) takes a straightforward approach to support teams in choosing their way of working (WoW). Process goals guide teams through the process-related decisions that they need to make to tailor agile strategies to address the context of the situation that they face. Some people like to call this capability-driven WoW, process outcomes-driven WoW, or a vector-driven approach.

Each of DAD's process goals define a high-level process outcome, such as improving quality or exploring the initial scope, without prescribing how to do so. Instead, a process goal indicates the issues you need to consider, what we call decision points, and some potential options you may choose to adopt.

Process goals guide teams through the process-related decisions that they need to make to tailor and scale agile strategies to address the context of the situation that they face. This tailoring effort should take hours at most, not days, and DAD's straightforward goal diagrams help you to streamline doing so. Process goals are a recommended approach to support teams in

Key Points in this Chapter
- Although every team works in a unique way, they still need to address the same process goals (process outcomes).
- Process goals guide you through what you need to think about and your potential options, they don't prescribe what to do.
- DAD process goals provide you with choices, each of which has trade-offs.
- Strive to do the best you can do right now in the situation that you face.
- The DAD process goals appear overly complicated at first, but ask yourself what you would remove?

choosing their WoW, and are a critical part of Disciplined Agile (DA)'s process scaffolding.

Why a Goal-Driven Approach?

In Chapter 1 we learned that there are several good reasons why a team should own their process and why they should choose and then evolve their WoW over time. First, every team faces a unique situation and therefore should tailor their approach to best address that situation and evolve their WoW as the situation evolves. In other words, context counts. Second, you need to have choices and know what those choices are — you can't own your process if you don't know what's for sale. Third, we want to be awesome at what we do, so we need the flexibility to experiment with ways of working so that we can discover how to be the most awesome team we can be.

Most teams struggle to truly own their process, mostly because they don't have the process expertise within the team to do so. So they need some help, and process goals are an important part of that help. Our experience is that there are several fundamental advantages to taking a goal-driven approach to agile solution delivery:
- It enables teams to focus on process outcomes, not on process compliance.
- It provides a concise, shared pathway to leaner, less wasteful process decisions.
- It supports choosing your WoW by making process decisions explicit.
- It makes your process options very clear and thereby makes it easier to identify

67

the appropriate strategy for the situation you find yourself in.

- It enables effective scaling by providing you with strategies that are sophisticated enough to address the complexities that you face at scale.
- It takes the guesswork out of extending agile methods and thereby enables you to focus on your actual job, which is to provide value to your Stakeholders.
- It makes it clear what risks you're taking on and thus enables you to increase the likelihood of success.
- It hints at an agile maturity model (this is important for any organization struggling to move away from traditional maturity models).

How Much Detail is Enough?

The amount of process detail that you require as a person, or as a team, varies based on your situation. In general, the more experienced you are the less detail you need. Figure 5.1 overviews how we've chosen to capture the details of DAD, starting with high-level, outcome-based process goals all the way down to the nitty-gritty details of a specific practice. This book addresses the first three level: process goals, process goal diagrams, and option tables. The fourth level, detailed practice/strategy descriptions, would be tens of thousands of printed pages – the agile/lean canon is very, very large and our aim with DAD is to help put it in context for you.

As you see in Figure 5.1, there are four levels of detail when it comes to describing process goals:

1. **Process goal**. The named process outcome, for example *Identify Architecture Strategy*, *Accelerate Value Delivery*, *Deploy the Solution*, or *Grow Team Members*. Named process goals are useful to provide a consistent language to discuss process-related issues across teams with potentially very different WoWs.

2. **Process goal diagram**. This is a visual depiction of the aspects you need to think through about the goal, what we call decision points, and several options for each decision point to choose from. We're not saying that we've identified every possible technique available to you, but we have identified enough to give you a good range of options and to make it clear that you do in fact have choices. In many ways a process goal diagram is an advanced version of a decision tree, and an example of one is depicted in Figure 5.4 later in this chapter. Process goal diagrams are useful for experienced practitioners, including agile coaches, as overviews of what they need to consider with tailoring the portion of their WoW addressed by that goal.

3. **Option tables**. An option table provides a brief summary of potential practices or strategies that you should consider adopting to address a given decision point. For each option the trade-offs associated with it are also provided so as to put it in context. There is no such thing as a best practice – every given practice/strategy works well in some contexts and is inappropriate in other contexts. Option tables help you to identify what you believe to be the best option for your team to experiment with in the current situation that you face. Table 5.1 provides an example of one later in this chapter.

4. **Practice/strategy descriptions**. Every technique is described through blogs, articles, and in some cases one or more books. For example, there are thousands of blog postings and articles about test-driven development (TDD) as well as several good books. Our aim is to point you in the right direction to these great resources, and very often Wikipedia proves to be a very good launch pad to do so.

68

Figure 5.1. Level of details with process goals.

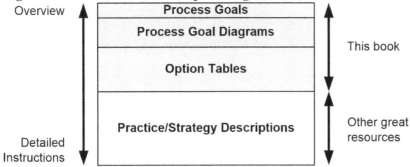

Context Counts: Disciplined Agile Teams are Goal-Driven

Figure 5.2 shows the goals for a DAD team grouped by the three phases of Inception, Construction, and Transition, as well as the goals that are ongoing throughout the lifecycle.

If you know your process history, you may have noticed that we adopted the phase names from the Unified Process (UP) [Kruchten]. More accurately, we adopted three of the four names from UP because DAD doesn't have an Elaboration phase, unlike UP. Some people will point to this as evidence that DAD is just UP, but if you're actually familiar with UP you'll recognize that this clearly isn't true. We choose to adopt these names because, frankly, they were perfectly fine. Our philosophy is to reuse and leverage as many great ideas as possible, including terminology, and not invent new terminology if we can avoid doing so.

Figure 5.2. The process goals of Disciplined Agile Delivery (DAD).

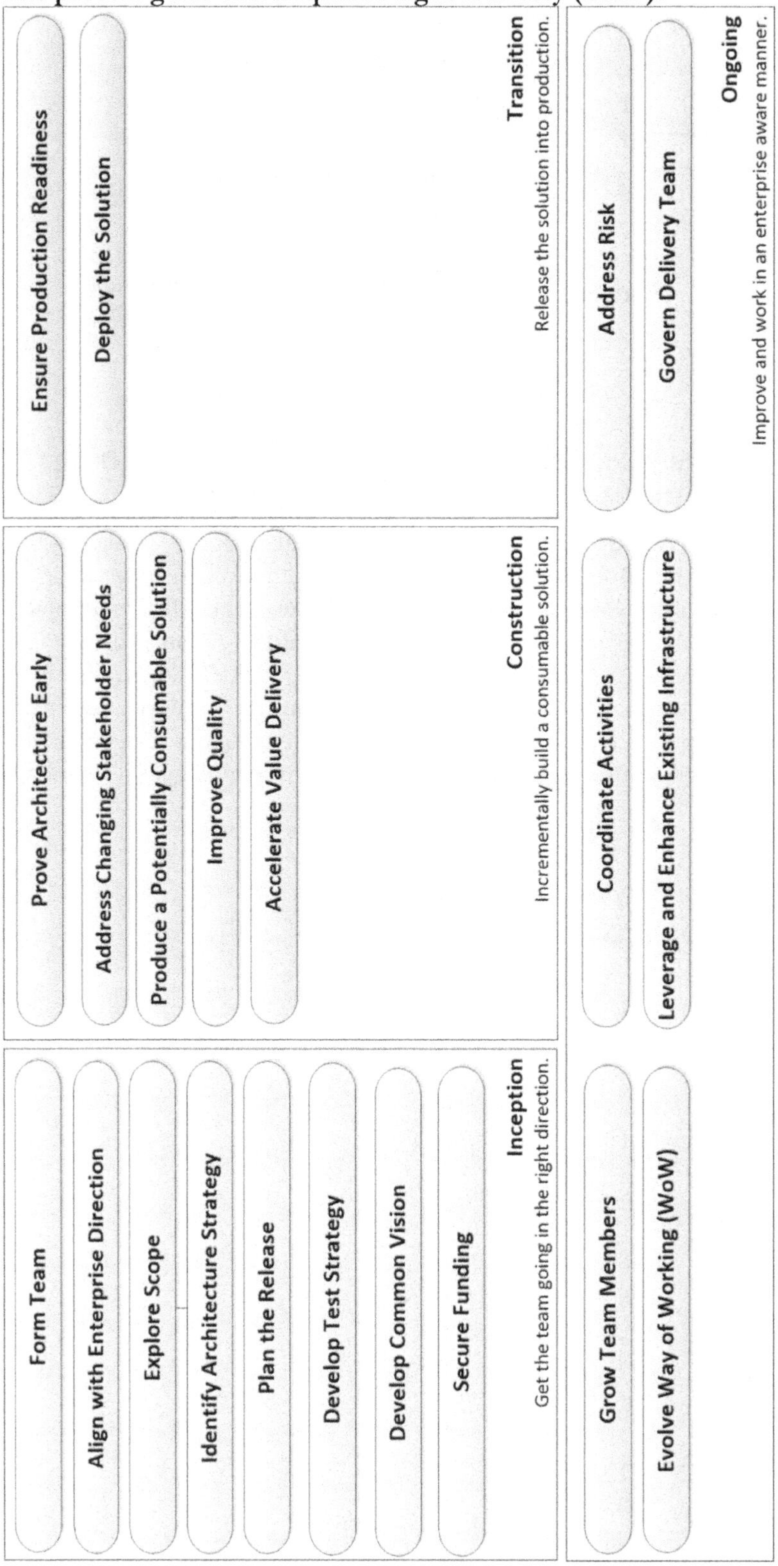

Inception
Get the team going in the right direction.

- Form Team
- Align with Enterprise Direction
- Explore Scope
- Identify Architecture Strategy
- Plan the Release
- Develop Test Strategy
- Develop Common Vision
- Secure Funding

Construction
Incrementally build a consumable solution.

- Prove Architecture Early
- Address Changing Stakeholder Needs
- Produce a Potentially Consumable Solution
- Improve Quality
- Accelerate Value Delivery

Transition
Release the solution into production.

- Ensure Production Readiness
- Deploy the Solution

Ongoing
Improve and work in an enterprise aware manner.

- Grow Team Members
- Evolve Way of Working (WoW)
- Coordinate Activities
- Leverage and Enhance Existing Infrastructure
- Address Risk
- Govern Delivery Team

70

Process Goal Diagrams

Although listing the high-level process goals in Figure 5.2 is a good start, most people need more information than this. To go to the next level of detail we use goal diagrams, the notation for which is described in Figure 5.3 and an example of which is shown in Figure 5.4. First, let's explore the notation:

- **Process goals**. Process goals are shown as rounded rectangles.

- **Decision points**. Decision points, which are process issues that you need to consider addressing, are shown as rectangles. Process goals will have two or more decision points, with most goals having four or five decision points although some have more. Each decision point can be addressed by practices/strategies that are presented in a list to the right. Sometimes there are decision points that you will not have to address given your situation. For example, the *Coordinate Activities* process goal has a *Coordinate Across Program* decision point that only applies if your team is part of a larger "team of teams."

- **Ordered option lists**. An ordered option list is depicted with an arrow to the left of the list of techniques. What we mean by this is that the techniques appearing at the top of the list are more desirable, generally more effective in practice, and the less desirable techniques are at the bottom of the list. Your team of course should strive to adopt the most effective techniques they are capable of performing given the context of the situation that they face. In other words, do the best that you can but be aware that there are potentially better techniques that you can choose to adopt at some point. From the point of view of complexity theory a decision point with an ordered option list is effectively a vector that indicates a change path. In Figure 5.4 the *Level of Detail of the Scope Document* decision point has an ordered set of options whereas the second one does not.

- **Unordered option lists**. An unordered option list is depicted without an arrow – each option has advantages and disadvantages, but it isn't clear how to rank the options fairly.

- **Potential starting points**. Potential starting points are shown in bold italics. Because there may be many techniques to choose from, we indicate "default" techniques in bolded italics. These defaults are good starting points for small teams new to agile that are taking on a straightforward problem – they are almost always strategies from Scrum, Extreme Programming (XP), Agile Modeling, with a few Unified Process ideas thrown in to round things out.

Figure 5.3. The notation of a process goal diagram.

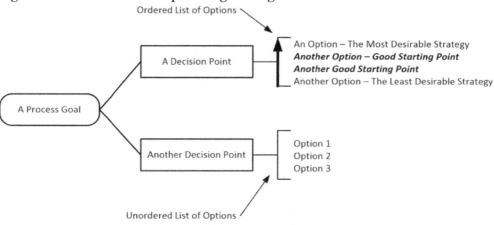

Figure 5.4. The goal diagram for Explore Scope.

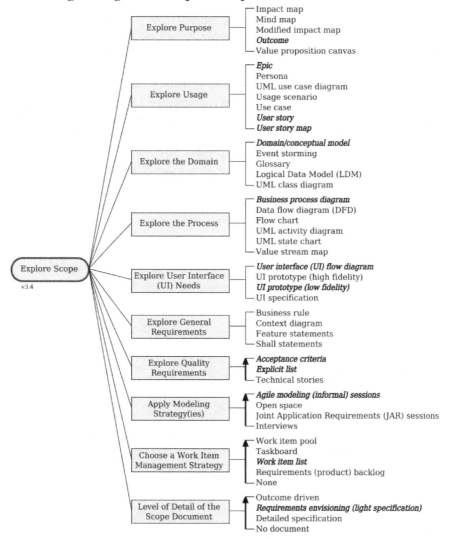

It is common to combine several options from a given list in practice. For example, consider the *Explore Usage* decision point in Figure 5.4 – it is common for teams that are new to agile to apply epics, user stories, and user story maps to explore usage requirements.

Let's explore the *Explore Scope* goal diagram of Figure 5.4 a bit more. This is a process goal that you should address at the beginning of the lifecycle during Inception (if you're following a lifecycle that includes an Inception phase, see Chapter 6). Where some agile methods will simply advise you to initially populate a product backlog with some user stories, the goal diagram makes it clear that you might want to be a bit more sophisticated in your approach. What level of detail should you capture, if any? How are you going to explore potential usage of the system? Or the UI requirements? Or the business process(es) supported by the solution? Default techniques, or perhaps more accurately suggested starting points, are shown in bold italics. Notice how we suggest that you likely want to default to capturing usage in some way, basic domain concepts (for example, via a high-level conceptual diagram) in some

> **But This is so Complex!**
> Our strategy with DA is to explicitly recognize that software development (and IT, and organizations in general) are inherently complex. DA doesn't try to dumb things down into a handful of "best practices." Instead, DA explicitly communicates the complexity that you face, the options that you have, and the tradeoffs that you're making and simplify the process of choosing the right strategies that meet your needs. DA provides scaffolding to help you make better process decisions.
>
> Yes, there are many process goals (21 in fact) depicted in Figure 5.2. Which would you take out? We've seen teams not address risk in any way, but that invariably went poorly for them. We've also seen teams choose not to address the goal *Improve Quality*, only to watch their technical debt rise. In practice you can't safely choose to ignore any of these goals. Similarly, consider the decision points in Figure 5.3, would you drop any of those? Likely not. Yes, it's daunting that there is so much to take into account to succeed at solution delivery long term, and what we've captured appears to be a minimal set for enterprise-class solution development.

way, and non-functional requirements in some way. There are different strategies you may want to consider for modeling – choose the ones that make sense for your situation and not that ones that don't. You should also start thinking about your approach to managing your work – a light specification approach of writing up some index cards and a few whiteboard sketches is just one option you should consider. In DAD, we make it clear that agile teams do more than just implement new requirements, hence our recommendation to default to a work item list over a simplistic requirements (product) backlog strategy. Work items may include new requirements to be implemented, defects to be fixed, training workshops, reviews of other teams' work, and so on. These are all things that need to be sized, prioritized, and planned for. Finally, the goal diagram makes it clear that when you're exploring the initial scope of your effort that you should capture non-functional requirements – such as reliability, privacy, availability, performance, and security requirements (among many) – in some manner. The *Explore Scope* process goal is described in greater detail in Chapter 9.

Getting to the Details: Option Tables and References

The next level of detail is the options tables, an example of which is shown in Table 5.1 for *Explore Scope*'s *Explore Quality Requirements* decision point. Each table lists the options, which are practices or strategies, and the trade-offs of each one. The goal is to put each option into context and where appropriate point you to more detail about that technique. We often point to Wikipedia, indicated by the [W] reference, and sometimes to a book or article (such as [ExecutableSpecs] for acceptance criteria).

Table 5.1. Describing the Explore Quality Requirements decision point.

Options (Ordered)	Trade-Offs
Acceptance criteria. Quality-focused approach that captures detailed aspects of a high-level requirement from the point of view of a Stakeholder [ExecutableSpecs].	• Motivates teams to think through detailed requirements. • Dovetails nicely into a behavior-driven development (BDD) or acceptance test-driven development (ATDD) approach. • Many quality requirements are cross-cutting aspects of several functional stories, so relying on acceptance criteria alone risks missing details, particularly in new requirements identified later in the lifecycle.
Explicit list. Enables us to capture quality requirements in a "reusable manner" that cross-cuts functional requirements.	• Not attaching quality requirements to specific functional requirements allows the option of using proof of technology "spikes" rather than waiting for an associated story. • Requires a mechanism, such as acceptance criteria, to ensure that the quality requirement is implemented across the appropriate functional requirements.
Technical stories. Simple strategy for capturing quality requirements that is similar to an explicit list.	• Works well when a quality requirement is straightforward and contained. • Not appropriate for quality requirements that cross-cut many functional requirements because we can't address the quality requirement in a short period of time.

How to Apply Process Goals in Practice

Disciplined Agilists can process goals in several common scenarios:

- **Identifying potential strategies to experiment with**. We described guided process improvement (GCI) in Chapter 1 where a team uses DAD as a reference to identify techniques to experiment with. Because DAD puts options into context, as you saw in Table 5.1, you are more likely to identify a technique that will work for you in your environment.
- **Enhancing retrospectives**. The goal diagrams, and supporting tables, provide a toolkit of potential options that you can choose to experiment with to resolve challenges identified by the team.
- **Checklists**. Goal diagrams are often used by experienced teams to remind them of potential techniques that they could choose to apply in their current situation.
- **Process tailoring workshops**. Described in Chapter 1, process tailoring

workshops are often used by new teams to identify or negotiate how they will work together. The process goals often prove to be great resources to help focus those workshops, and an easy way to use them is to print them out and put them up on the wall and then work through them as a team.

- **Maturity model**[6]. The ordered decision points effectively provide a focused maturity model around a given decision point. More importantly, ordered decision points are effectively vectors indicating an improvement path for teams to potentially follow.

- **Have productive discussions about process choices**. An interesting aspect of process goals is that some of the choices they provide really aren't very effective in practice. WHAT?!?!?! We sometimes find teams following a technique because they believe that's the best strategy available – maybe they've been told it's a "best practice," maybe it's the best strategy they know about, maybe it's the best they can do right now, or maybe it's been prescribed to them by their adopted methodology and they never thought to look beyond it. Regardless, this strategy plus other valid options are now provided to them, with the tradeoffs for each clearly described. This puts you in a better position to compare and contrast strategies and potentially choose a new strategy to experiment with.

In Summary

This book describes how you can choose your WoW, how your team can truly own its process. The only way you can own your process is if you know what's for sale. DAD's process goals help to make your process choices, and the trade-offs associated with them, explicit. In this chapter we explored several key concepts:

- Although every team works in a unique way, they still need to address the same process goals (process outcomes).
- Process goals guide you through what you need to think about and your potential options, they don't prescribe what to do.
- DAD process goals provide you with choices, each of which has trade-offs.
- Strive to do the best you can do right now in the situation that you face and to learn and improve over time.
- If the DAD process goals appear overly complicated at first, ask yourself: what you would remove?

---

[6] In DA, because we believe in pragmatism, we're not afraid to use "agile swear words" such as management, governance, phase, and yes, even "maturity model."

6 CHOOSING THE RIGHT LIFECYCLE

May your choices reflect your hopes, not your fears.
Nelson Mandela

We have the privilege of working with organizations all over the world. When we go into an organization, often to coach them in how to improve their way of working (WoW), we get to observe what is actually happening within these organizations. One thing we see over and over again, in all but the very smallest of enterprises, is that they have several delivery lifecycles in place across their teams. Some of these teams will be following a Scrum-based agile project lifecycle whereas others will have adopted a Kanban-based lean lifecycle. The more advanced teams, particularly those moving towards a DevOps mindset, will have adopted a continuous delivery approach [Kim]. Some may be working on a brand-new business idea and is following an experimental "lean startup" style of approach and some teams may still be following a more traditional lifecycle. The reason why this happens, as we described in Chapter 2, is because each team is unique and in a unique situation. Teams need a WoW that reflects the context that they face, and an important part of choosing an effective WoW is to select a lifecycle that best fits their situation. Disciplined Agile Delivery (DAD) scaffolding provides lifecycle choices to your delivery teams, while enabling consistent governance across them.

> **Key Points in this Chapter**
> - Some teams within your organization will still follow a traditional lifecycle – DAD explicitly recognizes this but does not provide support for this shrinking category of work.
> - DAD provides the scaffolding required for choosing between, and then evolving, six solution delivery lifecycles (SDLCs) based on either agile or lean strategies.
> - Project-based lifecycles, even agile and lean ones, go through phases.
> - Every lifecycle has its advantages and disadvantages, each team needs to pick the one that best reflects their context.
> - Common, lightweight, risk-based milestones enables consistent governance – you don't need to force the same process on all of your teams.
> - A team will start with a given lifecycle and often evolve away from it as they continuously improve their WoW.

A Quick History Lesson: The Traditional Lifecycle

First and foremost, the traditional lifecycle is not supported by DAD. There are several different flavors of the traditional lifecycle, sometimes called the serial lifecycle or the waterfall lifecycle. Figure 6.1 depicts what is known as the V model. The basic idea is that a team works through functional phases, such as Requirements, Architecture, and so on. At the end of each phase there is often a "quality gate" milestone review which tends to focus on reviewing documentation. Testing occurs towards the end of the lifecycle and each testing phase, at least in the V model, tends to correspond to an artifact creation phase earlier in the lifecycle. The waterfall lifecycle is based on 1960s/70s theories about how software development should work. Note that some organizations in the early 1990s and 2000s mistakenly instantiated Rational Unified Process (RUP) as a heavyweight process, so some practitioners think that RUP is a traditional process too. No, RUP is iterative and incremental, but was often implemented poorly by people who didn't move away from the traditional mindset.

Figure 6.1. The traditional software development lifecycle.

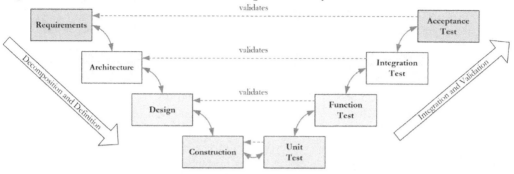

If the traditional approach is explicitly not included in DAD why are we talking about it? Because some teams are currently following a waterfall approach and need help moving away from it. Worse yet, there are many people who believe that traditional strategies are applicable to a wide range of situations. In one sense they are correct, but what they don't understand is that agile/lean strategies prove much better in practice for most of those situations. But, as you'll learn later in this chapter, there are a few situations where traditional strategies do in fact make sense. But just a few.

The Project Mindset Leads to Agile Phases, And That's OK

Many organizations choose to fund solution delivery in terms of projects. These projects may be date driven and have a defined start and end date, they may be scope driven in that they must deliver specific functionality or a specific set of outcomes, or they are cost driven in that they must come in on or under a desired budget. Some projects have a combination of these constraints, but the more constraints you put on a delivery team the greater the risk of project failure. Figure 6.2 depicts a high-level view of the project delivery lifecycle, and as you see it has three phases:

1. **Inception.** Inception is sometimes called "Sprint 0," "Iteration 0," startup, or initiation. The basic idea is that the team does just enough work to get organized and going in the right direction. The team will initially form itself, invest some time in initial requirements and architecture exploration, initial planning, aligning itself with the rest of the organization, and of course securing funding for the rest of the project. This phase should be kept as simple and as short as possible while

> **Agile History Lesson**
> The term "iteration 0" was first coined by Jim Highsmith, one of the creators of the Agile Manifesto, in his book *Agile Software Development Ecosystems* in 2002 [Highsmith]. It was later adopted and renamed Sprint 0 by the Scrum community.

coming to an agreement on how the team believes it will accomplish the outcomes being asked of it by their Stakeholders. The average agile/lean team spends 11 work days, so a bit more than two weeks, in Inception activities [SoftDev18].

2. **Construction.** The aim of Construction is to produce a consumable solution with sufficient functionality, what's known as a minimal marketable release (MMR), to be of value to Stakeholders. The team will work closely with Stakeholders to

understand their needs, to build a quality solution for them, to get feedback from them on a regular basis, and then act on that feedback. The implication is that the team will be performing analysis, design, programming, testing, and management activities potentially every single day. More on this later.

3. **Transition.** Transition is sometimes referred to as a "release sprint" or a "deployment sprint," and if the team is struggling with quality a "hardening sprint." The aim of Transition is to successfully release your solution into Production. This includes determining whether you are ready to deploy the solution and then actually deploying it. The average agile/lean team spends 6 work days on Transition activities, but when you exclude the teams that have fully automated testing and deployment (which we wouldn't do) it's an average of 8.5 days [SoftDev18]. Furthermore, 26% of teams have fully automated regression testing and deployment and 63% perform Transition in one day or less.

Figure 6.2. The agile project lifecycle (high-level).

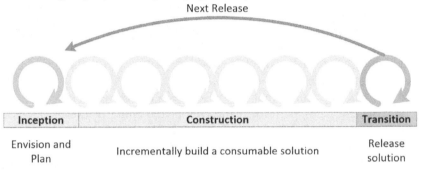

Although agile purists will balk at the concept of phases, and will often jump through hoops such as calling Inception "Sprint 0" and Transition a "release sprint," the fact is that agile project teams work in a serial manner at a high level. Teams need to invest some time at the beginning to get going in the right direction (Inception/Sprint 0), they need to spend time producing the solution (Construction), and they need to spend time deploying the solution (Transition/release sprint). This happens in practice and is very easy to observe if you choose to. The important thing is to streamline your Inception and Transition efforts as much as possible, and Construction too for that matter.

There is more to IT, and your organization in general, than solution delivery. For example, your organization is likely to have Data Management, Enterprise Architecture, Operations, Portfolio Management, Marketing, Procurement, Finance, and many other important organizational aspects. A full system/product lifecycle goes from the initial concept for the solution, through delivery, to operations and support and often includes many rounds through the delivery lifecycle. Figure 6.3 depicts the system lifecycle, showing how the delivery lifecycle, and the DevOps lifecycle for that matter, is a subset of it. Although Figure 6.3 adds the Concept (ideation), Production, and Retire phases the focus of DAD, and this book, is on delivery. Disciplined Agile (DA), however, includes strategies that encompass DAD, Disciplined DevOps, Disciplined Agile IT (DAIT), and the Disciplined Agile Enterprise (DAE) in general [AmblerLines2017].

Figure 6.3. The system/solution/product lifecycle (high-level).

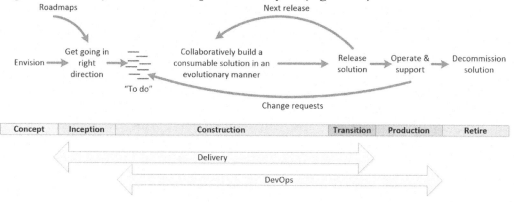

Shift Left, Shift Right, Deliver Continuously

Although some teams will take a project-based approach, not all of them do and over time we expect this trend to grow. When a team is allowed to stay together for a long period of time, typically longer than a single project, we call this a stable or long-standing team. When a long-standing team is allowed to evolve its WoW, we've seen some incredible things happen – they become teams capable of continuous delivery.

The term "shift left" is popular amongst agilists, often being used to indicate that testing and quality practices are being performed throughout the entire lifecycle. This is a good thing, but there's more to the "shifting" trend than this. There are several important trends, summarized in Figure 6.4, that will affect the way a team evolves its WoW:

1. **Testing and quality practices shift left.** Agilists are clearly shifting testing practices left through greater automation and via replacing written specifications with executable specifications via practices such as test-driven development (TDD) [W] and behavior-driven development (BDD) [W]. TDD and BDD of course are supported by the practice of continuous integration (CI) [W]. Adoption of these strategies are key motivators for an infrastructure as code strategy where activities that are mostly manual on traditional teams become fully automated on agile teams.

2. **Modeling and planning practices shift right.** Agilists have also shifted modeling/ mapping and planning practices to the right in the lifecycle so that we can adapt to the feedback we're receiving from Stakeholders. In DAD modeling and planning are so important that we do them all the way through the lifecycle in a collaborative and iterative manner [AgileModeling].

Figure 6.4. How lifecycles evolve when you shift activities left and right.

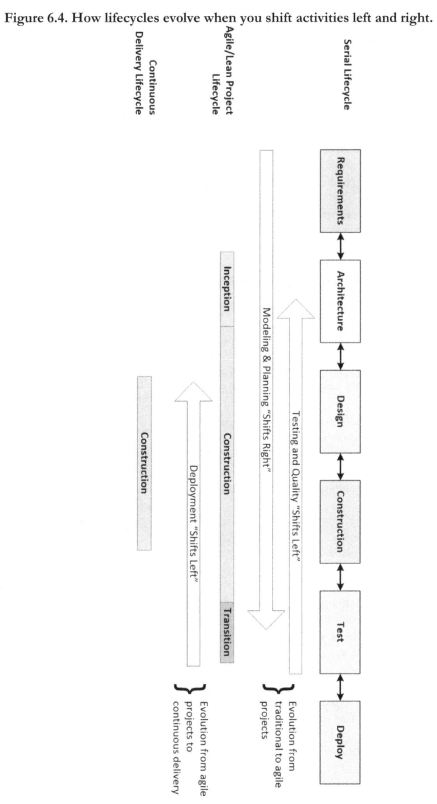

81

3. **Stakeholder interaction shifts right**. DAD teams interact with Stakeholders throughout the entire endeavor, not just during Requirements and Test phases at the beginning and end of the lifecycle.
4. **Stakeholder feedback shifts left**. Traditional teams tend to leave serious Stakeholder feedback to user acceptance testing (UAT) performed during the traditional Test phase. DAD teams, on the other hand, seek to gain Stakeholder feedback as early and as regularly as possible throughout the entire endeavor.
5. **Deployment practices shift left**. Deployment practices are being fully automated by agile teams, another infrastructure as code strategy, so as to support continuous deployment (CD). CD is a linchpin practice for DAD's two continuous delivery lifecycles described below.
6. **The real goal is continuous delivery**. All of this shifting left and shifting right results in teams that are able to work in a continuous delivery manner. Process improvement is about working smarter, not harder.

Choice is Good: DAD's Lifecycles

DAD supports several lifecycles for teams to choose from. These lifecycles, described in detail below and summarized in Figure 6.5, are:

1. **Agile**. Based on the Scrum construction lifecycle, teams following this project lifecycle will produce consumable solutions via short iterations (also known as sprints or time boxes).
2. **Continuous Delivery: Agile**. Teams following this agile-based lifecycle will work in very short iterations, typically one week or less, where at the end of each iteration their solution is released into production.
3. **Lean**. Based on Kanban, teams following this project lifecycle will visualize their work, reduce work in progress (WIP) to streamline their workflow, and pull work into the team one item at a time.
4. **Continuous Delivery: Lean**. Teams following this lean-based lifecycle will release their work into production whenever possible, typically several times a day.
5. **Exploratory**. Teams following this lifecycle, based on Lean Startup [Ries], will explore a business idea by developing one or more minimal viable product (MVP) which they run as experiments to determine what potential customers actually want. This lifecycle is often applied when a team faces a "wicked problem" [W] in their domain.
6. **Program**. A program is effectively a large team that is organized into a team of teams.

Figure 6.5. DAD's lifecycles.

Agile	Continuous Delivery: Agile	Exploratory

Lean	Continuous Delivery: Lean	Program

Now let's explore each of these lifecycles in greater detail. After that, then we'll discuss when to consider adopting each one.

DAD's Agile Lifecycle

 DAD's agile lifecycle, shown in Figure 6.6, is based largely upon the Scrum lifecycle with proven governance concepts adopted from the Unified Process (UP) to make it enterprise ready [Kruchten]. This lifecycle is often adopted by project teams focused on developing a single release of a solution, although sometimes a team will stay together and follow it again for the next release (and the next release after that, and so on). In many ways this lifecycle depicts how a Scrum-based project lifecycle works in an enterprise-class setting, we've worked with several teams that like to think of this as Scrum++, without being constrained by the Scrum community's cultural imperative to gloss over the activities of solution delivery that they find inconvenient. There are several critical aspects to this lifecycle:

- **The Inception phase**. As we described earlier, the team's focus is to do just enough work to get organized and get going in the right direction. DAD aims to streamline the entire lifecycle from beginning-to-end, including the initiation activities addressed by Inception. Inception ends when we have an agreed-to vision regarding the expected outcomes for the team and how we're going to achieve them.
- **Construction is organized into short iterations**. An iteration is a short period of time, typically two weeks or less, in which the delivery team produces a new, potentially consumable version of their solution. Of course, for a new product or solution you may not have something truly consumable until after having completed several iterations. This phase ends when we have sufficient functionality, also known as a minimal marketable release (MMR).
- **Teams address work items in small batches**. Working in small batches is a fundamental of Scrum, and because this lifecycle is based on Scrum it's an important aspect of it. DAD teams, regardless of lifecycle, are likely to work on a range of things: implementing new functionality, providing Stakeholders with positive outcomes, running experiments, addressing end-user change requests

83

coming in from usage of the current solution running in production, paying down technical debt, taking training, and many more. Work items are typically prioritized by the Product Owner (PO), primarily by business value although risk, due dates, and severity (in the case of change requests) may also be taken into account. The *Address Changing Stakeholder Needs* process goal (Chapter 16) provides a range of options for managing work items. In each iteration, the team pulls a small batch of work off of the work item list that they believe they can achieve during that iteration.

- **Critical ceremonies have a defined cadence**. Also like Scrum, this lifecycle schedules several agile ceremonies on specific cadences. At the beginning of each iteration the team performs detailed planning for the iteration and at the end of the iteration we hold a demonstration. We hold a retrospective to evolve our WoW, and we make a go-forward decision. We also hold a daily coordination meeting. The point is that by prescribing when to hold these important work sessions we take some of the guess work out of the process. The downside is that Scrum injects a fair bit of process overhead with ceremonies. This is a problem that the Lean lifecycle addresses.

- **The Transition phase**. The aim of the Transition phase is to ensure that the solution is ready to be deployed and if so then to deploy it. This "phase" can be automated away (which is exactly what happens when evolving towards the two continuous delivery lifecycles).

- **Explicit milestones**. This lifecycle supports the full range of straightforward, risk-based milestones as you see depicted along the bottom of the lifecycle . The milestones enable leadership to govern effectively, more on this later. By "lightweight" we mean that milestones do not need to be a formal bureaucratic review of artifacts. Ideally, they are merely placeholders for discussions regarding the status and health of the initiative. See the *Govern Delivery Team* goal in Chapter 27 for a more detailed discussion of how to keep milestones light.

- **Enterprise guidance and roadmaps are explicitly shown**. On the left-hand side of the lifecycle you see that important flows come into the team from outside of the delivery lifecycle. That's because solution delivery is just part of your organization's overall DevOps strategy, which in turn is part of your overall IT strategy. For example, the initial vision and funding for your endeavor may be coming from a Product Management group, and the roadmaps and guidance from other areas such as Enterprise Architecture, Data Management, and Security (to name a few). Remember, DAD teams work in an enterprise aware manner, and one aspect of doing so is to adopt and follow appropriate guidance.

- **Operations and support are depicted**. If your team is working on the new release of an existing solution then you are likely to receive change requests from existing end users, typically coming to you via your operations and support efforts. For teams working in a DevOps environment it may be that you're responsible for running and supporting your solution in production.

Figure 6.6. DAD's agile lifecycle.

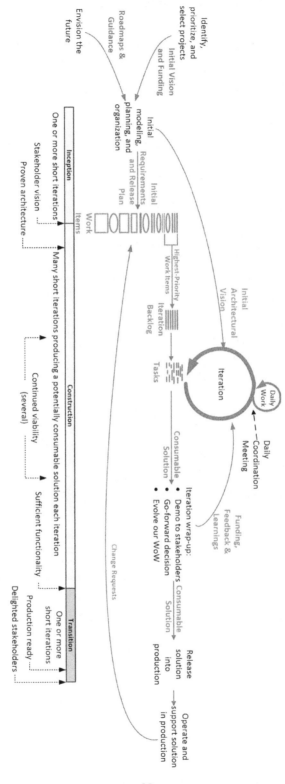

85

DAD's Continuous Delivery: Agile Lifecycle

 DAD's Continuous Delivery: Agile lifecycle, shown in Figure 6.7 is a natural progression from the Agile lifecycle of Figure 6.6. Teams typically evolve to this lifecycle from the Agile lifecycle, often adopting iteration lengths of one-week or less. The key difference between this and the Agile lifecycle is that the Continuous Delivery: Agile lifecycle results in a release of new functionality at the end of each iteration rather than after several iterations. There are several critical aspects to this lifecycle:

- **Automation and technical practices are key**. Teams require a mature set of technical practices around automated regression testing, continuous integration (CI), and continuous deployment (CD). To support these practices, investment in tools and paying down technical debt, and in particular writing the automated regression tests that are missing, needs to occur.

- **Inception occurred in the past**. When the team was first initiated, Inception would have occurred and it may have occurred again when significant change occurred such as a major shift in business direction or technical direction. So, if such as shift occurs again then yes, you should definitely invest sufficient effort to reorient the team – we see this as an activity, not a phase, hence Inception isn't depicted. Having said this, we do see teams stop every few months and explicitly invest several days to negotiate, at a high level, what they will do for the next few months. This is something that SAFe calls big room planning and Agile Modeling calls an agile modeling session. These techniques are discussed in the *Coordinate Activities* process goal (Chapter 23).

- **Transition has become an activity**. Through automation of testing and deployment the Transition phase has evolved from a multi-day or multi-week effort to a fully automated activity that takes minutes or hours.

- **Explicit milestones and incoming workflows**. There are still common, risk-based milestones to support consistent governance. Some milestones are no longer appropriate, in particular Stakeholder Vision and Proven Architecture would have been addressed in the past (although if major changes occur there's no reason why you couldn't address these milestones again). Incoming workflows from other parts of the organization are shown, just as with the Agile and Lean lifecycles.

Figure 6.7. DAD's Continuous Delivery: Agile lifecycle.

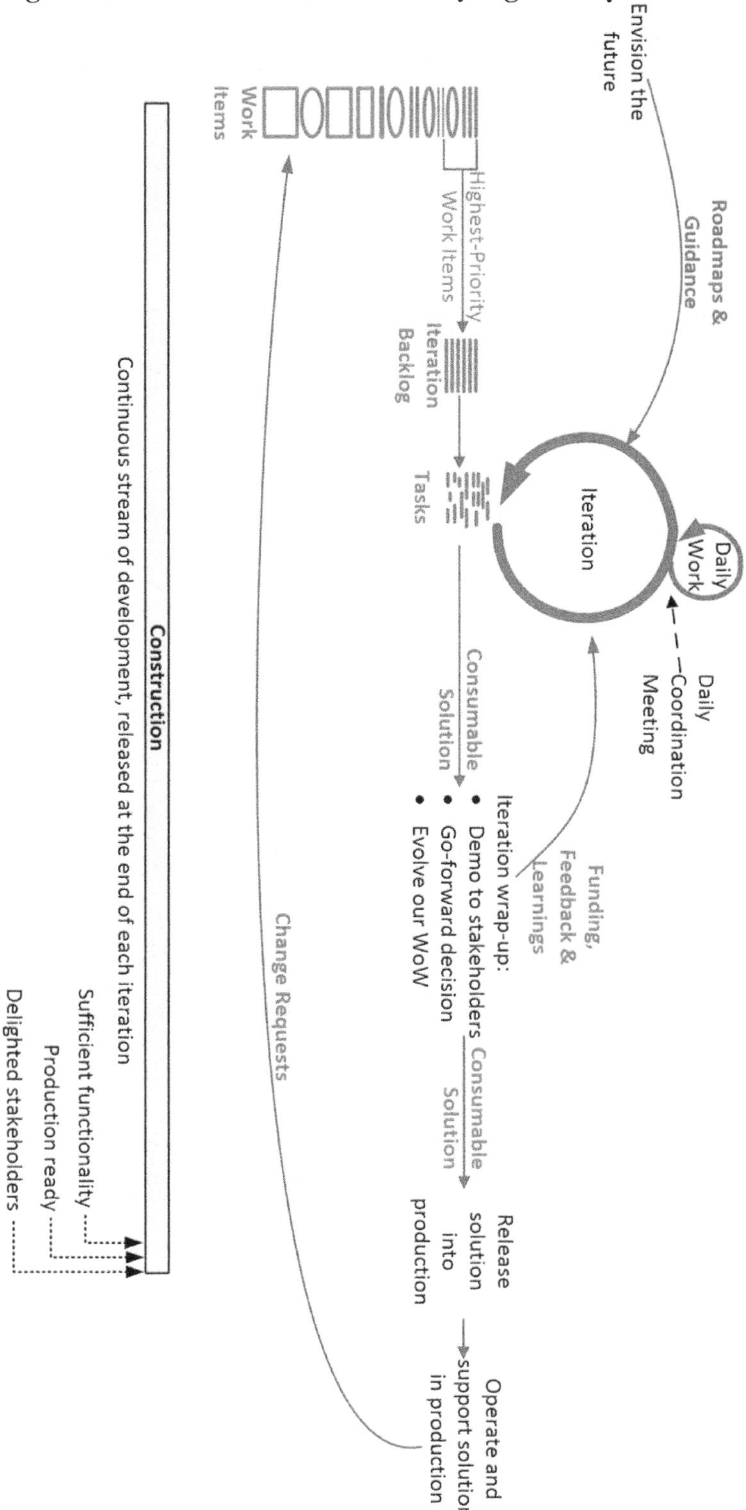

DAD's Lean Lifecycle

DAD's Lean lifecycle, shown in Figure 6.8 promotes lean principles such as minimizing work in progress, maximizing flow, a continuous stream of work (instead of fixed iterations), and reducing bottlenecks. This project-oriented lifecycle is often adopted by teams who are new to agile/lean who face rapidly changing Stakeholder needs, a common issue for teams evolving (sustaining) an existing legacy solution, and by traditional teams that don't want to take on the risk of the cultural and process disruption usually caused by agile adoption (at least not right away). There are several critical aspects to this lifecycle:

- **Teams address work items one at a time**. A major difference between the Lean and the Agile lifecycle is the lack of iterations. New work is pulled from the work item pool one item at a time as the team has capacity, as opposed to the iteration-based approach where it is pulled into the team in small batches.

- **Work items are prioritized just in time (JIT)**. Work items are maintained as a small options pool, often organized into categories by prioritization time – some work items are prioritized by value (and hopefully risk), by fixed delivery date, some must be expedited (often a severity 1 production problem or request from an important Stakeholder), and some work is intangible (such as paying down technical debt or going on training). Prioritization is effectively performed on a JIT basis, with the team choosing the most important work item at the time when they pull it in to be worked on.

- **Practices are performed when needed, as needed**. As with work prioritization, other practices such as planning, holding demos, replenishing the work item pool, holding coordination meetings, making go-forward decisions, look-ahead modeling, and many others are performed on a JIT basis. This tends to remove some of the overhead that teams experience with the Agile lifecycle but requires more discipline to decide when to perform the various practices.

- **Teams actively manage their workflow**. Lean teams use a Kanban board [W] to manage their work. A Kanban board depicts the team's high-level process in terms of state, with each column on the board representing a state such as Needs a Volunteer, Being Explored, Waiting for Dev, Being Built, Waiting for Test, Being Tested, and Done. Those were just examples, because teams choose their WoW every team will develop a board that reflects their WoW. Kanban boards are often implemented on whiteboards or via agile management software. Work is depicted in the form of tickets (stickies on the whiteboard), with a ticket being a work item from the options pool/backlog or a subtask of a work item. Each column has a work in progress (WIP) limit that puts an upper limit on the number of tickets that may be in that state. As the team performs their work they pull the corresponding tickets through the process on their Kanban board so as to coordinate their work.

- **Explicit phases, milestones, and incoming workflows**. There is still an Inception phase and a Transition phase as well risk-based milestones to support consistent governance. Incoming workflows from other parts of the organization are shown, just as with the Agile lifecycle.

Figure 6.8. DAD's Lean lifecycle.

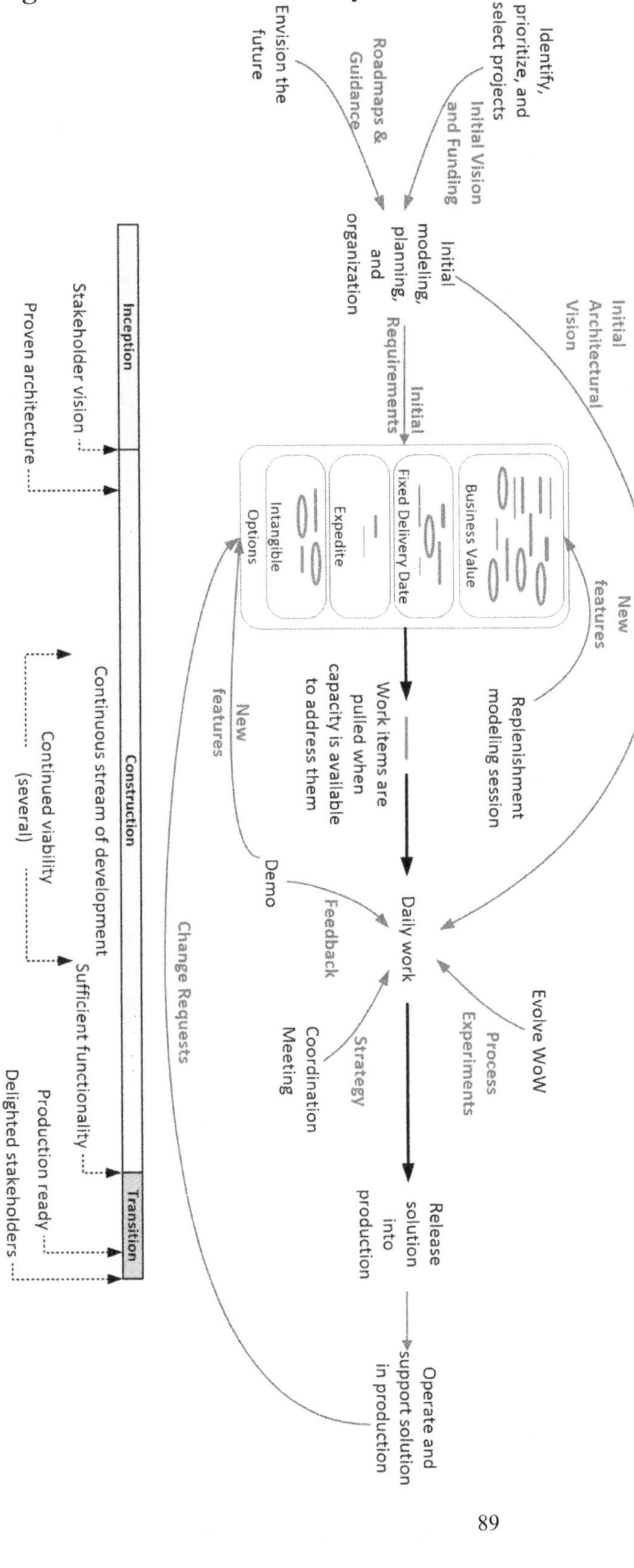

DAD's Continuous Delivery: Lean Lifecycle

DAD's Continuous Delivery: Lean lifecycle, shown in Figure 6.9 is a natural progression from the Advanced/Lean lifecycle. Teams typically evolve into this lifecycle from either the Lean lifecycle or the Continuous Delivery: Agile lifecycle. There are several critical aspects to this lifecycle:

- **Delivery of new functionality is truly continuous.** Changes to production are delivered several times a day by the team, although the functionality may not be turned on until it is needed (this is a DevOps strategy called feature toggles described in Chapter 19).

- **Automation and technical practices are key.** This is similar to the Continuous Delivery: Agile lifecycle.

- **Inception and Transition have disappeared from the diagram.** This occurred for the same reasons they disappeared for Continuous Delivery: Agile.

> **Outcomes Lead to Continuous Exploration**
> An interesting thing that we've observed is that when you capture work items as outcomes, instead of as requirements such as user stories, this lifecycle tends to evolve into continuous exploration of Stakeholder needs rather than continuous order taking that we see with requirements-driven strategies.

- **Explicit milestones and incoming workflows.** Once again, similar to the Continuous Delivery: Agile lifecycle.

Figure 6.9. DAD's Continuous Delivery: Lean lifecycle.

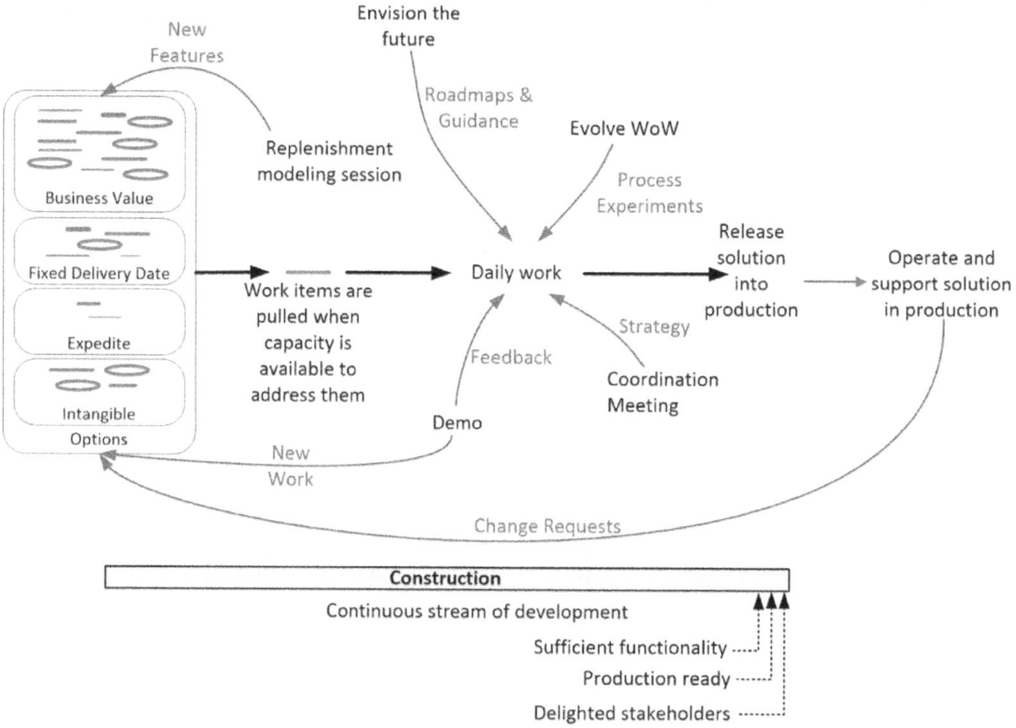

DAD's Exploratory Lifecycle

 DAD's Exploratory lifecycle, shown in Figure 6.10 is based on the Lean Startup principles advocated by Eric Ries. The philosophy of Lean Startup is to minimize up-front investments in developing new offerings in the marketplace in favor of small experiments [Ries]. The idea is to run some experiments with potential customers to identify what they want based in actual usage, thereby increasing our chance of producing something they're actually interested in. This approach of running customer-facing experiments to explore user needs is an important design thinking strategy for exploring "wicked problems" in your domain. There are several critical aspects to this lifecycle:

- **This is a simplified scientific method**. We come up with a hypothesis of what our customers want, we develop one or more minimal viable products (MVPs) which are deployed to a subset of potential customers, then we observe and measure how they work with the MVP(s). Based on the data we collect we decide how we will go forward – Do we pivot and rethink our hypothesis? Do we rework one or more MVPs to run new experiments based on our improved understanding of customer needs? Do we discard one or more ideas? Do we move forward with one or more ideas and "productize them" into real customer offerings?

- **MVPs are prototypes (at best)**. The MVPs we create are built hastily, often "smoke and mirrors" or prototype-quality code, whose sole purpose is to test out a hypothesis. It is not the "real thing" nor is it meant to be. It's a piece of functionality or service offering that we get out in front of our potential customers to see how they react to it. See Figure 6.11 for an overview of MVPs and related concepts.

- **Run several experiments in parallel**. Ideally this lifecycle entails running several experiments in parallel to explore our hypothesis. This is an improvement over Lean Startup which focuses on a single experiment at a time – although it is easier to run a single experiment at a time it takes longer to get to a good idea and worse yet runs the risk of identifying a strategy before other options have been considered.

Figure 6.10. DAD's Exploratory lifecycle.

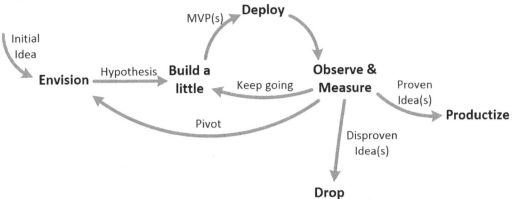

- **Failed experiments are still successes**. Some organizations are reluctant to run experiments because they are scared of failing, which is unfortunate because an exploratory approach such as this actually reduces your risk of product failure (which tend to large, expensive, and embarrassing). Our advice is to make it "safe to fail," to recognize that when an experiment has a negative result that this is actually a success because you have inexpensively learned what won't work, enabling you to refocus on looking for something that will.

- **Follow another lifecycle to build the real product**. Once we've discovered one or more ideas that it appears will succeed in the market, we now need to build the "real solution." We do this by following one of the other DAD lifecycles.

Figure 6.11. Exploring the terminology around MVPs.

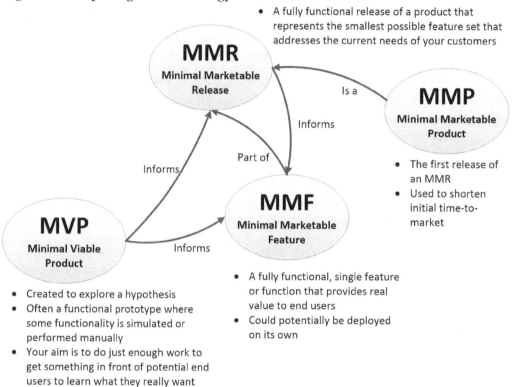

We've seen several different flavors, or perhaps several different tailorings is a better way of looking at it, over the years:

1. **Exploration of a new offering**. The most compelling reason, at least for us, is to apply this lifecycle to explore an idea that your organization has for a new product.

2. **Exploration of a new feature**. At a smaller scale the Exploratory lifecycle is effectively the strategy for running an A/B test or split test where you implement several versions of a new feature and run them in parallel to determine which one is most effective.

3. **Parallel proof-of-concepts (PoCs)**. With a PoC you install and then evaluate a package, sometimes called a commercial off-the-shelf solution (COTS), within your environment. An effective way to decrease the risk of software acquisition is to run several PoCs in parallel, one for each potential software package that you are

considering, and then compare the results to identify the best option available. This is often referred to as a "bake off."

4. **Strategy comparisons**. Some organizations, particularly ones in very competitive environments, will start up several teams initially to work on a product. Each team basically works through Inception and perhaps even a bit of Construction, the aim being to identify a vision for the product and prove out their architectural strategy. In this case their work is more advanced than an MVP but less advanced than an MMR. Then, after a period of time, they compare the work of the teams and pick the best approach – the "winning team" gets to move forward and become the product team.

DAD's Program Lifecycle for a "Team of Teams"

DAD's Program lifecycle, shown in Figure 6.12, describes how to organize a team of teams. Large agile teams are rare in practice, but they do happen. This is exactly the situation that scaling frameworks such as SAFe, LeSS, and Nexus address. There are several critical aspects to this lifecycle:

- **There's an explicit Inception phase**. Like it or not, when a team is new we need to invest some up front time getting organized, and this is particularly true for large teams given the additional risk we face. We should do so as quickly as possible, and the best way is to explicitly recognize what we need to do and how we'll go about doing so.

- **Subteams/squads choose and then evolve their WoW**. Subteams, sometimes referred to as squads, should be allowed to choose their own WoW just like any other team would. This includes choosing their own lifecycles as well as their own practices – to be clear, some teams may be following the Agile lifecycle, some the Continuous Delivery: Lean lifecycle, and so on. We may choose to impose some constraints on the teams, such as following common guidance and common strategies around coordinating within the program (captured by the *Coordinate Activities* process goal in Chapter 23). As Figure 6.13 implies we will need to come to an agreement around how we'll proceed with cross-team system integration and cross-team testing (if needed), options for which are captured by the *Accelerate Value Delivery* process goal (Chapter 19) and the *Develop Test Strategy* process goal (Chapter 12) respectively. Where a framework such as SAFe would prescribe a strategy such as a release train to do this, DAD offers choices and helps you to pick the best strategy for your situation.

- **Subteams can be feature teams or component teams**. For years within the agile community there has been a debate around feature teams versus component teams. A feature team works vertical slices of functionality, implementing a story or addressing a change request from the user interface all the way through to the database. A component team works on a specific aspect of a system, such as security functionality, transaction processing, or logging. Our experience is both types of teams have their place, they are applicable in certain contexts but not others, and the strategies can and often are combined in practice.

- **Coordination occurs at three levels**. When we're coordinating between subteams there are three issues we need to be concerned about: Coordinating the work to be done, coordinating technical/architectural issues, and coordinating people issues. In Figure 6.13 this coordination is respectively performed by the Product Owners, the

93

Architecture Owners, and the Team Leads. The Product Owners of each subteam will self-organize and address work/requirements management issues amongst themselves, ensuring that each team is doing the appropriate work at the appropriate time. Similarly the Architecture Ownership team will self-organize to evolve the architecture over time and the Team Leads will self-organize to manage people issues occurring across teams. The three leadership subteams are able to handle the type of small course corrections that are typical over time. The team may find that they need to get together occasionally to plan out the next block of work – this is a technique that SAFe refers to as program increment (PI) planning and suggest that it occurs quarterly. We suggest that you do it when and if it makes sense.

- **System integration and testing occurs in parallel**. Figure 6.12 shows that there is a separate team to perform overall system integration and cross-team testing. Ideally this work should be minimal and ideally entirely automated in time. We often need a separate team at first, often due to lack of automation, but our goal should be to automate as much of this work as possible and push the rest into the subteams. Having said that we've found that usability testing across the product as a whole, and similarly user acceptance testing (UAT), requires a separate effort for logistical reasons.

- **Subteams are as whole as they can be**. The majority of the testing effort should occur within the subteams just like it would on a normal agile team, along with continuous integration (CI) and continuous deployment (CD).

- **We can deploy any time we want**. We prefer a CD approach to this, although teams new to agile programs may start by releasing quarterly (or even less often) and then improve the release cadence over time. Teams who are new to this will likely need a Transition phase, some people call these "hardening sprints" or "deployment sprints" the first few times. The *Accelerate Value Delivery* process goal (Chapter 19) captures various release options for delivery teams and the *Release Management* process blade [AmblerLines2017] for organizations as a whole. A process blade encompasses a cohesive collection of process options, such as practices and strategies, that should be chosen and then applied in a context sensitive manner. Each process blade addresses a specific capability, such as Finance, Data Management, Reuse Engineering, or Procurement—just like process goals are described using process goal diagrams, so are process blades.

- **Scaling is hard**. Some problems require a large team, but to succeed you need to know what you're doing – if you're struggling with small-team agile then you're not ready for large-team agile. Furthermore, as we learned in Chapter 3, team size is only one of six scaling factors that our team may need to contend with, the others being geographic distribution, domain complexity, technical complexity, organizational distribution, and regulatory compliance. We cover these issues in greater detail at DisciplinedAgileDelivery.com.

Figure 6.12. The DAD Program lifecycle.

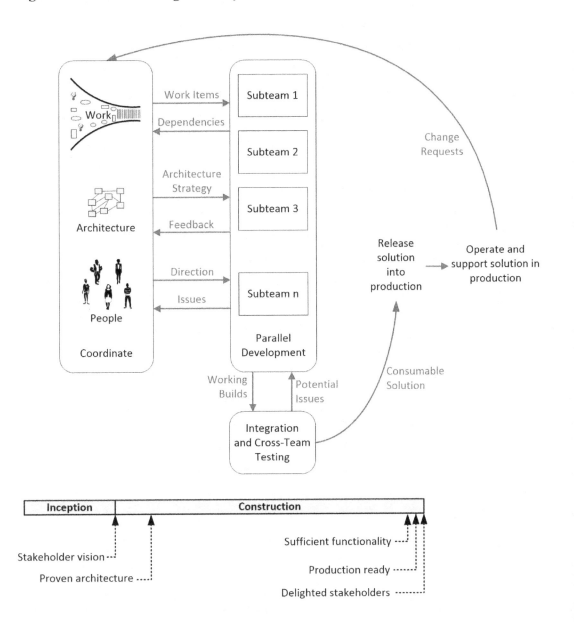

Figure 6.13. A potential structure for organizing a large team of teams.

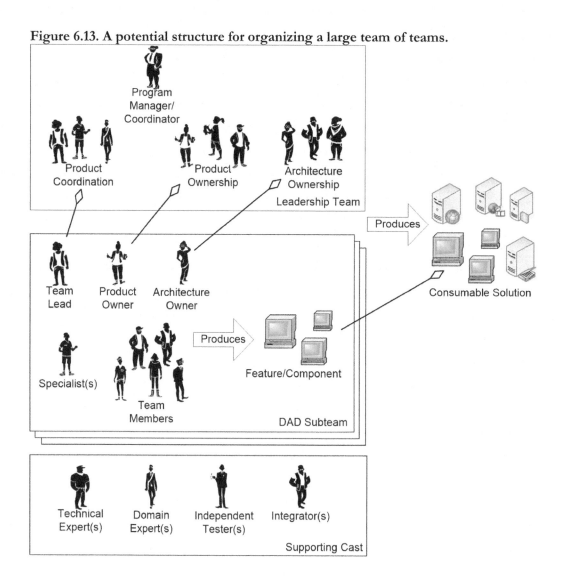

When Should You Adopt Each Lifecycle?

Every team should choose its own lifecycle, but how do you do this? It's tempting to have your portfolio management team to make this choice, well, at least it is for them. At best they should make a (hopefully solid) suggestion when they first initiate an endeavour, but in the end the choice of lifecycle should be made by the team if you want to be effective. This can be a challenging choice, particularly for teams new to agile and lean. An important part of the process decision scaffolding provided by DAD is advice for choosing a lifecycle, including the flow chart of Figure 6.14.

Figure 6.14. A flow chart for choosing an initial lifecycle.

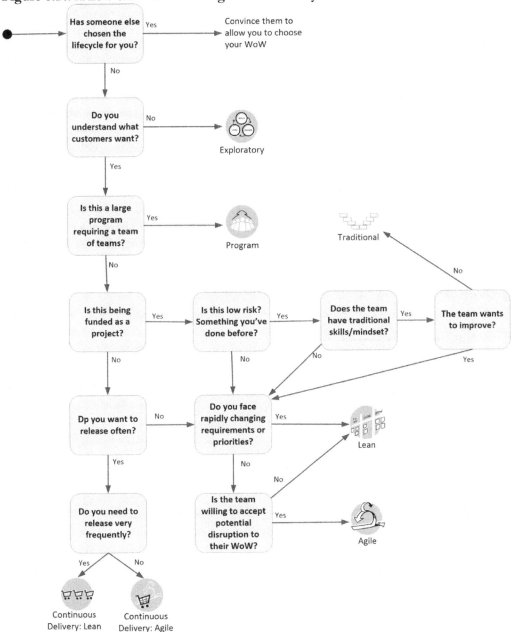

Of course there's a bit more to it than this flowchart. Figure 6.15 overviews what we've found to be important considerations, from the Software Development Context Framework (SDCF) [SDCF], to be taken into account when selecting a lifecycle. Constraining factors we keep in mind when choosing a delivery lifecycle include:

1. **Team skills**. The two continuous delivery (CD) lifecycles require the team to have a lot of skill and discipline. The other DAD lifecycles also require skill and discipline, although the two CD lifecycles stand out. With the traditional lifecycle you can get away with lower-skilled people – due to the hand-off oriented nature of

traditional you can staff each phase with narrowly-skilled specialists. Having said that we have seen many traditional teams with very skilled people on them.

2. **Team and organization culture**. The Agile and CD lifecycles require flexibility within the team and within the parts of the organization that the team interacts with. Lean strategies can be applied in organizations with a varying range of flexibility. Traditional can, and often is, applied in very rigid situations.

3. **The nature of the problem**. The CD lifecycles work very well when you can build and release in very small increments. The other DAD lifecycles work very well in small increments. Traditional is really geared for big releases.

4. **Business constraints**. The key issue here is Stakeholder availability and willingness, although financial/funding flexibility is also critical. The Exploratory lifecycle requires a flexible, customer-oriented and experimental mindset on the part of Stakeholders. Agile, because it tends to release functionality in terms of complete features, also requires flexibility in the way that we interact with Stakeholders. Surprisingly, the continuous delivery lifecycles require less Stakeholder flexibility due to being able to release functionality that is turned off, thereby providing greater control over when something is released (by simply toggling it on).

Figure 6.15. Selection factors for choosing a lifecycle.

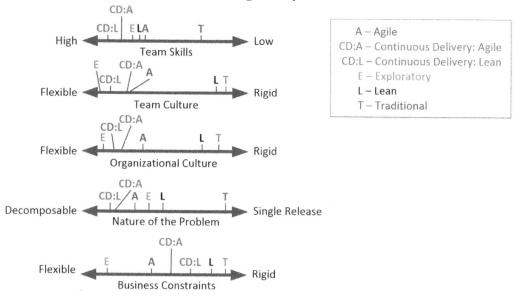

The *Evolve WoW* process goal (Chapter 24) includes a decision point that covers the trade-offs associated with the six DAD lifecycles plus a few others that are not explicitly supported by DAD (such as Traditional).

Different Lifecycles With Common Milestones

In many of the organizations that we've helped to adopt DA, the senior leadership, and often middle management, are very reluctant at first to allow delivery teams to choose their WoW. The challenge is that their traditional mindset often tells them that teams need to follow the same, "repeatable process" so that senior leadership may oversee and guide them. There are two significant misconceptions with this mindset: First, we can have common governance across teams without enforcing a common process. A fundamental enabler of this is to adopt common, risk-based (not artifact based) milestones across the lifecycles. This is exactly what DAD does, and these common milestones are shown in Figure 6.16. Second, repeatable outcomes are far more important than repeatable processes. Our Stakeholders want us to spend their IT investment wisely. They want us to produce, and evolve, solutions that meet their actual needs. They want these solutions quickly. They want solutions that enable them to compete effectively in the marketplace. These are the types of outcomes that Stakeholders would like to have over and over (e.g. repeatedly), they really aren't that concerned with the processes that we follow to do this. For more on effective governance strategies for agile/lean teams, see the *Govern Delivery Team* process goal (Chapter 27).

Figure 6.16. Common milestones across the lifecycles.

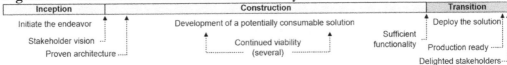

Let's explore DAD's risk-based milestones in a bit more detail:

1. **Stakeholder Vision**. The aim of the Inception phase is to spend a short yet sufficient amount of time, typically a few days to a few weeks, to gain Stakeholder agreement that the initiative makes sense and should continue into the Construction phase. By addressing each of the DAD Inception goals the delivery team will capture traditional project information related to *initial* scope, technology, schedule, budget, risks, and other information albeit in as simple a fashion as possible. This information is consolidated and presented to Stakeholders as a Vision statement as described by the *Develop Common Vision* process goal (see Chapter 13). The format of the vision and formality of review will vary according to your situation. A typical practice is to review a short set of slides with key Stakeholders at the end of the

> **Explicit Phases and Governance Make Agile More Palatable to Management**
> Daniel Gagnon has been at the forefront of Agile practice and delivery for almost a decade in two of Canada's largest financial institutions. He had this to say about using DA as an overarching toolkit: "At both large financials that I have worked in I set out to demonstrate the pragmatic advantages of using DA as a "top of the house" approach. Process tailoring in large, complex organisations clearly reveals the need for a large number of context-specific implementations of the four (now five) life cycles, and DA allows for a spectrum of possibilities that no other framework accommodates. However, we call this "Structured Freedom" as all choices are still governed by DA's application of Inception, Construction, and Transition with lightweight, risk-based milestones. These phases are familiar to PMOs, which means that we aren't carrying out a frontal assault on their fortified position, but rather introducing governance change in a Lean, iterative and incremental fashion."

Inception phase to ensure that everyone is on the same page with regard to the project intent and delivery approach.

2. **Proven Architecture**. Early risk mitigation is a part of any good engineering discipline. As the *Prove Architecture Early* process goal (see Chapter 15) indicates, there are several strategies you may choose to adopt. The most effective of which is to build an end-to-

99

end skeleton of working code that implements technically risky business requirements. A key responsibility of DAD's Architecture Owner role is to identify risks during the Inception phase. It is expected that these risks will have been reduced or eliminated by implementing related functionality somewhere between one and three iterations into the Construction phase. As a result of applying this approach early iteration reviews/demos often show the ability of the solution to support non-functional requirements in addition to, or instead of functional requirements. For this reason it is important that architecture-savvy Stakeholders are given the opportunity to participate in these milestone reviews.

3. **Continued Viability**. An optional milestone to include in your release schedule is related to project viability. At certain times during a project Stakeholders may request a checkpoint to ensure that the team is working towards the vision agreed to at the end of Inception. Scheduling these milestones ensures that Stakeholders are aware of key dates wherein they should get together with the team to assess the project status and agree to changes if necessary. These changes could include anything such as funding levels, team makeup, scope, risk assessment, or even potentially cancelling the project. There could be several of these milestones on a long-running project. However, instead of having this milestone review, the real solution is to release into production more often – actual usage, or lack thereof, will provide a very clear indication of whether your solution is viable.

4. **Sufficient Functionality**. While it is worthwhile pursuing a goal of a consumable solution (what Scrum calls a potentially shippable increment) at the end of each iteration, it is more common to require a number of iterations of Construction before the team has implemented enough functionality to deploy. While this is sometimes referred to as a minimal viable product (MVP) this not technically accurate as classically an MVP is meant to test the viability of a product rather than an indication of minimal deployable functionality. The more accurate term to compare to this milestone would be "minimum feature set" or "minimal marketable release (MMR)," as Figure 6.11 shows.

> **MVPs vs MMRs**
> Daniel Gagnon provides this advice: Think of an MVP as something the organization does for **selfish** reasons. It's all about learning, not about providing the customer with a fully-fledged (or sometimes even vaguely functioning!) solution. Whereas an MMF is **altruistic** – it's all about the customer's needs.

An MMR will comprise one or more minimal marketable features (MMFs), and an MMF provides a positive outcome to the end users of our solution. An outcome may need to be implemented via several user stories. For example, searching for an item on an ecommerce system adds no value to an end user if they cannot also add the found items to their shopping cart. DAD's sufficient functionality milestone is reached at the end of the Construction phase when a MMR is available plus the cost of transitioning the release to Stakeholders is justified. As an example, while an increment of a consumable solution may be available with every two week iteration, it may take several weeks to actually deploy it in a high compliance environment so the cost of deployment may not be justified until a greater amount of functionality is completed.

5. **Production Ready**. Once sufficient functionality has been developed and tested, transition related activities such as data conversions, final acceptance testing, production and support related documentation normally need to be completed. Ideally much of the work has been done continuously during the Construction phase as part of completing each increment of functionality. At some point a decision needs to be made that the

solution is ready for production, which is the purpose of this milestone. The two project-based lifecycles include a Transition phase where the Production Ready milestone is typically implemented as a review. The two continuous delivery lifecycles, on the other hand, have a fully automated transition/release activity where this milestone is addressed programmatically – typically the solution must pass automated regression testing and the automated analysis tools must determine that the solution is of sufficient quality.

6. **Delighted Stakeholders**. Governance bodies and other Stakeholders obviously like to know when the initiative is officially over so that they can begin another release or direct funds elsewhere. The initiative doesn't end when the solution is deployed. With projects, there are often closeout activities such as training, deployment tuning, support handoffs, post implementation reviews, or even warranty periods before the solution is considered completed. One of the seven principles of DA, see Chapter 2, is *Delighted Customers* which suggests that "satisfied" customers is setting the bar too low. The implication is that we need to verify whether we've delighted our stakeholders, typically through collection and analysis of appropriate metrics.

Lifecycles are Just Starting Points

DAD teams will often evolve from one lifecycle to another. This is because DAD teams are always striving to *Optimize Flow*, to improve their WoW as they learn through their experiences and through purposeful experimentation. Figure 6.17 shows common evolution paths that we've seen teams go through. The times indicated in 6.17 reflect our experiences when the team's are supported by Disciplined Agile (DA) training and support by Certified Disciplined Agile Coaches (CDACs) – without this expect longer times, and most likely higher total costs, on average. When helping a traditional team move to a more effective WoW, a common approach is to start with the Agile lifecycle. This is a "sink or swim" approach that experience shows can be very effective, but it can prove difficult in cultures that resist change. A second path shown in this diagram is to start traditional teams with a Lean Kanban

---

Lifecycle evolution is a good thing
To be clear, we think Scrum is great and it is at the heart of our two Agile lifecycles. However, we have seen a growing backlash in the agile community against its prescriptive aspects. As we describe in our Introduction to DAD book, in practice we regularly see advanced Agile/Scrum teams stripping out the process waste in Scrum such as daily meetings, planning, estimating, and retrospectives as they "lean up". The Scrum community is quick to ostracize such behavior as "Scrum but" – doing some Scrum but not all of it. However, we see this a natural evolution as the team replaces wasteful activities with added value delivery. The nature of these teams that naturally collaborate all day everyday means that they don't need to perform such ceremonies on a deferred cadence, preferring to do these things, when needed, on a JIT basis. We think this a good and natural thing.

[Anderson] approach wherein the team starts with their existing WoW and evolves it over time via small changes into the Lean lifecycle. While this is less disruptive, it can result in much slower rate of improvement since the teams often continue to work in a silo fashion with Kanban board columns depicting traditional specialties.

101

Figure 6.17. Common lifecycle evolution paths.

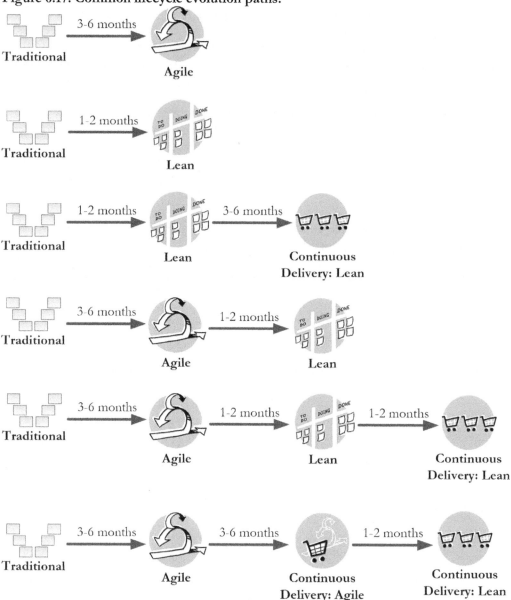

What Figure 6.17 doesn't show is where the Program or Exploratory lifecycles fit in. First, in some ways it does apply to the Program lifecycle. You can take an Agile Program approach (similar to what scaling Frameworks such as Nexus, SAFe, and LeSS do in practice) where the program releases large increments on a regular cadence (say quarterly). You can also take a Lean Program approach where the subteams stream functionality into production and then at the program level this is toggled on when it makes sense to do so. Second, the focus of the diagram is on full delivery lifecycles whereas the Exploratory lifecycle isn't a full delivery lifecycle in its own right. It is typically used to test out a hypothesis regarding a potential marketplace offering, and when the idea has been sufficiently fleshed out and it appears the product will succeed, then the team shifts into one of the delivery lifecycles of Figure 6.17. In that way it replaces a good portion of the Inception phase efforts for the team. Another common scenario is that a team is in the middle of development and realizes that they have a new idea for a major feature that needs to be better explored before investing serious development effort into it. So the team will shift into the Exploratory lifecycle for as long as it takes to either flesh out the feature idea or to disprove its market viability.

In Summary

In this chapter we explored several key concepts:

- Some teams within your organization will still follow a traditional lifecycle – DAD explicitly recognizes this but does not provide support for this shrinking category of work.
- DAD provides the scaffolding required for choosing between, and then evolving, six solution delivery lifecycles (SDLCs) based on either agile or lean strategies.
- Project-based lifecycles, even agile and lean ones, go through phases.
- Every lifecycle has its advantages and disadvantages, each team needs to pick the one that best reflects their context.
- Common, risk-based milestones enable consistent governance – you don't need to force the same process on all of your teams to be able to govern them.
- A team will start with a given lifecycle and often evolve away from it as they continuously improve their WoW.

SECTION 2: SUCCESSFULLY INITIATING YOUR TEAM

The aim of Inception is for a team to do just enough work to get themselves organized and to come to a general agreement around the scope, architectural strategy, and plan for the current release. The average agile/lean team spends on average 11 work days, so a bit more than two weeks, in Inception activities [SoftDev18]. This section is organized into the following chapters:

- **Chapter 7: Form Team**. Build and evolve an awesome team.
- **Chapter 8: Align With Enterprise Direction**. Ensure that the team understands and follows common roadmaps and guidance.
- **Chapter 9: Explore Scope**. Identify the potential scope for the current release of the solution.
- **Chapter 10: Identify Architecture Strategy**. Identify an architecture strategy to guide the construction of the solution.
- **Chapter 11: Plan the Release**. Create a sufficient, high-level release plan to guide the efforts of the team.
- **Chapter 12: Develop Test Strategy**. Identify a test strategy that reflects the scope, architectural strategy, and risk faced by the team.
- **Chapter 13: Develop Common Vision**. Develop a vision for what the team will accomplish for the current release of the solution.
- **Chapter 13: Secure Funding**. Obtain funding for the team.

105

7 FORM TEAM

The Form Team process goal, shown in Figure 7.1, provides options for how to build and eventually evolve our team. There are two reasons why this is important: First, we need people to get started. Although we expect the team to evolve over time, right now we need at least enough people to do the work involved with Inception. Second, we make key decisions early on. During Inception we make important decisions around scope, development strategy, and schedule amongst others. These are decisions that the team should make as they will be responsible for executing on them.

There are several reasons why this process goal is important:

1. **There is a lot to consider when you're building an awesome team**. Awesome teams are comprised of the right mix of people, with the requisite skills, with an open and safe culture, collaborating and learning together, and enabled to do so by the organizational ecosystem in which they work.

2. **We need time to build an awesome team**. We need to get started as soon as we can so that we can start inviting the right people to join the team as they become available. The mix of skills and collaborative style will evolve as we do so, and people will come in and out of the team as it evolves to meet the context of the situation that it faces.

> **Key Points in this Chapter**
> - You will need to decide whether your new initiative can be given to an existing team, or to evolve an existing team or create a new one.
> - You will need to appropriately size the teams and decide what type of work they are best suited for.
> - How whole are your teams and what is the strategy for accessing skills or responsibilities not held within the team?
> - You should strive for dedicated team members and if not, then understand the cost of this decision.
> - Your teaming strategies will vary based upon your enterprise realities such as outsourcing, distribution, and time zones.
> - You should consider strategies for adequate training, mentoring, coaching and obtaining access to stakeholders.
> - Who is responsible for evolving the team, and how will they do so?

3. **The people on the team, and the way we work together, will be the primary determinant of success**. The first value of the Agile Manifesto, adopted directly by the Disciplined Agile Manifesto (see Chapter 2) says it best – individuals and interactions over processes and tools.

Figure 7.1. The goal diagram for Form Team.

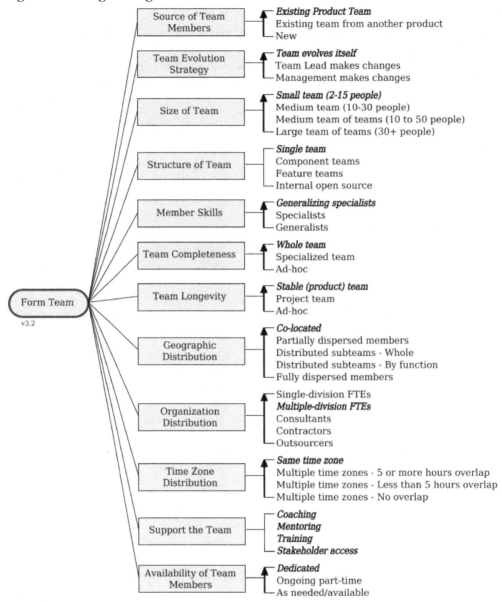

To form, and later evolve, our team we need to consider several important questions:
- Where will team members come from?
- How do we intend to evolve the team over time?
- How large should the team be?
- How will sub-teams be organized (if we need them)?
- What type of team members do we need?
- How complete will the team be?

108

- How long will the team exist?
- Where will team members be located?
- What organization(s) do the team members work for?
- What range of time zones are team members found in?
- How will we support the team?
- How available will team members be?

Source of Team Members

We need to how to source our team members. Is work taken to an existing team, or are team members selected for the work? This decision is one of the most important of all our organizational decisions. Using existing product teams is an important and fundamental step towards optimizing agility. Stable, long-term, small, co-located, dedicated teams should be our goal if we expect our teams to grow into high performance delivery machines, or "race car engines" in our racing car metaphor [RaceCar].

Options (Ordered)	Trade-Offs
Existing Product Team. Work is performed by an existing team that has worked on this previously and who understands the domain.	• The team understands the product domain and how to navigate the organization, making it more effective. • The team has an established velocity which makes forecasting more accurate. • The team has likely gelled and works well together. • Long-standing teams may make some team members feel trapped in their current role, necessitating opportunities to transfer between teams (People Management).
Existing Team from another product. The team has worked together for some time but on another product and perhaps even another domain.	• The team will likely perform better than a new team since they have a history of working together. • Not having worked in a new domain introduces a risk of miscommunication between the stakeholders and the delivery team. • The team may need to evolve to meet the demands of taking on new types of work.
New. The team has been assembled for this initiative and may have not worked together before. This is a traditional matrix-style of forming teams using a "project" approach rather than a release/product approach.	• The team will take some time to "Form, Storm, Norm, and Perform" resulting in having to work through trust issues, awkward collaboration, miscommunication, and often poor productivity and quality. • Inconsistent, but hopefully rising, velocity will be an initial characteristic of a new team. • This is the least effective choice as the effort to grow a high performance team is expensive and time consuming.

109

Team Evolution Strategy

Team turnover, even within "stable teams", will still occur over time. However, changing team members can be disruptive and can jeopardize our existing team dynamics.

Options (Ordered)	Trade-Offs
Team evolves itself. A manager may help to select candidates for a team but the team has the opportunity to make the final selection of who joins the team.	• Teams are motivated to identify people who are the best fit. • Teams are more likely to welcome new team members when they have a part in selecting them. • May be challenging to get team consensus. • Teams have to take time out for interviewing and selection.
Team Lead makes changes. A manager might help with shortlisting but the team lead makes the final selection.	• Works in an environment where the team trusts the Team Lead to make a good selection. • However, team dynamics are as important as domain knowledge so the team should still have the opportunity to vet candidates.
Management makes changes. A manager allocates or assigns "resources" to the team.	• Management is unlikely to appreciate the existing team dynamics. • Management may be motivated to place someone who is currently available rather than someone who is the best fit for the role.

Size of Team

The ideal situation is having small teams in a collocated work room. Mark likes to say, "I should be able to have conversations with any team member without my bum leaving my seat." However, we have also seen larger teams be quite successful despite "two-pizza strategies" or insistence on teams no larger than 7 +/- 2 people. Half of agile teams are ten or more people in practice. Having said that, team success rates drop the larger the team becomes. It's important to note that the size options in the following table purposefully overlap one another because there is no commonly accepted definitions for team size.

Options (Ordered)	Trade-Offs
Small team (2-15 people). A single team of people. See Figure 7.2 for a common organization structure.	• Small teams are most effective for collaboration. • May be more difficult to establish "whole teams" who have all the skills and authority to do the work required. • Small teams are likely to have dependencies on external teams to do work for them, requiring hand-offs that result in delays.
Medium team (10-30 people). A single team of people. See Figure 7.3 for a common organization structure.	• Slightly larger teams allow specialists such as UX designers, database and other technical or business specialists to join the team and still have enough work to be fully utilized. • Increased likelihood that the team can be a whole team. • Teams of this size are viable in practice, particularly when

	team members are near located, the team is allowed to grow into this size, and the team is following a lean lifecycle.
Medium team of teams (10 to 50 people). The medium-sized team is organized into a collection of small subteams. See Figure 7.4 for a common organization structure.	• Each subteam should be whole, thereby gaining the benefits of small teams. • Sometimes individuals will be members of several subteams. This adds scheduling complexity and risk to the subteams, and stress for the individuals. • Coordination is required between subteams, adding risk and overhead. Coordination can typically be accomplished via a "Scrum of Scrums (SoS)," which is a second daily coordination meeting comprised of a representative from each subteam.
Large team of teams (30+ people). The "large team" is organized into a collection of small subteams. See Figure 7.5 for a common organization structure.	• Typically requires more complex collaboration mechanisms than an SoS, in particular for requirements management, team management, and technical management. See the *Coordinate Activities* process goal in Chapter 23.

Figure 7.2. Potential organization of a small DAD team.

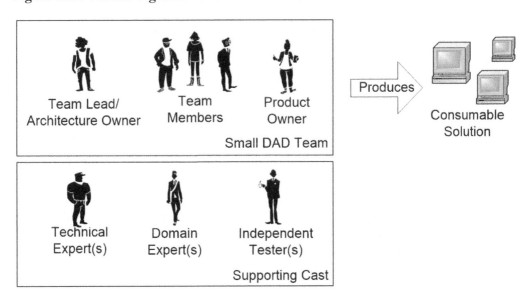

111

Figure 7.3. Potential organization of a medium-sized DAD team.

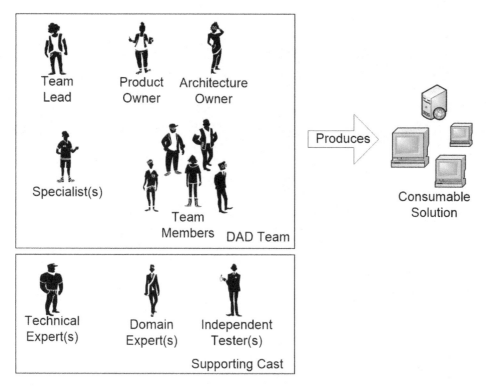

Figure 7.4. Potential organization of a medium-sized team of teams.

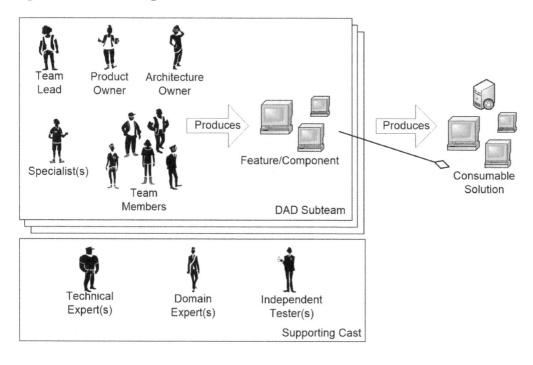

Figure 7.5. Potential organization of a large team of teams.

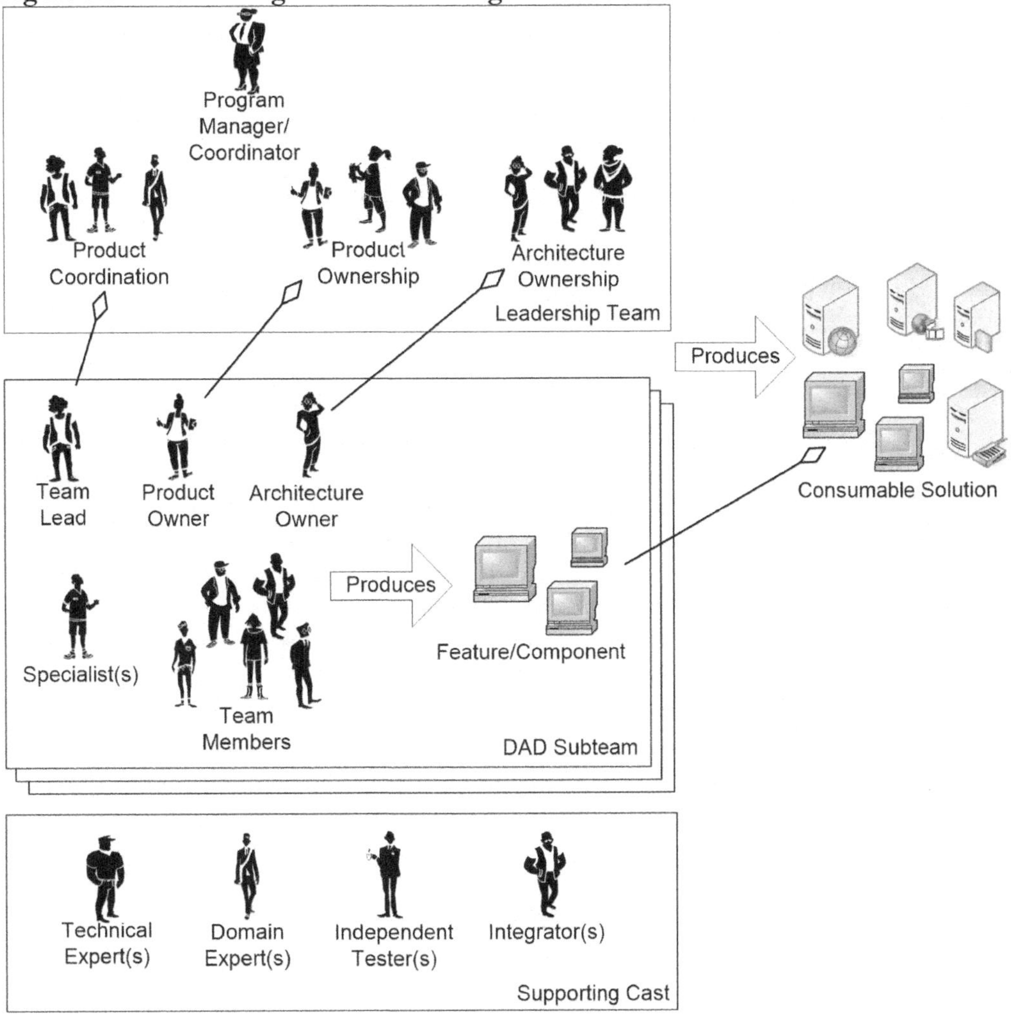

Structure of Team

We will need to decide if each of our teams build pieces of the solution end-to-end or whether we rely on other teams to complete our work.

Options (Ordered)	Trade-Offs
Single team. One "whole" team, where the team has all the skills required to get the job done, makes for the most effective team makeup.	• This greatly reduces, and sometimes eliminates, dependencies outside the team, which could inhibit the team's ability to delivery reliably. • Can be difficult to form a whole team, particularly in organizations where many staff members are still highly specialized.
Component teams. The team provides a component or part of	• Useful where there is a need to govern aspects of the solution, such as a security framework, so that they are appropriately designed and supported.

113

the solution, which is consumed by other teams or solutions. Also known as a services team.	• Can be efficient where there is a high degree of specialization involved. • Can result in bottlenecks and inefficient resourcing when other teams are dependent on the work of these teams.
Feature teams. These whole teams are responsible for creating all aspects of each feature from top to bottom.	• Ideal in that the teams are not dependent on individuals or other teams in order to deliver each part/feature of the solution. • Can result in organizational technical debt if each team is "doing their own thing." • Can be inefficient if teams are not experts in some technical areas. • There is a temptation to build everything from scratch if teams are not expected to consume services created by component teams. Hopefully our Architecture Owner (AO) will help to guide the team to work in an enterprise aware manner and avoid this mistake.
Internal open source. A component/framework is developed using an open source strategy within our organization (e.g., on our side of the firewall).	• Can be an effective way to encourage collective ownership of all organizational assets, not just within a team. This reduces business risk of some aspects of the solutions being poorly understood and supported. • Encourages reuse. • Requires expertise with open source development. • Very rare in practice; typically only applicable in large organizations with many teams working on a common platform.

Member Skills

Do our team members each have specific skills and can only work within their specialty or are they capable and comfortable with collaborating on work outside their specialty?

Options (Ordered)	Trade-Offs
Generalizing specialists. A generalizing specialist is skilled and experienced in one or more areas and also has general skills in other areas outside their specialty, e.g., a developer specialist who also can help with testing and analysis. Also known as "T-skilled," "E-skilled", "comb-shaped," or cross-functional people [GenSpec].	• Being able to contribute in areas outside of one's specialty means that the team is more effective overall. • A lower likelihood that work is delayed due to bottlenecks waiting for a skilled team member to complete work. • Requires people with a more robust set of skills.
Specialists. Individuals who are skilled only in one specialty such as testing, or	• Effective when there is little need to collaborate with others to complete work, e.g., we don't need to be

114

programming, or analysis.	agile.
	• When work has to be completed by multiple specialized team members the overall process tends to be slow and expensive, producing lower levels of quality.
Generalists. The person has general skills across disciplines but no expertise in any one.	• Generalists have the potential to be leaders or managers because they can often see the bigger picture.
	• A team made up solely of generalists is rarely able to produce a working solution due to lack of concrete skills.

Team Completeness

We should try to create a team that is complete in that it has all the skills, experience, and authority to get the job done. As you can see in the table below, there are several options for doing so. To determine whether a team has sufficient skills, a strategy that we've found effective is to first identify which process goals the team is responsible for addressing and then using the goal diagrams to assess whether the team has sufficient skills to address each goal.

Options (Ordered)	Trade-Offs
Whole team. A team that has all the skills required to complete the work. A whole team is responsible for addressing all of the process goals applicable to the lifecycle that they are following.	• Ideal in that the team is not dependent on others to get the work done. Dependencies create risk that the dependent work is not completed in a timely manner, and that its quality may jeopardize the team's own work. • For a team to be whole we may need to build a team that is larger than we had hoped (often breaking the "two pizza" rule – a team should be small enough to be fed with two pizzas). In organizations where people are still mostly specialized we will have larger "whole teams" compared with organizations where people are generalizing specialists with a more robust set of skills.
Specialized team. A team that is skilled in producing a particular type of work, such as a data group or a testing team. A specialized team is responsible for addressing the subset of process goals, and often a subset of the decision points of some goals, applicable to their specialty. For example, a testing team would be responsible for addressing *Develop Test Strategy*	• Useful in situations where the work is highly specialized. 4% of agile/lean teams are specialized "services" teams [SoftDev18]. • Results in dependencies across teams, which is inefficient, requires coordination, and increases delivery risk.

(Chapter 12) and a portion of *Accelerate Value Delivery* (Chapter 19).	
Ad-hoc. Teams are formed of people who may work well together but who may not have sufficient skills to complete the work.	• Less efficient than other approaches because of a lack of cohesion. • Teams who work well together can make up in part for a lack of cohesive set of skills and get the work done.

Team Longevity

This is one of the key decisions when building a team. Teams that stay together long term are most likely to gel and become high performing teams.

Options (Ordered)	Trade-Offs
Stable (product) team. The team stays together long term between releases with periodic rotation of team members for growth opportunities and knowledge sharing. Also called a long-lived team.	• Stable teams are more likely to be trusting and highly collaborative. 54% of agile/lean teams are stable/long-lived [SoftDev18]. • Avoids the tangible and substantial cost of disbanding teams. The forming, storming, norming, and performing journey for teams is expensive and time consuming.
Project team. Team is "resourced" and formed in	• Team productivity and quality is initially poor until the team gels. 42% of agile/lean teams are project

116

classic project style, specifically for a new initiative.	teams [SoftDev18]. • Potential for significant waste until the team optimizes a process that works for them.
Ad-hoc. A group of people delivering work without well-defined boundaries.	• Lack of commitment to the overall initiative that we should find in a team. • May be effective for ad-hoc work.

Geographic Distribution

The most effective method of communication is face-to-face discussion around a shared sketching environment, as you can see in Figure 7.6 below. The more geographic distance between people, the less able they are to adopt the most effective communication strategies which increases the risk of misunderstandings among team members. Similarly, organization distribution and time zone distribution of team members, described below, may affect our ability to choose communication strategies.

Figure 7.6. Comparing communication strategies between people.

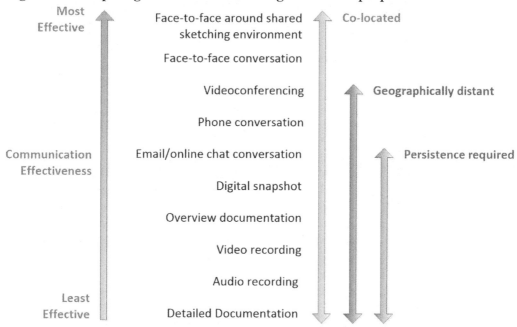

The reality in most organizations is that co-located teams are the exception rather than the rule due to flexible work at home policies and organizational distribution. We have several options for geographic distribution of the team, compared in the following table, which may be combined within a single team. When it's possible for team members to easily come together – perhaps dispersed members are within 1-2 hours driving distance – then they should come in periodically to work face-to-face (F2F) with the rest of the team. A common strategy that we've seen is to have certain days to be "office days" when everyone comes into the office to work together. The number of office days per week required to be effective will vary by team depending on how well the team has gelled and team member's ability to collaborate remotely. We suggest that you start by experimenting with allowing one day of remote work a week to see how that works, then adjust based on your experiences.

Options (Ordered)	Trade-Offs
Co-located. Team works in a common area.	• Most effective for collaboration. • The cost of creating a common work area for each team can be a barrier in many established organizations. • There is a fear, at least initially, that the work area will be too noisy and will not allow people to focus. • If teams are expected to evolve in size there will be a need for a flexible, movable wall/barrier strategy.
Partially dispersed members. Some team members work remotely from home or from another location.	• Less collaborative than co-located but allows remote workers to focus on their work. • Requires virtual tooling such as group chat, digital task boards, virtual whiteboards, and videoconferencing.
Distributed subteams – Whole team. Complete subteams where people are in two or more locations. Each subteam is whole, with sufficient skills to produce their portion of the working solution.	• Increases our ability to hire talented people given a larger candidate pool. • Difficult to coordinate work across team boundaries, but when the teams are whole the coordination required between teams is minimized. • Made worse if there are time zone differences between teams. Try to source distributed teams in the same general time zone. The process goal *Coordinate Activities* (Chapter 23) provides some strategies for subteam collaboration.
Distributed subteams – By function. Subteams/squads where people are in two or more locations. One or more of the subteams is organized by job function (e.g. a team is responsible just for testing, another just for requirements elicitation, and so on).	• Increases our ability to hire talented people given a larger candidate pool. • Very difficult to coordinate work across team boundaries because there will be significant coordination required between the teams. This coordination is often accomplished via detailed documentation or other forms of electronic communication. • Coordination is made worse if there are time zone differences between teams. Try to source distributed teams in the same general time zone. The process goal *Coordinate Activities* (Chapter 23) provides some strategies for subteam collaboration. •
Fully dispersed members. Everyone works from a unique location.	• Virtual tooling is critical for effective collaboration. • More difficult for the team to bond when not working together daily. • Consider bringing the team together periodically to work through critical decisions and to bond. This is particularly crucial when the team is first formed.

Organization Distribution

Sometimes people from several organizations, or several areas within the same organization, may be part of the team. As you see in the table below, there are several organization distribution strategies that may be combined. Because the organizations involved may be in different locations, this decision point may be correlated to both geographic distribution and time zone distribution.

Options (Ordered)	Trade-Offs
Single-division full time employees (FTEs). All of the people from our organization come from the same division or line of business (LOB).	• Simplifies People Management issues because everyone is in the same reporting structure. • The priorities and cultures of other divisions may not be well represented, leading to decisions that are not truly enterprise aware.
Multiple-division FTEs. People may come from several divisions/LOBs of our organization.	• Greater chance of working in an enterprise aware manner. • Often motivates creation of geographically distributed teams. • Often motivates addition of people to the team simply because they're from a certain group instead of being the best fit for their position. • Organizational politics and different organizational styles may hamper the team's ability to work together.
Consultants. These are typically experts in a certain specialty who join our team for a short period of time. Consultants typically come from external organizations although some may come from internal specialty groups such as Data Management, Reuse Engineering, or a Centers of Excellence (CoE).	• Great way to bring expertise into the team, particularly when members are tasked with sharing their skills and knowledge with others. • Consultants tend to have greater motivation to learn and be effective in their role. • Can motivate some of our FTEs to leave the organization to become consultants themselves. • Consultants and contractors often downplay long-term decisions around technical debt and sustainability because they won't be around to deal with the impact of these decisions. • Our organization may not be willing to pay for contractors or consultants to receive training or coaching, which can impact our ability to bring new knowledge and skills into the team. We may need to find a way where the contractors/consultants share the cost of the training (perhaps they aren't paid to be in the training with the rest of the team). • Regulations or policies may prevent us from treating external consultants and contractors as full team members, e.g., we can't invite them to team celebrations. • Regulations or policies may limit the amount of time that

	external consultants and contractors are allowed to work for our organization.
Contractors. These people are provided by an external service provider to augment our organization's staffing for a long period of time, usually for several months or years.	• Great way to bring expertise into the team, particularly when they are tasked with sharing their skills and knowledge with others. • Great way to address short-term staffing shortages, particularly when there is a clear plan to hire and train FTEs to replace the contractors. • See the concerns described for consultants around training/coaching, short-term thinking, and regulatory challenges.
Outsourcers. Some of the work, perhaps most of it, is performed by people external to our organization, many of whom will be offsite (and very likely paid lower wages).	• Outsourcers are motivated very differently than our organization. They want to maximize their profits and will act accordingly. • Outsourcers are often required to work (by our organization) under a project-based approach, thereby injecting all the associated risks and overhead of projects (see Chapter 6 for a discussion). • Outsourcers are often not as motivated by long-term concerns as they should be, particularly when there is the potential for follow-on work to fix any problems after the current project is completed. • Requires our management team to adopt agile contracting and contract governance practices (issues for the *Procurement* process blade [AmblerLines2017]), two areas which our organization is unlikely to be adept at and unlikely to even realize they need to be adept at.

Time Zone Distribution

Time zone differences, or more accurately differences in the common ranges of work hours for people at different locations, can reduce our ability to communicate effectively (see Figure 7.6). As you can see in the following table, there are several options available, the options becoming less effective as the overlap in working hours shrinks. Some people will choose to shift their working hours to compensate, putting potential stress on them and their families – Our advice is to share the "time zone pain" across locations and have everyone shift their working hours at some point, often rotating through locations. Geographic distribution and time zone distribution are often closely correlated, in particular when the geographic distribution is longitudinal rather than latitudinal. Having said that, latitude differences can cause time zone differences because of differences in how daylight savings times work – for example, depending on the time of year, Toronto Canada is either one, two, or three hours in time zone difference compared with Sao Paulo Brasil, even though Toronto is almost due north of Sao Paulo.

Options (Ordered)	Trade-Offs
Same time zone. Everyone works within the same time zone, although not necessarily the same location.	• The team is able to apply the more effective communication techniques. • Very easy to schedule virtual working sessions and coordination meetings with people in different locations. • Even if the team is not near-located, it may be fairly easy for people to get together face-to-face (F2F) as they may be within driving distance of each other.
Multiple time zones – 5 or more hours of overlap.	• Reasonably easy, although restricted ability to schedule virtual working sessions and coordination meetings. • Greater need for less effective communication strategies, such as email and documentation, during non-overlapping work periods.
Multiple time zones – Less than 5 hours of overlap.	• Offers the potential for our organization to staff the team from a wide range of locations. • The team will benefit from a wider range of views and cultures. • Opportunity to take a "follow the sun" approach to development where teams in different time zones hand-off to one another, potentially achieving a 24-hour development day across locations. • The team is forced to apply mostly ineffective communication strategies, thereby increasing cost and risk of lower quality due to misunderstandings. • Team morale likely to be lower with lower motivation for individuals to contribute to the team.
Multiple time zones – No overlap.	• Very similar to multiple time zones with less than 5 hours of overlap, but more extreme.

Support the Team

How will our organization enable the team to work effectively, to learn and to improve over time?

Options (Not Ordered)	Trade-Offs
Coaching. Accelerates learning about agile and lean ways of working. Coaching also helps teams to understand how to work effectively together [Adkins].	• Good coaching is like "success assurance" so that our early critical agile pilots are successful. • Typically requires a minimum three month investment to reap the benefits. • Good coaches can simultaneously coach multiple teams. • Can be difficult to find good, experienced coaches amongst the multitudes claiming to be agile coaches.
Training. Getting all stakeholders (both IT and business) on the same page is an important first step of	• Typically 2-4 days of Disciplined Agile training are required initially, with additional specialized training (such as Product Ownership or test-driven development) to follow as needed.

121

our agile transformation.	• Most Scrum training is inadequate for enterprise-class situations as it tends to gloss over the Inception and Transition portions of the lifecycle and all but ignores technical topics such as architecture, testing, and development.
Mentoring. One-on-one guidance to help transfer knowledge to all team members.	• Best done for all stakeholders such as executives, managers, and team members. • Both Business and IT should receive mentoring. • The most expensive but valuable team support option. • Requires that the mentor have a deep understanding of Disciplined Agile and years of experience in many contexts.
Stakeholder access. Access to stakeholders is necessary to ensure that the team receives timely information and feedback.	• Stakeholders will need to be educated on the importance of sharing all relevant information and the impact of their decisions.

Availability of Team Members

We will need to determine the availability of each team member to the team. A critical consideration is whether our aim is for our team to be productive, or whether our aim is to ensure that everyone is fully utilized (possibly through assigning them to multiple teams) – people need slack to have time to reflect, learn and improve [Demarco].

Options (Ordered)	Trade-Offs
Dedicated. The team member is dedicated to working only on this team.	• Very important for agile teams so that they can focus on meeting their commitments. • There is no hidden work when everyone is dedicated because stakeholders know what all team members are working on.
Ongoing part-time. The team member is a part of multiple teams.	• Context switching between teams has a tangible cost. • Difficult for the team to make commitments. • Waste is incurred for team members who need to attend multiple coordination and other meetings. • When someone is working on work items from multiple teams then the team does not have good visibility into what they are working on.
As needed/available. The person is brought into the team on an as-needed basis.	• Common with highly-specialized people who are required by multiple teams. • Difficult to plan for because availability of the person can be hard to predict. • Disruptive to the team, resulting in long, drawn out efforts.

8 ALIGN WITH ENTERPRISE DIRECTION

The Align With Enterprise Direction process goal, summarized in Figure 8.1, provides options to help our team ensure that what we're about to do reflects the overall strategy of our organization. There are two reasons why this is important:

	Key Points in this Chapter

1. **Ensure we're doing the right thing**. We want to understand both the technical and business strategies that are relevant to our situation. We also want to follow appropriate conventions and controls to streamline our interactions with others in the organization. In other words, we want to work in an "enterprise aware" manner.

- We can increase quality, consistency, and speed up our delivery by adopting common guidelines and templates, and taking advantage of reuse opportunities.
- WE should understand our enterprise governance strategies and look for opportunities to help leadership to understand and support lean governance strategies.

2. **Ensure we're taking advantage of everything available to us**. We want to identify existing assets that we can leverage, thereby enabling the team to focus on adding new value.

Figure 8.1. The goal diagram for Align With Enterprise Direction.

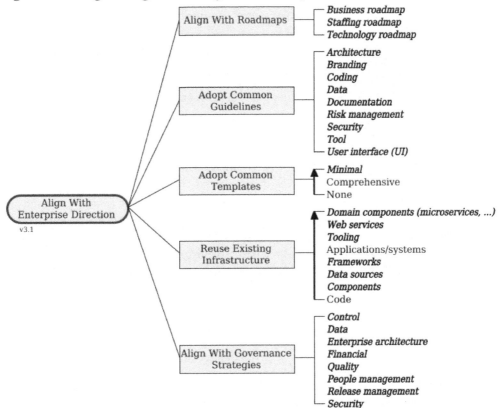

123

As you can see in the Align With Enterprise Vision goal diagram, we need to address several important questions:

- What is our overall organizational direction?
- What are the standards and guidelines we should follow?
- What templates should we adopt?
- How will we go about reusing existing enterprise assets?
- What governance strategies will we need to work under?

Align with Roadmaps

Mature organizations will have strategies in place, often captured by roadmaps or high-level plans, that capture their vision for where they are headed. These potential roadmaps, several of which are described in the following table, will often describe both what your organization hopes to do as well as what it hopes to not do. Effective roadmaps take a rolling-wave approach, with detailed information describing the vision for the near future with less and less detail for portions of the future that are further in the future. These roadmaps are continuously updated by the leadership teams responsible for them.

Options (Not Ordered)	Trade-Offs
Business roadmap. This roadmap captures the organizational vision for what lines of business, or value streams, it intends to be in and which ones it intends to reduce or exit.	• Provides guardrails for business architecture decisions. • Critical input for anyone, such as product owners, making scoping or prioritization decisions. • Contains strategic information that senior leadership does not want to share with the competition and may not want to share with all staff.
Staffing roadmap. This roadmap captures the staffing needs for the organization, often indicating the split between employees and contractors, the desired staffing levels for certain skillsets, and staffing by geography.	• Provides guardrails for staffing decisions. • Critical input for anyone making people management decisions [AmblerLines2017]. • Staffing roadmaps need to be fluid because the staffing needs for a team will vary depending on the needs of the market. • Contains strategic information that senior leadership does not want to share with service providers and may not want to share with all staff.
Technology roadmap. Captures the organizational vision for your technology infrastructure, including the desired technologies to move towards, the technologies to move away from, and potential new technologies that still need to be experimented with [AmblerLines2017].	• Provides guardrails for technical decisions. • Critical input for anyone making or guiding architecture and design decisions. • Some team members may feel overly constrained by an enterprise technology roadmap. This is an indication that our team needs to work closely with the enterprise architects, who are typically responsible for this roadmap, to understand and evolve it where appropriate. • Contains strategic information that your organization does not want to share with technology vendors.

Adopt Common Guidelines

Guidelines are more likely to be followed when they're practical, concise, and developed collaboratively with the people meant to follow them. As you can see in the following table, there are many potential categories of guidelines applicable to delivery teams. Following these guidelines appropriately is an important aspect of our overall governance efforts.

Options (Not Ordered)	Trade-Offs
Architecture. Explains the "to be" architectural vision for the organization, recommended architectural styles, and recommendations for solution adaptiveness. Also indicates the technologies that are considered acceptable to work with, the technologies and systems slated for retirement, and potentially an indication of upcoming technologies that may be available for teams to experiment with.	• Increases the chance that teams follow a common architectural strategy, thereby reducing technical debt and increasing reuse. • The architectural vision needs to evolve as our organizational needs evolve and as technology options evolve.
Branding. Captures important marketing decisions around the usage of color, words/phrases, and our corporate logo.	• Increases the chance that teams will develop solutions with a common look and feel. • Tendency to make these guidelines overly formal.
Coding. Describes programming conventions for a given language.	• Promotes consistent coding style and conventions within and across teams, increasing overall quality. • Less experienced developers will often chafe at having to follow coding conventions.
Data. Describes naming and design conventions for our data sources as well as recommended technologies. May also list recommended sources of data and data sources slated for retirement.	• Increases the consistency across data sources, thereby increasing overall quality. • Many existing data professionals will chafe at the idea of delivery teams being allowed to do data work, even if they are following guidelines. • Many developers lack a sufficient background in data to appreciate the need for data guidelines.
Documentation. Potentially indicates writing style guidelines, dictionary/language options,	• Increases consistency of documents, improving their readability and maintainability. • Following common guidelines is critical for deliverable documentation to increase its consumability by your stakeholders.

internationalization requirements, tool choices, and available templates.	• Many "agilists" are anti-documentation and unwilling to invest the time to understand documentation conventions.
Risk management. Describes the organizational approach to how risks are addressed at various organizational levels. Often includes a checklist of common potential risks to be considered by teams.	• Increases the consistency of how risks are identified, classified, and reported. • Tendency to make these guidelines overly formal or overly detailed, particularly in regulatory environments.
Security. Overviews conventions around data privacy, encryption, security tooling, authentication, confidentiality, and more. Also called InfoSec guidelines.	• Increases the chance that teams will build secure solutions. • Delivery teams will still need help from experienced security engineers, particularly in complex situations. • Security guidelines need to evolve regularly to reflect the changing nature of security threats to our organization.
Tool. Describes strategies for accomplishing common tasks with a given tool.	• Increases the chance that tools are used appropriately. • Consistent tool usage patterns enable pairing and other non-solo collaboration strategies. • Potential to miss, misuse, or underuse some tool features.
User interface (UI). Describes conventions around report layout, screen layout, color application, supported platforms, selected UI frameworks, and other UI-related issues.	• Increases the likelihood that teams will develop UIs with a consistent look and feel, thereby improving end user experience. • Strict adherence to UI guidelines can prevent opportunities for building creative solutions.

Adopt Common Templates

Templates can be an accelerator for teams in that they don't have to figure everything out from scratch. However, templates shouldn't overly constrain teams from doing what makes sense in their given context. In many situations, particularly when regulatory compliance is an issue or when our team is part of a larger program, we will find that adopting some templates is a firm requirement. Furthermore, our organization is likely to have a different set of templates for traditional teams than for agile teams, albeit with some overlap (in particular, documents for operating and supporting our solution).

Options (Ordered)	Trade-Offs
Minimal. Simple templates that address the common 80% of what teams	• A good balance between the freedom of the teams to do what makes sense for them and the need for consistent documentation. • Documents across teams will vary, reflecting the fact that

need to capture.	each team needs to capture some information unique to them.
Comprehensive. Heavy-weight templates that address everything that a team may encounter, or that has been encountered in the past by teams.	• May make sense where standard approaches across multiple teams is desired and artifacts from these teams are reviewed by a common stakeholder. • Many of the sections in the template won't apply to a team's unique situation, resulting in members having to indicate that it's not applicable or worse yet filling in low-value information to cater to reviewers.
None. A template is not available for the type of document we need to create.	• Simple or unique situations will not benefit from templates. • When the type of documentation is needed by multiple teams but a template doesn't exist, the team should invest the time to develop one so that it can be reused by others.

Reuse Existing Infrastructure

There are many assets that can potentially be leveraged by a team. Increased reuse within our organization results in higher-quality assets, higher productivity, lower maintenance costs, and quicker development times. Some organizations will have a Reuse Engineering team that works with delivery teams, or a reuse repository in which reusable assets are stored [Reuse].

Options (Ordered)	Trade-Offs
Domain components (microservices, …). An independently deployable set of functionality, with a well-defined interface, that addresses a cohesive business or technical goal.	• Organizes common, reusable functionality into evolvable, loosely coupled components. • A proven architectural approach from the 1990s (e.g., CORBA), with Microservices being the latest technological incarnation. • Requires significant investment in initial architectural modeling, then continued adherence to following and evolving the architectural strategy. • Without enterprise-level architectural guidance this strategy often results in a morass of disparate technologies, particularly in the case of Microservices.
Web services. A Web service is a loosely coupled, highly cohesive function that is accessed via web-based protocols.	• Extends reusable functionality to a wide range of consumers by wrapping disparate, underlying technologies via cross-platform web protocols • The Web protocols used inject significant overhead, particularly around data transport.
Tooling. Tools, and the support thereof, can be reused across teams.	• Potential to reduce licensing costs. • Enables our organization to focus on maintaining and supporting a reasonable number of tools. • Restricting tools too tightly results in (highly paid) professionals working in less effective ways due to

	not having access to appropriate tooling.
Applications/systems. The functionality within applications/systems can be reused, particularly when a defined application programming interface (API) to do so, and better yet a service level agreement (SLA), is available.	• It's very difficult to "wrap access" to a legacy application because they are rarely architected with this in mind, and as a result the functionality it could potentially provide has too many side effects due to high coupling with other functionality.
Frameworks. Frameworks for user interface (UI) development, security, logging, and many other purposes are commonly available.	• Easy way to reuse important and often specialized functionality. • Frameworks often offer far more functionality than what we need, adding to our solution's overall footprint. • Similar frameworks are often difficult to use together. • Often language or platform specific.
Data sources. Production data sources – including databases, data files, test data, configuration files, and more – can and should be reused wherever possible.	• Reusing existing data can avoid significant development overhead and the creation of additional technical debt (in this case around duplicated data) within our organization. • Production data sources are often used as a source of test data, but we may need to cleanse/obfuscate the data for privacy reasons (see *Develop Test Strategy* in Chapter 12). • Owners of existing data sources can often be difficult to work with (they likely don't have the resources required to help other teams), documentation can be out of date or non-existent, and the data semantics of the data source will vary from what we need.
Components. Small-scale components, in particular UI widgets, can be easily reused by developers.	• Easy to understand and apply due to being small and cohesive. • Components are often platform dependent. For UI components we typically need to adopt a single library or framework to achieve a common look and feel.
Code. Copying, and often modifying, source code is a form of reuse.	• Quick way to get some code written initially. • Very difficult to consistently update common logic when the code has been copied many times.

Align with Governance Strategies

While "governance" is often thought of as a dirty word by agilists, the reality is that our team will be governed. For instance, sharing our status is a type of governance and in the agile world we share status using techniques such as daily coordination meetings (verbally) and task boards (visually). Reporting on progress is also part of governance and one way we do this in an agile fashion is through regular demonstrations of new functionality. Standards and guidelines, which every responsible enterprise has, are also part of governance.

Effective governance is based on motivation and enablement, not on command and control, and we believe that you should be governed effectively [ITGovernance]. As you see in the following table, there are various aspects to governing IT delivery teams to be aware of. The groups that are involved with governance should push as much skill, knowledge, responsibility, and automation into delivery teams as they can. This puts them in a position where they can focus on assisting delivery teams to address any difficult challenges that they run into. For more about agile/lean governance, see the *Govern Delivery Team* process goal (Chapter 27).

Options (Not Ordered)	Trade-Offs
Control. How does our organization monitor and guide IT delivery teams? What milestones are teams expected to fulfill (and how do they do so)?	• Improves the chance that delivery teams are aligned with organizational goals. • We may need to work closely with our "control tribe" to help them rework their approach as many existing control strategies are documentation-based "quality gate" reviews, not the straightforward risk-based approach promoted by DA.
Data. What data quality and availability goals are to be met? How will Data Management support the rest of the organization?	• Helps delivery teams increase the quality of the data being produced and decrease organizational technical debt within existing data sources. • We may need to work closely with our Data Management team to help it adopt more collaborative and evolutionary strategies.
Enterprise architecture. How will the Enterprise Architecture (EA) team collaborate with and guide IT delivery teams? How will it collaborate with and guide the business?	• Increases the chance that delivery teams will build solutions that leverage and integrate well into the existing IT ecosystem. • The Enterprise Architects need to get ahead of the delivery teams, and then support them in a collaborative and evolutionary manner. • Team Members often need to be coached by their Architecture Owner to appreciate and leverage EA guidance.
Financial. How will Finance allocate and monitor funds? What reporting needs, perhaps around CAPEX/OPEX, do they need?	• Increases the chance that the organization will focus on spending their IT investment wisely as opposed to ensuring they come in on (an often artificial) budget. • Increases the chance that delivery teams will streamline their strategy to secure funding and any needed reporting for CAPEX/OPEX tracking.

	• Finance may not realize the impact that misaligned finance strategies, such as fixed price projects, have on team behavior
Quality. How should quality conventions be met by development teams? What monitoring/reporting requirements must be met? What tooling exists to do so?	• Increases the chance that the team leverages existing testing assets and processes. • Potential to hamper agile teams when the existing quality team has not yet adopted modern agile strategies, included automated regression testing and continuous integration (CI).
People Management. What are our organization's strategies around "human resource (HR)" matters such as training, education, compensation, roles and responsibilities, legal constraints, and conflict resolution (to name a few).	• Streamlines how teams evolve and how our organization helps people grow their skills. • Educates teams on legal regulations around how they evolve their team and treat each other, and when to get assistance from our People Management team.
Release Management. What are our organization's strategies and tooling for deploying solutions into production? What are the potential release windows and blackout periods? What continuous integration (CI)/continuous deployment (CD) tooling and support exists?	• Decreases the chance that collisions will occur when releasing into production. • Enables teams to adopt CI/CD and other release/deployment practices effectively. • Potential to reinforce existing, more traditional release practices that tend to be slow and costly.
Security. How will our organization ensure that our staff, systems, and assets are trustworthy? How will our organization ensure the safety of such?	• Increases the chance that delivery teams will work with Security staff when appropriate throughout the lifecycle to ensure their solutions are secure.

9 EXPLORE SCOPE

The Explore Scope process goal, shown in Figure 9.1, provides options to elicit and capture the initial requirements for our solution. Very often an initial vision will have been developed by our Product Management team (if we have one) and prioritized and initially funded by our Portfolio Management team (if we have one). The point is that there may already have been some initial thinking about the scope of our initiative. There are several reasons why we need explore the initial scope in a bit more detail:

> **Key Points in this Chapter**
> - We need to do just enough requirements exploration so that we understand what we're trying to achieve as a team.
> - User stories and epics often need to be supplemented with other models to explore domain, user experience, and business process concerns.
> - You should have a strategy to agree upon and manage quality requirements.
> - Consider what technique and tools you will need to prioritize and manage your work.

1. **We need to answer common stakeholder questions**. Before providing funding for the rest of the effort, our stakeholders are likely to ask us fundamental questions such as: What are we going to deliver? How much will it cost? and When will we deliver it? To answer these questions we will need to work through what we believe the initial scope of our next release will be.

2. **We need to know what to work on initially**. We want to do just enough requirements elicitation to understand what our stakeholders want so that we can confidently begin Construction. We will also have to do some detailed, look-ahead modeling, to explore the high-priority work items that we will work on for the first few weeks of Construction. Basically, we will need to have a sufficient understanding of these requirements so that we can do the work to implement them.

3. **We want to set reasonable expectations as to what we'll deliver**. Both the team and our stakeholders need to come to an agreement around a reasonable scope for the current effort that is being funded so that we're all working towards the same vision.

131

Figure 9.1. The goal diagram for Explore Scope.

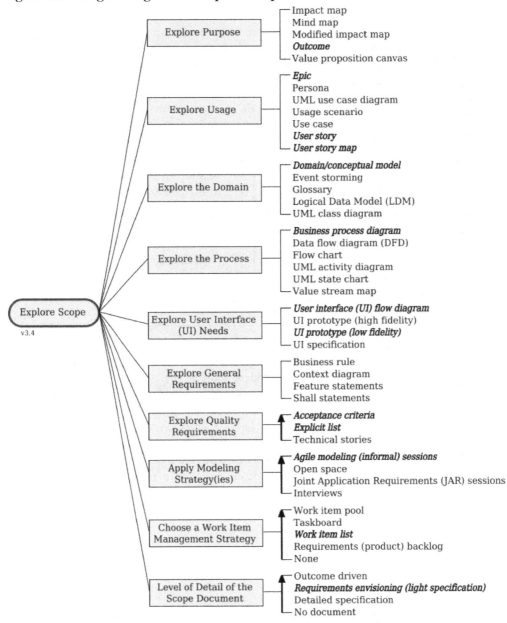

As you can see in the Explore Scope goal diagram, we need to consider several important process outcomes:

- What is the purpose of our solution?
- How will we explore the ways that people will potentially use the solution?
- How will we explore domain concepts, the business process(es) to be supported by the solution, UI requirements, and general requirements?
- How will we capture quality requirements?
- How will we approach modeling activities?

132

- How will changing requirements be managed throughout Construction?
- What level of detail do we need to capture?

Explore Purpose

An important question to answer early on is "Why are we creating this solution?" or "What is the value we will produce?" In other words, what is our purpose? The purpose of a potential solution is often initially explored at a high level during the concept or "ideation" phase before a solution delivery team is initiated (see Chapter 6 for an overview of the phases of the system lifecycle) as part of our Portfolio Management efforts to identify solutions/products that are potentially worth investing in. While we explore the scope of our solution we will also need to explore the purpose, which arguably guides the focus of our requirements elicitation efforts and work prioritization. Several common techniques for exploring purpose are compared in the table below.

Options (Not Ordered)	Trade-Offs
Impact map. An application of a mind map to explore a goal (what), the actors involved (who), the impact (why), and the deliverables (how) [ImpactMap].	<ul><li>Great way to visually work through the analysis of a high-level requirement or strategy.</li><li>Helps teams to explore their assumptions and align their activities with the overall business roadmap.</li><li>See mind map.</li></ul>
Mind map. Brainstorm and organize ideas and concepts [W].	<ul><li>Very visual and easy to understand notation.</li><li>Used to structure similar ideas during a conversation.</li><li>Supports collaborative idea generation, particularly when used with tools such as whiteboards and sticky notes.</li><li>Can lead to categorization of an idea earlier than is optimal, thereby shutting down lines of inquiry.</li><li>Allows capture of off-topic ideas without losing context of current discussions</li></ul>
Modified impact map. An impact map (see above) where the focus is on outcomes rather than deliverables.	<ul><li>By focusing on outcomes, rather than deliverables, a team can explore requirements effectively without diving into solution design too early.</li><li>Complimentary to user experience (UX) design thinking strategies.</li><li>See impact map.</li></ul>
Outcome. An outcome describes a desired, measurable result that is pertinent to our stakeholders.	<ul><li>Outcomes describe what stakeholders would like to achieve and why they would like to achieve that, but not how to do so.</li><li>Provides teams flexibility in how to achieve the desired outcome.</li><li>Useful to capture high-level stakeholder needs.</li></ul>
Value proposition canvas. Used to explore, typically via sticky notes, the fit between a product/solution and the	<ul><li>Enables you to identify the value proposition of your solution/product, the needs of your (potential) customers, and to explore the fit between them.</li><li>Simple tool that is straightforward and easy for</li></ul>

customer(s) it is meant to delight [ValueProposition].	• You still need to validate your value proposition with actual (potential) customers, perhaps via the Exploratory lifecycle, via prototyping, or similar means. • Often used in combination with a business value canvas, which explores the long-term vision for a product, by Product Managers [AmblerLines2017].
(continued: stakeholders to learn.)

Explore Usage

There are many ways to explore how people will work with our solution. Although there is significant focus within the Agile community on user stories and epics, and a growing appreciation for design thinking, these aren't our only choices. Disciplined Agilists prefer to use the best technique for the situation they face, and as you can see in the table below there are several options available to us.

Options (Not Ordered)	Trade-Offs
Epic. Large stories that take a lot of effort, often multiple iterations, to complete. Epics are typically organized into a collection of smaller user stories [W]. Sometimes Epics are referred to as Features or User Activities.	• Useful for high-level program planning. • Appropriate level of detail for low priority work since the details are likely not well understood yet and are likely to change anyway.
Persona. Detailed descriptions of fictional people who fill roles as stakeholders of the solution being developed [W].	• Used as a technique to build empathy for users as real people, and to understand the optimal user experiences for each. • Useful when we don't have access to actual end users, or potential end users. • Can be used as an excuse not to work with actual users.
Unified Modeling Language (UML) use case diagram. Diagrammatic notation for a textural use case [W, ObjectPrimer].	• Puts use cases, and potentially usage scenarios and epics if we're flexible, into context. • Can promote requirements reuse via <<include>> and <<extend>> relationships. • Can motivate unnecessary complexity via <<include>> and <<extend>> relationships.
Usage scenario. Describes the step-by-step interaction between a user/actor and the solution. Similar to acceptance criteria, although tends to cross the equivalent of several stories. Also known as a use-case scenario [W, ObjectPrimer].	• Useful to flush out all the different ways that a solution can be used, often putting granular requirements such as stories or features into context. • Danger of becoming a set of detailed requirements. • Scenarios are typically less structured than acceptance criteria, making the testing of them more difficult.

134

Use case. Textural specification describing all different usage scenarios for the goals of the system [W, ObjectPrimer].	• Puts requirements into the context of actual usage scenarios. • Traditional use cases can require significant effort to write, although it is possible and highly desirable to write simple use cases instead.
User story. One or two sentences to describe something of value to a user [W, ObjectPrimer].	• The most common technique to organize the agile usage requirements. • Very high-level depiction of usage requirements, often requiring detailed modeling at some point in the future before the story is sufficiently understood, or ready, for development. • Due to the granularity of stories it can be difficult to understand their context without another artifact such as an epic or usage scenario.
User story map. User stories are placed on a flat surface (a wall in the case of sticky notes, a table in the case of index cards, or a screen in the case of digitally captured stories). They are then organized to indicate the epic they are part of and the production release they are assigned to [Patton].	• Puts stories into context. • Enables planning and scoping.

Explore the Domain

We may wish to create an information model to capture key concepts and relationships within our business domain, particularly when that domain is complex. These models/artifacts should be kept as simple as possible and only created when they provide valuable insight for the team. You may even consider adopting a Domain Driven Design (DDD) approach where the primary focus is on domain concepts and logic [DDD], rather than the usage-driven approach based on user stories/epics common on agile teams. The following table captures several options for exploring domain concepts.

Options (Not Ordered)	Trade-Offs
Domain/conceptual model. A high-level data model showing the entities and the relationship between them. Attributes of the entities are optionally indicated [W, ObjectPrimer].	• A simple way to explore the entities and their relationships. • Experienced data modelers will often want to capture far more information than is required, leading to wasted effort.
Event storming. A collaborative Agile Modeling session focused on exploring business domain events and the business domain itself. Often used with a Domain Driven Design (DDD)	• Inclusive, collaborative modeling session involving a range of stakeholders. • Originally focused on a handful of modeling techniques, in particular event and domain modeling, it has since expanded into something very similar to an Agile Modeling session.

approach [EventStorming].	• Requires facilitation, planning, and an agile modeling room.
Glossary. A collection of the definitions of key terms, often captured in a Wiki [W, ObjectPrimer].	• Useful to ensure alignment on terminology. • Can lead to excessive documentation – we don't need the level of precision of a professionally written dictionary.
Logical data model (LDM). A diagram showing data entities and their attributes without depicting the actual physical implementation and types for the entities [W, ObjectPrimer].	• Suitable to get agreement on basic data entity relationships without the need for upfront understanding of the actual physical representation. • The need to capture logical data information is often overblown. Concise data guidance and a practical approach to physical data model will often suffice.
UML class diagram. Similar to a domain model with a notation that supports adding more detail around data attributes, relationships, aggregation, and composition [W, ObjectPrimer].	• Suitable in more sophisticated domains or where a certain amount of upfront data design is required. • Usually overkill for most situations and the more robust notation (compared with other models listed above) can motivate BRUF.

Explore the Process

When our existing business processes, or potential solution processes, are complex we should consider investing some time exploring them. Our aim should be to understand how people currently work and more importantly to consider if there are better ways to achieve the same outcomes. We must also strive to ensure that the business process supported by our solution reflects the overall direction of our organization, often captured by our business roadmap (see the *Align with Enterprise Direction* process goal in Chapter 8). The following table overviews several common options for exploring or capturing processes.

Options (Not Ordered)	Trade-Offs
Business process diagram. Used to depict the activities and the logical flow between them within a process. Could be done in freeform format or with a notation such as Business Process Modeling Notation (BPMN) [W].	• Useful to understand current and future state business processes. • Formal notation can be useful for understanding hand-offs, responsibilities, delays and other valuable information about the business processes but can be time consuming. • Some modeling notations, particularly BPMN, can be overly complex and difficult for business stakeholders to work with.
Data flow diagram (DFD). Shows movement of data through a business or solution process, depicting activities/sub-processes, data flows, data stores, and external entities/actors. Popularized in the 1970's for	• May be useful in modeling legacy information flows. • Can often lead to BRUF, particularly when modelers have a Structured Analysis and Systems Design (SASD) background.

structured analysis and design approaches [W, ObjectPrimer].	
Flow chart. A technique popularized in the 1970s to explore detailed process logic, showing activities, decisions, and flow between them [W, ObjectPrimer].	• A traditional way of exploring business logic and business rules. • Easy to teach stakeholders. • Difficult to depict complex scenarios in a comprehensible manner (use UML activity diagrams instead).
UML activity diagram. Explores processes/activities and the control flow between them [W, ObjectPrimer].	• Useful for modeling sequence of process steps. Includes mechanisms to model processes by responsibility with swim lanes as well as to model parallelism of activities. • Notation can become complex, increasing the chance that stakeholders will not understand them.
UML state chart. Describes the lifecycle of the key entity statues of the solution [W, ObjectPrimer].	• Suitable for modeling complex behaviors and states in real-time systems. • Can be difficult for stakeholders to understand due to the level of abstract thinking.
Value stream map. Depicts processes, the time spent performing them, the time taken between them, and the level of quality resulting from processes. Used to explore the effectiveness of existing processes and to propose improved ways of working [W, MartinOsterling].	• Identify potential inefficiencies in a process. • Can be very illuminating when there is disagreement around the effectiveness of a process. • Suitable when the focus of the solution is on improving the process flow.

Explore User Interface (UI) Needs

Understanding the usability of the solution is critical to ensure that what we are producing is consumable (it is functional, usable, and desirable). Our team should be following organizational user interface (UI) and user experience (UX) guidelines where appropriate, see *Align with Enterprise Direction* (Chapter 8), to increase consistency across solutions. It should also embrace an agile "design thinking" strategy where we purposefully work with potential end users to explore how they will work with our solution and better yet be delighted by it [W].

Options (Not Ordered)	Trade-Offs
User interface (UI) flow diagram. Explores how the various screens and reports all fit together. Often created as a sketch on a whiteboard or with sticky notes on a drawing surface. Sometimes called a	• Provides a high-level view of how major UI elements fit together to support one or more scenarios. • Provides insight into potential consumability problems long before the solution is built.

137

wireframe diagram [W, ObjectPrimer].	
UI prototype (high fidelity). Identifies the user-facing design of screens and reports and the flow between them. Often requires a digital prototyping tool or a UI development tool [W, ObjectPrimer].	• Concrete way to explore what people want our solution to do. • Explores the solution's look and feel to ensure we're building something desirable. • Provides a mechanism to stakeholders to take portions of the solution for a "test drive" long before they're coded. • Can motivate significant up-front UI exploration and design, thereby taking on the risks associated with BRUF.
UI prototype (low fidelity). Identify requirements for screens and reports using inclusive tools such as paper and whiteboards. Also called a screen sketch [W, ObjectPrimer].	• Easily explore requirements for the UI in a platform-independent manner. • Quickly explore potential UI design options without the overhead of high-fidelity UI prototyping.
UI specification. Define exactly how a screen or report is to be built by the development team.	• High potential to jump into design long before it's appropriate. • Motivates over-documentation of the UI. • Changing UI requirements (which is very common) can make it very difficult to keep UI specifications up to date.

Explore General Requirements

There are several strategies with which we can organize and support our other requirements techniques. Several common techniques are compared in the table below.

Options (Not Ordered)	Trade-Offs
Business rule. Defines a domain-oriented constraint on our solution, often part of the "done" criteria for functional requirements [W, ObjectPrimer].	• Often acceptance criteria for one or more usage requirements. • Sometimes implemented as automated developer unit tests, particularly for a granular business rule. • Can result in over modeling at the beginning of the endeavor when using a formal business rule modeling approach.
Context diagram. Shows the primary users of the solution, their main interactions with it, and any critical systems that the solution interacts with [W, ObjectPrimer].	• Useful as high-level overview of how the solution fits into the overall organizational ecosystem. • Often a key diagram for a vision statement.
Feature statements. Captures the solution's key capabilities	• Straightforward approach to capturing functional requirements at a level our key stakeholders

138

and benefits at a high level. Can provide a high-level description of scope to our stakeholders in a vision statement [W, ObjectPrimer].	understand. • Feature statements will often stray into design through inadvertently specifying an aspect of the implementation.
Impact map. An application of a mind map to explore a goal (what), the actors involved (who), the impact (why), and the deliverables (how) [ImpactMap].	• Great way to visually work through the analysis of a high-level requirement or strategy. • Helps teams to explore their assumptions and align their activities with the overall business roadmap. • See mind map.
Mind map. Brainstorm and organize ideas and concepts [W].	• Very visual and easy to understand notation. • Used to structure similar ideas during a conversation. • Supports collaborative idea generation, particularly when used with tools such as whiteboards and sticky notes. • Can lead to categorization of an idea earlier than is optimal, thereby shutting down lines of inquiry. • Allows capture of off-topic ideas without losing context of current discussions
Modified impact map. An impact map (see above) where the focus is on outcomes rather than deliverables.	• By focusing on outcomes, rather than deliverables, a team can explore requirements effectively without diving into solution design too early. • Complimentary to user experience (UX) design thinking strategies. • See impact map.
Shall statement. Formal approach to capture functional or quality requirements. Traditionally captured in a detailed Software Req. Specification (SRS) [W, ObjectPrimer].	• Supports contractual documentation requirements in some government and defense environments. • Can motivate over documentation/BRUF. • Often ambiguous as they typically do not put the requirements into a context of usage, leading to difficulties prioritizing them.
Value proposition canvas. Used to explore, typically via sticky notes, the fit between a product/solution and the customer(s) it is meant to delight [ValueProposition].	• Enables you to identify the value proposition of your solution/product, the needs of your (potential) customers, and to explore the fit between them. • Simple tool that is straightforward and easy for stakeholders to learn. • You still need to validate your value proposition with actual (potential) customers, perhaps via the Exploratory lifecycle, via prototyping, or similar means. • Often used in combination with a business value canvas, which explores the long-term vision for a product, by Product Managers [AmblerLines2017].

Explore Quality Requirements

139

"What is quality?" Answering this question can be difficult because quality is in the eye of the beholder, or as Gerry Weinberg was wont to say, "Quality is value to some person." The implication is that we need to work closely with our stakeholders to discover what quality means to them. Quality requirements – also known as non-functional requirements (NFRs), system-wide requirements, quality of service (QoS) requirements, or "ilities" – address issues such as security, availability, reliability, performance, usability, and other key concerns. Figure 9.2 shows potential categories of quality requirements. Quality requirements drive many of the acceptance criteria for our functional requirements as well as architectural decisions (see the *Identify Architecture Strategy* process goal in Chapter 10) and test strategy (see the *Develop Test Strategy* process goal in Chapter 12) decisions. As you can see in the following table, there are several ways to capture quality requirements.

Figure 9.2. Potential categories of quality requirements.

• Accessibility	• Environment (green)	• Regulatory
• Accuracy	• Exclusive access/locking	• Reliability
• Availability	• Historical data tracking	• Reusability
• Auditability	• Internationalization	• Scalability
• Capacity	• Interoperability	• Security
• Concurrency	• Maintainability	• Serviceability
• Consumability	• Operability	• Supportability
• Customer experience	• Performance	• Timeliness
• Data integrity	• Recoverability	• Traceability
• Deployability		• Usability

Options (Ordered)	Trade-Offs
Acceptance criteria. Quality-focused approach that captures detailed aspects of a high-level requirement from the point of view of a stakeholder.	• Motivates teams to think through detailed requirements. • Dovetails nicely into a behavior-driven development (BDD) or acceptance test-driven development (ATDD) approach. • Many quality requirements are cross-cutting aspects of several functional stories, so relying on acceptance criteria alone risks missing details, particularly in new requirements identified later in the lifecycle.
Explicit list. Enables us to capture quality requirements in a "reusable manner" that cross-cuts functional requirements.	• Not attaching quality requirements to specific functional requirements allows the option of using proof of technology "spikes" rather than waiting for an associated story. • Requires a mechanism, such as acceptance criteria, to ensure that the quality requirement is implemented across the appropriate functional requirements.
Technical stories. Simple strategy for capturing quality	• Works well when a quality requirement is straightforward and contained.

140

requirements that is similar to an explicit list.	• Not appropriate for quality requirements that cross-cut many functional requirements because we can't address the quality requirements in a short period of time.

Apply Modeling Strategy(ies)

There are several techniques that we can apply to work with stakeholders to elicit the information required to scope our solution. These modeling strategies often require pre-planning, you at least need to schedule and invite people to them, and often require follow-up to share the results of the session with the participants.

Options (Ordered)	Trade-Offs
Agile Modeling (informal) sessions. An informal, collaborative approach to modeling where stakeholders are often actively involved using simple, inclusive modeling tools such as whiteboards and paper [AgileModeling].	• Works well when the people involved can be brought together in a modeling room. • Works well with small groups of people, but can be scaled to "teams of teams" with the proper coordination. • Requires some facilitation to ensure that a range of issues are addressed. • Modeling sessions, even informal ones, can require some scheduling lead time.
Open space. An open space is a facilitated meeting or multi-day conference where participants focus on a specific task or purpose (such as sharing experiences about applying agile strategies within an organization). Open spaces are participant driven, with the agenda being created at the time by the people attending the event. Also known as open space technology (OST) or an "unconference" [W].	• Works well with a disparate group of people that need to hear each other. • Often produces important insights that leadership may not have been aware of and innovative ideas. • Requires some up-front planning, facilitation, and follow-through to share the results. • Some people will not like what appears to be the "unplanned" nature of open space.
Joint Application Requirement (JAR) sessions. Formal modeling sessions, led by a skilled facilitator, with defined rules for how people will interact with one another.	• Scales to dozens of people. • Works well in regulatory environments due to the creation of defined agendas, requirements documentation, and other artifacts. • Can require significant overhead to schedule. • Can sometimes be overly focused on the JAR process and documentation format rather than the collaboration.
Interviews. Someone interviews stakeholders individually or in small	• Works well when we need to clarify information provided by a stakeholder in previously.

141

groups to identify their needs.	<ul><li>May be the only option for geographically distributed stakeholders.</li><li>Interviews are expensive and time consuming.</li><li>Doesn't provide the opportunity for disparate stakeholders to interact with one another, to hear one another, and to prioritize together.</li><li>Sometime not everyone's opinion is equally respected. The Highest Paid Person's Opinion (HIPPO) may skew the findings. We often need to remind senior stakeholders that they must listen to the other stakeholders.</li></ul>

Choose a Work Item Management Strategy

Early in the lifecycle we need to identify how changing stakeholder needs will be dealt with. As requirements are identified, how are they going to be recorded, prioritized and managed? This decision is highly related to the level of detail that we choose to capture – the more flexible our work item management approach the less detailed our requirements documentation needs to be.

Options (Ordered)	Trade-Offs
Work item pool. A lean approach that enables team to implement several prioritization strategies simultaneously. Examples of prioritization strategies include business value, items to be expedited, fixed date, and intangible items such as paying down technical debt or attending training.	<ul><li>Requires teams to consider a variety of issues, including stakeholder value, risk, team health, and enterprise issues.</li><li>Done properly requires discipline to manage work in progress (WIP).</li></ul>
Taskboard. A lean strategy where the lifecycle, including prioritization, of work items is managed visually by the team.	<ul><li>Prioritization is visible and transparent to the team and to stakeholders.</li><li>Taskboard effectively does double duty – a place where we prioritize our work as well as manage it.</li><li>Supports highly collaborative planning and coordination sessions.</li><li>Simple approach that can be implemented with sticky notes, index cards, or agile management software.</li></ul>
Work item list. Similar to a Scrum product backlog but includes all types of work, not just requirements. In addition to value, work is also prioritized to implement risk-related items early.	<ul><li>Helps to ensure that all work is made visible and prioritized, not just new requirements.</li><li>Can be frustrating to stakeholders to see how much non-new work, such as fixing defects or paying down technical debt, needs to be done by delivery teams.</li></ul>

142

Requirements (product) backlog. A unique, ranked, stack of work that needs to be implemented for the solution. Traditionally comprised of a list of requirements in Scrum, although now some "requirement-like" work such as fixing defects is also included.	• Simple to understand and implement. • Typically doesn't include the concept of risk in the prioritization scheme, thereby reducing the team's chance of success. • Non-requirement, or requirement-like work, still needs to be managed somehow.
None. Changing stakeholder needs will not be supported during Construction.	• Viable for short-term, straightforward efforts where the requirements are known up front and stakeholders are comfortable with them not evolving over time. These situations are very rare in practice. • Very often the requirements do in fact need to evolve, even when you believe that is not the case. • Typically results in a solution that meets the original requirements specification but is not desired/used by the end users because the solution doesn't meet their actual needs.

Level of Detail of the Scope Document

How much detail, if any, will we need to capture in our requirements artifacts? This decision will be driven primarily by issues such as regulatory compliance, geographic distribution of team members, and our organizational culture. We recommend the Agile Modeling advice of "less is more" – aim to have requirements documentation that is just barely good enough for our situation, recognizing that it's more effective to explore the details when we actually need them.

Options (Ordered)	Trade-Offs
Outcome driven. The requirements are captured in the form of high-level outcomes or goals, and there is explicit agreement to explore the details later. Outcomes are typically captured as a simple point-form list that is easily available to anyone involved with the initiative.	• Provides significant flexibility in how the team will approach implementation. • The team, and their stakeholders, must be very comfortable with ambiguity. • Requires a very skilled and organized team.

Requirements envisioning (light specification). A set of simple models, typically captured as sketches and minimal text descriptions (such as those described by Agile Modeling). Examples include user stories, personas, story maps, low-fidelity UI prototypes [AgileModeling].	• A way to quickly and inexpensively explore and come to an agreement around initial requirements. • When the team is not co-located in the same area as where the requirements are captured we will likely need to capture our work somehow (perhaps via digital pictures or via input into a tool). Note that we should consider getting the team together face-to-face during Inception to work through key issues around scope, architecture, and the plan – this is referred to as "big room planning" or simply "agile modeling."
Detailed specification. This includes the traditional approach to requirements, often referred to as big requirements upfront (BRUF), where detailed documents are written to capture the requirements before development begins. In a small number of cases this may be a tradition Model-Driven Development (MDD) strategy where the specifications are captured using sophisticated modeling tools.	• Only effective in situations where the solution is very well understood and the requirements are unlikely to change (which is rare in practice). • Often requires expensive and time consuming requirements management efforts to update, typically resulting in change prevention rather than change management. • May be required in life-critical regulatory situations or when solution delivery is being outsourced.
No document. The stakeholders describe their needs to the team and the team produces something based on that conversation.	• Appropriate in situations where the effort is low risk, there is tolerance for minimal governance, or when the stakeholders are collocated with the delivery team full-time, allowing for easy face-to-face collaboration. • Shortens the Inception effort.

144

10 IDENTIFY ARCHITECTURE STRATEGY

The Identify Architecture Strategy process goal, formerly known as Identify Initial Technical Strategy, is shown in Figure 10.1. This process goal provides options for how we will identify a potential architecture strategy, or sometimes strategies, for producing a solution for our stakeholders. There are several reasons why this is important:

1. **It enables effective evolutionary architecture.** We can avoid major problems later on in Construction by doing a bit of thinking up front to get going in the right direction while allowing the details to evolve later.

2. **We want to identify, and hopefully eliminate key architectural risks early.** A little bit of up-front modeling goes a long way towards identifying critical technical risks early on. We can then mitigate them later through strategies such as proving the architecture with working code early in Construction or via spikes.

3. **Avoid technical debt.** By thinking through critical technical issues before we implement the solution, we have the opportunity to avoid a technical strategy that needs to be reworked at a future date.

> **Key Points in this Chapter**
> - We should invest a minimal yet sufficient amount of time to consider our architectural strategy.
> - We should keep architectural exploration as lightweight and minimal as possible.
> - There are many ways to explore architecture opportunities such as modeling, mobbing, and spikes.
> - There are various types of architectural models relevant to our context in the areas of technology, business, and user interface (UI).
> - Look for opportunities to increase quality and accelerate delivery by leveraging proven architectural assets.

The most effective way to deal with technical debt is to avoid it in the first place.

4. **Improved DevOps integration.** Because DAD teams are enterprise aware they understand the importance of the overall system lifecycle, which includes both development and operations activities. During architecture envisioning, DAD teams will work closely with operations staff to ensure that their solution addresses their needs. This potentially includes mundane issues such as backup and restore of data and version control of delivered assets, as well as more complex issues such as monitoring instrumentation, feature toggles, and support for A/B testing. DAD teams strive to address DevOps issues throughout the entire lifecycle, starting with initial envisioning efforts.

5. **Enables us to answer key stakeholder questions.** Our teams are being governed, like it or not. It's very likely that at some point our stakeholders will want to know how we believe we will build the solution before they will fund the team. Furthermore, our architectural strategy is important input into answering similar questions around how much money we need and how long we think this will take.

6. **Enhance initial scoping and planning efforts.** Our solution architecture will inform our scoping efforts, motivating questions about requirements as well as suggestions for better options. Similarly, architecture also affects our plan in that some architecture strategies take longer to implement than others, architectural activities such as proof-of-concept (PoC) efforts may need to be scheduled, and the cost of new architectural assets may need to be taken into account.

To successfully address this goal, we need to consider several important questions:

- What is our overall strategy for producing a solution? Will we buy, extend, or build new?
- How many architectural strategies should we consider?
- What level of detail do we need to go to?
- What will our approach to exploring the architecture be?
- What models, or views, should we produce (if any)?
- How will we go about understanding the legacy assets that we'll work with?

Figure 10.1. The goal diagram for Identify Architecture Strategy.

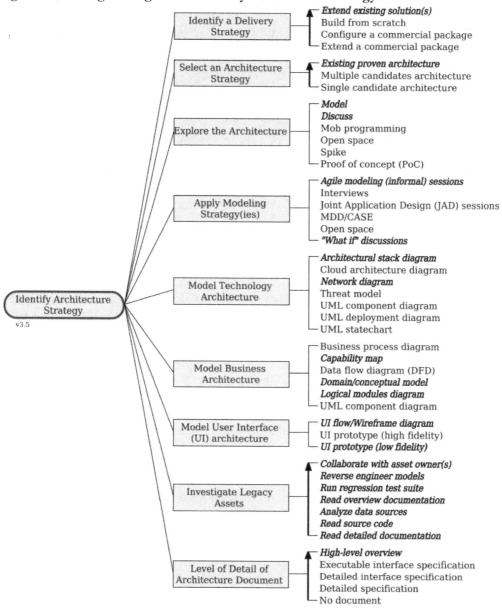

Identify a Delivery Strategy

Not all IT solutions require building everything new from scratch. In fact, the majority of teams extend existing solutions to provide improved value to their stakeholders. As you can see in the table below we have several options to choose from.

Options (Ordered)	Trade-Offs
Extend existing solution(s). If we have an existing solution, or existing legacy assets that can be integrated together, we may choose to extend or customize them.	• Typically requires very little architectural modeling. • We may have a team in place that already understands the existing solution and can efficiently extend it. • The existing technology may be stale and has accrued technical debt.
Build from scratch. Some solutions are "bespoke," built new to address the needs of stakeholders.	• Often requires significant investment in exploration of the architecture (via modeling, mob programming, ...) due to the potential architectural risks involved. • Allows maximum tailoring of the solution for the stakeholders. • Due to the uncertainty of the technology and perceived needs, this may be our most risky option.
Configure a commercial package. Configure a new or existing package such as SAP or Oracle PeopleSoft to meet stakeholder needs.	• Potentially our least risky option since configuration does not require changing the software and potentially injecting defects. • Packages often offer greater sophistication than we require and a greater range of functionality that we require, while missing some functionality and being inflexible in portions of their implementation. • Suitable when we don't have in-house developers who can build or extend a package.
Extend a commercial package. Some customization of a commercial package may require extending or modifying the source code of the package.	• Enables us to take advantage of a sophisticated package while tailoring it to our needs. • Often requires investment in spikes (see below) or a proof-of-concept (PoC) to explore how the package works in our environment. • May be difficult to remain on the package's release path when extensive modifications have been made. • May require redoing some changes when new versions are released. • May be more cost effective than building from scratch, particularly when a small number of changes are required.

Select an Architecture Strategy

Our overall architectural strategy is an important deciding factor in how much effort we need to put into initial architecture modeling. When we are extending an existing solution there is very likely little architecture exploration required – the architecture is already known. However, a new solution, particularly one in a complex space, is likely to require a bit of up-front thinking before we dive into Construction. As you can see in the following table, we have several options available to us.

Options (Ordered)	Trade-Offs
Existing proven architecture. This is the most common approach, with roughly 80% of agile teams being in this situation.	• Modeling will be required when there is the intent to make architecturally significant changes to the current approach. • People unfamiliar with the existing architecture will need to be given help to learn about it (often a discussion led by our Architecture Owner).
Multiple candidate architectures. Several architectural strategies are identified and worked through, ideally leading to the selection of the most likely architectural strategy. This is a form of set-based design.	• Enables us to have several delivery teams work on the problem, often leading to a "bake off" where the best strategy to move forward with is chosen. • Provides us with a "plan B," a "plan C," … that we can shift to when our architectural strategy is disproved early in Construction. • Increases the cost and expense of initial architecture modeling, but potentially reduces long-term risk through considering a wide range of options.
Single candidate architecture. Although the team will discuss a range of options, they focus their efforts on a single approach that they feel is best.	• The most common option, particularly for teams that have a limited budget, when architectural modeling is required. • Focusing on a single strategy is less expensive in the short term, but risks cutting options off early and requiring future rework. • Can be hard to get agreement around a single vision, requiring leadership from the Architecture Owner to guide the team through difficult discussions.

Explore the Architecture

There are several options available to us for how we may decide to explore our architectural strategy. This exploration effort will be led by our architecture owner (AO). The AO on our team should work closely with our organization's enterprise architects (EAs), if our organization has any, to understand the architectural direction of our organization so as to guide how we explore the architecture. In fact, our AO might also be an EA. Several architecture exploration strategies are compared in the following table.

Options (Not Ordered)	Trade-Offs
Model. One or more people discuss and capture an abstraction of what someone	• Enables people to work through problem or solution domain issues, thereby reducing risk. • Face-to-face (F2F) discussion around a shared

would like produced (requirements/needs) or how the team will produce it (architecture/design). A model, or portion thereof, may be captured as a sketch on a paper or a whiteboard, as a drawing in a digital tool, as text on sticky notes, index cards, paper, or even a digital tool.	sketching environment is known to be the most effective way for people to communicate [Communication]. • Often perceived by developers as something we need sophisticated, digital tooling for (whereas most modeling is done on paper and whiteboards in practice). • Potential for traditionalists to take modeling too far, to do too much of it too early, because that is what they are familiar with.
Discuss. Two or more people gather, either physically or virtually, to talk with one another about an issue.	• Enables people to work through problem or solution domain issues, thereby reducing risk. • F2F discussion is a very effective way for people to communicate. • Discussions can go in circles. When this happens consider shifting to modeling to help us focus. • To persist the conversation we will need to record it, take notes, or model somehow.
Mob programming. The team gathers around a single workstation, with one team member coding while the others observe, discuss, and provide advice. The programmer is swapped out regularly and everyone codes at some point. The code is often projected onto a large screen [W].	• Enables teams to work through a complex technical issue. • Enables teams to develop an example of how to implement an important, and often reusable, technical strategy. • Arguably a F2F discussion around a shared sketching environment, where the "sketch" is the source code being projected on the screen. • Often misunderstood by management, and seen as wasteful, as it is perceived as a technique for "many people programming" instead of "many people thinking." This is due in most part to the name of the technique.
Open space. An open space is a facilitated meeting or multi-day conference where participants focus on a specific task or purpose (such as sharing experiences about applying agile strategies within an organization). Open spaces are participant driven, with the agenda being created at the time by the people attending the event. Also known as open space technology (OST) or an	• Works well with a disparate group of people that need to hear each other. • Often produces important insights that leadership may not have been aware of and innovative ideas. • Requires some up-front planning, facilitation, and follow-through to share the results. • Some people will not like what appears to be the "unplanned" nature of open space.

"unconference" [W].	
Spike. Code is written to explore a technology, or combination of technologies, that is new to the team. Spikes typically take a few hours or a day or two. In effect an informal and small PoC [ExtremeProgramming].	• Enables teams to quickly and cheaply learn about how a technology works (or doesn't) in their environment. • Reduces technical risk by (dis)proving parts of our architectural strategy. • The code is often low-quality, on purpose, and thrown away afterwards.
Proof of concept (PoC). A technical prototype that is developed over several days to several weeks to explore a technology. Formal success criteria for the PoC should be developed before it begins.	• Reduces risk by exploring how a major technical feature, often an expensive software package or platform, works in practice within our environment. • PoCs can be large, expensive efforts that are sometimes run as a mini project. • Success criteria is often politically motivated and sometimes even oriented towards a pre-determined answer.

Apply Modeling Strategy(ies)

Similar to the Explore Scope goal, we will want to decide how to explore the potential architectural approach(es) for our solution. There are several options available to us for

150

approaching the modeling or exploration of our architecture strategy.

Options (Not Ordered)	Trade-Offs
Agile modeling (informal) sessions. Modeling/planning performed via face-to-face (F2F) using inclusive tools such as whiteboards and paper [AgileModeling].	<ul><li>Works very well with groups of up to seven or eight people, but can be scaled to much larger with skilled facilitation.</li><li>Potential for very collaborative and active modeling with stakeholders.</li><li>Requires some facilitation to ensure that a range of issues are addressed.</li><li>Can require significant lead time to schedule.</li><li>Experienced architects, including enterprise architects who our team relies on, may not be comfortable with informal modeling.</li></ul>
Interviews. Someone interviews stakeholders individually or in small groups to identify their technical requirements and guidance.	<ul><li>Expensive way to derive our strategies because it often requires a lot of going back and forth between the people involved.</li><li>Risk missing someone in important discussions, or at least requires additional interviews with the appropriate people involved.</li><li>An option when people are geographically distributed or when people are unwilling to collaborate with a wider group.</li></ul>
Joint Application Design (JAD) sessions. Formal modeling sessions, led by a skilled facilitator, with defined rules for how people will interact with one another [W].	<ul><li>Scales to dozens of people.</li><li>Many people may get their opinions known during the session, enabling a wide range of people to be heard.</li><li>Works well in regulatory environments.</li><li>Works well in contentious situations where extra effort is required to keep the conversation civil or to avoid someone dominating the conversation.</li><li>"Architecture by consensus" often results in a mediocre technical vision.</li><li>Formal modeling sessions risk devolving into specification-focused, instead of communication-focused, efforts.</li></ul>
Model Driven Development (MDD)/Computer Aided Software Engineering (CASE). Detailed requirements, architecture, and design are captured using complex, software-based modeling tools [W].	<ul><li>Works very well for complex solutions being developed in a narrow technical domain, in particular systems engineering.</li><li>Requires significant skill and sophisticated tools, on a long-term ongoing basis, to accomplish.</li><li>Many of the modeling tools do not have a comprehensive testing solution available.</li></ul>
"What if"	<ul><li>Enables us to think through potential situations, and thereby</li></ul>

discussions. Identify potential technical and business changes that could impact our architecture.	steer our architecture in a better direction. • Supports a lean "think before we act" approach. • Potentially motivates teams, particularly those new to agile, to overbuild their solution.

Model Technology Architecture

As you can see in the following table, there are many potential model types available to explore and capture the technology aspects of our architecture. Our strategy for the technology aspects of our architecture should reflect our organization's technology roadmap (see *Align with Enterprise Direction* in Chapter 8). We will likely want to do some minimal modeling of the technical architecture for new solutions when:

- Material changes to the architecture of an existing solution are needed.
- Significant integration is required between existing legacy assets.
- A package often requires significant integration with existing legacy assets..

Options (Not Ordered)	Trade-Offs
Architectural stack diagram. Describe a high-level, layered view of the hardware or software (or both) of our solution [ObjectPrimer].	• Explores fundamental issues around architecture. • Best suited for layered architectures. • Well understood by most IT and systems professionals. • Not well suited to describe architectures based on a network of components or services.
Cloud architecture diagram. A style of deployment diagram used to explore how a solution is deployed across on-premises infrastructure and cloud-based infrastructure. Typically a freeform diagram.	• Critical for any team where a portion of the "back end" for their solution is deployed to the cloud. • Easier to understand than UML deployment diagrams. • Should be combined with threat boundaries (see threat model below) so as to address security concerns. • This is an emerging architectural view, so most of the advice around this technique is vendor-focused at present. • Can be overly simplistic, particularly when "the cloud" is treated as a nebulous black box.
Network diagram. Model the layout of major hardware elements and their interconnections (network topology) [W, ObjectPrimer].	• Well understood by most IT and systems professionals. • Can become very large and unwieldy.
Threat model. Consider security threats via a form of deployment/network diagram [W].	• Straightforward way to explore security threats to our solution long before we build/buy it. • Threat boundaries can be indicated on any type of diagram, although a specific diagram is often useful. • Can mask a lack of security expertise within the team by making it appear that we've considered the issues.

152

UML component diagram. Describe software components or subsystems, and their interrelationships (software topology) [W, ObjectPrimer].	• Can be used to explore either technical or business architecture issues. • Can easily become overly complex.
UML deployment diagram. Explore how the major hardware components work together and map major software components to them (solution topology) [W, ObjectPrimer].	• Well understood by most IT and systems professionals • Diagrams can become quite large in complex environments
UML state chart. Explore the dynamic nature of our architecture. Also known as a state machine diagram [W, ObjectPrimer].	• Particularly useful in real-time systems to explore or even simulate potential behaviors of interacting systems. • Usually used at the detailed design level for smaller components.

Model Business Architecture

In Disciplined Agile we remind people that we are delivering solutions, not just software. In many situations the solution being delivered supports new or changed business processes. Our strategy for the business aspects of our architecture should reflect our organization's business roadmap (see *Align with Enterprise Direction* in Chapter 8). Our team's Product Owner (PO) will be a primary stakeholder of the business architecture and should be actively involved in its exploration. The following table provides a range of potential model types to explore and capture our business architecture..

Options (Not Ordered)	Trade-Offs
Business process diagram. Identify business processes, data sources, and the data flow between them. Common notation options include Business Process Modeling Notation (BPMN) and UML activity diagrams [W].	• Effective way to visually explore existing or potential processes supported by the solution. • When sketched collaboratively, process diagrams can be an effective way to communicate with business stakeholders. • Complex BPMN notation can motivate over modeling.
Capability map. Depicts what a business does to reach its strategic objectives (its capabilities) rather than how it does it (its processes). Sometimes called a business capability map [CapabilityMap].	• Captures a stable and long-lasting view of the enterprise that can be used to guide prioritization decisions. • Easily understood by both business and technical people. • Can be used to explore both future capabilities as well as existing capabilities. • At the solution level connects solution capabilities to implementation.

153

	• At the enterprise level connects business strategy to execution.
Data flow diagram (DFD). Explore the data flows between major processes, subsystems, and the people and organizations that interact with the solution [W, ObjectPrimer].	• Effective way to explore the high-level processing that the solution is involved with. • When the notation is kept simple this tends to be a very intuitive technique to use with stakeholders.
Domain/conceptual model. Identify major business entities and their relationships. Typically captured using data models, entity relationship diagrams (ERDs), or Unified Modeling Language (UML) class diagrams [W, ObjectPrimer].	• Promotes a common understanding of domain terminology, which helps us to simplify our other artifacts through consistent terminology. • Provides a high level start at our data schema and business class schema. • Supports a Domain-Driven Design (DDD) approach to development [DDD]. • Can motivate over modeling by people with a traditional data background.
Logical modules diagram. Depicts the critical modules (systems, data sources, micro services, frameworks, …) or our architecture at a functional level. Sometimes called a logical architecture diagram [W, ObjectPrimer].	• Promotes a common, high-level understanding of the architecture. • Useful for thinking through important aspects of the architecture without making implementation decisions about it. • Can often become too abstract to anyone beyond the people who created it.
UML component diagram. Describes software components or subsystems, and their interrelationships (software topology) [W, ObjectPrimer].	• Can be used to explore either technical or business architecture issues. • Can easily become overly complex.

Model User Interface (UI) Architecture

The user interface (UI) is the system to most end users. The UI architecture drives the usability, and hence consumability, of our solution – so it behooves us to invest a bit of time thinking it through up front. The following table provides several common options for exploring and capturing the UI aspects of our architecture. Although these options are also applicable to the Explore Scope process goal described earlier, in this case our focus is on the architectural applications of these techniques.

Options (Not Ordered)	Trade-Offs
UI flow/wireframe diagram. Depicts the flow between major UI elements (such as pages/screens and reports) [W, ObjectPrimer].	• Explore a high-level view of how major UI elements will fit together to support one or more usage scenarios, enabling us to explore potential consumability issues long before the UI is built. • On its own this technique can be too abstract for stakeholders, so it needs to be supported via prototyping.
UI prototype (high fidelity). A mockup of one or more major UI elements using software to explore the detailed screen design [W, ObjectPrimer].	• Concrete way to quickly explore what people want our solution to do and thereby identify a more consumable solution early in the lifecycle. • When used to design a few key pages/screens this is an effective way to explore UI design details with stakeholders. • When used to design all or most of the pages/screens this leads to a lengthy "big design up front (BDUF)" strategy that often produces a detailed design that proves to be brittle in practice. • UI designers often fall into the trap of showing stakeholders a beautiful prototype that can't actually be built, thereby setting unreasonable expectations. • Prototyping tools may not exist for our platform, requiring potentially slower coding. • Some users believe that the system is "almost done" when they see high-fidelity screen prototypes.
UI prototype (low fidelity). A user-centered design technique where we use paper and sketches to mock out the requirements for, or design of, major UI elements. For example, requirements for a report could be identified by manipulating sticky notes on whiteboard [W, ObjectPrimer].	• A quick and easy approach that avoids the problems associated with high-fidelity prototypes. • Can be too abstract for some stakeholders, so we often find we still need to develop high-fidelity prototypes of a few pages/screens to show stakeholders that we understand how they want the UI to be built.

155

Investigate Legacy Assets

The majority of agile delivery teams work with one or more legacy assets, be they web services, legacy data sources, or legacy systems. Many times agile teams are responsible for extending and paying down the technical debt within those assets. Unfortunately in some cases our team is not familiar with the legacy assets and therefore must learn about them. The following table compares common strategies for investigating legacy assets.

Options (Not Ordered)	Trade-Offs
Collaborate with asset owner(s). The team works with the people who know the legacy assets best to understand the implications of working with them	• Very effective way to learn about how the asset is actually built and what challenges we're likely to run into working with it. • Assets owners, or at least people knowledgeable about the asset, often aren't available.
Reverse engineer models. Modeling tools are used to visually explore the architecture and design of the asset based on the existing code and data schema.	• Can be a great way to learn about an asset and the dependencies it is involved with. • These tools often aren't available for all of the technologies used to build the asset or if they are, they are often expensive. • The models generated can often be overly detailed (a reflection of the architectural problem we face working with it).
Run regression test suite. The team works with the regression test suite for the asset to understand the impact of potential changes.	• Automated regression tests are effectively executable specifications that are in sync with the implementation, meaning we can trust them. • Regression tests work well for people who can understand and work with code. • Regression test suites rarely exist, or when they do they're often not sufficient for legacy assets.
Read overview documentation. The team reads the available high-level documentation, or the overview portions of detailed documentation, to understand the asset.	• Overview documentation provides a high-level description, including key diagrams, that can be quickly read by team members. • Likely to be reasonably accurate because of its high-level nature, so can be trusted. • Enables team members to make reasonable guesses as to where to dive into the implementation to make changes. • We still need some way to understand the details.
Analyze data sources. The team uses data visualization and query tools to explore what is actually stored in a data source. Also called data archaeology.	• Effective way to discover what data is actually being stored within a data source. • Can be very time consuming, particularly for a large data source.
Read source code. The team works with the source	• Some legacy source code can be difficult to work with, particularly code that has been worked on by

156

code for the legacy asset to understand how it is built. Also called code archaeology.	• There may be significant reluctance to change the source code due to high coupling within it and a lack of automated regression tests to identify potential problems when we do. • We may not have the actual code used to build the currently running version of the asset.
Read detailed documentation. The team works with the detailed documentation associated with the asset to understand how it's built.	• Can be a good starting point to understand a legacy asset, in particular the high-level overview portions of the documentation. • The detailed portions of it are likely out of sync with the implementation so shouldn't be trusted.

Level of Detail of Architecture Document

Similar to other goals like Explore Scope, we will need to decide what level of detail is appropriate for describing our initial architecture strategy.

Options (Ordered)	Trade-Offs
High-level overview. Capture our architecture strategy with a few key diagrams and concise supporting documentation [AgileModeling].	• Increases the chance that the architecture model will be used and evolved over time. • Enables team to coalesce around a technical vision. • Enables flexibility, particularly when architectural options are left open. • Detailed design decisions can be deferred to when they can be most appropriately made, consistent with the lean "defer commitment" practice. • Requires team members to have greater design and architecture skills. • Team members making deferred decisions must be aware of enterprise architectural direction and guidelines. • Can motivate over-building our solution early in the lifecycle, particularly when the team is new to agile. • May not be sufficient in regulatory situations.
Executable interface specification. Capture the interface definitions of critical architectural components (such as micro services, services, or frameworks) using automated tests [APIFirst].	• Enables teams to safely work on architectural components in parallel. • Executable specifications are more likely to remain in sync with the application and when run as part of our automated testing strategy, they reduce the feedback cycle when changes to the interface do occur. • Requires time to develop and test the executable specifications and mocks/stubs for the architectural components. • Potentially increases the chance that we will overbuild our solution, which increases both cost and delivery time. • In regulatory situations, it requires auditors who understand

	this approach.
Detailed interface specification. Capture the interface definitions of critical architectural components using detailed documentation [APIFirst].	• Enables teams to work on architectural components in parallel. • Enables us to mock or stub out the interfaces to components early. • The interface will still need to evolve throughout the project, although hopefully not much, requiring negotiation between the owning subteam and customers of the evolving component. • Requires time to develop and write the documentation. • Potentially increases the chance that we will overbuild our solution, which increases both cost and delivery time.
Detailed specification. Define, in detail, exactly how we intend to build the solution before we actually do so. This typically includes detailed interface specifications, internal designs, and specifications of cross-cutting concerns. Sometimes referred to as "big design up front (BDUF)."	• Enables teams to work on architectural components in parallel. • Details can deceive people into believing that the architecture will actually work (when it still hasn't been proven), thereby increasing risk. • Important decisions are made early in the lifecycle based on information that is likely to evolve, thereby increasing risk. • Decreases morale of developers by taking away the challenges associated around architectural work. • Increases overhead to evolve the architecture when the requirements change or the chosen technologies evolve. • Supports a documentation-based governance strategy, increasing organizational risk. • Requires significant time (and cost) to perform. • Potentially increases the chance that we will overbuild our solution, which increases cost, delivery time, and overall risk.
No document. Don't capture our up-front architectural thinking at all.	• Works well for very simple solutions produced by very small teams. • Shortens the Inception effort. • Team members don't have a common architectural vision to work towards, resulting in confusion and wasted effort. • Too many decisions are deferred to Construction, increasing the chance of rework.

11 PLAN THE RELEASE

The Plan the Release process goal, shown in Figure 11.1, provides options for creating an initial plan for our team. There are several reasons why this is important:

1. **Our stakeholders will require answers to fundamental management questions**. In particular, the majority of agile teams are asked how long a release will take and how much it will cost.

2. **We can help our stakeholders to evolve their agile mindset**. Initial release planning often proves to be a useful time to help our stakeholders move away from a cost/budget mindset towards a value delivered mindset, and similarly away from a schedule/date mindset towards a delivered outcomes mindset. This mindset shift, which can be difficult at first, supports a partnership relationship between our team and our stakeholders, which will enable us to streamline how we work together.

> **Key Points in this Chapter**
>
> - Our team should create a release plan that we believe we can reasonably be expected to work to.
> - We should strive for continuous, rolling wave plans maintained at a high level.
> - We will need to make decisions regarding our need for phases, releases, iterations, and their cadences.
> - There are many estimating strategies, including #NoEstimates that we consider.
> - There are many options for capturing and managing our plans.

3. **We want to have a viable strategy**. Our primary goal should be to think things through before we do them, not to produce documentation (a plan) describing what we think we're going to do.

4. **We need to set reasonable expectations**. Our stakeholders, including other delivery teams, will make important decisions based on our plan. Similarly, during Inception the team decides how it will work together and the plan will reflect several key decisions such as choice of lifecycle, governance strategy, and risk mitigation efforts.

159

Figure 11.1. The goal diagram for Plan the Release.

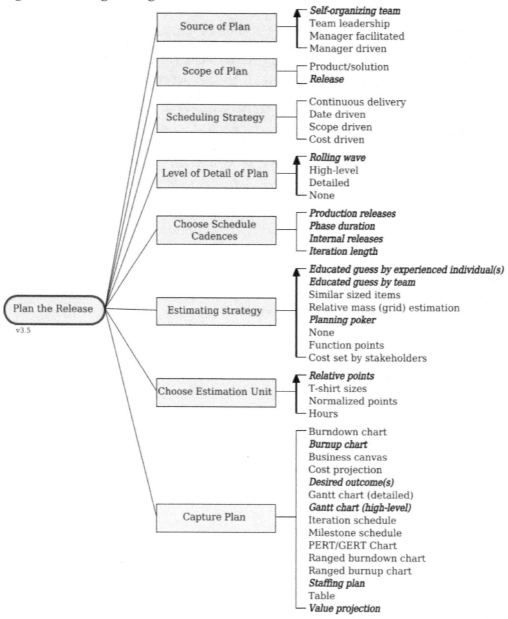

160

Although the details will emerge throughout Construction, we should still think about the general timing of our work and what, if any, dependencies are involved. When we are developing an initial release plan, we need to consider several important questions:

- Who will be involved in planning?
- What is the scope of our planning effort?
- What is our overall strategy driving this plan?
- How detailed should our plan be?
- What cadences will the team adopt?
- What approach to estimating will we take?
- What units will we estimate in?
- What artifacts/views will we capture about our plan?

Source of Plan

We need to decide who will be responsible for formulating our release plan. This decision will have a significant impact on the realism of the plan and the acceptability of it to the team.

Options (Ordered)	Trade-Offs
Self-organizing team. The team, with someone to facilitate, creates the plan.	• Produces a realistic plan that is acceptable to the people who have to execute on it, but it may not be what senior management and stakeholders want to hear. • Still needs someone to facilitate the planning effort, and team members may need some coaching in the various planning techniques (this typically takes a few hours). • When facilitated by the Team Lead (TL), there is a danger that the TL may push the plan in a direction that they prefer. • Teams new to agile run the risk of insufficient initial planning – detailed planning during Construction supports initial release planning, it doesn't replace it.
Team leadership. The Team Lead, Product Owner, and Architecture Owner develop the plan for the team.	• This is a reasonably low-cost option as fewer people are involved (compared with the entire team doing it). • Realistic plan will likely be developed, albeit not as good as one developed by a self-organizing team. • Team members may not "own" the plan because they weren't involved.
Manager facilitated. A manager, often from outside the team, leads the team through planning [PMI].	• Produces a plan that is acceptable to senior management and stakeholders. • The team may be intimidated by the manager, particularly if a reporting relationship exists, and be unwilling to be fully honest in development of the plan. • The plan may be overly optimistic due to aggressive goals. • Beware of manager-driven plans with a façade of being manager facilitated.

161

Manager-driven. A manager produces the plan, often with some input from team members, and presents the plan to the team [PMI].	• Produces a plan that is acceptable to senior management and stakeholders. • The plan is often overly optimistic due to aggressive goals, increasing the risk that the team won't deliver on plan. • The team may not accept the plan given to them, decreasing their motivation to follow it. • The plan doesn't reflect the realities faced by the team. • Significant effort invested throughout the project tracking actual results against the plan. • Plans based on generic positions/people are often inaccurate as the productivity of developers has been shown to range by more than an order of magnitude between individuals within an organization. • Watch out for plans that make unrealistic assumptions about staff availability, dependencies on deliveries by other teams, or implementation technologies.

Scope of Plan

We need to identify the scope of our release plan so that we know where to focus our planning efforts. During Inception, DAD teams typically produce a plan for the current release they are working on and may consider, at a very high level, future releases.

Options (Not Ordered)	Trade-Offs
Product/solution. The plan addresses long-term issues that go beyond a single release. These plans are best done at a high level.	• Sets stakeholder expectations, at least at a high level, as to the long-term strategy of the team. • There is better alignment with the organization's long-term strategy. • The further out in time that we plan, the less realistic the plan becomes due to the impact of change.
Release. The plan focuses on the effort required for the next major release of the solution into production. These plans are best done in rolling-wave fashion. This is often referred to as a "project plan."	• Enables the team to come to an agreement around reasonably short-term strategy, particularly when releases are frequent. • Does not address long-term planning needs for some stakeholders, particularly other teams or organizations with dependencies on our releases.

162

Scheduling Strategy

Our releases will typically be driven by either a fixed date, a minimum amount of scope, or by a fixed cost. It may even be driven by two of these three factors, although our risk increases when we do so. It should not be driven by all three factors, otherwise risk of failure is almost certain.

Options (Not Ordered)	Trade-Offs
Continuous delivery. The solution is to be delivered incrementally by the team, as needed by the stakeholders [W].	• Provides significant flexibility as all three of scope, schedule, and cost are allowed to vary. • Reflects the way that teams following either the Continuous Delivery: Agile or Continuous Delivery: Lean lifecycles (see Chapter 6) work. • Stakeholders must actively monitor what the team is producing, provide feedback, and identify when to deploy. • Provides significant control to stakeholders over scope, schedule, and cost (assuming they're willing to do so). • Can appear as "unpredictable" to people unfamiliar with the approach. In fact this is very predictable given the transparency and control provided to stakeholders.
Date-driven. The solution is to be delivered on a predetermined date (or sooner), therefore either scope or cost (or both) will need to vary.	• Provides some degree of certainty around the delivery date to stakeholders so that they can be prepared to receive and support the solution. See *Accelerate Value Delivery* goal (Chapter 19). • Works well with one of DAD's project-oriented lifecycles: Agile (Scrum-based) lifecycle or the Lean (Kanban-based) lifecycle (see Chapter 4). • Useful for product companies where their customers expect releases on predetermined dates.
Scope-driven. The solution is to be delivered when a minimum amount of acceptable functionality has been produced, therefore either the cost or the schedule (or both) must vary.	• Useful where time to market is paramount and delivering the minimal acceptable functionality is desired. • Works well with one of DAD's project-oriented lifecycles: Agile (Scrum-based) lifecycle or the Lean (Kanban-based) lifecycle (see Chapter 4). • Effective for regulatory projects where the scope is driven by an outside organization (typically the government). Note that a delivery date is often also set on such projects. • Typically results in a difficult-to-predict timeline, at least initially, until the capacity of the team is determined.
Cost-driven. The solution is to be delivered for a specific amount (or less), therefore at least one of schedule or scope must vary.	• Useful when our organization is focused on coming in on budget as opposed to spending our IT investment wisely (the nuance is important). • Typically results in poor quality or a solution that doesn't meet the needs of stakeholders due to management going with the lowest cost service provider (in the case of outsourcing).

163

Level of Detail of the Plan

What level of detail is required for our release plan? This decision will determine the amount of initial effort that we put into documenting our planning efforts as well as how much effort we will need to maintain the documented plan over time. We want to take advantage of planning, which is to think through critical issues in advance, but not take on the risks of overthinking or making commitments too early that is associated with overly detailed planning. In short, aim for just enough planning.

Options (Ordered)	Trade-Offs
Rolling wave. Plans are continuously updated (like waves), with more detail for upcoming work, and less for work further out [W, PMI].	• Very effective in fluid environments where requirements are evolving over time. • Works well with rolling wave budgeting, aligning continuous funding practices with continuous planning. • Enables teams to produce honest timelines and budgets for their stakeholders. • Requires flexibility on the part of stakeholders, removing their (comforting) sense of false predictability in favor of providing them the ability to steer and guide the team to success.
High-level. The release plan does not address the detailed work to be performed, trusting the team to self-organize and do whatever is appropriate.	• Useful to give stakeholders a high-level forecast for what will be delivered over time and to identify dependencies with other teams. • Provides some sense of "predictability" without taking on the costs of detailed planning. • May be uncomfortable for people seeking the false sense of security that comes with detailed plans.
Detailed. The release plan contains significant details around the work to be done and may even assign that work to specific roles or people.	• Only practical for trivial initiatives where the degree of uncertainty related to requirements and technology are low and the schedule is actually predictable. • Provides a false sense of predictability to stakeholders. • Requires significant, and usually unnecessary, effort to maintain later in the lifecycle as the situation evolves. • Drives down morale of team. • Often justified by need to be regulatory compliant, even though the regulations very likely don't require detailed up-front planning.
None. The release plan is not documented at all.	• Appropriate for simple, low risk initiatives in a very highly collaborative environment. • No documentation overhead. • Does not provide transparency to stakeholders who are not actively collaborating with the team.

Choose Schedule Cadences

We will need to pick our cadences for how we are going to work as a team. This will help to drive our release dates, opportunities for feedback, testing cycles, and other critical planning aspects. The following table captures potential cadence levels for us to consider.

Options (Not Ordered)	Trade-Offs
Production releases. How often will we release our solution into production?	• Enables our team to coordinate our deployment strategy with our organization's Release Management team (if any). • DAD teams prefer small, regular releases because they provide more frequent opportunities for feedback, thus increasing the chance they will build the right solution. On average, an agile/lean team releases into production every 45 calendar days, 30% of teams release at least weekly, and 68% at least monthly [SoftDev18]. • Helps to set expectations with stakeholders. • Runs the risk of disappointing stakeholders if we don't release when we promised.
Phase duration. How long do we believe Inception, Construction, and Transition will take (if applicable)?	• Applicable for project-based lifecycles (the continuous delivery lifecycles are effectively phase-less). • It is difficult for a new team to predict how long Inception and particularly Transition efforts will take. The average agile/lean team spends 11 days in Inception activities and 6 in Transition activities [SoftDev18]. • Evolving requirements will often extend Construction, particularly when we are not following a date-driven planning strategy.
Internal releases. How often will we deploy internally into our demo and testing environments?	• If parallel independent testing will occur, then we need to negotiate how often we need to make our working builds available to that team. The average agile/lean team releases internally every 9 calendar days, although 54% release internally one or more times a day [SoftDev18]. • We will need to negotiate with our stakeholders how often they would like the demo environment refreshed. • Teams with a continuous integration (CI) and continuous deployment (CD) pipeline in place will be able to effortlessly deploy frequently (perhaps many times a day).
Iteration length. If we have selected an Agile (Scrum-based) lifecycle, how long will our iterations/sprints be?	• Shorter iterations are better because they provide more frequent opportunities for feedback and learning. • An iteration carries an amount of overhead with it, sometimes called process taxes, so shorter iterations can increase overhead percentage. • Of the teams doing iterations, 82% have two-week iterations and 5% one-week iterations [SoftDev18].

Estimating Strategy

If we are required to estimate our release then we have many options for doing so. It is worth noting that there is much debate in the agile community regarding the value of estimating, popularized by the hashtag #NoEstimates on Twitter (see Chapter 2), so understanding the tradeoffs associated with the various strategies is critical. Recently the terms "forecasting" of releases and "sizing" of work items have been replacing the term estimating, given the baggage associated with the term. For people with a good sense of humor, and honesty for that matter, the term "guesstimate" is also popular. The following table compares and contrasts several estimating strategies available to you.

Options (Ordered)	Trade-Offs
Educated guess by an experienced individual(s). The team designates someone(s) to provide a guess based on their experience.	• A quick approach and often realistic estimate. • Requires a high degree of trust by the team that the estimator will provide an estimate reflective of the average team member.
Educated guess by team. The team provides an estimate based on consensus and their collective experience.	• Quick way to get to an estimate that is acceptable to the team. • Tends to be overly optimistic, particularly when there is little experience within the team with what they are estimating. • The estimate can be easily swayed by the more senior or the most loud person in the room. • Should be updated incrementally throughout the lifecycle as the team gains more information.
Similar sized items. All work items are created so that they are close to the same amount of effort.	• This is a form of #NoEstimates because we merely have to count the number of similarly sized work items (everything is effectively of size 1). • Sometimes a work item is broken down too much in an effort to have similarly sized items, resulting in the need to track the various parts that make up the whole.
Relative mass (grid) valuation. Relative point estimates are developed by putting work items on a grid using the Fibonacci sequence for sizes [Estimation].	• Effective for there is a need for very rapid estimating. • Resulting estimate is almost as good as that produced by planning poker. • Much faster due to the parallel nature of the estimation effort – everyone on the team puts work items onto grid cells at once, discussing anything they disagree on while doing so.
Planning Poker. Based upon a technique called Wideband Delphi, work items are sized	• Well known technique that is widely adopted by Scrum practitioners. • Very good way to size the work because many people discuss what needs to be done, the people who will do the work estimate it, and the work items tend to be reasonably

166

based upon "relative points." Point estimate is identified by a team estimate, not individual [Cohn].	small. Furthermore, the shared discussion improves the team's understanding of what needs to be done. • Very slow due to the serial nature of the technique – the team discusses each work item one at a time.
None. No estimate is produced. A #NoEstimates strategy [NoEstimates].	• Appropriate where stakeholders are not asking the team to project their schedule or cost. • Lean-based teams may choose to derive forecasts from measured lead and cycle times rather than manually estimate individual work items.
Function points. Traditional estimating technique based upon number of outputs, inquiries, inputs, internal files, and external interfaces [W].	• Relies on a history of estimating similar efforts and technologies. • Appropriate where a third party is requested to provide an estimate with limited understanding of the domain. • The formula relies on "fudge factors," so functional point counts aren't as comparable as many will claim.
Cost set by stakeholders. The stakeholders, typically a senior leader, sets the cost (more accurately an upper limit on the cost) for the release.	• Appropriate with a cost-driven scheduling strategy, but scope or schedule (or both) must be allowed to vary. • Tends to motivate high-risk plans due to unrealistic cost request by decision makers.

167

Choose Estimation Unit

An important decision to make when estimating or sizing work items is the unit in which you are doing so. Regardless of whether you're estimating the complexity of the work, the value of it to your stakeholders, or the amount of work to be performed the team will need to use a consistent measurement unit to do so. The following table presents several estimation options available to us. It's important to note that the trade-offs listed below are for release planning, not iteration or detailed planning during Construction.

Options (Ordered)	Trade-Offs
Relative points. The team develops its own point system. It does this by choosing a work item, assigning it a number of points, and then sizing everything else based on how it compares with the first work item.	• Increases the chance that the team will believe in their estimate because they define the estimation unit. • Enables the team to quickly and inexpensively estimate at a high-level. • Points-based estimates can be easily used to provide cost or time projections via strategies such as (ranged) burn up/down charts. • People new to points-based estimates can become confused with how points are then "converted" into hours during detailed planning (see the Produce a Potentially Consumable Solution process goal in Chapter 17 for how to do so).
T-shirt sizes. The team uses sizes such as Small, Medium, Large, and Extra Large [Cohn].	• Enables the team to quickly and inexpensively estimate at a high-level. • Easy to get going with this technique. • Can be difficult to project cost or schedule because sizes can't be easily added to one another (Small + Extra Large = ??). This can be overcome by converting sizes to points or hours. • People new to this strategy can become confused with how points are then "converted" into hours during detailed planning.
Normalized points. The team uses a common pointing system that is in use by other teams. Very often implemented as relative points across a program or even entire IT department. Can also be implemented as an hours-based strategy (i.e. 1 point = 8 hours) [SAFe].	• Useful across a program so that estimates performed by subteams/squads may be rolled up into an overall program estimate. • Injects the overhead of defining, and then maintaining, a common estimation unit across teams. Difficult to keep teams consistent without a regular planning session, such as program increment (PI) planning, across the teams. • This isn't exact – The units will still vary a bit across teams based on their different understanding of what a point represents. • Very questionable strategy when teams are not part of a larger program.
Hours. The team estimates in terms of	• Enables easy rollup of estimates across teams because they're using a consistent unit (hours).

hours of work effort to implement or perform the work item.	<ul><li>Tends to be a very expensive form of estimation due to the tendency to dive down into detailed implementation issues.</li><li>Tends to promote detailed up-front planning, which in turn proves to be wasteful due to evolving requirements later in the lifecycle.</li><li>You need to know who is doing the work, because the productivity of an experienced developer can be an order of magnitude greater than that of a novice.</li></ul>

Capture Plan

Throughout our planning efforts we will consider several critical views: outcomes, staffing (people), financial (cost and value), and schedule (time). As we discussed earlier, we prefer an outcome/value-based mindset over a cost/schedule-based mindset amongst our stakeholders – stakeholder mindset will influence what our planning efforts focus on as well as what aspects of our plan we choose to capture. The following table explains several potential artifacts that we may choose to create in order to capture our plan for our endeavor (which may be a project, the next release of our solution, or our team's work for a given period of time). As always, the true value is in planning (the collaborative thinking), not in the plan itself. For any artifacts that we do create, we should follow agile documentation strategies and keep them as minimal and focused as possible.

Options (Not Ordered)	Trade-Offs
Burndown chart. Projects/indicates the expected number of Construction iterations left given the current size of the required work for this release and the team's current velocity [W].	<ul><li>Provides a reasonable estimate as to the time required to implement the functionality.</li><li>A straightforward visualization that is easily understood.</li><li>Common report that is automatically generated by agile management tools.</li><li>Provides a point-specific estimate instead of a ranged estimate. This is relatively poor practice because estimates are actually probability distributions.</li><li>The projected schedule tends to shift over time, usually negatively, due to changing stakeholder needs. As a result the initial estimates tend to be overly optimistic.</li><li>Requires significant work on the part of the team to size the work that is being depicted in the chart.</li></ul>
Burnup chart. Projects/indicates the expected number of Construction iterations left given the minimum required work for this release and its intersection with the team's projected delivery of functionality [BurnUp].	<ul><li>Same as for burndown chart.</li><li>The choice of burndown or burnup is a matter of preference. Some people believe that burnup charts provide a more positive depiction than burndowns.</li></ul>

Business canvas. Captures critical information about the endeavor, potentially including the expected outcomes, a summary of the scope, the sponsor(s), and why the endeavor is important.	• Straightforward, text-based planning/strategy artifact. • Provides an excellent summary of the endeavor, and can be an important information radiator moving forward. • Often used to develop and then maintain the vision for the endeavor. • Typically requires a facilitated planning session to develop (see the *Coordinate Activities* process goal in Chapter 23).
Cost projection. The estimated cost of the endeavor.	• A simple, text-based artifact usually developed using a spreadsheet. • Important part of a business canvas. • The quality of the cost project is directly related to our understanding of the scope, the people on the team, and our architectural strategy.
Desired outcome(s). Our stakeholder's expectations of what they hope our team will produce.	• Straightforward, text-based list that is easy for stakeholders to understand. • Provides greater flexibility for the team by allowing them to make critical promises about what stakeholder value will be delivered without committing to how it will be delivered. • Important part of a business canvas. • Key information radiator for the team and stakeholders.
Gantt chart (detailed). A diagram depicting the scheduled activities, dependencies between them, and potentially even the people assigned to the activities at a minute level [W, PMI].	• Appropriate for high-risk endeavors with a low rate of change. • Visual representation that is well understood by management. • Motivates too much planning up front, which leads to making commitments too early and thereby restricting the flexibility of the team.
Gantt chart (high-level). A diagram depicting the major activities and the dependencies between them for our endeavor. See Figure 11.2 for an example [W, PMI].	• Visually depicts key information, particularly dependencies and milestone dates • Helps the team to think through critical issues that will need to be worked through in the future. • Helps to set stakeholder expectations. • Common diagram that is well understood by management. • Good information radiator. • Critical events, in particular the projected end of Construction and potential delivery date, should be presented as a range if stakeholders are able to understand that strategy. See Figure 11.3 for an example.
Iteration schedule. An overview of how a typical iteration will work, including when	• Text-based representation of a schedule that is easy to create. • For agile teams only (lean teams don't have iterations).

the planning, demo, retrospective, wrap up, and coordination meetings will be held.	• Often maps expected work items/stories to the iteration, but this tends to be difficult to maintain over time as the stakeholder needs evolve. • Dependencies can be difficult to depict.
Milestone schedule. Projected milestone review dates.	• A focused, text-based list of milestones and expected dates for them. • Sets stakeholder expectations as to when the team intends to address key milestones. • Potential aspect of a business canvas. • As stakeholder needs evolve, dates will shift moving milestones further out in time. Expected dates should be given as a range.
PERT/GERT chart. Alternatives to Gantt charts that provide different views on the schedule [W].	• A Program Evaluation Review Technique (PERT) chart depicts the tasks and activities within a schedule that is often used to identify the critical path within a plan. Can be automatically generated from a Gantt chart in a traditional project management tool such as Microsoft Project. • A Graphical Evaluation and Review Technique (GERT) chart is a probabilistic treatment of a complex plan that contains many dependencies and even loops. • These two diagrams have fallen out of favor within the IT project management community.
Ranged burndown chart. A burndown chart showing a ranged projection for when Construction will end. The range is calculated via the gross velocity (the number of points delivered) and the net velocity (the change in the number of points of functionality remaining) [Ranged].	• Provides a ranged estimate as to the time required to implement the functionality. • The projected ranges tend to vary, often dramatically, early in the lifecycle. After a few iterations they tend to focus in on a range that tightens over time. • The chart is a straightforward visualization. • Many people do not like the idea of a ranged estimate, preferring the often false predictability of a point-specific estimate instead.
Ranged burnup chart. A burnup chart with a ranged projection for when Construction will end based on the projected delivery of the minimum scope to be delivered and the changed minimum scope.	• Same as for ranged burndown chart.
Staffing plan. A matrix/table that maps	• Enables the team to identify the requisite skills, and any gaps in skills, for the endeavor.

(potential) team members and their skills. May also indicate availability dates, for the team members.	• Critical input into estimating the cost of the endeavor. • Increases the chance of building a whole team. • Only works when you have a good idea as to the scope of the endeavor, the architectural strategy, and the process the team will be following. The DAD process goals can provide insight into the required skills.
Table. A listing of the critical activities, dependencies, dates, and potential people associated with the activities.	• Text-based representation of the schedule. Basically the text-based equivalent of a Gantt chart (and often produced automatically by traditional project planning tools). • Works well for a high-level schedule or as a reference for a detailed schedule.
Value projection. The estimated value of the endeavor. Can be graphical or text-based.	• Critical input into determining the potential financial benefit of the endeavor (benefit = value – cost). • Potential aspect of a business canvas.

Figure 11.2. An example of a high-level Gantt chart.

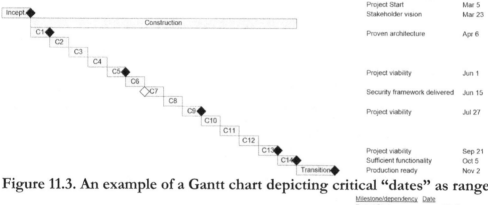

Figure 11.3. An example of a Gantt chart depicting critical "dates" as ranges.

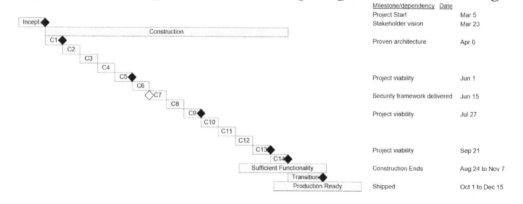

172

12 DEVELOP TEST STRATEGY

The Develop Test Strategy process goal, shown in Figure 12.1, provides options for how our team should plan how we will approach verification and validation. There are several reasons why this is important. We want to ensure:

1. **We have sufficient skills within the team**. Our testing strategy will drive whether we need people with the skills to write automated tests, the skills to perform specialized types of testing such as performance testing, security testing and exploratory testing, test-first development skills, and so on.

2. **We have sufficient technical resources**. We need to determine whether we have sufficient access to resources such as testing tools, test data, and testing environments. Figure 12.2 depicts the test automation pyramid [GregoryCrispin], which indicates the various levels of testing and tooling support our team will need to consider. Exploratory testing is depicted as a cloud because it can occur at any time or level.

3. **We build quality in**. We want to build quality into the way that we work, rather than inspect it in after the fact. Important strategies to do this including preferring test-first or test-driven strategies over

> ## Key Points in this Chapter
> - Before beginning construction it is important to consider the many aspects of testing our solution. We may wish to outline a plan and strategy in a lightweight fashion.
> - We want to understand what types of testing will be done by whom and what skills are required.
> - Everyone helps test but we may additionally see a need for independent testing of our work.
> - We need to consider what types of tooling and environments will be required and how they will be provisioned.
> - A strategy needs to be in place to test quality requirements.
> - We must identify a strategy for manual and automated testing.
> - We need to determine what our strategy is for capturing and managing defects, along with the associated tooling.

testing after the fact, coaching people in design and usability skills, testing throughout the entire lifecycle rather than testing at the end, and adopting a mindset that quality is everyone's responsibility. Of course, this begs the question "What is quality?" The challenge is that quality is in the eye of the beholder, or as Gerry Weinberg was wont to say, "Quality is value to some person." The implication is that we need to work closely with our stakeholders to discover what quality means to them (see *Explore Scope* in Chapter 9 for some thoughts on this).

4. **We fulfill our organizational needs**. Our team may have regulatory compliance, governance procedures, and organizational standards around security and data that need to be addressed.

5. **We test to the risk**. Our testing strategy should be driven by the risk that we face – the more complex the domain problem we face or the more complex the technology that we're working with, the more robust our testing strategy will need to be.

6. **We reduce the feedback cycle between defect injection and defect identification**. In the 1970s, Dr. Barry Boehm, a computer science researcher, discovered that the average cost of fixing defects rises exponentially the longer it takes us to find the defect. Dr. Boehm continued researching this into the early 2010s and found, not surprisingly, that it holds true for agile as well as traditional teams. The implication is that we want to

adopt testing and quality techniques that have a short feedback cycle, and as we can see in Figure 12.3, which map various techniques to the cost of change curve.

Figure 12.1. The goal diagram for Develop Test Strategy.

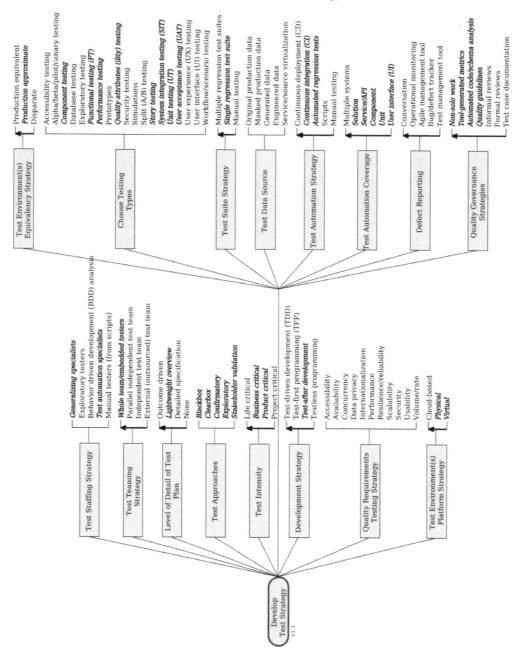

Figure 12.2. The test automation pyramid.

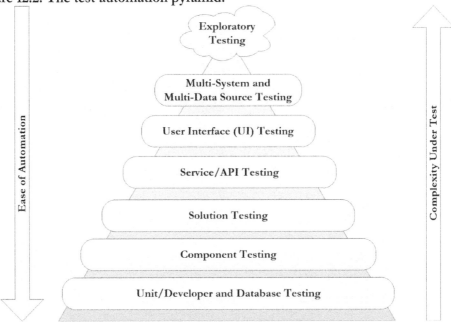

Figure 12.3. Comparing the average cost to fix potential defects based on when and how they are found.

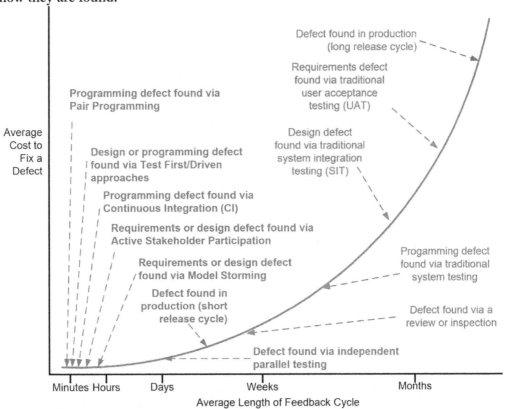

175

To be effective, we need to consider several important questions:
- How will we staff our team?
- How will we organize our team?
- How will we capture our plan?
- How will we approach testing?
- How intense will our testing be?
- How will we approach development/programming?
- How will we choose a platform for test environment(s)?
- How will we choose a platform equivalency strategy?
- How will we test non-functional requirements?
- What types of testing do we expect to perform?
- How will we automate testing?
- What type of automated tests will we have?
- How will we obtain test data?
- How will we automate builds?
- How will we report defects?
- How will we govern our quality efforts?

Test Staffing Strategy

We need to determine the type of people we intend to have performing testing activities so that we can bring the right people onto the team when needed.

Options (Not Ordered)	Trade-Offs
Generalizing specialists. A team member with one or more deep specialties, in this case in testing, a general understanding of the overall delivery process, and the desire to gain new skills and knowledge [GenSpec].	• Provides greater flexibility for staffing, greater potential for effective collaboration, greater potential for overall productivity, and greater career opportunities. • It takes time for existing specialists to grow their skills and some people prefer to be specialized. • This option requires people with the development skills to be able to write automated tests, not just manual testing.
Exploratory testers. Someone who is skilled at probing solutions to identify how they work and any unexpected or broken behavior. Often includes ad hoc manual regression for dependent functionality [W].	• Finds potential defects that the stakeholders may not have thought of, often problems that would have only been found in production, where they are typically more expensive to fix. • Requires significant time and effort to gain this skill. • Exploratory testing is a manual effort, making it slow and expensive at first, but it in turn identifies checks that can then be automated and run inexpensively from then on.
Behavior driven development (BDD) analysts. Someone who is	• When written before the functionality, the acceptance tests both specify and validate the functionality. • Requires significant skill and discipline on the part of

176

skilled at analyzing stakeholder needs and capturing them as executable specifications (tests) [ExecutableSpecs].	the analyst.
Test automation specialists. Someone with the ability to write automated tests/checks.	<ul><li>Supports the creation of automated regression tests, which in turn enables teams to safely evolve their solutions.</li><li>Requires investment in the automated tests themselves, which may appear expensive in the short term when it comes to legacy assets.</li></ul>
Manual testers (from scripts). Someone with the skill to develop test cases from requirements, write manual test scripts, and follow test scripts to identify and record the behavior exhibited by the solution under test.	<ul><li>The solution is validated to some extent and supports a structured approach to user acceptance testing (UAT).</li><li>Very slow and expensive strategy for solution validation.</li><li>Provides very poor support for agile software development.</li></ul>

Test Teaming Strategy

We need to decide how testing and quality assurance (QA) professionals will work with or as part of the delivery team so that everyone involved knows how the team(s) are organized. Although a whole team approach is preferred for Disciplined Agile teams, you can see in the following table that there are other options available to us.

Options (Ordered)	Trade-Offs
Whole team/embedded testers. People with testing skills are embedded directly into the delivery team to test the solution as it's being developed.	<ul><li>Improved collaboration within the team, leading to greater productivity and quality.</li><li>Promotes the mindset that quality is the team's responsibility, not just the testers'/QA's responsibility.</li><li>Enable people to learn from one another, enabling them to become more effective generalizing specialists.</li><li>Can be difficult when we are first working in an agile manner because we're likely to have a lot of people with specialized skills, requiring a larger team than we would normally build.</li></ul>
Parallel independent test team. An independent test team works in parallel with the delivery team to handle the more difficult or expensive testing activities. Completed work is normally passed	<ul><li>Can fulfill regulatory requirements around independent verification without requiring significant end of lifecycle testing.</li><li>Decreases the cost of some forms of test & fix, in particular around integration, by reducing the feedback cycle.</li><li>Enables highly skilled testers, such as security testers or exploratory testers, to focus on their specialty.</li></ul>

to the independent test team on iteration boundaries but more advanced testing teams can accept new, completed items at any time [PIT].	• Useful where the team does not have access to a production-like environment, where it is difficult for the team to test sophisticated transactions across systems such as legacy integrations (for example, end of month batch processing) or where a traditional, cycle-based regression of test cases is required. • Increases complexity of the testing process (compared with whole team testing). • Requires a strategy to manage potential defects discovered by the independent testers. • Can lengthen Transition phase because we will need to perform one last round of independent testing before we can deploy. • Complicates what it means to be "done." • When there are many teams delivering work to the independent test team, there will likely be a need for support by someone doing integration.
Independent test team. Some testing activities, often user acceptance testing (UAT) and system integration testing (SIT), are left to the end of the lifecycle to be performed by a separate team [PIT].	• Easy strategy for existing, traditional testers to adopt. • Focuses UAT and SIT efforts to end of delivery lifecycle, resulting in significantly more expensive defect fixing. • Lengthens the Transition phase substantially. • Increases overall risk due to key testing activities being pushed to end of lifecycle. • Increases average cost of fixing defects due to long feedback cycle.
External (outsourced) test team. An independent test team staffed by a different organization, often in a different time zone, typically an IT service provider.	• The manual testing effort may be less expensive due to wage differences. • May be only way to gain access to people with testing skills. • Requires significant (and expensive) requirements documentation to be provided to the testing team, and ongoing communication and management effort, negating any cost savings from inexpensive testing staff. • Lengthens the Transition phase substantially. • Increases overall risk due to key testing activities being pushed to end of lifecycle. • Increases average cost of fixing defects due to long feedback cycle.

Level of Detail of Test Plan

We need to identify the level of detail we require to capture our test strategy. The following table compares several common approaches for doing so.

Options (Ordered)	Trade-Offs
Outcome driven. A high-level collection of testing and quality assurance (QA) principles or guidelines meant to drive the team's decision making around testing and QA.	• Provides sufficient guidance to skilled team members. • Insufficient guidance for low-skilled team members (they will require coaching or help via non-solo strategies). • By itself it is insufficient for some regulations, particularly life-critical ones, but can be part of the overall strategy.
Lightweight overview. A concise description of our test strategy, potentially in point form.	• Provides sufficient guidance for most team members. • Often sufficient for regulatory environments. • May not be read by senior team members who believe they already know what to do.
Detailed specification. A descriptive and thorough test strategy document.	• Provides sufficient guidance for outsourced/external testing and for low-skilled team members. • Very expensive to create and maintain. • A high risk of getting out of sync with other team artifacts. • Very likely to be ignored by skilled team members who believe they know what to do.
None. The test strategy is not captured.	• Appropriate for simple situations or in situations where we have a standard testing infrastructure and a team experienced at using it. • Won't be sufficient for most regulatory compliance situations. • In outsourcing situations, leaves us at the mercy of the service provider.

179

Test Approaches

We need to identify the general testing approaches/categories that we intend to follow so that we know what skills people need and potentially to identify the type of test tools required.

Options (Not Ordered)	Trade-Offs
Black box. The solution is tested via its external interface, such as the user interface (UI) or application programming interface (API) [W]. Note: Acceptance criteria are typically implemented at the black box level.	• Enables us to test a large percentage of scenarios. • Can be a very good starting point for our testing efforts. • Very common approach for database testing. • Difficult to test internal components, or portions thereof. • Often has a slow feedback cycle.
Clear box. The internals of the solution are tested [W]. Also known as white-box testing. Note: Developer unit tests are typically at the clear box level.	• Potential to test all scenarios as we can get into the innards of the solution. Note that by pairing testers together we're more likely to avoid unnecessary scenarios. • Requires intimate knowledge of the design and implementation technologies.
Confirmatory. The validation that the solution works as requested. Sometimes called "testing to the specification" or positive testing [W].	• Confirms that we've produced what we said we would. • Falsely assumes that our stakeholders are able to identify all of the requirements. • Test-driven development (TDD), and behavior-driven development (BDD) are a confirmatory approach to testing. • Can unfortunately motivate an expensive BRUF approach, but does not require written specifications in practice.
Exploratory. An experimental approach to testing that is simultaneously learning, test design, and test execution [W].	• Enables us to test for the things that the stakeholders didn't think of. • Often identifies problems that would have escaped into production (and are hence expensive to fix). • Requires significant skill, so it can be hard to find exploratory testers and require a long time to grow.
Stakeholder validation. Our stakeholders, in particular our end users, validate how well the solution meets their needs.	• Enables us to determine how effective our solution will be in practice, providing valuable feedback that we can use to improve the solution. • Potential testing strategies include field testing, alpha/beta testing, pilot testing, and user acceptance testing (UAT). • Requires stakeholders to be actively involved with testing, often throughout the lifecycle.

Test Intensity

An important decision that needs to be made early on, albeit one that may evolve as we understand our stakeholder needs better, is how much do we care about testing? The fundamental issue is that the greater the complexity or risk that we face, the more testing intensity or sophistication required. Interestingly, the greater the intensity of your testing effort the more effective it tends to be. The following table captures the potential intensity levels that we may face.

Options (Ordered)	Trade-Offs
Life critical. Our solution is very high risk, with the potential to adversely affect the health or physical well-being of people. This includes, but is not limited to, medical devices, health-oriented data processing, transportation systems, and food processing systems.	• Testing must be very thorough. • Regulations exist that will guide the minimal required levels of verification and validation (V&V). • Validation efforts will be thorough and potentially time consuming. • There is likely to be comprehensive specifications, ideally executable ones, which will need to be validated. • Sophisticated configuration management (CM) control, with support for granular control of configuration items (CIs), will be required.
Business critical. Our solution is high risk, with the potential to adversely affect the financial health or public image of our organization.	• Testing must be thorough. • Regulations exist that will guide the minimal required levels of V&V. • Specifications should ideally be executable, and the portions thereof that describe high-risk aspects of the solution will need to be validated. • Robust CM will be required, with ability to restore previous versions of CIs.
Product critical. Our solution is medium risk, with the potential to adversely affect the overall product or service offering.	• Testing will focus on the high-risk aspects of the solution, with less thorough testing for less risky aspects. • Regulations, or at least organizational guidelines, may exist to guide V&V. • Simple CM control is likely sufficient.
Project critical. Our solution is low-risk, with potential adverse affects being limited to the loss of the investment in the team itself.	• Testing will focus on the high-risk aspects of the solution, if any, with less thorough testing for less risky aspects. • Regulations, or at least organizational guidelines, may exist to guide V&V. • Simple CM control is sufficient.

Development Strategy

We need to identify how our team will approach development so that we know how to properly staff the team with people who have testing and programming skills. This decision point is also part of the *Accelerate Value Delivery* process goal (see Chapter 19).

Options (Ordered)	Trade-Offs
Test-driven development (TDD). A combination of test-first programming (see below) to add any new functionality and refactoring to improve the quality of existing functionality. This includes developer TDD and acceptance TDD (ATTD)/behavior driven development (BDD) [W].	• See trade-offs with test-first programming. • Refactoring supports a continuous approach to paying down existing technical debt. • Refactoring will slow down current work but resulting quality improvements will increase development productivity and maintainability in the future and potentially reduce overall cost.
Test-first programming (TFP). The developer(s) write(s) one or more tests before writing the production code that fulfills those tests. Sometimes called test-driven programming [W].	• Drives the solution requirements (via acceptance tests) and design (via developer tests) based on the requested functionality. • Produces detailed, executable design specifications while supporting a confirmatory approach to testing. • Enables the team to safely evolve their solution by supporting automated regression testing. • Results in better design by forcing team members to think through design before committing to code. • Ensures writing of unit tests are not "forgotten" or not done due to time constraints. • Requires significant discipline and skill among team members. • Requires ongoing maintenance of the tests which may slow down new work as the design evolves over time. • May require significant investment in writing tests when working with legacy software, although that can be spread out over time and does not need to be done all at once.
Test-after development. The developer(s) write some production code, typically for a few hours, then write the test(s) that validate the code works as requested.	• Easier for the team to get going with regression testing as it requires less discipline than test-first approaches. • Requires testing skills within the team. • May result in more bugs compared to TFP or TDD. • Test code coverage tends to be less as compared with TFP or TDD. • Lengthens the feedback loop (compared with TFP

	and TDD). • May require significant investment in writing tests when working with legacy software.
Testless programming. The developer(s) write some code then provide it to someone else to validate.	• Potential starting point for teams made up of specialists (i.e., some team members are programmers, others just focus on testing). • Often supports a slow, mini-waterfall approach to development. • Motivates longer iterations as result of mini-waterfall. • Motivates less-effective testing strategies (i.e., manual testing). • Results in more expensive fixing, on average, due to increased feedback cycle.

Test Environment(s) Platform Strategy

We need to identify our strategy or strategies for how we intend to deploy new test platforms or better yet leverage existing test platforms.

Options (Ordered)	Trade-Offs
Cloud-based. The test environment is hosted in a private or public cloud environment.	• Potential for very efficient use of test platform resources. • Potential for quick and easy access to testing platforms on an as-needed basis. • Good fit for project-based development because the environment can be run for period required by the team. • A private cloud environment will need to be maintained or a public cloud environment contracted for and operated. • May not be possible to fully approximate production. • There may be data sovereignty issues with public clouds. • There may be security and data tenancy concerns with public cloud offerings.
Physical. Separate hardware and software is provided for testing.	• Provides greatest opportunity to approximate production. • With a project-based approach to development this can be expensive to set up and then tear down. • Testing environments are often underfunded and difficult or slow to access for development teams (injecting bottlenecks into our process).
Virtual. Virtualization software is used to provide a test environment.	• Very flexible way for multiple teams to share physical testing environments. • It may not be possible to fully approximate our production environments. • We will still need a physical environment available where the virtual environment(s) can run.

Test Environment(s) Equivalency Strategy

We need to identify our approach to how close the test environments will represent production environments. In general, the closer to production an environment is the better the quality of the testing it enables but the more expensive it is. The following table captures several common options available to us.

Options (Ordered)	Trade-Offs
Production equivalent. The test environment is an exact, or at least very close, approximation of production. This includes both identical hardware and software configurations compared with what is available in production.	• Provides greatest level of assurance. • Enables a hot switchover (blue/green) deployment strategy (see *Deploy the Solution* in Chapter 21). • Usually prohibitively expensive and therefore an unrealistic strategy. • Appropriate for pre-production test environments in high-risk situations.
Production approximate. A test environment built using significantly less hardware, and sometimes less capable versions of software, than what is currently available.	• Our tests will miss production problems, risking very expensive fixes later on. • Requires significantly less investment. • Appropriate for team integration test environments and pre-production test environments for low-risk situations.
Disparate. The testing environment is significantly different than production. Disparate test environments are often built using inexpensive hardware or are simply a partition on a developer's workstation.	• Very inexpensive testing environments. • Appropriate for developer workstations. • Very poor at finding integration problems due to poor approximation of production.

Quality Requirements Testing Strategy

We need to identify our approach(es) to validating quality requirements, also known as quality of service (QoS) or non-functional, requirements for our solution [W]. A critical thing that our team needs to do is to work with our stakeholders to define what quality means to them – quality is in the eye of the beholder. Quality requirement categories include, but are not limited to, the options listed in the table below. It is important to note that most of these testing strategies require an explicit skillset and special tooling to perform.

Options (Not Ordered)	Trade-Offs
Accessibility. Ensure that our solution is usable by people with challenges such as color blindness, blindness, hearing loss, old age, and other	• Respects and supports the full range of our potential user base, increasing the inclusivity of our solution. • Typically requires access to people with those disabilities, or at least intimate knowledge of those disabilities, to perform the testing. • Often an afterthought for many teams, leading to

potential disabilities [W].	expensive changes to address accessibility problems.
Availability. Ensure service reliability and our solution's fault tolerance (the ability to respond gracefully when a software or hardware component fails) [W].	• Ensure that our solution fulfills availability and reliability requirements. • Often requires long-running tests. • May require production monitoring functionality built into our solution (which we likely want to support DevOps anyway).
Concurrency. The aim is to detect problems around locking, deadlocking, semaphores and single-threading bottlenecks. Sometimes called multi-user testing.	• Ensure that our solution works when many simultaneous users are working with it. • Often requires long-running, complex tests.
Data privacy. Ensure that people have access to only the data, no more and no less, than they have the right to access [W].	• Discover data privacy/access problems before they occur. • Data privacy testing requires a deep understanding of the access rights of the roles supported by the solution as well as appropriate regulatory compliancy. • Ability to create, read, update, or delete given data may vary by role. For example, we can see our salary but not update it.
Internationalization. Ensure that our solution supports multiple languages and cultures, often referred to as locales. Sometimes called localization, I18n, or globalization [W].	• Increases the potential market or user base for our solution. • Requires someone who understands each locale to be supported by the solution. • Increases the burden of manual testing as each locale will potentially need to be tested.
Performance. Determine the speed or effectiveness of our solution or portion thereof [W].	• Discover performance problems before our solution is released into production. • May require significant amounts of test data, data that may need to be generated or copied from production (with privacy issues addressed accordingly).
Resilience/reliability. Determine whether our solution will continue to operate over the long term [W].	• Ensure that our solution will operate for a long period of time. • Often requires long-running tests used to detect memory leaks. • May require production monitoring functionality built into our solution (which we likely want to support DevOps anyway).
Scalability. Ensure that the solution will meet or exceed the demands	• Identifies potential limits to usage of our solution, and more importantly identifies the criteria to detect when we will need to extend or refactor the architecture once

placed upon it by the growing needs of our user base [W].	the solution is in production. • Requires an understanding of the architecture. • Difficult in practice because it requires a prediction of the expected usage patterns of end users. Note that usage patterns are much easier to predict when we already have a version running in production.
Security. Typical security issues include confidentiality, authentication, authorization, integrity, and non-repudiation [W].	• Discover security problems before they occur, perhaps via penetration testing via third-party "ethical hackers." • Security testing often requires deep expertise in security and potentially expensive testing tools.
Usability. End users are asked to perform certain tasks to explore issues around ease of use, task time, and user perception of the experience [W].	• Discover usability problems while they are still relatively easy to address. • Usability testing often requires deep experience in user experience (UX) and design skills. • Requires access to potential end users or development of realistic personas.
Volume/rate. Determine that our solution will perform properly under heavy load or large volumes of data. Sometimes called load testing or stress testing [W].	• Ensure that our solution works under heavy load. • May require significant amounts of test data, data that may need to be generated or copied from production (with privacy issues addressed accordingly).

Choose Testing Types

An important question that we need to answer is what types of testing will we need to perform while building our solution. The agile testing quadrants of Figure 12.4, modified from [Marick] and [GregoryCrispin], overview some potential types of testing that we should consider adopting within the team. The following table overviews and contrasts these strategies.

Figure 12.4. The agile testing quadrants.

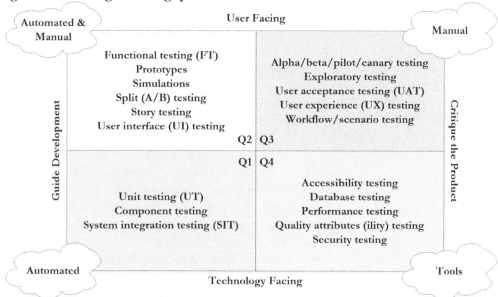

Options (Not Ordered)	Trade-Offs
Accessibility testing. A subset of user experience (UX) testing where the focus is on ensuring that people with accessibility challenges, such as color blindness, vision loss, hearing loss, or old age can work with the solution effectively [W].	• Helps to ensure our solution addresses appropriate regulatory issues regarding accessibility. • Requires skills and knowledge around accessibility issues and design thinking. • Often requires collaboration with people who have accessibility challenges.
Alpha/beta/pilot/canary testing. Test in production with a subset of the overall user base. Alpha, beta, and pilot testing is typically a full release of the system to a subset of users. A canary test is typically a release of a small subset of functionality to a subset of users [W].	• Increases the chance you will build what stakeholders want by getting feedback based on actual usage. • Limits the impact of a poor release to just the subset of users. • Requires the solution be architected to limit access to a subset of users. • In case of alpha, beta, and pilot testing people will likely need to be informed that they are involved with such a release.
Component testing. Test a	• Limits the scope of your testing effort, enabling

187

cohesive portion of the overall solution in isolation. A "component" may be a web service, a micro-service, a user interface (UI) component, a framework, a domain component, or a subsystem. This is a combination of unit testing and system integration testing where the component is simultaneously the unit and the system under test [W].	you to focus on that specific functionality. • A form of functional testing that determines how well a component works in isolation. • Does not determine how well a component will work when integrated with the rest of the solution/environment.
Database testing. Databases are often used to implement critical business functionality and shared data assets and therefore need to be validated accordingly. Also called data testing [W].	• Ensures that data semantics are implemented consistently within a shared database. • Identifies potential problems with data sources before production usage. • Database tests are often written as part of application testing efforts, thereby increasing the chance that localized data rules are validated rather than organization-wide rules. • Automated regression test suites for the data source itself are required to ensure data consistency across systems. • Difficult to find people with database testing skills because few existing data professionals have database testing skills, and few application developers understand the nuances of databases.
Exploratory testing. An experimental approach to testing that is simultaneously learning, test design, and test execution [W].	• Finds potential issues that would otherwise have slipped into production, thereby reducing the overall cost of addressing the problem (see Figure 12.3 earlier). • Requires highly skilled testers who are good at exploring how something works. • Expensive form of testing that is mostly manual, but the learning part can often be the most efficient way to discover things quickly.
Functional testing (FT). Test the functionality of the solution as it has been defined by the stakeholders. This is a form of black-box testing. Sometimes called requirements testing, validation testing, or testing against the specification [W].	• Validates that what we've built meets the needs of our stakeholders as they've communicated them to us so far. • The requirements often change, implying that our automated functional tests will need to similarly evolve. • Behavior driven development (BDD) and test-driven development (TDD) strategies support FT very well.

Performance testing. Testing to determine the speed/throughput at which something runs, and more importantly where it breaks. This is a form of quality attribute (ility) testing. Sometimes called load or stress testing [W].	• It can demonstrate that our solution meets *performance* criteria. • It can compare two or more solutions to determine which performs better. • It can identify which components of the solution perform poorly under specific workloads, enabling us to identify areas that need to be refactored. • Performance testing is highly dependent upon the robustness of our test environment, the implication being that we may need to make significant investment to test properly. • Test results are short lived in that they are potentially affected by any change to the implementation of the system.
Prototypes. A prototype of the solution is developed so that potential end users may work with it to explore the design. The prototype typically simulates potential functionality [W].	• Enables the team to explore the user interface (UI) design without investing significant effort to build it. • Very effective when it isn't clear how to approach one or more aspects of the design. • Potential to reduce the feedback cycle by getting prototyped functionality into the hands of stakeholders quickly. • Requires investment in the development of "throw-away" prototype code, which can be seen as a waste.
Quality attributes (ility) testing. The validation of the solution against the quality requirements, also called quality of service (QoS) requirements or non-functional requirements (NFRs), for it. Figure 12.5 summarizes categories of potential quality requirements [W].	• Because quality requirements drive critical architecture strategies, this is a critical strategy to ensure that our solution's architecture meets the overall needs of our stakeholders. • Quality attributes apply across many functional requirements, making testing difficult. • Requires automated regression testing to ensure compliancy as the functionality evolves.
Security testing. Testing to determine if a solution protects functionality and data as intended. This includes confidentiality, authentication, authorization, availability, and non-repudiation. Security testing is a form of quality attribute (ility) testing [W].	• Helps to identify potential security holes in our solution. • Security testing is a sophisticated skill. • Commercial security testing tools are often expensive.
Simulations. Simulation software, sometimes called	• Common approach when the component or system under test involves human safety, or

189

large-scale mocks, is developed to simulate the behavior of an expensive or risky component of the solution [W].	when the component is not available (perhaps it is still under development), or when large amounts of money are involved (such as a financial trading system). • Enables the team to test aspects of their solution early in the lifecycle because they don't need to wait for access to the actual component that is being simulated. • Can be expensive to develop and maintain the simulator. • You're not testing against the real functionality. • The results from testing are only as good as the quality of the simulation.
Split (A/B) testing. We produce two or more versions of a feature and put them into production in parallel, measuring pertinent usage statistics to determine which version is most effective. When a given user works with the system they are consistently presented with the same feature version each time, even though several versions exist [W]. This is a traditional strategy from the 1980s, and maybe even farther back, popularized in the 2010s by Lean Start-Up.	• Enables us to make fact-based decisions on actual end-user usage data regarding what version of a feature is most effective. • Supports a set-based design approach (see Explore Solution Design below). • Increases development costs because several versions of the same feature need to be implemented. • Prevents "analysis paralysis" by allowing us to concretely move on. • Requires technical infrastructure to direct specific users to the feature versions and to log feature usage.
Story testing. This is a form of functional testing (FT) where the functionality under test is described by a single user story. Can be thought of as a form of acceptance testing when a stakeholder representative, such as a product owner, performs it.	• Validates that we've implemented the story as required by our stakeholders. • The details of the story will evolve over time, implying that our automated tests will need to similarly evolve. • Danger that this is effectively component testing for a story – cross-story integration testing will need to still be performed, such as workflow/scenario testing.
System integration testing (SIT). Testing that is carried out across a complete system, the system typically being the solution that our team is currently working on [W].	• Requires skill and knowledge on the part of the person(s) doing the testing. • Integration tests can be long running and often must be run in their own test suite. • Integration testing requires a sophisticated test environment that mimics production well.
Unit testing (UT). Testing of a very small portion of functionality, typically a few	• Many developers still need to gain this skill (so pair with testers). • Ensures that code conforms to its design and

lines of code and its associated data [W]. Sometimes called developer testing, particularly in the scope of test-driven development (TDD).	behaves as expected. • Limited in scope but critical, particularly for clear-box testing.
User acceptance testing (UAT). The solution is tested by its actual end users to determine whether it meets their actual needs (which may be different than what was originally asked for or specified). UAT should be a flow test performed by users [W].	• Provides valuable feedback based on actual usage of the solution. • Expensive because it is performed manually. • Very expensive form of regression testing (you're much better to automate regression tests). • Requires stakeholder participation, or at least stakeholder representatives such as product owners (POs). • Often repeats FT efforts, so potentially a source of process waste.
User experience (UX) testing. Testing where the focus is on determining how well users work with a solution, the intention being to find areas where usage can be improved. Sometimes called usability or consumability testing [W].	• Requires UX skills and knowledge that is difficult to gain. • May require significant investment in recording equipment and subsequent review of the recordings to identify exactly what people are doing. • Enables us to determine how the solution is used in practice, and more importantly where we need to improve the UX.
User interface (UI) testing. Testing via usage of the user interface. This can be performed either manually or digitally using UI-based testing tools. Sometimes called glass testing or screen testing [W].	• Straightforward step to move from manual testing to automated testing because the manual test scripts can be written as automated UI tests. • Expensive way to automate functional testing (FT), even given record/playback tools. • Tests prove to be very fragile in practice. • Difficult to maintain automated tests because the tests break whenever the user interface evolves.
Workflow/scenario testing. Testing where the focus is on determining how well a solution addresses a specific business workflow or usage scenario. A scenario is described to one or more end users and they are asked to work through that scenario using the solution. This is a form of UX testing [W].	• We need to have an understanding of the overall workflow, which typically goes beyond stories and even epics. • See the tradeoffs associated with UX testing.

Figure 12.5. Potential categories of quality requirements.

• Accessibility	• Environment (green)	• Regulatory
• Accuracy	• Exclusive access/locking	• Reliability
• Availability	• Historical data tracking	• Reusability
• Auditability	• Internationalization	• Scalability
• Capacity	• Interoperability	• Security
• Concurrency	• Maintainability	• Serviceability
• Consumability	• Operability	• Supportability
• Customer experience	• Performance	• Timeliness
• Data integrity	• Recoverability	• Traceability
• Deployability		• Usability

Test Suite Strategy

We need to identify the approach that we're taking to organize our test suites so that we know how the regression test tools need to be configured. Important issues to consider are the amount of time that regression tests take to run and where in our WoW we are running the tests. For example, the regression test suite that runs on my workstation when I commit code needs to run in a few minutes, whereas a test suite that runs at night on our team integration server could run for many hours.

Options (Ordered)	Trade-Offs
Multiple regression test suites. There are several regression test suites, such as a fast running suite that runs on developer work stations, a team integration suite that runs on the team integration sandbox (this suite may run for several minutes or even hours), a nightly test suite, and even more.	• Enables quick test suites to support team regression testing. • Supports testing in complex environments. • Supports the running of test suites on different cadences (run on commits, run at night, run on weekends, ...). • Requires several testing environments, thereby increasing cost. • Requires strategy for deploying across testing environments. • Often requires defect reporting strategy.
Single regression test suite. All tests are invoked via a single test suite.	• Supports testing in straightforward situations. • Requires creation and maintenance of a test environment.
Manual testing. Tests are run manually, often by someone following a documented test script.	• Appropriate for very simple systems. • Very ineffective for regression testing (automate our tests instead). • Very slow and expensive. • Does not work with modern iterative and agile strategies.

192

Test Data Source

We need to identify our approach to obtaining test data to support our testing efforts. Obtaining test data can be a tricky issue, particularly given privacy and sovereignty issues, and engineering data requires skill. As you can see in the following table there are several options for sourcing test data.

Options (Not Ordered)	Trade-Offs
Original production data. A copy, often a subset, or actual "live" data is used.	• Easy source of accurate test data. • Subsets of production data are protected by privacy regulations such as Health Insurance Portability and Accountability Act (HIPAA) in the US. • Current production data may not cover all test scenarios. • Often too much data, requiring us to take a subset of it.
Masked production data. Original production data is used, where some data elements, typically data that can be used to identify an individual or organization, are transformed into non-identifying values (this is called obfuscation).	• Easy source of accurate test data with privacy concerns addressed. • Current production data may not cover all test scenarios. • Often too much data, requiring us to take a subset of it.
Generated data. Large amounts of test data, often with random data values, is generated.	• Very effective for volume testing. • Very ineffective for anything other than volume testing unless the generated data is also engineered.
Engineered data. Test data is purposefully created to provide known values to support specific scenarios.	• Potential to cover all testing scenarios. • Many problems that we haven't predicted occur with production data.
Service/source virtualization. Application of mock or simulation software to enable testing of difficult-to-access solution components (i.e., hardware components or external systems).	• Simulates systems that we cannot safely or economically test. • May not fully simulate the actual system. • We still need to test against the actual system.

Test Automation Strategy

We need to determine the level of automation we intend to implement for our test and possibly deployment suites so that we know what tools support we need and what our team's potential ability to evolve the solution will be. Note that test automation requires the people writing the tests to have the skills and appropriate mindset to do so. A significant challenge for many teams moving to Disciplined Agile ways of working is to help bring such skills and mindset into the team as it requires investment and time to do so.

Options (Ordered)	Trade-Offs
Continuous deployment (CD). When the solution is successfully integrated within a given environment or sandbox, it is automatically deployed (and hopefully automatically integrated via CI) in the next level environment [W].	• Automates "grunt work" around deployment. • Supports regression testing in complex environments. • Enables the continuous delivery lifecycles. • Requires investment in CD tools.
Continuous integration (CI). When something is checked in, such as a source code file or image file, the solution is automatically built again. The changed code is compiled, the solution is integrated, the solution is tested, and optionally code analysis is performed [W].	• Automates "grunt work" around building the solution. • Supports regression testing in each of our test environments. • Important step towards continuous delivery. • Key enabler of agile solution delivery. • Requires investment in CI tools.
Automated regression tests. Automated tests are written to ensure that a given percentage of the source code is invoked.	• Enables teams to run their regression tests regularly, often many times a day. This in turn enables them to safely evolve their solution with the knowledge that they will be able to detect potential problems. • Requires significant skill and discipline to write the tests and keep them up to date as the requirements evolve. • Requires investment in paying down the technical debt of writing any missing tests that should have been developed in the past but unfortunately were not. • Can be difficult to write automated tests at the user interface (UI) level, particularly when the UI is rapidly evolving or is graphically complex, without code automation tools.

Scripts. One or more scripts are manually run to build the solution.	• Important step towards CI (we need the scripts for our CI tool(s) to invoke). • Overhead of running the scripts means team members will do it less often, leading to longer feedback cycles.
Manual testing. Test scripts for manually-performed tests are developed with the goal of validating certain portions of the solution.	• Often used to validate complex UI functionality. • Manual testing is expensive and slow in practice, thereby reducing a team's ability to regression test continuously.

Test Automation Coverage

An important consideration regarding automated regression testing is how we intend to approach it, or in other words in what levels of the testing pyramid (see Figure 12.2 above) will we automate our tests?

Options (Ordered)	Trade-Offs
Multiple systems. Tests invoke functionality, or use data from multiple systems to determine whether they work together as expected. A form of black-box testing at the production level.	• Reduces the risk that a new release of our solution into production will adversely affect other systems within our organizational ecosystem. • Effectively integration tests for our production environment. • Enables us to release into production more often. • Requires a sophisticated, and potentially expensive, approximation of our production environment.
Solution. Tests are written to ensure that our solution works as expected. A form of black-box testing at the system level. Also known as end-to-end tests.	• Helps to verify that our solution meets the high-level requirements and expectations of our stakeholders. • Effectively integration tests for the solution. • Solution-level tests are an important part of the executable requirements specification for a solution. • Typically confirms architecture-level requirements and decisions. • Requires an understanding of the requirements for the overall solution.
Service/application programming interface (API). Tests are written to ensure that services or API calls work as expected within the context of our solution. A combination of clear-box testing (within the solution) and black-box testing (of the services/API).	• Helps to verify that the services/API work as desired. • Effectively integration tests for the services/API. • These tests form an executable specification for the services/API. • Typically validates design-level decisions. • Requires an understanding of the design and requirements for it, in particular the semantics of the data being passed/returned.

195

Component. Tests are written to validate that components/subsystems of our solution work as expected. A component may be internal to a solution or part of the external user interface (UI) [W].	• Helps to verify that the component works as desired. • Effectively integration tests for the component. • These tests form an executable specification for the component/subsystem. • Typically validates design-level decisions. • Requires an understanding of the requirements for the component.
Unit. Tests are written that directly invoke our source code, often using the xUnit test suite. A form of clear-box testing. Sometimes called developer tests [W].	• Helps to verify that the "unit" we are building – an operation/function or part of one – works as desired. • Tends to be the fastest automated tests. • Often the easiest types of tests to maintain when requirements are evolving. • These tests form an executable design specification for the service, component, or solution under test. • Typically validates design-level decisions. • Requires an understanding of the design of the unit that we're testing.
User interface (UI). Tests are written that invoke the UI, often simulating the interactions that an end-user would have with the solution. Sometimes called glass testing [W].	• Helps to validate that the UI exhibits the desired behavior. • These tests form an executable requirements specification for a solution or even collection of solutions (when used for production-level integration testing). • Typically validates requirements or UI-design decisions. • UI tests can be very fragile when they are implemented in black-box fashion (often via record-and-playback tools), but are less fragile when implemented via clear box test tools (such as Jasmine for JavaScript testing). • Danger of being over-applied, particularly by organizations that are moving away from specification-based manual testing, to (sort of) replace testing that is better done via the strategies defined above.

Defect Reporting

We need to identify how we intend to report/record defects, if at all, so that the team knows how they will do so and what tools they will require. Defects found by the team during Construction are typically not tracked, they are instead fixed on the spot, although defects that escape the team and are caught by independent testing or that are found in production are tracked, particularly in financial or life-critical situations. Tools can be a contentious issue as existing quality professionals are likely to have their preferred tools whereas agile teams have different preferences. Our advice is to optimize the overall workflow and not just locally optimize portions of it – consider the larger picture for defect reporting.

196

Options (Ordered)	Trade-Offs
Conversation. The defect is reported to the appropriate developer(s) by speaking to them.	<ul><li>Fast and efficient way to communicate the issue.</li><li>Even with the other options listed below, there is very likely always a need for the person who found a potential issue to be available to explain it to the person fixing it.</li><li>Not sufficient if we require documentation about the defect (for contractual reasons or for regulatory reasons).</li><li>Does not support defect tracking measurements.</li></ul>
Operational monitoring. Tools that track/log end-user usage of a solution. Sometimes called a crash analytics tool.	<ul><li>Helps teams to identify the cause of potential problems/defects.</li><li>Provides real-time, operational intelligence to developers to help identify what functionality is being used in practice.</li><li>Supports Exploratory lifecycle and experimentation practices such as canary testing and split (A/B) testing.</li><li>Requires architectural scaffolding for event logging.</li><li>Potential for performance degradation due to logging.</li></ul>
Agile management tool. A management tool such as Atlassian Jira, Jile, or VersionOne is used to document and report the defect and then add it as a work item for the team.	<ul><li>Developers are likely already using such a tool to manage their other work items.</li><li>Defects can be easily treated as a work item type.</li><li>Supports defect tracking and reporting.</li><li>Existing testers may not be familiar with these tools.</li><li>Test teams that have to support a multi-modal IT department may need to use different tools to report defects back to different teams.</li></ul>
Bug/defect tracker. A defect tracker, such as Bugzilla or QuickBugs, is used to document and report the defect.	<ul><li>Specific tools, including reporting, around defect tracking offer potential for best of breed (for silo work).</li><li>Possible to track quality metrics such as escaped defects into independent testing or production.</li><li>Requires the team to adopt one more tool.</li><li>May not integrate well, if at all, with any agile work management software being used.</li><li>May make it harder to make all work visible due to integration challenges.</li></ul>
Test management tool. A test management tool such as HP Quality Center/ALM is used to document and report the defect.	<ul><li>Existing testers will be familiar with existing test management software.</li><li>Possible to track quality metrics such as escaped defects.</li><li>Test management tools often automate unnecessary traditional test management bureaucracy.</li><li>Requires the team to adopt one more tool.</li><li>May not integrate well, if at all, with any agile work management software being used.</li><li>May make it harder to make all work visible.</li></ul>

Quality Governance Strategies

We need to identify the quality strategies that the team intends to adopt to govern the quality of the work they will produce. Quality governance typically focuses on examining the proof/evidence that the artifacts created by the team are of sufficient quality.

Options (Ordered)	Trade-Offs
Non-solo work. People work together via practices such as pairing, mob programming, and modeling with others.	• Enables knowledge, skill, and information sharing between team members. • Potential defects/issues found and hopefully addressed at point of injection, leading to higher quality and lower cost of defect removal. • Development can be a bit slower and more expensive than people working alone (although this is often more than made up for in lower cost of addressing defects).
Tool-generated metrics. Our continuous integration (CI) tools can provide important development intelligence regarding the quality of our work. CI tools include the CI server itself, automated regression testing tools, code analysis tools, and schema analysis tools.	• The tools generate critical information such as build status, test status (pass/fail), code quality metrics, security ratings, and data quality metrics that can be captured and reported on in real time. • Improved information enables the team to make better decisions and thereby to self-organize more effectively. • Improved information enables leadership to govern more effectively. • Requires investment in data warehouse (DW) and business intelligence (BI) technologies to capture and report the information.
Automated code/schema analysis. Code analysis tools such as CAST and SonarQube are used to either statically or dynamically evaluate the source code or database schema to identify potential quality problems.	• Automates a lot of the "grunt work" of code reviews. • Potential to find a very wide range of common defect types. • Effective way to ensure common coding conventions are followed. • Not all potential defects can be found automatically.
Quality guidelines. Quality guidelines – including but not limited to code quality, data quality, and documentation quality	• Simple way to capture common values and principles to motivate improved quality and consistency. • Captures common, cross-team attributes for Definition of Done (DoD) [Rubin]. • Some developers require detailed instructions (so codify them with code analysis tools).

– are shared with delivery teams.	
Informal reviews. Work is reviewed and feedback is provided, often in a straightforward manner.	<ul><li>Great technique for sharing skills, promoting common values within the team, and for finding potential defects.</li><li>May be sufficient for some regulatory compliance situations.</li><li>Longer feedback cycle than automated code analysis or non-solo strategies.</li></ul>
Formal reviews. Work is reviewed in a structured manner, often following defined procedures.	<ul><li>Supports some regulatory compliance requirements.</li><li>Long feedback cycle.</li><li>Can require significant planning and documentation overhead.</li></ul>
Test case documentation. Test cases, particularly manual test cases, may be captured as static documentation (instead of as automated tests).	<ul><li>This is better, usually, than not capturing test cases.</li><li>Written test cases provides governance people with potential insight into the testing approach being taken by the team.</li><li>Test case documentation suffers from the CRUFT challenges associated with all forms of documentation (see the *Accelerate Value Delivery* process goal in Chapter 17).</li><li>Test case documentation can be expensive to write and maintain.</li></ul>

13 DEVELOP COMMON VISION

The Develop Common Vision process goal, shown in Figure 13.1, provides options for how we will come to, and communicate, a common vision about the purpose of the team. An initial vision for this team was very likely developed by our Product Management team (if we have one) and prioritized by our Portfolio Management team (if we have one) long before our team started into Inception. This initial vision is a starting point for us, effectively forming a high-level promise to our stakeholders that was sufficiently compelling for them to provide the funds required to initiate, or bring new work to, our team. Now we need to explore and evolve this vision in sufficient detail. There are several reasons why this is important:

> **Key Points in this Chapter**
> - We may wish to capture our findings in Inception and review it with our stakeholders to obtain agreement on the vision.
> - A vision statement typically includes traditional elements of a project charter albeit in lightweight fashion, such as scope, schedule, budget, risks, and other supporting information.
> - A vision statement as a summary of our Inception work can be an extremely effective way to get all stakeholders on the same page with regard to the expected outcome of our initiative.

- **Our stakeholders want to know what they're going to get**. Chances are very good our stakeholders will want to know what we're going to do, how we're going to do it, how much it will cost, and how long it will take. We will need to provide them with plausible answers to those questions if we hope to have Construction funded.

- **Our team should have purpose**. In *Drive*, Dan Pink argues that autonomy, mastery, and purpose are what motivate people. One aim of this process goal is to come to an agreement about what we hope to achieve as a team. Note that the *Coordinate Activities* process goal, see Chapter 23, enables autonomy and the *Grow Team Members* process goal, see Chapter 22, provides opportunities for gaining mastery.

- **Our team should agree on how we're going to proceed**. As a team we should agree on what we're supposed to be producing and how we're going to do so. This is particularly important when people are working at different locations or when the team is large and organized into subteams.

- **We want to capture key decisions**. Early in the lifecycle we often make important promises about the projected business benefits, the payback period, the scope, and even the technologies to be used or supported. We should strive to fulfill the promises that we make, and disciplined teams (and stakeholders for that matter) will track progress against them.

- **We want to stay on track**. Having a vision in place, particularly one that is sufficiently captured/documented, provides the team with something to check against during Construction – some people like to call this a guiding "North Star." When we allow the requirements to evolve over time, when the design evolves in step, and when our plan similarly evolves it is easy to get off track and start going in a different direction. Throughout Construction the team should ask itself if they're still heading in the direction they said they would, and if not then either adjust the direction or the vision accordingly.

Figure 13.1. The goal diagram for Develop Common Vision.

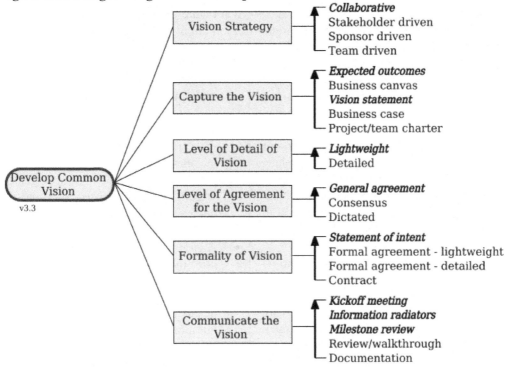

To be effective, we need to consider several important questions:

- What strategy will we follow to develop the vision?
- How are we going to capture the vision?
- How much detail must we capture?
- What level of agreement must we come to with our stakeholders before we can move on into Construction?
- What level of formality must we use for this agreement?
- How will we communicate the vision with our stakeholders?

Vision Strategy

We need to identify who will be responsible for developing the vision. Preferably this should be a collaborative effort between the team and its stakeholders, but as you can see in the following table there are several other less attractive options as well.

Options (Ordered)	Trade-Offs
Collaborative. Business and IT work together to develop a shared vision.	• This is the ideal situation when both business stakeholders and the IT delivery teams have a stake in the vision. • Can be difficult to get key stakeholders to be actively involved.
Stakeholder driven. The stakeholders drive the vision for the initiative(s).	• The stakeholders may not have an understanding about what is truly possible so the vision may not be practical. • The delivery team may not accept a vision that is handed to them, particularly the technical and schedule aspects of it.
Sponsor driven. The people with the money or authority define the vision.	• Decision making is easier when the ones sponsoring the initiative are driving it. • Often sponsors are not close enough to the stakeholders to adequately understand their detailed needs. • The delivery team may not accept a vision that is handed to them.
Team Driven. The delivery team defines the vision.	• The vision can often be developed very quickly. • The team will very likely identify a vision that the stakeholders won't accept. • Might be appropriate in rare circumstances if the team is an expert in the domain and it is not possible to obtain feedback from the stakeholders.

Capture the Vision

We need to identify how we are going to capture the vision. This decision is often driven by the expectations of our stakeholders, and when an organization is new to agile the expectations are often towards the heavier, less effective options. The implication is that we may need to negotiate a better option, and as you see in the table below there are several choices available.

Options (Ordered)	Trade-Offs
Expected outcomes. We capture the vision as high-level outcomes that describe what we intend to achieve rather than how we intend to achieve it.	• Provides direction to the team while providing sufficient flexibility for them to find the best way to delight their customers. • Requires strong trust between the team and stakeholders. • Works well with experienced, long-standing teams.

	• Opportunity for differing opinions as to how the outcomes will be achieved, requiring significant coordination and collaboration between people during Construction.
Business canvas. Captures critical information about the endeavor, potentially including the expected outcomes, a summary of the scope, the sponsor(s), and why the endeavor is important to our organization.	• Straightforward, text-based planning/strategy artifact. • Provides an excellent summary of the endeavor, and can be an important information radiator moving forward. • Requires a facilitated planning session to develop (see the *Coordinate Activities* process goal in Chapter 23).
Vision statement. A summary of key information about the initiative, typically overviewing the plan, architecture, scope, and teaming strategy.	• Often documented in a concise manner, perhaps as several slides in a presentation deck or on Wiki pages containing key diagrams and points, making it easy to maintain over time. • Provides stakeholders with concise but sufficient documentation of the vision, thereby increasing their confidence in the team. • Usually sufficient for regulatory compliance.
Business case. An exploration of whether the initiative, often a project, makes sense from economic, technical, organizational, and operational points of view [W].	• Forces the team and stakeholders to think through the viability of their strategy. • Often required by traditional-leaning governance strategies, but often proves to be a work of fiction that is rarely consulted in practice. • Usually sufficient for regulatory compliance.
Project/team charter. A detailed overview of key information about the initiative, potentially including the plan, architectural strategy, scope, teaming strategy, process, expected deliverables, and more [W].	• Typically motivates too much modeling and planning early in an initiative, increasing cost, time to delivery, and very often overall risk. • Often required by traditional-leaning governance strategies, but often proves to be a work of fiction that is rarely consulted in practice. • Often more than what is needed for regulatory compliance.

204

Level of Detail of the Vision

We need to decide what level of detail to capture in the vision. Because less is generally more, we should strive to keep the amount of documentation we create sufficient for our needs and no more [AgileDocumentation]. In other words, follow common agile documentation strategies for capturing the viesion. Time boxing an Inception phase is a good way to avoid the trap of going into too much detail, which is sometimes referred to as WaterScrumFall, wagile, or even Scrumifall.

Options (Ordered)	Trade-Offs
Lightweight. Created in a document or presentation for review with stakeholders. Initial scope should be summarized rather than a list of stories that may not be of interest at the vision level.	• Likely the most common approach. • Easy to distribute for feedback.
Detailed. A traditional detailed description of the vision. Usually captured as a project charter or formal cost-benefit analysis study.	• Many decisions will be made earlier in the lifecycle than they needed be, increasing waste and inefficiency. • Gives stakeholders a false sense of security. • Because the requirements are very likely to change, a detailed vision artifact tends to lead to significant overhead later in the lifecycle to address any changes. • Increases the length of time invested in Inception, thereby increasing our overall cost of delay (opportunity cost) and increasing the chance that we'll miss the window of opportunity for the solution. • May be appropriate in situations where the work is being outsourced and the details are important, or for a complex multi-year initiative (which we should organize into smaller initiatives).

Level of Agreement

How do we obtain agreement among our stakeholders that the vision makes sense? The following table compares several strategies available to us.

Options (Ordered)	Trade-Offs
General Agreement. Most, but not all stakeholders agree with the vision.	• It is usually easier to obtain general agreement than consensus. • Some people may not be happy with the vision.
Consensus. All stakeholders and the delivery team agree on the vision.	• It may be time consuming or even impossible to get consensus from all stakeholders. • Consensus-based decision making tends to lead to poor-quality decisions.
Dictated. The delivery team is not consulted about the value of the vision or if it is achievable.	• Stakeholders and the delivery teams may not fully engage if they are not permitted input into the vision, particularly if they perceive the vision to be unrealistic. • In regulatory situations portions of the vision, particularly the scope and the delivery date, may be mandatory.

Formality of Vision

How formally does the vision need to be presented and reviewed? The more formal the presentation the greater the level of preparation needed, and more likely the greater the amount of detail captured.

Options (Ordered)	Trade-Offs
Statement of intent. Stakeholders verbally agree to the vision without a formal review process.	• A simple conversation may be all that is required to conclude Inception and begin delivery. • The most agile approach and suitable for straightforward initiatives. • The word 'intent' implies that the vision may be revisited and adjusted, and is suitable in situations where a degree of uncertainty exists regarding the details in the vision.
Formal agreement - lightweight. The team and stakeholders have a sit-down meeting to formally review and agree to the vision, which has been captured in a concise and often high-level manner. A sign-off may be part of this review.	• The most common approach where key stakeholders wish to be walked through the details of the vision before committing to funding the delivery of the initiative. • Suitable in situations for complex initiatives requiring alignment across teams and stakeholder groups. • The vision might be used to overly constrain the team, often to the detriment of the stakeholders.
Formal agreement – detailed. The team and	• Often used in regulatory situations where there is a desire for a rigorous vision that has been formally accepted by

stakeholders have a sit-down meeting to formally review and agree to the vision, which has been captured in detail. A sign-off is usually part of this review.	stakeholders. • Suitable in situations for complex initiatives requiring alignment across teams and stakeholder groups. • The vision might be used to overly constrain the team, often to the detriment of the stakeholders themselves. • Aligns with a more formal approach to governance, which in turn tends to increase risk and overhead for the team.
Contract. A signed agreement regarding the vision is made between the team and stakeholders.	• Often required when working with a vendor. Some regulatory environments, particularly life-critical ones, require contract-like sign-offs and tracking of key artifacts. • Can inject needless overhead into the process, increasing both cost and time to deliver. • Often motivates a more formal approach to governance, which in turn leads to increased risk and overhead for the team.

Communicate the Vision

An important part of developing a common vision is to ensure that it's been effectively shared with, or communicated to, everyone involved. Our goal is to ensure that our stakeholders are aligned with the strategy that we intend to follow.

Options (Ordered)	Trade-Offs
Kickoff meeting. The team, often with key stakeholders in attendance, meets and publicly summarizes their strategy for how they intend to proceed. Kickoff meetings are often held at the beginning of Inception to initially align people and may also be held at the end of Inception to signal the start of Construction [W].	• Effective way for people to meet one another if the team is recently formed or if a lot of people are added all at once. • Often seen as an official start for a new team. • Public way to communicate the overall vision.
Information Radiators. Capture the vision on whiteboards or on sheets of flip chart paper. Posting this information on walls "radiates" the vision to anyone interested	• Very easy to do and stresses a desired low-formality agile approach to upfront planning and modeling. • Digital snapshots of the radiator can be taken to persist a static version of the radiator, which is useful for archiving. • Less useful if the vision is created by and for distributed teams; needs to be reviewed formally with stakeholders,

[CockburnAgile].	or needs to be persisted for later editing. • Not easily viewable outside the team's work area. • People need to know where the information radiators are and that they're allowed to look at them. • It isn't always clear what information is being "radiated," requiring discussion with people who understand the context of what's being shared.
Milestone review. Gather critical stakeholders together to review the vision, accept it, and decide whether to continue with the effort. We want to keep the review as straightforward as possible (see *Govern Delivery Team* in Chapter 27).	• Motivates stakeholders to either support the team or make it clear what their concerns are. • Often requires communication with the key decision makers beforehand so that they know what they're being asked to decide on. • Often adds time to the length of the Inception phase, particularly if the review results are negative and the team is asked to rework the vision.
Review/walkthrough. The vision is reviewed with key stakeholders, often as a prelude to a milestone review (see above) [W].	• Communicates the direction the team believes it is going in. • Good way to get feedback from stakeholders who aren't actively involved with the development of the vision. • Likely need supporting documentation, although it is possible to do a wall walk (a walkthrough) of our information radiators if we've been developing the vision in an Agile Modeling/planning room.
Documentation. The vision is captured in a document, or via a browser-based strategy such as a wiki, and made available to interested stakeholders.	• Having a documented vision gives the team something to refer back to during Construction, which is useful to determine if we're staying on track. • Supports geographically distributed stakeholders. • According to Media Richness Theory (MRT), detailed documentation is the least effective means of communication available to us [W].

14 SECURE FUNDING

The Secure Funding process goal, shown in Figure 14.1, provides options for how we can obtain funding for the team to continue on into Construction (and beyond). The Secure Funding process goal is important to most agile teams because, at least initially, they need the money to pay for development of the solution. In the case of product teams, discussed below, they may eventually become self-funding, where the revenue or cost savings from their solution is sufficient to pay for the ongoing cost of development. Until the team is self funding, they need some "seed funding" to get started.

> **Key Points in this Chapter**
> - We should gain agreement on the funding strategy for our initiative.
> - Fixed-price funding is the riskiest option available to us, and luckily we have much better options available.
> - Stable funding of value streams, rather than project-based funding of software teams, is an extremely effective approach.

Figure 14.2 shows the high-level flow between the Finance process blade, the Portfolio Management process blade, and our team [AmblerLines2017]. The team will have received sufficient funding for Inception – this is typically provided by our organization's Portfolio Management activities – but additional funding will need to be justified based on the vision for the team (see Chapter 13). In fact, the Portfolio Management effort itself, as well as any efforts to explore potential product ideas, would also need to have been funded in some way in order to get us to this point. As you can see in Figure 14.2 this funding is typically provided by our organization's Finance efforts. Note that in smaller organizations Finance and Portfolio Management efforts are often addressed by a single team, whereas larger organizations are likely to spread these functions across multiple collaborating teams.

Figure 14.1. The goal diagram for Securing Funding.

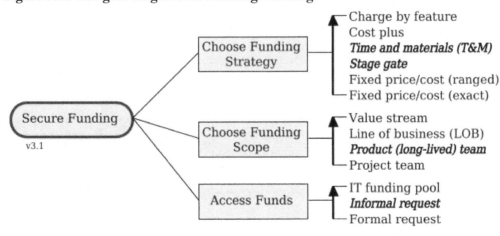

209

Figure 14.2. Funding flows between Finance, Portfolio Management, and a team.

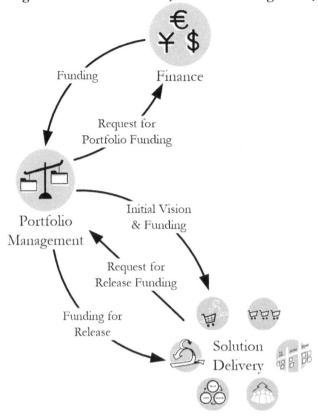

When securing initial funding for a team we need to consider three important questions:
- How will we fund the team?
- What type of team are we funding?
- How will we access those funds?

Choose Funding Strategy

We need to select the strategy that will be used to fund our solution delivery team. The strategy selected will have a significant impact on the behavior of the delivery team in terms of quality delivered and willingness to embrace changing requirements. The following table compares and contrasts several strategies for funding solution delivery teams.

Options (Ordered)	Trade-Offs
Charge by feature. Features, such as addition of a new report or implementation of a new user story, are funded individually.	• Enables bidding on individual features, supporting a very flexible approach to evolving requirements. • Suitable for outsourcing but generally not used for internal development. • Requires significant involvement and sophistication of stakeholders. • Funding to address technical issues, such as paying down

210

	technical debt, is likely to be starved out.
Cost plus. A variation on time and materials where a low rate is paid for developer's time to cover their basic costs with delivery bonuses paid for production of consumable solutions. This is also called "outcome based" or "cost reimbursement" [W].	• Works very well for outsourced development, spreading the risk between the customer and the service provider because the service provider has their costs covered but won't make a profit unless they consistently deliver quality software. • Low financial risk for both the team and for stakeholders. • Requires active governance by stakeholders and a clear definition of how to determine whether the project team has met their service level agreement (SLA) and therefore has earned their performance bonus.
Time and Materials (T&M). With this approach we pay as we go, paying an hourly or daily rate ("the time") plus any expenses ("the materials") incurred [W].	• Low financial risk when teams are governed appropriately. • Requires stakeholders to actively monitor and govern the team's finances. • In the case of outsourcing, vendors should provide complete transparency such as task boards so that stakeholders are confident that they are getting value for their money.
Stage Gate. With this strategy we estimate and then fund the project for a given period of time before going back for more funding. This is effectively a series of small fixed cost funding increments [W].	• Medium-level financial risk as it provides stakeholders with financial leverage over a delivery team. • Some organizations have an onerous funding process, so requiring teams to obtain funding in stages can increase their bureaucratic overhead and risk of delivering late. • Except for the Inception phase, funding should be tied to delivery of increments of working solutions, not paper based artifacts – the stage gates could coincide with DA's Stakeholder Vision, Proven Architecture and/or Continued Viability milestones as a component of our agile governance.
Fixed price/cost (ranged). At the beginning of the project we develop, and then commit to, an initial estimate that is based on our up-front requirements and architecture modeling efforts.	• Ranges provide stakeholders with a more realistic assessment of the uncertainty faced by the team. • High financial risk due to the initial estimate being based on initial requirements that are very likely to change and potential for technical unknowns. • To narrow the range we will need to do significant up front modeling and planning, thereby increasing our cost of delay and overall risk of incurring waste. • Many stakeholders will focus on the lower end of the estimate range. • Many stakeholders don't understand the need for ranged

211

The estimate should be presented as a fairly large range, often +/- 25% or even +/- 50% to reflect the riskiness of "fixed price" estimates [W].	estimates and we will likely need to educate them on the concept.
Fixed price/cost (exact). An initial estimate is created early in the lifecycle and presented either as an exact figure or as a very small range (e.g. +/- 5% or +/- 10%) [W].	• Very high financial risk due to likelihood of changing requirements and technical unknowns. • Provides stakeholders with an exact, although almost always unrealistic, cost to hope for. • Works well when we are allowed to drop scope to come in on budget, otherwise quality will suffer, which eventually drives up total cost of ownership (TCO) in the long run. • Doesn't communicate the actual uncertainty faced by the project team and sets false expectations about accuracy.

Choose Funding Scope

We need to select the type of team that we will be funding, and as you can see in the table below we have options.

Options (Ordered)	Trade-Offs
Value stream. The funding is for the entire value stream, include solution development, IT operations of the solution, and the business operations of the solution [W].	• Supports a more holistic view of value generation within our organization. • Works very well with modern, rolling-wave budgeting processes • Value streams often cross organizational boundaries, yet funding mechanisms in many organizations do not, making it difficult to adopt this approach
Line of business (LOB). Provide funding for a LOB or division and let them fund teams accordingly [W].	• Provides significant flexibility to the LOB. • Still requires the LOB to fund teams in some manner.
Product (long-lived) team. The funding is for a team to develop multiple releases of the solution over time, potentially many years.	• Estimating costs for a product team is very easy (it's the number of people times our charge-out rate). • Works very well with modern, rolling-wave budgeting processes. • Out of sync with the annual budgeting process in most traditional organizations.
Project team. The funding is for a team to	• Limits the scope and time frame for funding. • Fits in well with organizations still taking a project-based

212

develop a single release of the solution. Project-based funding is often, but not always, limited to a single fiscal year at most [W].	approach to solution delivery. • Estimating costs for a project team can be quite complicated due to the variable staffing needs throughout a project and the difficulty involved with predicting the schedule of a project.

Access Funds

There are various ways in which we can provide access to funds.

Options (Ordered)	Trade-Offs
IT funding pool. Funds are drawn as needed from an organizational budget (such as the IT or LOB budget). This is basically a "take what we need" approach.	• Works well for high-competition situations where time to market is critical. • Requires ongoing monitoring of how the funds are being invested. • Requires a high-trust environment.
Informal request. Straightforward and simple request for funds is submitted by the team. This request is often made via a presentation to our Finance team.	• Low overhead and potential to be fairly responsive; supports lean financial governance. • Does not provide the documentation, and the false sense of predictability that accompanies it, that traditional governance people often expect.
Formal request. Comprehensive request for funds, often requiring documented value assessment or cost/benefit calculations and a presentation to our Finance team.	• Fits with more formal or traditional approaches to financial governance. • High overhead, particularly for smaller efforts. • Provides a false sense of control or predictability.

SECTION 3: PRODUCING BUSINESS VALUE

The aim of Construction is to produce a minimal marketable release (MMR) of a consumable solution that is ready to be transitioned into production or the marketplace. This section is organized into the following chapters:

- **Chapter 15: Prove Architecture Early**. Show that the team's architectural strategy works in practice, evolving it as necessary, early in Construction to reduce overall technical risk.
- **Chapter 16: Address Changing Stakeholder Needs**. Act on stakeholder feedback to ensure that the team produces something that stakeholders desire.
- **Chapter 17: Produce a Potentially Consumable Solution**. Incrementally and collaboratively build or configure the solution.
- **Chapter 18: Improve Quality**. Improve overall quality by avoiding the injection of new technical debt and by paying down existing technical debt.
- **Chapter 19: Accelerate Value Delivery**. Ensure the quality of the solution being produced by following good software engineering practices.

15 PROVE ARCHITECTURE EARLY

The Prove Architecture Early process goal, shown in Figure 15.1, provides options for determining whether our architectural strategy is viable. There are several reasons why this goal is important:

1. **Reduces technical risk**. There is a big difference between thinking that our architecture works and knowing that it does. This is particularly important when we are making significant architectural decisions, typically during the first release of a solution or when we are reworking or replacing important aspects of an existing solution. By addressing architecturally risky functionality early in the lifecycle, we reduce the overall risk profile of our endeavor. Figure 15.2 shows the risk profile of a typical DAD team following one of the project-based lifecycles (the Agile lifecycle based on Scrum or the Lean lifecycle based on Kanban, see Chapter 6). It shows how the risk on a DAD team drops substantially early in Construction due to proving the architecture (ideally with working code). Figure 15.3 compares the risk profiles of the DAD, Scrum, and Traditional lifecycles.

> **Key Points in this Chapter**
> - Building a "walking skeleton" of a solution by prioritizing architecturally risky functionality and implementing it first will pay down most, if not all, of the technical risk faced by a team.
> - Reviewing architecture models or documents is an ineffective strategy for mitigating architectural risk.

2. **Increases the chance the team is aligned**. By proving that the architecture works in practice we will remove many, if not all, of the doubts that people may have about our strategy.

3. **Supports appropriate governance**. As you can see in Figure 15.2, there is an explicit Proven Architecture milestone built into DAD – as you learned in Chapter 6, risk-based milestones are an important part of DAD's lean governance strategy.

4. **Reduces political risk**. When a team is perceived as low risk, particularly when we've taken concrete steps to address the risks that we face, an interesting side effect is that it makes it difficult for any detractors to attack the work that we're doing. In short, we're not an easy target for them.

217

Figure 15.1. The goal diagram for Prove Architecture Early.

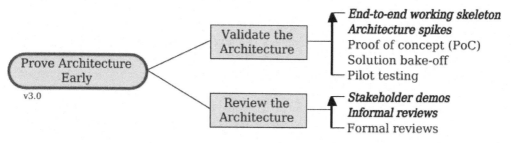

Figure 15.2. DAD's risk-value lifecycle.

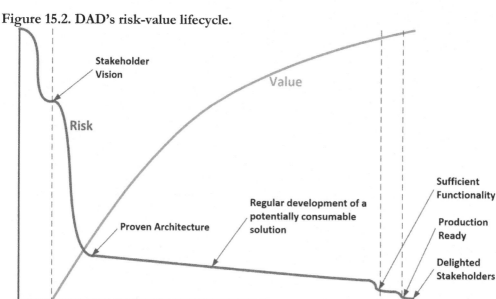

Figure 15.3. Comparing the risk profiles of different lifecycles.

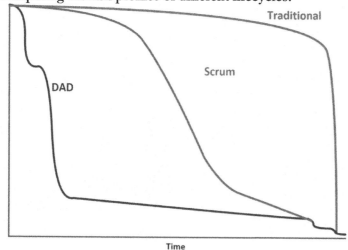

To prove the architecture early in the lifecycle we may need to address two important questions:

- How can we concretely validate that our architecture works?
- Do we need to review our strategy with key stakeholders?

Validate the Architecture

The only way that we can be sure that our architecture strategy truly meets our stakeholders' needs is to have working code that addresses the architecturally risky aspects. This decision point focuses on a collection of pragmatic, concrete strategies to prove our architecture via running code. As you can see in the following table we have several options for doing so.

Options (Ordered)	Trade-Offs
End-to-end working skeleton. Implement high-risk business functionality that stresses the architecturally significant aspects of our solution [Kruchten]. This is sometimes called a "walking skeleton."	• Requires the team to have an understanding of the target architecture and the quality requirements for their solution. • This strategy (dis)proves your architectural strategy early in Construction. • The team, often led by the architecture owner (AO), needs to be able to justify to the product owner (PO) that the architecturally risky functionality should be implemented first. • Easy to accomplish because all it requires is the reprioritization of a few functional requirements. • This works very well with an "integration tests first" testing strategy (see the _Accelerate Value Delivery_ process goal in Chapter 19). • Architecturally risky functionality may be difficult to implement, competing with the strategy of implementing a few easy requirements early in the lifecycle to give the team some quick wins.
Architecture spikes. One or more people on the team write quick prototyping code to explore a new technology or combination of technologies [Beck]. Sort of a "mini-PoC."	• Explores a targeted technical issue. • Teams are tempted to keep the (low-quality) code. • Inexpensive, but still requires an explicit decision. • This is a just-in-time (JIT) strategy that can be applied at any point in the lifecycle.
Proof-of-concept (PoC). An architecturally significant component – often a commercial package, a framework, or platform – is implemented within our existing environment to determine how well it works in practice [W].	• Explores a large technical issue, often the integration of a package into your environment. • Typically an Inception phase, or even pre-Inception, strategy. • May require specific funding for a "mini-project" as it can be expensive and time consuming. • In some cases the decision to move forward with the component is pre-determined by senior management and the PoC is run to make it appear that you're following "the process."

Solution bake-off. The team runs multiple PoCs in parallel to hopefully identify the best strategy available.	• Increases the chance that you identify the best solution early on. • Often reveals that every option has trade-offs and may not result in a clear "winner." • Often requires a mini-project for funding. • Typically an Inception phase, or even pre-Inception strategy. • Very expensive. • In some cases the winner is pre-determined by senior management.
Pilot test the solution. The actual solution is deployed into production for a small group of end users. Sometimes called alpha-testing or beta-testing [W].	• Typically requires significant development to get to the point of having a deployable solution. • Typically a late Construction strategy, with the potential that any identified changes will be expensive to address.

Review the Architecture

It is also possible to reduce some of your risk via reviewing your architectural strategy. These strategies are less concrete, and as a result less effective, than the strategies for validating our architectural strategy presented above.

Options (Ordered)	Trade-Offs
Stakeholder demos. Demonstrate the working solution to "architecturally savvy" stakeholders.	• Basically a normal demo, but with stakeholders who have an architectural background. • A good way to get feedback about the user experience (UX) aspects of the architecture. • Not sufficient for reviewing non-visible aspects of the architecture.
Informal reviews. A walkthrough of the team's architecture artifacts. This can be as simple as a "wall walk" of your architecture sketches or a summary presentation.	• Straightforward, inexpensive and quick. • Can be performed in an impromptu manner for quick feedback, although when scheduling of reviewers is required it has a medium-term feedback cycle.
Formal reviews. Architecture documents or models are developed by the team and shared with reviewers who are given time to read and prepare feedback to the team. This feedback may be provided in a variety of formats, but typically is given via a formal meeting of the reviewers with the team.	• The more comprehensive the artifacts the lower the chance that people will review them thoroughly. • Agile teams often create these documents only to pass through an organization's traditional governance strategy. • Burdensome, expensive, and time consuming. • This strategy typically has a long, multi-week feedback cycle, thereby increasing the average cost to address any identified issues.

220

16 ADDRESS CHANGING STAKEHOLDER NEEDS

The Address Changing Stakeholder Needs process goal, overviewed in Figure 16.1, provides options for DAD teams to react to changing needs effectively. Change happens. Sometimes a change is a completely new piece of work, sometimes it's a modification to work you haven't started yet, sometimes it's a modification to work you're currently doing, and sometimes it's a modification to work you've already delivered.

Of course, new information isn't always a requirement change. The reality is that as a team works on something the stakeholder's understanding, and in turn the team's understanding, of the true requirements will evolve and new or changed details will surface. In an effort to maintain a sustainable pace we have seen some "purist" Team Leads disallow new requirement details to be brought into an iteration to motivate Product Owners to do a better job of look-ahead modeling. In these situations they ask the PO to create a new work item and add it to the backlog to be estimated and prioritized for development in a future iteration. Obviously this doesn't help to build a good working relationship between the business and the delivery team. A better approach is for the team to expect details to emerge during the iteration, often via just in time (JIT) model storming or impromptu feedback sessions/demos, and ensure that they allocate a buffer as a contingency during their iteration planning session. When new information about an existing work item proves to be too large, at that point the team can ask the PO to introduce new work items. These decisions are described as options in the Accept Changes decision point.

> **Key Points in this Chapter**
> - A team will receive feedback on a regular basis that reflects the changing understanding of what stakeholders believe they need.
> - On many teams Product Owners are responsible for eliciting and prioritizing changing stakeholder needs, but there are other (and sometimes better) options to accomplish these things.

There are several reasons why this goal is important:

- **Teams do more than implement new requirements**. Yes, stakeholders need our team to implement the new requirements that they come up with. But they also need us to fix the defects that are found when using the solution, they need us to support other teams working in parallel to our own, they need us to learn and grow as professionals, and they need us to improve the quality of our implementations. The implication is that their needs will generate a range of work item types, or "classes of service." This includes, but is not limited to, new requirements, changed/evolved requirements, defect fixes, growing team members through training or education events, paying down technical debt, and running experiments.

- **Stakeholder needs will change**. There is a variety of reasons why stakeholder needs change, including gaining insight during a demo, your competitors releasing a competing offering that your stakeholders need to react to, technology changes, legislation changes, and many more good reasons. Jeff Patton has been known to say requirements change is not scope creep, but rather that our understanding of the true needs grows. Disciplined Agilists embrace the fact that change is natural.

- **The changes need to be managed**. Part of embracing change is managing those changes so that we react appropriately to them. Change is good and natural, but uncontrolled change is not. We need to exhibit some degree of discipline with regard to change so that we can meet the delivery expectations of your stakeholders. As always, the trick is to be as agile with requirements change as possible. As you

221

can see in Figure 16.1, teams often discover that there's a bit more to it than having a simplistic stack of requirements prioritized by business value.

Figure 16.1. The goal diagram for Address Changing Stakeholder Needs.

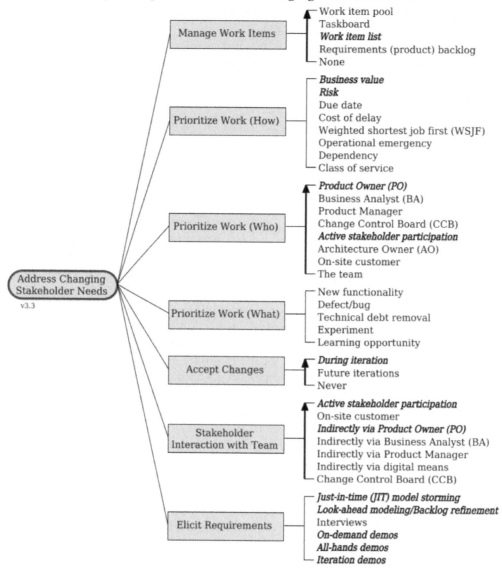

To be effective, we need to consider several important questions:
- How are we going to manage work items?
- How are we going to prioritize changes?
- Who will prioritize the changes?
- What types of changes need to be prioritized?
- When are we going to accept any changes?
- How will we work with stakeholders?
- How will our team elicit feedback from stakeholders?

222

Manage Work Items

There are several strategies for how our team may go about managing work items. These options are overviewed in Figure 16.2 and compared in the following table.

Figure 16.2. Strategies for managing work items.

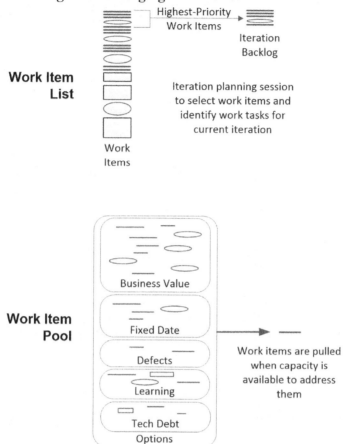

223

Options (Ordered)	Trade-Offs
Work item pool. One or more pools of work items grouped by class of service such as expedite, business value, fixed date, and intangible. Work is then pulled in a lean, just-in-time fashion based on highest priority at the time [Anderson].	• Best where priorities are changing continually. • Easily supports several prioritization schemes in parallel. • Harder to see the work as one stacked-rank list of priorities if there are multiple pools. • Requires discipline to pull new work fairly from the various categories – it's common to see one or more categories, such as paying down technical debt, starved in favor of implementing new functionality.
Task board. All work items are visually shown in one of the columns on a task board. The task board may be either manual (e.g. stickies on a whiteboard) or digital. Sometimes called a Scrum board or Kanban board [Anderson].	• All work, including both upcoming work and in progress work, is managed in one place. • Increases transparency for the stakeholders. • Works very well for teams working within short time frames (i.e. following one of the lean lifecycles or an agile team with a small backlog). • Works with both a work item pool and a work item list approach (as you see in Figure 16.2). • May be too detailed for prioritization by business stakeholders.
Work item list. Work items are managed as an ordered list/stack, including all types of work items (new requirements, defects, technical debt removal, …). Work at the top of the list should be captured in greater detail than work at the bottom of the list [ScrumGuide].	• Best suited where the team follows one of the DAD agile lifecycles. • Clearly indicates the order in which work will be performed, enabling effective prioritization discussions with stakeholders. • Supports the projection of cost and schedule estimates via techniques such as burndown or burnup charts.
Requirements (product) backlog. A unique, ranked, stack of work that needs to be implemented for the solution. Traditionally comprised of a list of requirements in Scrum, although now some "requirement-like" work such as fixing defects is also included.	• Clearly indicates the order in which work will be performed, enabling effective prioritization discussions with stakeholders. • Supports the projection of cost and schedule estimates via techniques such as burndown or burnup charts.
None. Work is not persisted anywhere for sharing purposes, i.e., no requirements are	• Useful only in straightforward situations where work and priorities are communicated in an extremely collaborative fashion such as a Product Owner pairing

documented, organized and managed. Requirements are typically communicated verbally or via temporary models.	with a developer full-time.

Prioritize Work (How)

Our work items need to be prioritized in some manner so that we implement the most important ones first. As you can see in the following table there are many strategies for prioritizing work items, strategies that can be combined as needed.

Options (Not Ordered)	Trade-Offs
Business value. The value to the organization is estimated, usually in terms of money or sometimes via points.	• Increases the chance that the team focuses on the most valuable work items, increasing ROI. • Often hard to define business value. • Not all stakeholders value the same things.
Risk. The risk profile of work items is identified so that riskier work is mitigated appropriately.	• Increases the chance that the team will succeed by mitigating risks early in the lifecycle. • People perceive risk differently. • Requires effective risk management strategy (see *Address Risk* in Chapter 25).
Due date. The delivery or completion date for some work items is mandated, either due to imposed regulations or promises made to stakeholders.	• Increases the chance that the team gets the work done on time (if the dates are reasonable). • Supports regulatory compliance. • May cause stress for the team if the dates are not reasonable.
Cost of delay. The opportunity costs of delaying the work, such as forgoing revenue or missing the market entirely, are identified. Cost of delay considers that implementing something now may provide significantly more value than if you wait for six months [W].	• Increases the chance that the team focuses on the most valuable work items, increasing ROI by capturing revenue that wouldn't have been realized if not implemented early enough. • Just like it's difficult to estimate value, it's even harder to estimate cost of delay.
Weighted shortest job first (WSJF). Work items vary in value and size, making them hard to compare. To normalize the estimates, divide the	• Increases the chance that the team maximizes overall ROI by focusing on the most valuable combination of work items. • Enables you to prioritize different work items fairly. • A "low hanging fruit" type of strategy to deliver high value to duration ratio work.

225

business value (hopefully taking into account the cost of delay) by the size/cost of implementation [W].	• Requires reasonably straightforward math (once you've calculated business value).
Operational emergency. The majority of teams are working on the new release of an existing solution, and as a result, they receive defect reports from end users. Some of these production issues need to be dealt with quickly.	• Ensures that the team addresses critical problems when they arise. • Challenging for iteration-based lifecycles since it can result in not meeting the team's iteration goals. • Works well for teams following Lean lifecycles. • Requires a consistent strategy for determining problem severity (see the *Operations* process blade [AmblerLines2017]).
Dependency. Sometimes one piece of functionality depends on the existence of other functionality. When A depends on B, you may want to prioritize the work so that B is implemented first.	• Potentially makes development easier by building functionality in a convenient order. • Risks building lower-value functionality earlier than other prioritization strategies would warrant. • Strive to minimize dependencies, especially on any work outside of the team. If possible, bring this external work into the team so that the team controls its destiny. • Reduces the need to mock out missing functionality.
Class of service. There are different categories of work, such as implementing new functionality, fixing defects, and so on. See Prioritize Work (What) below. With this strategy we set percentage goals for each of the major work item types to fairly address each category.	• Ensures that some classes of service, also called work item types, such as paying down technical debt or growing team members, don't get starved out. • Difficult to justify when there are time or cost pressures on the team. • Very appropriate for Lean lifecycle where work can be organized by class or type of work.

Prioritize Work (Who)

Work items should be prioritized by someone who understands and represents the needs of the stakeholders. Although most agile methods will prescribe that the Product Owner (PO) is responsible for this, a strategy first proposed by Scrum in the mid-1990s, as you can see in the following table there are several options available to you.

Options (Ordered)	Trade-Offs
Product Owner (PO). As we saw in Chapter 4, the PO is	• Clear who the team goes to for priorities. • Size/cost of the work item typically doesn't matter. • May not initially understand how to, or be willing to,

226

responsible for prioritizing the work for the team [ScrumGuide].	prioritize technical, team health, or solution health work items. • May need to work with senior stakeholders or a change control board (CCB) to prioritize critical/expensive work items. • Can be difficult to staff the PO role. • In many organizations the PO is not given the authority to prioritize work items and instead the team must rely on a Product Manager or senior business leader to do so.
Business Analyst (BA). At scale, either a team of teams situation or a team that is geographically distributed, a subteam may not have a dedicated PO and instead have a BA or junior PO to interact with. This strategy is promoted by LeSS.	• Similar issues to the PO approach, but BAs often aren't used to having the authority to make prioritization decisions. • BAs will often bring a disciplined approach to requirements elicitation. • BAs will often bring a documentation-heavy approach to requirements capture.
Product Manager. A Product Manager is responsible for the long-term vision of an overall product/solution, the marketing of the solution, and potentially sales.	• Product Managers are typically adept at prioritization of high-level outcomes or features for a product, but may not be experienced working with detailed requirements. • Increases the chance that tactical prioritizations will reflect the overall vision for the product. • Product Managers are often not available to make the tactical, day-to-day decisions required by a team. Product management is already a challenging job, adding this responsibility may not be realistic.
Change Control Board (CCB). A CCB is a group of people who meet regularly, typically at least once a month although as often as weekly is common, who are responsible for prioritizing changes to a solution [W].	• Clear who the team goes to for priorities. • Often a bottleneck because the team needs to wait for the CCB to decide. This in turn introduces delay (waste) in the process. • May not be willing to prioritize "small" work items. • Often focuses on business-oriented changes
Active stakeholder participation. The team works directly with stakeholders on a daily basis, and the stakeholders are	• Not clear which stakeholder should prioritize. • Team often gets conflicting priorities when several stakeholders provide direction. • Some stakeholders may not have the authority to prioritize and will need to defer to someone more senior, slowing things down.

actively involved with decision making, modeling, and testing activities. Similar to on-site customer, albeit with a greater level of participation [AgileModeling].	• Stakeholders are often focused on their area and may not see the larger organizational picture.
Architecture Owner (AO). As we saw in Chapter 4, the AO is responsible for guiding a team in architecture decisions. Because this is often a senior person they may be able to prioritize the work as well.	• A valid option when nobody else is available to prioritize the work or for straightforward, technically oriented efforts such as infrastructure upgrades. • Clear who the team goes to for priorities. • The AO is likely to inappropriately focus on technical decisions, such as paying down technical debt or running experiments rather than implementing new functionality. • The AO likely doesn't have the authority to prioritize business functionality.
On-site customer. An Extreme Programming (XP) practice where the team is near-located with their customers, the XP term for stakeholders [Beck].	• Similar to active stakeholder participation, although the "customer" isn't as likely to be as willing to make the decisions. • Not clear who should prioritize when there are multiple customers/stakeholders. • Business stakeholders are often unaware of the IT and process implications and will struggle to prioritize the work as a result.
The team. The team prioritizes their work, typically lead by the Team Lead or AO.	• Works in situations like startups where the team collectively has the vision for the product. In some product companies, we have seen that the development team has a better understanding of the change requirements than users or other stakeholders. • Often a strategy of last resort when stakeholders are unable or unwilling to work with the team. Very likely an indication that you shouldn't be building this solution at this time if you can't get stakeholders involvement. • Often leads to gold plating, the addition of "cool features" identified by team members. • Often leads to too much focus on technical work items. • The team may appear out of control to senior leaders, and it very often is.

Prioritize Work (What)

There are several reasons, or considerations, that may need to be taken into account when prioritizing work items. These considerations, which align with work item types or classes of service, must be balanced by whomever is responsible for prioritizing the work.

Options (Not Ordered)	Trade-Offs
New functionality. A new requirement, often captured (at a high level) as a user story, epic, or other form of usage requirement.	• Supports the vision, or the day-to-day work, of stakeholders. • Teams new to agile can make the mistake of believing they only need to implement new functionality. • Some POs new to the role may choose to prioritize new functionality over other types of work items, effectively starving out the other work.
Defect/bug. A perceived inadequacy or improper implementation of existing functionality, typically identified by someone outside of the development team such as an independent tester or end user.	• Supports addressing existing end users' perceived or actual issues with the existing solution. • Defects are often perceived to be the team's fault, which can complicate the issue of how the work is paid for in a contracting situation.
Technical debt removal. An explicit decision to improve the quality of an existing asset.	• Supports all stakeholders in the long run in that it increases the quality and evolvability of the solution, thereby reducing cost and time to market. • Often not related to implementing new functionality, so can be seen by stakeholders as a waste.
Experiment. A decision to try something to discover how well it works within your current environment. Experiments may focus on new or different functionality, or on potential process or organizational improvements.	• Reduces overall risk. • Supports continuous improvement, and better yet guided continuous improvement (GCI) (see Chapter 1). • Often not related to implementing new functionality, so can be seen by stakeholders as a waste. • Enables team to learn how well something works in our environment.
Learning opportunity. Work is prioritized to provide learning experiences, such as "hackathons" or training, for one or more team members. This may also include prioritizing "easy" work to give the team an opportunity to learn how to work together effectively.	• Can help the team to gel. • Can be used to give team a chance to learn how to work together. • Training and other forms of education often come out of a different budget, complicating the prioritization process because the person(s) who should do the prioritization may not own the budget. • When it's not directly related to implementing new functionality it can be seen by stakeholders as a waste.

Accept Changes

When it comes to actual changes the question is: when should we do the work? Scrum used to discourage change during an iteration/sprint since the team has committed to the delivery of a set of work items based on agreed upon acceptance criteria at the iteration planning session. In 2012 this changed and the people behind the Scrum method accepted that sometimes change is so common that we should consider accepting new work into the current iteration, a strategy that was the norm in the Extreme Programming (XP) and Unified Process (UP) methods since the late 1990s. DAD, as you can see in the following table, has always supported both approaches.

Having said all this, this decision point typically only applies to teams following one of the Agile, iteration-based lifecycles due to the small-batch nature of that approach. When following one of the Lean lifecycles, priorities can change at any time. This only impacts the team if they are asked to pause work in progress in favor of a new work item (such as addressing a severity one production defect).

Options (Ordered)	Trade-Offs
During iteration. The team accepts new work during the current iteration.	• Enables the team to respond immediately to critical changes. • Can require the team to work overtime if they have not been allowed to move an equivalent (or greater) amount of work to a future iteration.
Future iterations. The team defers any new work to future iterations.	• Enables the team to respond to changing stakeholder needs. • Can result in schedule slippage and changes to release plans if substantial changes occur.
Never. Scope is locked down and change is not allowed without formal change management procedures.	• Supports, or more accurately motivated by, cost-driven funding strategies. • Supports schedule-driven or cost-driven plans. • Increases the chance that what the team produces won't actually meet stakeholder needs.

Stakeholder Interaction with Team

We need to identify how we're going to work with our stakeholders to understand the changes that they're asking for. Figure 16.3 shows that the strategies where team members can interact directly with stakeholders tend to be more effective than the strategies where there is an intermediary, which in turn tend to work better than the documentation-based strategies. The following table overviews and compares the various strategies that our team can adopt to interact with stakeholders.

Figure 16.3. Comparing the effectiveness of communication strategies between people (from Media Richness Theory (MRT)).

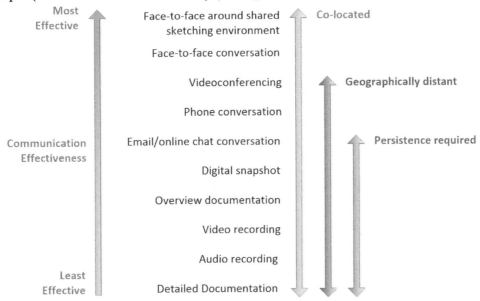

Options (Ordered)	Trade-Offs
Active stakeholder participation. Stakeholders work with the team and actively participate in modeling sessions, demos, testing, and other activities. An Agile Modeling practice that extends on-site customer.	• Quick and direct, get robust information quickly that the team can act on. • Stakeholders see the team acting on their input, increasing their confidence. • Team members need robust communication skills. • Some stakeholders do not have the time nor inclination to work directly with the team.
On-site customer. Stakeholders are readily available to discuss issues with team members, and are typically in the same building if not the same floor as the team. An	• Very similar to active stakeholder participation, albeit with less involvement of stakeholders. • Team members need robust communication and analysis skills to explore needs with stakeholders.

Extreme Programming (XP) practice.	
Indirectly via Product Owner (PO). The PO interacts directly with stakeholders, eliciting details from them, then communicates the stakeholder needs to the team. A Scrum practice.	<ul><li>Requires less communication skill of team members because they don't interact directly with stakeholders.</li><li>Can be difficult to secure someone from the business to staff the PO role.</li><li>The PO will interpret the stakeholder needs, effectively acting as a filter between the team and the stakeholders.</li><li>The PO acts as a communication conduit between the team and stakeholders, distilling the valuable information from the chaff/noise.</li></ul>
Indirectly via Business Analyst (BA). The BA interacts directly with stakeholders, eliciting details from them, then communicates the stakeholder needs to the team.	<ul><li>Very similar to PO strategy, but can lead to more documentation due to some BA cultures.</li><li>BA serves as a link to the PO, or as a junior PO, when stakeholders are geographically distributed from team.</li><li>Business analysts (BAs) often come from the business so may not have the best understanding of IT needs.</li><li>Business system analysts (BSAs) often report through IT so may not have the best understanding of the true business needs.</li></ul>
Indirectly via Product Manager. A Product Manager is responsible for the long-term vision of an overall product/solution, the marketing of the solution, and potentially sales.	<ul><li>Very similar to the PO strategy.</li><li>Product Managers are already very busy people, asking them to also perform requirements elicitation may not be realistic.</li><li>Appropriate strategy for a small organization or for a start-up project.</li></ul>
Indirectly via digital means. Stakeholder needs are communicated to the team via digital means such as online chat, "agile management" tools, or documents.	<ul><li>Supports stakeholders who are geographically distributed.</li><li>Greater chance of misunderstanding due to using less effective communication strategy.</li><li>Documentation can support regulatory compliance (if any).</li></ul>
Change control board (CCB). Stakeholder needs flow through a CCB to the team, often in combination with indirect means via a PO, BA, or digital tool [W].	<ul><li>Supports strict regulatory compliance strategies.</li><li>Suffers from issues around poor communication.</li><li>Adds another level of indirection between the team and stakeholders, increasing the chance of misunderstandings.</li><li>Slow, increasing cost of delay and waste due to waiting.</li><li>The CCB often becomes a bottleneck.</li><li>Expensive way to manage change.</li><li>Adds process complexity (and cost and time) because CCBs often require a triage process so that only critical changes are routed to the CCB.</li></ul>

Elicit Requirements

We need to choose how we're going to elicit requirements details from our stakeholders. The following table compares several common strategies for doing so, all of which can be done face-to-face (F2F) or in a distributed manner via digital tools. As always, we recommend F2F whenever possible (see Figure 16.3 above).

Options (Not Ordered)	Trade-Offs
Just-in-time (JIT) model storming. One or more people work with the stakeholders directly [AgileModeling].	• Direct, interactive way to explore requirements, increasing the chance they will be understood. • JIT increases efficiency by enabling the team to focus on what needs to be produced. • At least some team members need robust communication and analysis skills.
Look-ahead modeling/Backlog refinement. The PO/BA performs sufficient work to get the work item ready for implementation.	• Need easy access to stakeholders. • Works very well with an active stakeholder participation approach. • Ensures that work items conform to the Definition of Ready (DoR) [Rubin], the minimum criteria that a work item must meet before the team will work on it.
Interviews. Stakeholders are interviewed, typically by a PO or BA, to obtain details about work items.	• Enables stakeholders to focus small periods of time on supporting the team. • You will miss information, requiring you to go back to the stakeholders for more. • Harder to see the big picture. • Harder to negotiate conflicting priorities when you are working with stakeholders one-on-one.
On-demand demos. The current version of our solution is made available to stakeholders in a known and easy-to-access environment.	• Requires a working CI/CD pipeline to deliver changes to an accessible environment. • Increases transparency and potentially reduces the feedback cycle with stakeholders as they can view and test the solution at any time. • Enables stakeholders to see work in progress. • Helps to ensure that there are no unpleasant surprises at end-of-iteration demos.
All-hands demos. Show the solution to a wide range of stakeholders.	• We gain feedback from a wide range of people. • Great way to validate that your PO/BA/CCB represents the stakeholders well (or not). • Increases transparency, thereby reducing political risk (for successful demos).
Iteration demos. Show the solution, usually at the end of an iteration for agile teams, to a targeted group of stakeholders.	• The team gains feedback from subset of stakeholders interested in what you're building (assuming you invited the right ones). • Medium-length feedback cycle for agile teams (dependent on iteration length).

17 PRODUCE A POTENTIALLY CONSUMABLE SOLUTION

The Produce a Potentially Consumable Solution process goal is overviewed in Figure 17.1. Wait a minute, shouldn't we be talking about "potentially shippable software?" That's a good start, but in the enterprise space we need to do a lot better. It isn't enough to be potentially shippable; what our stakeholders want is something that is usable (it is easy to work with), that is desirable (they want to use it), and that is functional (it meets their needs). Furthermore, our stakeholders need solutions, not just software. Yes, software is part of the solution. But we may also be updating the hardware or platform that it runs on, writing supporting documentation, changing the business processes around the usage of the

> **Key Points in this Chapter**
> - The team will collaboratively produce the solution incrementally, seeking and acting on feedback as they do so.
> - The requirements, design, and plan will evolve over time based on your, and your stakeholders, changing understanding of what they want.

system, and even evolving the organization structure of the people using it. Working software is nice but a consumable (usable + desirable + functional) solution (software + hardware + documentation + process + organization structure) actually gets the job done.

There are several reasons why this process goal is important:

- **We need to incrementally produce a consumable solution.** One of the key agile principles is "Simplicity—the art of maximizing the amount of work not done—is essential." It is important to keep this in mind when choosing whether to work on an artifact and to what level of detail. Show your users a working solution as quickly as possible and at regular intervals. For agile teams this begins in the first iteration of Construction and continues for each subsequent iteration. For lean teams it may begin even sooner, perhaps just a few days into Construction. Stakeholders will soon tell us whether we are on the right track. Often they will tell us that we have missed the mark. This is a natural outcome. It is a good thing that we found this out early while we still have the opportunity to adapt our solution toward what they truly need and expect.

- **We want to explore requirements details at the last most responsible moment.** By doing so, we can focus on what our stakeholders actually need. The longer we wait to gather the details the more we'll know about the domain and therefore are able to ask more intelligent questions. Likewise, our stakeholders will have seen the solution developed over time so will be able to give us better answers. The bottom line is that by waiting we can focus and have better conversations.

- **We want to explore design details at the last most responsible moment.** Because we're exploring requirements just in time (JIT), we similarly evolve our design JIT.

- **We need to plan and coordinate our work.** Disciplined Agilists plan at the "long term" release level and the intermediate term iteration level (if they're following one of the agile lifecycles). We coordinate with other teams when it makes sense to do so and internally on at least a daily basis.

Figure 17.1. The goal diagram for Produce a Potentially Consumable Solution.

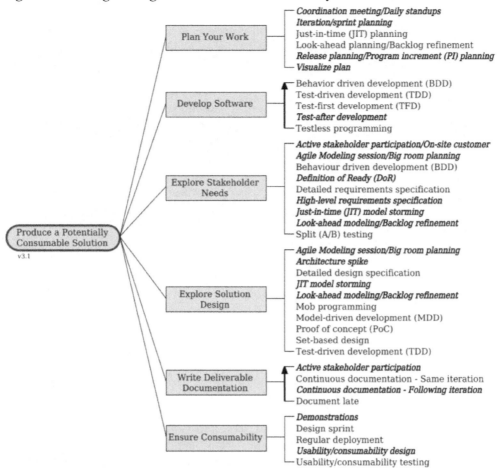

To be effective, we need to consider several important questions:

- How will we plan how we'll work together?
- What programming approach will we take?
- How will we explore the problem space?
- How will we architect and design the solution?
- How will we approach writing deliverable documentation?
- How will we ensure that our solution is consumable?

Plan The Work

As a team we need to plan what we are going to do and how we're going to do it. There are different ways that we can plan, different times that we can do it, and different scopes that we can address. Although planning can be hard, and plans often prove to be inaccurate in practice, the act of planning is quite valuable because we think through what we're doing before we do it. Here are several heuristics about planning that will help guide our decision making:

- It's easier to plan small things than large things.

236

- The people who are responsible for doing the work are more likely to produce a good plan than people who aren't.
- It's easier to plan work that you're just about to do compared with work in the future.
- People who have done similar work before are likely to produce a better plan than people who haven't.
- Multiple people are likely to produce a better plan than someone planning alone.

Several common planning options are compared in the table below. Coordination is highly related to planning, options for which are captured by the *Coordinate Activities* process goal (Chapter 23).

Options (Not Ordered)	Trade-Offs
Coordination meetings/Daily standups. The team gets together to quickly coordinate what we're doing for the day. These meetings typically take 10-15 minutes. The primary aim is to coordinate, although in many ways this is detailed planning. Also called a Scrum meeting, a Scrum, or a huddle [W].	• Keeps the team on track so that there are no surprises. • Enables the team to eliminate waste of waiting by identifying potential dependencies between the work of team members that day, thereby allowing us to organize accordingly. • People new to self-organization, or more accurately new to being a true team member, see this as a waste of time. • Coordination meetings quickly become overhead when performed poorly – your goal is to coordinate the work, not to do the work during the meeting. • Potential to become micro-management if the team doesn't actively focus on self-organization AND senior management actively chooses to allow that.
Iteration/sprint planning. The team performs detailed planning at the beginning of each iteration, identifying the work items that they intend to perform that iteration and the detailed tasks required to do so [Cohn].	• Identifies who will be doing what during the current iteration. • Increased acceptance by the team because it's their plan. • Often requires look-ahead planning and look-ahead modeling sessions to ensure that the work items are ready to be worked on. • Often seen as overhead by developers, particularly those new to self-organization.
Just-in-time (JIT) planning. Similar to iteration/sprint planning, except performed as needed and typically for smaller batches of work [Anderson].	• Identifies the work to be done and often who will be doing it. • Increased acceptance by the team because it's their plan. • A work item will need to be sufficiently explored, typically via Agile Modeling strategies, before the work to fulfill it can be planned.
Look-ahead planning/Backlog	• Identify potential dependencies between work

refinement. Detailed planning is performed for an upcoming work item, perhaps one that looks like it will be worked on within the next few weeks [AgileModeling].	items, which can be important information for prioritization of work. • Shortens iteration/sprint or JIT planning sessions. • Appropriate for complex work items, potentially leading to the work item being simplified or broken into smaller (and simpler) items. • Potential to be wasted effort if the work item is deprioritized or even removed from backlog/work item pool. • Enables teams to eliminate waste of waiting by identifying missing information or availability of people or resources. • Enables teams to eliminate waste by more efficiently negotiating scope through de-prioritization of less important work items.
Release planning/Program increment (PI) planning. Planning for the current/forthcoming release of a solution. Typically performed by the team with the participation of key stakeholders when appropriate. Release planning is the Extreme Programming (XP) version of the practice and PI planning the SAFe version [Beck, SAFe].	• Often includes modeling and other organizational tasks so it tends to become a mini-Inception phase in practice. • Particularly effective when the team and key stakeholders gather physically. • Enables the team to plan/coordinate their work for the next few weeks or months. • Requires facilitation and pre-planning to run successfully.
Visualize plan. The plan/schedule is captured, shared, and updated in a visual manner that is understandable by both team members and stakeholders. For a detailed plan, this is often a collection of stickies on a physical task board or a digital representation of such in a software-based "agile management" tool. For a high-level plan this is often a simple Gantt chart or PERT chart [Anderson].	• Increases transparency internally within team and externally with stakeholders. • Provides an easy mechanism for the team to update their release plan or iteration plan as needed. • Enables the team to know who is doing what, to look for and then address bottlenecks, to stay on track. • Requires the team to be sufficiently disciplined to update the plan or the information that goes into it.

Develop Software

We want to build our solution as a series of high-quality increments. As you see in the following table, there are several strategies to choose from as to how our team can approach development. It's important to notice that we distinguish between the concepts of programming and development (programming + testing).

Options (Ordered)	Trade-Offs
Behavior driven development (BDD). BDD is the combination of test-first development (see below), where you write acceptance tests, and refactoring. Also known as acceptance test-driven development (ATDD) or specification by example [ExecutableSpecs].	• The acceptance tests do double duty – because you write them before the code, the tests both specify the detailed requirements and validate that your solution conforms to them. • Refactoring reduces your velocity in the short term. • Refactoring increases velocity and evolvability in the long term by reducing technical debt. • Takes discipline to ensure tests are actually written before the code. Takes time, tests may have their own defects, or be poorly designed.
Test-driven development (TDD). TDD is the combination of test-first development (see below), where you write developer-unit tests, and refactoring [W].	• The unit tests do double duty (see BDD above). • TDD results in better code since it needs to conform to the design of the unit tests. • Gives greater confidence in the ability to change the system knowing that defects injected with new code will be caught. • Refactoring is a necessary discipline to ensure longevity of the application through managing technical debt.
Test-first development (TFD). Writing automated developer unit tests before the code that needs to pass the tests [W].	• Takes discipline and skill. • Many developers will not have a testing mindset so they may need training and opportunities to pair with people with testing skills. • Many existing legacy assets, including both systems and data sources, will not have a sufficient automated test suite in place. This is a form of technical debt that makes it difficult to adopt agile development strategies.
Test-after development. The developer writes a bit of code (perhaps up to a few hours) and then writes the tests to validate that code.	• Reduces the feedback cycle between injecting a defect into code and finding it. This in turn reduces the average cost of fixing defects. • A good first step towards TFD. • Teams often find reasons to not write tests, such as time pressures.
Test-less programming. The developer writes the code, often does some nominal testing,	• Leads to poor quality designs, which in turn are more difficult and expensive to evolve later. • Valid approach for prototyping code that will be

but then hands their work to someone else to do the "real testing."	discarded afterwards. • Valid for production code only if your stakeholders knowingly accept the consequences, perhaps because time to market is a greater consideration for them than quality and long-term evolvability.

Explore Stakeholder Needs

We want to explore our changing stakeholder needs throughout Construction, and this decision point captures techniques for doing the work of needs elicitation. We want to keep this effort as simple and collaborative as we can, doing just enough exploration to understand what we need to produce and no more. To do this we need to work with someone who understands the stakeholder needs, ideally stakeholders themselves and if not a surrogate such as a Product Owner (PO). Note that the *Address Changing Stakeholder Needs* process goal (Chapter 16) captures the details around organizing and managing evolving requirements.

Options (Not Ordered)	Trade-Offs
Active stakeholder participation/On-site customer. Stakeholders can be actively involved with requirements modeling when you adopt inclusive tools such as whiteboards and paper. Active stakeholder participation is Agile Modeling's extension to XP's On-site customer practice [AgileModeling].	• Opportunity to significantly improve the quality of the information because the stakeholders are the ones best suited to explore their needs. • Modeling enables people to think through the "big issues" that they face. • Difficult to convince stakeholders to be actively involved or even to be available to the team. • Best performed when several stakeholders are involved.
Agile Modeling session/Big room planning. Stakeholder needs are explored face-to-face (F2F) via Agile Modeling strategies. Key stakeholders and the team gather in a large modeling room that has lots of whiteboard space to work through the stakeholder needs. Several modeling rooms may be required for "breakouts" when large groups of people are involved. This is one of several aspects of "big room planning" in SAFe [AgileModeling, SAFe].	• Organizations new to agile often need to build one or more agile work spaces, and may have organizational challenges doing so. • Modeling enables people to think through the "big issues" that they face. • It is easy to measure the cost but difficult to measure the value of doing this. • Often need to fly key people in, and make them available for several days. • Requires facilitation and organization/planning beforehand to run a successful session.
Behavior driven development (BDD). Detailed stakeholder needs are captured in the form of executable specifications via	• Enables teams to capture stakeholders needs via automated tests in a "human readable" format. • Tests are very useful for thinking through, and capturing, detailed ideas.

240

acceptance test tools. The tests are written before the production code required to implement the functionality being tested. Also called acceptance test driven development (ATDD).	• Forces the stakeholders or product owner to clearly define how to validate that the solution meets their expectations. • With a BDD approach the acceptance tests do double duty as requirements. • A large number of automated tests may need to be maintained and updated as the solution evolves.
Definition of Ready (DoR). Our DoR defines the minimum criteria that a work item must meet before our team will work on it [Rubin].	• A DoR is a simple "quality gate" that protects the team from poorly formed work items. • A DoR provides transparency to stakeholders in that it communicates what the team requires from them to do their jobs. • DoRs can be difficult to meet when Product Owners are new to the job or are overwhelmed with work (the implication is that the team will need to help them). • DoRs can be an excuse for POs to produce artifacts instead of sitting down with the team and having a conversation.
Detailed requirements specification. Requirements are captured as static documentation, often using a word processor or Wiki. Requirement details may be captured at the beginning of the lifecycle or as needed throughout Construction. When the requirements are captured at the beginning of the lifecycle this approach is referred to as "big requirements up front (BRUF)" [AgileModeling].	• May be useful in contractual situations to create a requirements baseline for the solution. Of course, you would be better advised to adopt agile contracting strategies that don't require this. • Difficult to keep up to date as requirements continually change. • Duplication of requirements and test cases makes maintenance difficult. • It is very difficult to create accurate requirement documents before starting to build the solution. • Supports documentation-heavy interpretations of regulatory requirements. • This is often a symptom of teams working in mini-waterfalls, not in a truly iterative manner.
High-level requirements specification. Typically composed of several critical diagrams with concise descriptions of each. The aim is to present an overview of the requirements to provide context.	• Provides sufficient information to begin development of one or more work items. • Details are evolved during the iteration in parallel to the requirement being implemented. • When combined with a BDD/executable specification approach it supports regulatory compliance very well. • Some team members may be uncomfortable with lack of detail if they are used to coding from a detailed specification.
Just-in-time (JIT) model storming. Requirements are	• Enables us to focus on what needs to be built, and on most current needs.

241

explored as needed, often in an impromptu and simple manner – usually a team member asks the Product Owner (PO) or one or more stakeholders to explain what they need, and everyone gathers around a whiteboard or similar tool to share their ideas [AgileModeling].	<ul><li>Stakeholder needs are elicited at the last most responsible moment.</li><li>Modeling enables people to think through the "big issues" that they face.</li><li>Requires easy access to stakeholders or their proxies (such as POs or business analysts).</li></ul>
Look-ahead modeling/Backlog refinement. Performed for work items to be delivered in upcoming iterations to get them ready. Ideally we model at most one or two iterations ahead of time. The amount of modeling that we do is inversely proportional to how far ahead we model – the further ahead we look, the less detail we need right now. Look-ahead modeling is an Agile Modeling practice, and backlog refinement (formerly called backlog grooming) is the corresponding Scrum practice [AgileModeling, ScrumGuide].	<ul><li>Reduces the risk of being caught off guard by domain complexities.</li><li>Can improve effectiveness of upcoming iteration planning.</li><li>Modeling enables people to think through the "big issues" that they face.</li><li>Enables teams to eliminate the waste of waiting through identification of dependencies on other teams, new technologies, forthcoming information, and so on. The team can address the dependencies before the implementation work begins, or reprioritize the work accordingly.</li><li>Distracts team members from delivering work committments for the current iteration.</li><li>If the work item becomes a lower priority and is not implemented the modeling work becomes a waste. The further ahead you model the greater the risk that the requirements will change and your modeling will be for naught.</li></ul>
Split (A/B) testing. We produce two or more versions of a feature and put them into production in parallel, measuring pertinent usage statistics to determine which version is most effective. When a given user works with the system they are consistently presented with the same feature version each time, even though several versions exist. This is a traditional strategy from the 1980s, and maybe even farther back, popularized in the 2010s by Lean Start-Up.	<ul><li>Enables us to make fact-based decisions on actual end-user usage data regarding what version of a feature is most effective.</li><li>Supports a set-based design approach; see Explore Solution Design below.</li><li>Increases development costs because several versions of the same feature need to be implemented.</li><li>Prevents "analysis paralysis" by allowing us to concretely move on.</li><li>Requires technical infrastructure to direct specific users to the feature versions and to log feature usage.</li></ul>

Explore Solution Design

Because our stakeholder needs evolve over time our solution design must similarly evolve to address these new ideas. Our aim is to explore the design collaboratively in a manner that is as simple as we can make it while still being sufficient for our needs. The following table compares potential design strategies that Disciplined Agile teams should consider adopting.

Options (Not Ordered)	Trade-Offs
Agile Modeling session/Big room planning. Architectural issues, and sometimes design issues, are worked through face-to-face (F2F) via Agile Modeling strategies. See Explore Stakeholder Needs above for more information [AgileModeling, SAFe].	• Organizations new to agile often need to build one or more agile work spaces, and may have organizational challenges doing so. • It is easy to measure the cost, but difficult to measure the value, of doing this. • Often need to fly key people in, and make them available for several days. • Requires facilitation and organization/planning beforehand to run a successful session.
Architecture spike. Write a minimal amount of code to validate one or more technical approaches. Often used with set-based	• Reduces technical risk by quickly proving, or disproving, a specific aspect of the architecture. • It takes time and effort that instead could be invested in building new functionality. • Results in code that should be discarded but sometimes

243

design (see below) [Beck].	isn't for the sake of "saving time."
Detailed design specification. Designs are captured as static documentation, often using a word processor or Wiki. Details may be captured at the beginning of the lifecycle or as needed throughout Construction. When the design is captured at the beginning of the lifecycle this approach is referred to as "big design up front (BDUF)".	• Reduces the time required for iteration planning because it helps to get a work item ready to be worked on. • Useful in regulatory situations that require design specifications. • When performed as a hand-off between senior and junior team members the junior team members may become demotivated because they don't get to do the "fun design stuff." • Detailed design specifications and the actual code can easily get out of sync. • This can often be a symptom of a lack of collaboration or trust between team members. When team members are collaborating closely they don't need detailed specifications to drive their work. • Often a symptom of over specialization of some team members (in this case in modeling) which in turn leads to overhead and risk.
Just in time (JIT) model storming. JIT agile design modeling for a work item as it is about to be implemented [AgileModeling].	• Team members think through what they're about to build, streamlining the development process. • Modeling enables people to think through the "big issues" that they face. • Consistent with lean's principle of deferring commitment until the last moment, when the most up to date information about the requirements is known.
Look-ahead modeling/Backlog refinement. Team members, often led by the Architecture Owner (AO), model the design of upcoming, technically complex requirements. The amount of modeling that we do is inversely proportional to how far ahead we model – the further ahead we look, the less detail we need right now. See Explore Stakeholder Needs above for more information [AgileModeling, ScrumGuide].	• Allows teams to consider how designs need to evolve to meet upcoming requirements. • Reduces the risk of being caught off guard by technical complexities. • Modeling enables people to think through the "big issues" that they face. • Can improve effectiveness of upcoming iteration planning because team members investigate design alternatives before committing to an approach during iteration planning. • Enables teams to eliminate the waste of waiting through identification of dependencies on other teams, new technologies, forthcoming information, and so on. The team can address the dependencies before the implementation work begins, or reprioritize the work accordingly. • If the requirement becomes a lower priority and is not implemented, the modeling work becomes a waste. The further ahead you model the greater the risk that the requirements will change and your modeling work will be for naught.

	• Distracts team members from delivering work committments for the current iteration.
Mob programming. The whole team works on the same thing, at the same time, in the same space, and at the same computer. Everyone on the team will drive the keyboard at some point, rotating in for short periods (10-15 minutes) at a time [W].	• May be useful to ensure the quality of very technical, high-risk work. • Very useful for exploring a new technology or technique and then determining how to move forward with it (or not) as a team. • Useful for sharing knowledge within the team. • Very difficult to convince management that this is an efficient way to work (so don't ask for permission, experiment with the technique and discover how well it works in practice).
Model-driven development (MDD). Detailed visual models are created via sophisticated software-based modeling tools (formerly called Computer Aided Software Engineering (CASE) tools). Code is generated by the tool(s) and typically reverse-engineered so that the models stay in sync with the code. This is sometimes call Model Driven Architecture (MDA), a strategy promoted by the Object Management Group (OMG).	• Analysis and design models allow for portability by transforming code to multiple platforms. Visual models that are synchronized with code result in detailed system documentation. • Can be time consuming to perform detailed modeling. • Requires team members to have sophisticated modeling skills. • MDD is fairly common in embedded software development and systems engineering environments but not very common in IT environments.
Proof-of-concept (PoC). A technical prototype is developed over several days to several weeks to explore a new technology. Formal success criteria for the PoC should be developed before it begins.	• Reduces risk by exploring how a major technical feature, often an expensive software package or platform, works in practice within your environment. • PoCs can be large, expensive efforts that are sometimes run as a mini project. • Success criteria is often politically motivated and sometimes even oriented towards a pre-determined answer.
Set-based design. The team considers several design strategies concurrently, eliminating options over time until the most effective design	• Very appropriate for architecture-level design decisions and for high-risk detailed design decisions. • Enables the team to identify the most effective design strategy. • Split (A/B) testing (see Explore Stakeholder Needs above) can be used to explore the effectiveness of

remains [W].	design options in practice. • More expensive and time consuming than single-option design strategies.
Test-driven development (TDD). TDD is the combination of test-first development (TFD), where you write developer-unit tests before production code, and refactoring [W].	• TDD leads to higher-quality code. • Refactoring code as a matter of course throughout the Construction phase keeps technical debt manageable. • Tests are very useful for thinking through, and capturing, detailed ideas. • Requires skill and discipline on the part of team members. • Existing legacy code and data sources may not have existing regression test suites, requiring investment in them. • This can be a difficult, albeit incredibly valuable, practice to adopt.

Write Deliverable Documentation

An important part of our solution is deliverable documentation, the kind of documentation needed by our stakeholders to work with, operate, and sustain the solution. This may include system overview documentation, user guides/help, training manuals, and operations guidelines etc. There are several agile documentation strategies to keep in mind:

- **Invest in quality over documentation**. The better designed our solution is the easier it will be for stakeholders to understand it, and therefore generally less documentation will be required.
- **Work closely with stakeholders**. Figure 17.2 summarizes the CRUFT formula for calculating the effectiveness of a document, as a percentage. The only way we can write effective documentation is if we know what stakeholders actually need and how they will work with the deliverable documentation that we produce. Effective documents tend to be single purpose and targeted at a specific audience.
- **Write documentation that is just barely good enough (JBGE)**. When we do create documentation ii should be JBGE, or just barely sufficient, to fulfill the needs of our stakeholders and no more. Any investment in an artifact to make it more than good enough is a waste – keep your documentation concise.

Figure 17.2. The CRUFT formula.

Effectiveness of a document = C*R*U*F*T

Where:
  C = The percentage of the content that is correct
  R = The chance that the document will be read
  U = The chance that the document will be understood
  F = The chance that the advice will be followed
  T = The chance that the advice will be trusted

The following table compares several Agile Modeling practices that our team can adopt when writing documentation [AgileModeling].

Options (Ordered)	Trade-Offs
Active stakeholder participation. Stakeholders work with team member(s) who have technical writing skills to write "their" documentation.	• Difficult to convince stakeholders to be actively involved. • The act of writing will help stakeholders learn the details of the solution. • Significantly greater chance that the team will develop useful documentation for stakeholders.
Continuous documentation – same iteration. Deliverable documentation is evolved throughout the lifecycle. Updates to documentation are made in the same iteration as corresponding changes to other aspects of the solution.	• It is easier to write documentation when it is fresh in your mind. The effort to write documentation is spread throughout the project. • Ensures that your solution is up-to-date and potentially shippable at the end of the iteration. • Documentation update efforts during Transition are significantly reduced, if not eliminated. • Evolving requirements may motivate changes to previously written documentation, slowing us down (XP would say we're travelling heavy). • This approach is hard to make work in short iterations because the information to be documented may not stabilize in time for it to be documented that iteration.
Continuous documentation – Following iteration. Deliverable documentation is evolved throughout the lifecycle. Updates to documentation are made in the iteration following the corresponding changes to other aspects of the solution.	• Evolving requirements may motivate changes to previously written documentation. • This approach works well for short iterations. Our solution is in effect not consumable until the documentation is up to date, so with a short iteration we don't need to wait too long before the solution is "done." • Makes it very difficult to properly test the solution if it isn't yet "complete" at the end of the current iteration.
Document late. The creation of deliverable documentation is left until just before releasing the solution into production.	• Minimizes the overall effort to write the documentation because the information to be captured will have stabilized. • We run the risk of being unable to finish the documentation due to schedule pressures. • We may have forgotten important information from earlier in the project. • Increases the manual work during Transition, preventing us from automating Transition into an activity instead of a phase (see Chapter 6). • This approach effectively prevents us from fully adopting the practice of continuous delivery.

Ensure Consumability

Design thinking tells us that we need to ensure that our solution is consumable – that it is be functional, usable, and desirable. We will do this by applying a combination of user experience (UX) strategies in an agile manner and by reducing the feedback cycle with our stakeholders. Figure 17.3 shows the feedback cycle that we experience when working with stakeholders during Construction, and our aim should be to tighten the cycle however we can. The following table compares strategies that we could adopt.

Figure 17.3. The stakeholder feedback cycle.

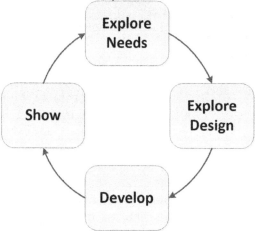

Options (Not Ordered)	Trade-Offs
Demonstrations. The team shows (demos) their working solution to a group of interested stakeholders. Demos can be run at any time on an impromptu basis or scheduled (perhaps at the end of an iteration). Demos may be focused on the interests of a small group of specific stakeholders or broad and presented for a wider, "all-hands", group. Demos may be face-to-face (F2F) or virtual/remote, and they may be scripted or ad-hoc.	• Concrete feedback provided to the team, particularly when stakeholders are invited to work with the solution during the demo. • Provides transparency to stakeholders. • Enables the team to discuss consumability issues with stakeholders throughout the lifecycle. • Stakeholders need to make time to attend the demo.
Design sprint. A multi-day Agile Modeling session typically focusing on UX (so it's really a narrowly focused, mini-Inception). Typically run before Inception (for ideation) or during Inception to focus on UX. Often includes usability/consumability	• Explore, and hopefully address, significant UX issues during Construction. • For many teams this is a step in the right direction towards agile design thinking. • Requires significant involvement of stakeholders over several days, which can be difficult to schedule.

248

design and testing [W].	<ul><li>Effectively "big UX design," running the risks associated with over modeling and committing to decisions too early.</li><li>Symptom that you didn't do Inception well enough.</li></ul>
Regular deployment. The team deploys their working solution on a regular basis into an internal environment(s), perhaps a testing or demo environment, and better yet, into production. This deployment occurs at least once an iteration, although at least daily/nightly is preferred, and better yet, several times a day via a continuous delivery (CD) strategy.	<ul><li>Reduces the feedback cycle by making the solution available to others more often.</li><li>Provides opportunities for the team to streamline and potentially fully automate the deployment process.</li><li>Supports strategies such as parallel independent testing and demonstrations.</li><li>Initially adds overhead to the team to do the deployment work.</li></ul>
Usability/consumability design. The user interface (UI) of the solution is designed taking the user experience into account. This is a UX/design practice, albeit one that you want to keep as agile as possible [W].	<ul><li>Increases the chance that you will build a usable and desirable solution.</li><li>Requires significant stakeholder involvement, on an ongoing and regular basis if you're really taking an agile approach to your UX efforts, which can be difficult to get.</li><li>Usability design, and design thinking in general, is a sophisticated skill that can be difficult to find.</li></ul>
Usability/consumability testing. The usability of the solution's UI is validated, often through observing potential users working with the solution to perform common tasks. This is a UX practice, albeit one that you want to keep as agile as possible [W].	<ul><li>Verifies that you have built a usable and desirable solution.</li><li>Requires significant stakeholder involvement, on an ongoing and regular basis if you're really taking an agile approach to your UX efforts, which can be difficult to get.</li><li>Usability testing is a sophisticated skill that can be difficult to find.</li></ul>

18 IMPROVE QUALITY

The Improve Quality process goal, depicted in Figure 18.1, shows strategies for addressing the technical debt and related quality issues faced by a Disciplined Agile Delivery (DAD) team. The focus of this goal is to capture specific techniques, rather than general strategies such as increasing collaboration, comprehensive testing, and reducing the feedback cycle. These general strategies pervade the rest of the book, for example the *Accelerate Value Delivery* process goal (Chapter 19) encompasses a large number of testing techniques and strategies, the *Produce a Potentially Consumable Solution* process goal (Chapter 17) addresses consumability techniques and executable specification strategies such as test-driven development (TDD) and behavior driven development (BDD) that reduce the feedback cycle a DAD team has with its stakeholders. Our point is that quality strategies pervade DAD.

> **Key Points in this Chapter**
> - Technical debt is slowly choking the life out of your organization, reducing your ability to respond to opportunities in the marketplace and increasing your cost of IT.
> - The easiest technical debt to pay down is the debt that you don't incur in the first place.
> - Consider paying down technical debt gradually over time, making it part of what you normally do as a matter of course.

To properly improve quality we must consider all aspects of our work, not just the source code that we write, and we must be enterprise aware in that we recognize quality goes beyond the confines of the solution that we're producing. This goal is important because it enables us to:

1. **Pay down technical debt**. Technical debt refers to the implied cost of future refactoring or rework to improve the quality of an asset to make it easy to maintain and extend. We want to pay down technical debt, in other words fix the quality problems within our assets, to enable us to evolve them safely and quickly. High-quality assets are easier and cheaper to work with than low-quality assets.

2. **Avoid new technical debt**. At a minimum we shouldn't make our organization's technical debt problem any worse than it already is. By being quality focused, by quickly addressing any quality problems that we do inject into our work (often via refactoring), we can avoid adding new technical debt.

3. **Work in a more enterprise aware manner**. Quality problems affect everyone – they affect our team's ability to evolve our solution to meet the changing needs of our stakeholders, they affect the user experience of our solution, and they reduce the value of our solution to our organization. By looking beyond code quality problems we increase the chance of addressing quality challenges that impact our stakeholders.

251

Figure 18.1. The process goal diagram for Improve Quality.

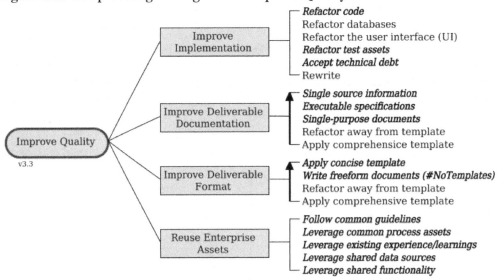

To improve the quality of our work we need to address four important questions:
- Can we improve the implementation of our solution?
- Can we improve our deliverable documentation?
- Can we improve the format of our (non-code) deliverables?
- Can we improve our solution quality by reusing existing assets?

Improve Implementation

A fundamental agile principle is for our team to maintain a sustainable pace that enables us to swiftly react to changing stakeholder needs (see Chapter 16). To do this our assets need to be of sufficiently high quality so that they are easily evolved. Therefore, we must develop high-quality assets and when we find technical debt in those assets we should address that debt appropriately. This can be difficult because technical debt can appear in multiple locations – in our code, in our data, and even in our user interfaces (UIs). Important questions that we need to ask ourselves are:
- Why does this technical debt exist?
- What can we learn from this debt so that we can avoid injecting similar technical debt in the future?
- How much of this debt do we need to pay down now and how much of this debt can we live with?

The following table compares several strategies for improving our implementation.

Options (Not Ordered)	Trade-Offs
Refactor code. A code refactoring is a simple change to the source code, such as renaming an operation or introducing a variable, that improves the quality without	• Pays down code-based technical debt safely in small increments. • Improves readability and maintainability of the code. • Developers need to understand and follow common code quality conventions so that they

252

changing the semantics of the code in a practical manner [Refactoring].	know what to refactor. • Developers on the team may not have the requisite skills and knowledge to pay down technical debt in the code, requiring coaching and potentially training.
Refactor databases. A database refactoring is a simple change to a database schema, such as renaming a column or adding a lookup table, that improves the quality without changing the semantics of the database in a practical manner [DBRefactoring].	• Pays down data technical debt safely in small increments. • Developers need to understand and follow data quality conventions. • Few developers have a data background, nor may they be sufficiently aware of enterprise data issues, risking inappropriate refactoring. • Requires long-term database refactoring process support, a Data Management activity, to remove the implementation scaffolding.
Refactor the user interface (UI). A UI refactoring is a simple change to the UI, such as aligning fields or applying a consistent font, that improves the quality without changing the functionality of the UI in a practical manner.	• Pays down UI-based technical debt safely in small increments. • Improves the usability/consumability of a solution. • Developers need to understand and follow UI quality conventions. • This requires participation of the Product Owner (PO), but they may not be aware of your organizational UI conventions or of user experience (UX) concerns. • Developers on the team may not have the requisite skills and knowledge to pay down UI technical debt, requiring coaching and potentially training in UI, UX, and design thinking.
Refactor test assets. The team improves the implementation of their test assets by replacing manual tests with automated tests, by migrating automated tests to the most appropriate place, and by automating other aspects of the testing process.	• Reduces the cost of regression testing. • Reduces the feedback cycle. • Automated regression test suites act as a safety check, increasing our ability to find injected defects when we make changes. • Reduces the delays associated with releasing into production. • Requires investment in paying down technical debt associated with testing.
Accept technical debt. The team makes a conscious decision to not remove technical debt at the current time, which as you can see in the technical debt quadrant of Figure 18.2 is a valid option. This is a decision that should be led by the Architecture Owner	• Increases speed to delivery in the short term at the cost of decreasing maintainability in the long term. • Agile purists may not accept this as a valid trade-off, leading to arguments within the team.

(AO) and confirmed by the PO.	
Rewrite. Technical debt is addressed in a large scale manner by redeveloping a large portion of a system (or even the entire system).	<ul><li>Pays down technical debt quickly in large increments.</li><li>In practice it's difficult to find a reasonably sized "asset" to rewrite due to high coupling with other assets.</li><li>Often needs to be treated as a project to obtain funding.</li><li>Tends to be risky due to the large change required.</li><li>Tends to be difficult to size and to cost due to unforeseen side-effects from coupling.</li></ul>

Figure 18.2. Martin Fowler's technical debt quadrant.

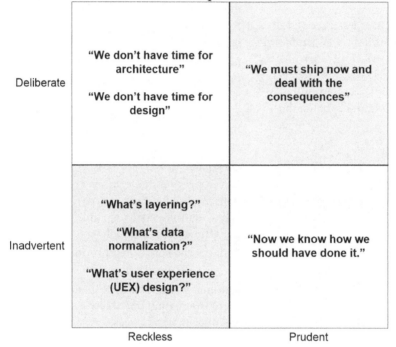

Improve Deliverable Documentation

Our documents, our "non-code assets," can also suffer from technical debt problems. Furthermore, you may find that the required documentation surrounding an existing system may not even exist yet and we may need to take responsibility for addressing that problem. The following table compares several strategies for potentially increasing the usefulness of the documents that we create.

Options (Ordered)	Trade-Offs
Single-source information. Information is captured in one place and one place only and then referenced as needed. This is effectively the normalization of documentation [AgileModeling].	• Difficult to do given disparate documentation and specification technologies. • Requires sophisticated tools and integration in some cases to produce consumable documentation from the information components. However, Wikis are a great tool for single-sourcing information because we can write a single wiki page for a cohesive piece of information and then reference it from a variety of places, even from outside of the Wiki tool. • Greatly increases accuracy and maintainability of documentation.
Executable specifications. Specifications are captured in the form of automated tests. Detailed requirements are captured via acceptance tests and detailed designs as developer tests [ExecutableSpecs].	• Requires team members to have automated testing skills, and better yet test-driven development (TDD) or behavior-driven development (BDD) skills. • Increased accuracy and value of the specifications because they also validate your implementation. • Specification documents, if needed, can be generated from the tests. This is an example of single-sourcing information or what Gojko Adzic calls "living documentation." • Team members are motivated to keep the specifications in sync with the implementation. • Legacy implementations will likely require investment in writing the missing automated tests.
Single-purpose documents. A document is written with a single purpose in mind, such as a user manual, a training manual, or an operations manual [AgileModeling].	• The resulting documents are easy to work with, increasing the consumability of the documentation. • Often results in several, smaller documents that need to be maintained. • Likely to have overlapping information between documents, making the information harder to keep in sync.
Multi-purpose documents. A document is written to serve several purposes. For example, a single document might be written so that it is used as a training manual, help manual, and a user reference guide [AgileModeling].	• Often results in a handful of large documents. • Less chance of overlapping information between documents. • People more likely to know where to go to for information because of the small number of documents. • Documents are less consumable and harder to maintain.

Improve Deliverable Format

We can potentially increase the readability and usability of our documentation through the effective application of common templates. The following table compares several strategies for improving the format of our deliverables.

Options (Ordered)	Trade-Offs
Apply concise template. The template contains the 20% of the fields that capture 80% of the information required. The additional 20% of the information is then captured as the team sees fit.	• Documents will vary between teams. • The majority of information is consistently captured between teams. • The team is prompted to capture the critical information. • Potential that some of the fields are not required, resulting in "not applicable" being filled in or worse yet unnecessary information filled in.
Write freeform documents (#NoTemplates). The team creates documentation using whatever style and approach that they believe is appropriate.	• Works very well for simple documents or for small organizations with few systems. • Becomes confusing at scale due to inconsistencies between teams, particularly for people who need to work with documentation produced by different teams. • Enables team to capture only the specific information required. • Can miss key information because there's no prompting from the template.
Refactor away from template. Remove or modify the fields of a comprehensive template to fit the needs of the team.	• Increases the consumability of the document as it avoids input in the inappropriate sections. • Focuses the document on the valuable information. • Decreases consistency between teams. • May motivate teams to refactor existing documentation that is currently based older versions of the template.
Apply comprehensive template. The template is designed to (try to) capture all possible information that may need to appear in the document.	• Likely to have many "not applicable" sections. • Onerous to fill out and review. • Often results in questionable documentation because teams feel the need to provide input into all sections of the template.

Reuse Enterprise Assets

A relatively easy strategy for improving the quality of our solution is to reuse existing, high-quality assets. Assets that are reused/leveraged by multiple solutions are tested more thoroughly, have often "stood the test of time," and tend to get the investment required to keep them of high quality. Reuse has the added benefit of shortening our development time and lowering our costs. The following table describes several strategies that our team can adopt to increase reuse, and the ongoing goal *Leverage and Enhance Existing Infrastructure* (Chapter 26 goes into greater detail).

Options (Not Ordered)	Trade-Offs
Follow common guidelines. The team adopts and follows common guidelines or standards. This includes coding conventions, data standards, security standards, UI standards, and more. These guidelines may be in the form of written documentation, configuration files (used by code or schema analysis tools), or via word of mouth.	• Results in increased quality of assets being developed. • Guidelines provide guardrails for teams and can act as enabling constraints. • Some team members, particularly the inexperienced ones, may not like being required to follow the guidelines. • When the guidelines do not yet exist, the team may be required to begin the creation of them, hopefully based on existing industry guidelines, slowing down development in the short term. • Existing guidelines may need to be updated, often by collaborating with the team responsible for them. • The team need to know about, and have access to, the guidelines.
Leverage common process assets. The team adopts, and tailors where necessary, existing process assets such as procedures, templates, lifecycles, governance conventions, or similar.	• Speeds up the team's learning by not requiring them to reinvent the process wheel. • Supports regulatory regimes that require a defined process. • When there are many teams in our organization, we will need a strategy in place to share common process elements (something covered in the Continuous Improvement process blade).
Leverage existing experience/learnings. Our organization has many knowledgeable and experienced people working here. We should take advantage of that and reach out to them for help and advice whenever appropriate, and to learn from them when they share their experiences with us.	• We can avoid common mistakes, and speed up our own improvement, by learning from others. • It is easy to fall into the "common best practices" trap where we assume that because something worked for another team it will work for us too. A better strategy is to experiment with the idea to see whether and how well it works in our situation. • See the *Evolve WoW* process goal (Chapter 24) and the *Continuous Improvement* process blade [AmblerLines2017]. • Requires humility on the part of the team to accept the idea that others have already worked through similar challenges that we currently face and therefore we can learn from them.

257

Leverage shared data sources. The team reuses existing data sources, including databases, data files, and configuration files (or other implementations) in the creation of the solution.	• Increases overall data quality across our organization. • Lowers the overall cost of development. • Team members need to know about and be able to access shared data sources. • Data quality problems will affect multiple systems (therefore refactor the data sources). • A strategy to evolve and support the shared data sources over time is required. • Requires common quality conventions across the organization. • Requires effective enterprise architecture (EA) and Data Management to be truly effective.
Leverage shared functionality. The team reuses existing functionality, such as web services, micro services, frameworks, or components (or other forms of implementation) in the creation of the solution.	• Increases overall quality across our organization. • Lowers the overall cost of development. • Shared functionality across solutions is easier to evolve because it is in one place. • A strategy to evolve and support the shared assets over time is required. • Requires common quality conventions across teams. • When shared functionality fails many systems could be affected. • Requires effective EA and Reuse Engineering efforts to be truly effective. • Team members need to be able to find the shared functionality.

19 ACCELERATE VALUE DELIVERY

The aim of the Accelerate Value Delivery process goal, formerly called Move Closer to a Deployable Release[7], is to optimize technical aspects of how our team works (interpersonal aspects are address by the *Coordinate Activities* process goal in Chapter 23). As a result, this process goal encompasses critical decision points around deployment, configuration management, and quality assurance (QA). The Accelerate Value Delivery goal is important because it enables us to:

- **Streamline deployment**. For our deployment efforts to be effective we must choose the best strategy that our team is capable of and actively plan our approach with applicable stakeholders such as operations engineers and release managers. We will need a strategy for how we release internally, such as into a demo environment or testing environment(s), and how we will release into production.

> **Key Points in this Chapter**
> - Teams actively streamline development through automation.
> - When deployment isn't (yet) fully automated then it will need to be planned for with appropriate stakeholders from operations.
> - Teams actively test their work throughout Construction, building quality into the entire lifecycle.

- **Support a DevOps strategy through streamlining and automation**. A key component of any DevOps strategy is automation of operational functionality to monitor and control running systems. In combination with automating your continuous integration (CI)/continuous deployment (CD) pipeline, this is often referred to as an "infrastructure as code" strategy.

- **Build quality activities into our process**. We want to build quality into our process from the very beginning of the lifecycle, including both validation and verification (V&V) strategies. Ideally we want to avoid injecting quality problems to begin with, typically through continuous collaboration, but failing that we want to find any potential defects as early as possible to reduce the average cost of fixing them. This is often referred to as a "shift left" strategy.

---

[7] Why the name change? The original name wasn't clear and quite frankly it was a mouthful.

Figure 19.1. The goal diagram for Accelerate Value Delivery.

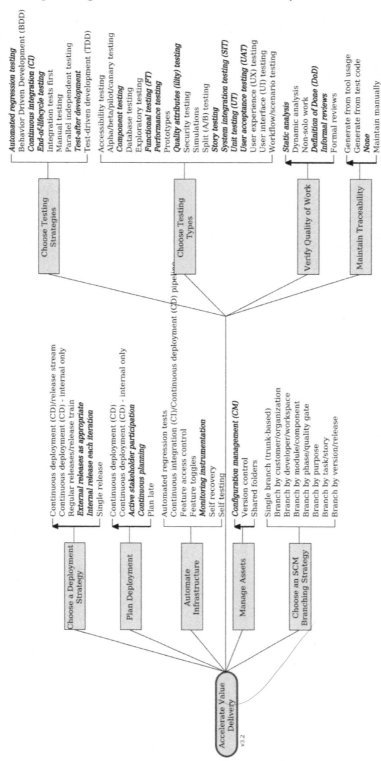

To be effective, we need to consider several important questions:
- How will we deploy our solution?
- How can we automate our technical infrastructure?
- How will we manage the assets that we produce?
- How will we manage the configuration of our assets?
- What strategies will we follow to validate our work?
- What types of testing will we need to perform?
- How will we assure stakeholders that the quality of our work is sufficient?
- How will we maintain traceability, if at all?

Choose a Deployment Strategy

We need to identify how often we intend to deploy our solution both internally (into demo or testing environments) and into production. Will we only deploy once? Will we deploy several times a day? Somewhere in between? Another key question we need to answer is how automated will our deployment be?

When it comes to the cadence of deployments we like to distinguish between three categories:
1. **Irregular deployment**. There is a long time between deployments, often weeks or months or even years. Deployments may be planned, perhaps to hit a fixed delivery date, or may be impromptu.
2. **Regular deployment**. There is a consistent cadence to when we deploy our solution. For example, we could choose to have nightly releases, weekly releases, bi-weekly releases, monthly releases, quarterly releases, and so on.
3. **Continuous deployment**. We deploy our solution, or at least portions of it, many times a day – if something builds successfully in one environment/sandbox then it is automatically deployed to the next environment.

Our aim is to reduce the feedback cycle between the team and our stakeholders to identify potential changes as soon as we can, thereby reducing the average cost to make those changes. Figure 19.2 depicts common deployment strategies mapped to Boehm's average cost of change curve – as you can see, the more often we release the lower the average cost to make a change and thereby the greater the likelihood that we'll be able to evolve our solution to meet the changing needs of our stakeholders.

Lean software development also provides significant insight into the importance of increasing the cadence of releases. A fundamental principle of lean is to reduce work in progress (WIP), and a key way to do that is to have smaller production releases. Reducing WIP increases quality, which in turn leads to reduced cost, both of which enable you to release faster – it is a virtuous improvement cycle. Reduced WIP also leads to reduced need for managing the work and for any re-planning due to changed stakeholders needs, resulting in less overhead and cost.

Figure 19.2. The average cost to make changes.

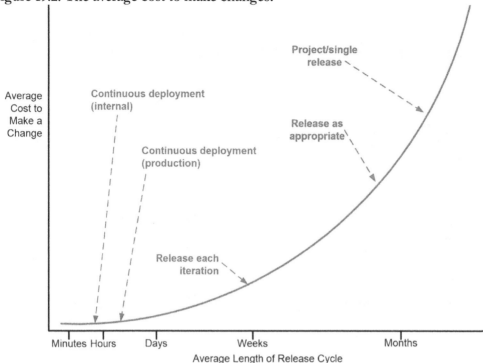

Options (Ordered)	Trade-Offs
Continuous deployment (CD)/release stream. The solution is automatically deployed through all internal testing environments and into production without human intervention.	• Low risk, inexpensive way to deploy into production. 14% of agile/lean teams report that they release into production whenever they want to and an additional 7% indicate that they release at least daily [SoftDev18]. • Requires a continuous integration (CI)/continuous deployment (CD) pipeline and, by implication, sophisticated automated regression testing. • Enables the team to receive continuous feedback from end users. • Enables us to potentially remove our internal demo environment (we can just use production for that). • This is a fundamental practice that enables team to adopt either one of the Continuous Delivery: Agile or Continuous Delivery: Lean lifecycles.
Continuous deployment (CD) – internal only. The solution is automatically deployed through all internal testing environments with human intervention but is NOT deployed automatically	• Requires a continuous integration (CI)/continuous deployment (CD) pipeline and, by implication, sophisticated automated regression testing. • Enables teams to streamline their (internal)

262

into production [W].	<ul><li>deployment processes, which in turn informs external deployment into production.</li><li>Enables teams to move towards adopting the CD practice. 32% of agile/lean teams report that they release internally whenever they want to and an additional 21% indicate that they release internally at least daily [SoftDev18].</li></ul>
Regular releases/release train. The solution is released on a regular schedule – i.e. quarterly, bi-monthly, monthly, bi-weekly – into production [W, SAFe].	<ul><li>Release schedule becomes predictable, thereby setting stakeholder expectations and making it easier for external teams to coordinate with our team.</li><li>Important step towards a continuous delivery (CD) approach, particularly when the releases are very regular (such as monthly or better).</li><li>The cycle time from idea to delivery into production may not be sufficient, particularly with longer release cycles (such as quarterly releases).</li></ul>
External release as appropriate. The solution is released manually (often by someone running one or more deployment scripts) into production at the behest of stakeholders. This may be an impromptu decision at the end of an iteration (i.e., an irregular deployment) or may be pre-planned (i.e., an irregular deployment with a fixed delivery date or a regular deployment, perhaps as quarterly).	<ul><li>Enables opportunities for regular feedback from end users.</li><li>Helps the team move closer to continuous deployment.</li><li>Changes identified by end users can be expensive (on average) to implement.</li><li>Requires regression testing infrastructure, some of which may still be manual (which is problematic).</li><li>Requires automation of deployment scripts for production releases.</li></ul>
Internal release as appropriate. The solution is manually released (often by someone running one or more scripts) into internal testing and demo environments. Often driven by desire for feedback, this is a form of irregular deployment.	<ul><li>Enables opportunities for regular feedback from internal stakeholders.</li><li>Helps the team move closer to continuous deployment (internal only).</li><li>Changes identified by end users can be expensive (on average) to implement.</li><li>Requires regression testing infrastructure, some of which may still be manual (which is problematic).</li><li>Requires automation of deployment scripts for production releases.</li></ul>
Single release. The solution is released into production a single release at a time, with following releases (if any) planned out as	<ul><li>This is a very risky way to release because the team will have no experience releasing this solution into production.</li><li>Changes identified by end users can be very</li></ul>

separate efforts. Often driven by promises to a customer, regulatory requirements, or a project mindset. Also called a project release, this is a form of irregular deployment.	expensive (on average) to implement, and with a project approach there may not even be budget to do so after the release. • Deployment often includes expensive and slow manual processes. • Appropriate for solutions that are truly one-release propositions, but they are few in practice.

Plan Deployment

We need to decide how we will go about planning how to deploy our solution. When will we plan? Who will be involved? Can we potentially automate away the need for deployment planning? In organizations with dozens, if not hundreds of delivery teams working in parallel, we will need to coordinate our deployment plan with any common *Release Management* strategies [AmblerLines2017].

Options (Ordered)	Trade-Offs
Continuous deployment (CD). The solution is automatically deployed through all internal testing environments and into production without human intervention [W].	• Effectively no planning is required because "the plan" is to allow the deployment scripts to run automatically. • Production releases are automatic and therefore predictable. • Requires sophisticated testing, continuous integration (CI), and continuous deployment (CD) infrastructure.
Continuous deployment (CD) – internal only. The solution is automatically deployed through all internal testing environments with human intervention but is NOT deployed automatically into production.	• Production releases still need to be planned. • Internal releases are automatic and therefore predictable. • Requires sophisticated testing, CI, and CD infrastructure.
Active stakeholder participation. The stakeholders who are affected by our deployment strategy work with our team in a "hands on" manner to plan the deployment. These stakeholders include Operations staff, Support staff, and Release Managers (if any exist in the organization). This planning typically occurs throughout the lifecycle [AgileModeling].	• Results in a high-quality, realistic plan because the people with the knowledge and skills participated. • Acceptance of the plan is very high. • Deployment stakeholders may not be available to the required extent (because they have their "real jobs" to do), or when their participation is most needed.
Continuous planning. Our team will work closely with deployment stakeholders for	• This is slow and potentially expensive due to the need for multiple reviews.

input into our plan, often via reviews.	• Significant potential for injecting wait time into our overall delivery efforts. • Results in a workable and acceptable plan.
Plan late. Deployment planning is left late in the lifecycle, typically the last few weeks of Construction or even early in Transition.	• Risky, may miss deployment windows because the team could miss a cut-off date through not getting into the release queue. • If mistakes have been made, such as missing a required task during development, they won't be found until late in the lifecycle when they are expensive to address. • Potential to lengthen Transition due to injecting wait time.

Automate Infrastructure

To make it easier to operate, monitor, and control our solution in production we want to build the appropriate scaffolding into our solution. By doing so we make the operations and support of our solution easier, thereby supporting our organization's overall DevOps strategy. This is often referred to as "infrastructure as code." This infrastructure should be architected into our solution, see *Identify Architecture Strategy* (Chapter 10) and *Produce a Potentially Consumable Solution* (Chapter 17), and it may even be possible to reuse existing infrastructure (see the *Leverage and Enhance Existing Infrastructure* process goal in Chapter 26).

Figure 19.3. The process of continuous integration.

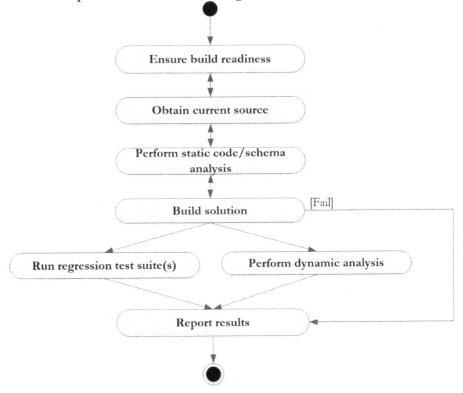

265

Figure 19.4. The process of continuous deployment (CD).

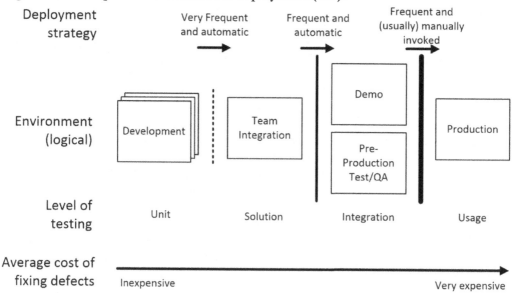

Options (Not Ordered)	Trade-Offs
Automated regression tests. Tests/checks are automated and run regularly by the team, often several times a day. There is typically one or more test suites developed for each environment in Figure 19.4 [W].	• Increases confidence within the team to make changes to their work because they know that mistakes are likely to be caught quickly. • Enables practices such as test-driven development (TDD), behavior driven development (BDD), and continuous integration (CI). • Requires skill and discipline to automate tests. • Very often legacy assets do not have sufficient tests (yet), requiring investment to pay down that technical debt.
Continuous integration (CI)/Continuous deployment (CD) pipeline. The combination, and integration, of CI and CD tools. CI tools automatically build, run regression tests, and run static/dynamic analysis tools (if any) when something is checked in (see Figure 19.3). CD tools automatically deploy updated assets to the next sandbox/environment when CI succeeds at the current level (see Figure 19.4) [W].	• The CI/CD pipeline automates a lot of onerous and repetitive work, thereby freeing developers to focus on adding value. • CI ensures that your quality checks, such as automated regression test suites and code/schema analysis tools, are invoked regularly. • CD ensures that your work is regularly pushed into more sophisticated environments and quality assurance strategies, enabling us to find potential problems quickly when they are less expensive (on average) to address. • Requires investment in CI/CD tools, configuration, and education.

Feature access control. The solution gives access to only the features and data that an end user is allowed to have – no more and no less. Access control is a fundamental security aspect [W].	• Enables granular and often real-time access control to functionality (sometimes called permissioning). • Supports experimentation strategies such as canary tests and split (A/B) tests by limiting end-user access to certain features.
Feature toggles. A feature toggle is effectively a software switch that allows you to turn features on (and off) when appropriate. Also called feature flags, feature bits, or feature flippers [W].	• A common strategy is to turn on a collection of related functionality that provide cohesive business value, often described by an epic or use case, all at once when end users are ready to accept it. • Supports turning off individual features when it's discovered that the feature isn't performing well (perhaps the new functionality isn't found to be useful by end users, perhaps it results in lower sales, and so on). This can alleviate the need to invest in backout and restore logic when we go to deploy. • Enables us to test and deploy functionality into production on an incremental basis.
Monitoring instrumentation. This includes logging and real-time alert functionality built into a solution. The purpose is to enable monitoring, in (near) real-time, of solutions operating in production [Kim].	• Enables people responsible for operating a solution to detect when a problem starts to occur before it becomes too serious. • Logging provides valuable intelligence for anyone debugging and fixing operational problems. • Supports real-time operations dashboards. • Enables canary tests and split tests as it provides the data required to determine the effectiveness of the functionality under test.
Self recovery. When a system runs into a problem it should do its best to automatically recover and continue on as before. Ideally end users never know that something was wrong.	• Provides a better/consistent experience to end users. • Reduces the operational burden on your organization. • Increases the reliability and availability of your solutions.
Self testing. Each component of a solution includes basic tests to validate that it can properly operate while in production. When a problem is detected it should be communicated via your monitoring instrumentation.	• Increases the robustness and reusability of your solutions. • Supports deployment testing efforts once a solution has been deployed into production (see the *Deploy the Solution* process goal of Chapter 21).

267

Manage Assets

Our team will need to manage the assets that we create – source code, tests, deliverable documentation, and so on – in some manner. The following table compares several common options available to us.

Options (Ordered)	Trade-Offs
Configuration management (CM). We track and control changes to our assets, with versioning and support for baselines across assets [W].	<ul><li>Requires some discipline and skill, and more importantly a shared understanding within the team as to how to use the CM tool consistently.</li><li>Can be difficult for non-technical stakeholders to understand (at first).</li><li>Enables us to improve the reliability of our assets.</li><li>Enables baselining of related groups of assets and restoration thereof.</li><li>Supports regulatory compliance.</li></ul>
Version control. We track and control changes to our assets, including versioning [W].	<ul><li>Requires some discipline and skill, including a shared understanding within the team to use the version control tool consistently.</li><li>Can be difficult for non-technical stakeholders to understand (at first).</li><li>Supports restoration and low-risk forms of regulatory compliance.</li></ul>
Shared folders. We maintain our assets in a collection of folders that are easily accessible by team members and potentially stakeholders.	<ul><li>Straightforward approach.</li><li>Very difficult to restore previous versions of artifacts without the use of tools that support versioning, such as Dropbox or Google Drive.</li><li>Does not support regulatory compliance.</li></ul>

Choose an SCM Branching Strategy

We need to identify our team's branching strategy for our source code repository. A branch is a copy or clone of all, or at least a portion of, the source code (and other assets that are used to build our solution) within the repository. We branch our code to support concurrent development, capture of solution configurations, multiple versions of a solution, and multiple production releases of a solution so that it may be worked on in parallel. When we branch we eventually need to integrate our changes back into the mainline branch/trunk – the longer we wait to do so, the greater the chance of a "collision/merge conflict" with changes made by someone else. A great resource is the book *Configuration Management Best Practices* by Bob Aiello and Leslie Sachs [CM]. As you can see in the following table there are many branching strategies available to us, strategies that may be applied in combination.

Options (Not Ordered)	Trade-Offs
Single branch (trunk based). As the name suggests there is only the mainline branch (the trunk).	<ul><li>Straightforward approach.</li><li>Well suited for DevOps-friendly strategies such as continuous delivery (CD) and feature toggles.</li><li>Merge conflicts are usually straightforward and</li></ul>

	easy to address.
Branch by customer/organization. A customized release created for a customer or organization. Standard features are developed on the mainline branch, while customer-specific features are maintained on their branches.	<ul><li>Short-term solution to delight a customer.</li><li>Supports customer-specific functionality that is more complex than what can be implemented via configuration data.</li><li>Requires a tenancy strategy that ensures privacy for each customer.</li><li>Potential to create a significant maintenance burden over time as the number of supported customer versions grows.</li><li>Defects need to be analyzed to determine if they pertain to standard functionality or customer-specific functionality.</li><li>Strategy needed to promote customer-specific features to become "standard product" features on the mainline branch.</li></ul>
Branch by developer/workspace. Developers have their own private branches to work on.	<ul><li>A promotion strategy, where you update ancestor/parent code versions, is required.</li><li>A rebasing strategy, how we update descendent/child code versions, is required.</li><li>Often used in combination with other branching strategies.</li><li>Enables experimentation by developers.</li><li>Enables review of changes in staging areas before they are promoted to the trunk.</li></ul>
Branch by module/component. A branch is created for a specific module (or cohesive functionality such as a component, subsystem, library, or service) of the larger solution. Effectively a single branch strategy for a module.	<ul><li>Enables parallel, component-based development teams.</li><li>Requires a clean architecture.</li><li>Requires system integration testing (SIT) across the modules to ensure the overall solution works together.</li></ul>
Branch by phase/quality gate. A branch is created for a specific project phase or approval stage. Sometimes called a "waterfall branching model."	<ul><li>Enables the team to continue working on new code while we wait for the previous version to be reviewed and approved.</li><li>Any changes required by the review will need to be implemented in the reviewed version of the code, reviewed again and, when accepted, merged into the mainline branch.</li><li>May be required under strict interpretations of regulatory compliance.</li></ul>
Branch by purpose. We only create a new branch when it is absolutely necessary – we must start work on a new version but still need to maintain the current	<ul><li>Supports baselining of previous versions/releases if required.</li><li>Works well when we have a single release of a solution that we wish to maintain, but still may</li></ul>

269

version.	need to temporarily branch for defect fixes or to temporarily support parallel development. • All development can occur via a single branch strategy when previous releases are not maintained.
Branch by task/story. A branch is created to work on a piece of functionality, perhaps described as a user story or usage scenario.	• Enables feature-based development teams. • Code needs to be merged back into the mainline branch. • Opportunity for significant collisions when features developed in parallel cause changes to the same code files.
Branch by version/release. A new branch is created for a release of a solution while maintenance of previous versions still occurs. Version/release branches are often created at the start of the Transition phase (if you still have one) so that developers can begin working on the next/upcoming release.	• Enables us to maintain multiple versions of your solution in production. • Requires serial changes to code, with sequential check ins/outs. • Adds overhead to maintenance of released versions due to need to make changes in the version branch and then promote to the trunk and any appropriate version/release branches.

Choose Testing Strategies

We need to validate that our work meets the needs of our stakeholders via testing against the needs of our stakeholders. The focus of this decision point is the overall approaches, or strategies, that we choose to follow to write the tests. As you can see in the following table we have many choices available to us to combine as appropriate.

Options (Not Ordered)	Trade-Offs
Automated regression testing. Tests/checks are automated and run regularly, potentially many times a day [W].	• Requires skill and investment to write automated tests. • Existing legacy assets may not have sufficient tests, a form of technical debt.
Behavior driven development (BDD). BDD is the combination of test-first development (see below), where we write acceptance tests before we write the production code, and refactoring. Basically a form of requirements-level functional testing. Also known as acceptance test-driven development (ATDD) [W].	• The acceptance tests do double duty – Because we write them before the code the tests both specify the detailed requirements and validate that our solution conforms to them. • Refactoring reduces our velocity in the short term. • Refactoring increases velocity and evolvability in the long term by reducing technical debt. • It takes discipline to ensure tests are actually written before the code. • It takes time to write the tests. • The tests themselves may have their own defects or be poorly designed, increasing technical debt.

Continuous integration (CI). Upon something being checked into configuration management (CM) control, the CI tool automatically rebuilds the solution by recompiling, running regression test suite(s), and running dynamic or static analysis tools. See Figure 19.3 for an overview of the CI process [W].	• Automates the onerous work involved with building our solution. • CI is a fundamental technical practice for agile teams. • Requires investment in setting up our CI strategy, in particular the development of automated regression tests. • Requires investment in training and team process improvement, particularly around adoption of agile quality practices and automated regression testing.
End-of-lifecycle testing. Any testing activities that occur during Transition or, if we have them, during "hardening sprints." Note that Transition is minimally "run our regression tests one more time and deploy if successful."	• When regression tests are fully automated then this proves to simply be one last check before deploying. • When significant testing and fixing occurs, it is an indication that we need to improve our approach to quality assurance earlier in the lifecycle. In other words, "shift testing left" in the lifecycle.
Integration tests first. We will focus our testing efforts by writing integration tests first.	• Motivates the team to think through, and show, how they are going to integrate their work, hopefully early in the lifecycle, thereby reducing overall technical risk. • Works well with a prove the architecture with working code strategy (see *Prove the Architecture Early* process goal in Chapter 15). • Requires the team to identify and agree to an initial architecture strategy early in the lifecycle (see Chapter 10) so that they know what needs to be integrated. • Requires integration test skills.
Manual testing. This is scripted testing based on the requirements for the solution.	• Very expensive and time-consuming form of testing. • Does not support agile/lean software development very well because it doesn't handle change easily. • Although manual testing can often be outsourced to people in low-cost countries, it often proves to be the most expensive approach to testing due to the overhead of producing detailed requirements documents from which to base the scripts.
Parallel independent testing. An independent test team works in parallel to the delivery team(s), see Figure 19.5, to perform testing activities that the development teams can't easily do. The delivery team(s) make	• Supports legal regulations that require some testing to be performed by someone who is independent of the development team, a separation of concerns (SoC) issue. • Enables organizations to support forms of testing that are not economically viable for development teams to perform. This includes system integration

their builds available to the parallel independent test team (PITT) on a regular basis (perhaps nightly or at least at the end of an iteration). The PITT takes these builds, integrates them into their test environment, tests them, and reports potential issues back to the delivery teams(s) [PIT].	testing (SIT) across a large program (a team of teams) or testing requiring highly skilled people or expensive tools (such as security testing). • Great way to identify problems that got past the team before the solution is shipped to production, offering the opportunity for the team to learn and improve their testing approach. • Potential for the delivery team to become sloppy regarding testing because they believe the PITT will find any problems. • Lengthens the time required for end-of-lifecycle testing because the PITT needs to take one last run at the solution, and maybe more if significant problems are found, before it can be shipped.
Test-after development. A developer writes a bit of code (perhaps up to a few hours) and then writes the tests to validate that code.	• Reduces the feedback cycle between injecting a defect into code and finding it. This in turn reduces the average cost of fixing defects. • A good first step towards TDD. • Teams often find reasons to not write tests, often due to time pressure. • Requires skill and discipline. • Many developers do not have a "testing mindset" so they need to work closely, often through pair programming, with people who do.
Test-driven development (TDD). TDD is the combination of test-first development (TFD), which is writing automated developer unit tests before the production code, and refactoring. Basically a form of design-level functional testing [W].	• The automated tests do double duty in that they both specify (because we write them before the production code) and validate. • TDD results in better code since it needs to conform to the design of the unit tests. • Gives greater confidence in the ability to change the system knowing that defects injected with new code will be caught. • Refactoring is a necessary discipline to ensure longevity of the application through managing technical debt.

Figure 19.5. Parallel independent testing.

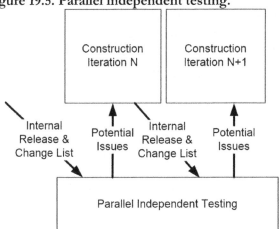

Whole-Team Testing
- Behavior driven development (BDD)
- Developer TDD
- Developer regression testing
- Other solution-focused testing

Independent Testing:
- Pre-production integration testing
- Other expensive/skillful testing

Choose Testing Types

An important question that we need to answer is what types of testing will we need to perform while building our solution. Figure 19.6 depicts the Test Automation pyramid and Figure 19.7 the Testing Quadrants [GregoryCrispin]. The test automation pyramid indicates the various levels of testing our team will need to consider. Exploratory testing is depicted as a cloud because it can occur at any time and any level. Note that some people consider exploratory testing, the act of probing a solution to see if it behaves in unexpected ways, to be the only true form of testing. When we are manually following a test script, or when we are running automated regression tests, then these "tests" are really checks that we run to ensure that the solution still works as expected. For the sake of simplicity, in Disciplined Agile (DA) we still refer to all of this work as testing (as opposed to testing and checking) .

Figure 19.6. The test automation pyramid.

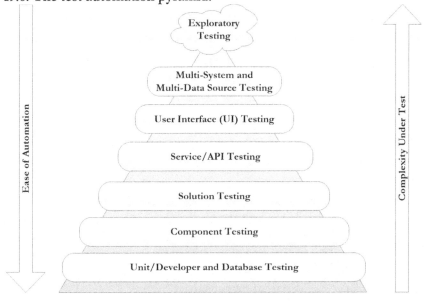

The agile testing quadrants of Figure 19.7, originally developed by Brian Marick, overview some potential types of testing that we should consider adopting within the team. The following table overviews and contrasts these strategies.

Figure 19.7. The agile testing quadrants.

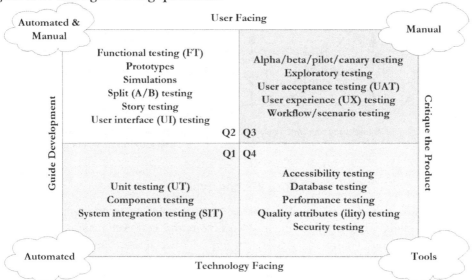

Options (Not Ordered)	Trade-Offs
Accessibility testing. A subset of user experience (UX) testing where the focus is on ensuring that people with accessibility challenges, such as color blindness, vision loss, hearing loss, or old age can still work with the solution effectively [W].	• Helps to ensure our solution addresses appropriate regulatory issues regarding accessibility. • Requires skills and knowledge around accessibility issues and design thinking. • Often requires collaboration with people who have accessibility challenges.
Alpha/beta/pilot/canary testing. Test in production with a subset of the overall user base. Alpha, beta, and pilot testing is typically a full release of the system to a subset of users. A canary test is typically a release of a small subset of functionality to a subset of users [W].	• Increases the chance you will build what stakeholders want by getting feedback based on actual usage. • Limits the impact of a poor release to just the subset of users. • Requires the solution be architected to limit access to a subset of users. • In case of alpha, beta, and pilot testing people will likely need to be informed that they are involved with such a release.
Component testing. Test a cohesive portion of the overall solution in isolation. A "component" may be a web service, a micro-service, a user	• Limits the scope of your testing effort, enabling you to focus on that specific functionality. • A form of functional testing that determines how well a component works in isolation.

274

interface (UI) component, a framework, a domain component, or a subsystem. In some ways this is a combination of unit testing and system integration testing where the component is simultaneously the unit and the system under test [W].	• Does not determine how well a component will work when integrated with the rest of the solution/environment.
Database testing. Databases are often used to implement critical business functionality and shared data assets and therefore need to be validated accordingly. Also called data testing [W].	• Ensures that data semantics are implemented consistently within a shared database. • Identifies potential problems with data sources before production usage. • Database tests are often written as part of application testing efforts, thereby increasing the chance that localized data rules are validated rather than organization-wide rules. • Automated regression test suites for the data source itself are required to ensure data consistency across systems. • Difficult to find people with database testing skills because few existing data professionals have database testing skills, and few application developers understand the nuances of databases.
Exploratory testing. An experimental approach to testing that is simultaneously learning, test design, and test execution [W].	• Finds potential issues that would otherwise have slipped into production, thereby reducing the overall cost of addressing the problem (see Figure 19.2 earlier). • Requires highly skilled testers who are good at exploring how something works. • Expensive form of testing that is mostly manual, but the learning part can often be the most efficient way to discover things quickly.
Functional testing (FT). Test the functionality of the solution as it has been defined by the stakeholders. This is a form of black-box testing. Sometimes called requirements testing, validation testing, or testing against the specification [W].	• Validates that what we've built meets the needs of our stakeholders as they've communicated them to us so far. • The requirements often change, implying that our automated functional tests will need to similarly evolve. • Behavior driven development (BDD) and test-driven development (TDD) strategies support FT very well.

275

Performance testing. Testing to determine the speed/throughput at which something runs, and more importantly where it breaks. This is a form of quality attribute (ility) testing. Sometimes called load or stress testing [W].	• It can demonstrate that our solution meets *performance* criteria. • It can compare two or more solutions to determine which performs better. • It can identify which components of the solution perform poorly under specific workloads, enabling us to identify areas that need to be refactored. • Performance testing is highly dependent upon the robustness of our test environment, the implication being that we may need to make significant investment to test properly. • Test results are short lived in that they are potentially affected by any change to the implementation of the system.
Prototypes. A prototype of the solution is developed so that potential end users may work with it to explore the design. The prototype typically simulates potential functionality.	• Enables the team to explore the user interface (UI) design without investing significant effort to build it. • Very effective when it isn't clear how to approach one or more aspects of the design. • Potential to reduce the feedback cycle by getting prototyped functionality into the hands of stakeholders quickly. • Requires investment in the development of "throw-away" prototype code, which can be seen as a waste.
Quality attributes (ility) testing. The validation of the solution against the quality requirements, also called quality of service (QoS) requirements or non-functional requirements (NFRs), for it. Figure 19.8 summarizes categories of potential quality requirements.	• Because quality requirements drive critical architecture strategies, this is a critical strategy to ensure that our solution's architecture meets the overall needs of our stakeholders. • Quality attributes apply across many functional requirements, making testing difficult. • Requires automated regression testing to ensure compliancy as the functionality evolves.
Security testing. Testing to determine if a solution protects functionality and data as intended. This includes confidentiality, authentication, authorization, availability, and non-repudiation. Security testing is a form of quality attribute (ility) testing [W].	• Helps to identify potential security holes in our solution. • Security testing is a sophisticated skill. • Commercial security testing tools are often expensive.
Simulations. Simulation	• Common approach when the component or

276

software, sometimes called large-scale mocks, is developed to simulate the behavior of an expensive or risky component of the solution [W].	system under test involves human safety, or when the component is not available (perhaps it is still under development), or when large amounts of money is involved (such as a financial trading system). • Enables the team to test aspects of their solution early in the lifecycle because they don't need to wait for access to the actual component that is being simulated. • Can be expensive to develop and maintain the simulator. • You're not testing against the real functionality. • The results from testing are only as good as the quality of the simulation.
Split (A/B) testing. We produce two or more versions of a feature and put them into production in parallel, measuring pertinent usage statistics to determine which version is most effective. When a given user works with the system they are consistently presented with the same feature version each time, even though several versions exist. This is a traditional strategy from the 1980s [W], and maybe even farther back, popularized in the 2010s by Lean Start-Up [Ries].	• Enables us to make fact-based decisions on actual end-user usage data regarding what version of a feature is most effective. • Supports a set-based design approach (see Explore Solution Design below). • Increases development costs because several versions of the same feature need to be implemented. • Prevents "analysis paralysis" by allowing us to concretely move on. • Requires technical infrastructure to direct specific users to the feature versions and to log feature usage.
Story testing. This is a form of functional testing (FT) where the functionality under test is described by a single user story. Can be thought of as a form of acceptance testing when a stakeholder representative, such as a product owner, performs it.	• Validates that we've implemented the story as required by our stakeholders. • The details of the story will evolve over time, implying that our automated tests will need to similarly evolve. • Danger that this is effectively component testing for a story – cross-story integration testing will need to still be performed, such as workflow/scenario testing.
System integration testing (SIT). Testing that is carried out across a complete system, the system typically being the solution that our team is currently working on [W}.	• Requires skill and knowledge on the part of the person(s) doing the testing. • Integration tests can be long running and often must be run in their own test suite. • Integration testing requires a sophisticated test environment that mimics production well.
Unit testing (UT). Testing of a	• Many developers still need to gain this skill (so

very small portion of functionality, typically a few lines of code and its associated data. Sometimes called developer testing, particularly in the scope of test-driven development (TDD) [W].	pair with testers). • Ensures that code conforms to its design and behaves as expected. • Limited in scope but critical, particularly for clear-box testing.
User acceptance testing (UAT). The solution is tested by its actual end users to determine whether it meets their actual needs (which may be different than what was originally asked for or specified). UAT should be a flow test performed by users [W].	• Provides valuable feedback based on actual usage of the solution. • Expensive because it is performed manually. • Very expensive form of regression testing (it's much better to automate regression tests). • Requires stakeholder participation, or at least stakeholder representatives such as product owners (POs). • Often repeats FT efforts, so potentially a source of process waste.
User experience (UX) testing. Testing where the focus is on determining how well users work with a solution, the intention being to find areas where usage can be improved. Sometimes called usability or consumability testing [W].	• Requires UX skills and knowledge that are difficult to gain. • May require significant investment in recording equipment and subsequent review of the recordings to identify exactly what people are doing. • Enables us to determine how the solution is used in practice, and more importantly where we need to improve the UX.
User interface (UI) testing. Testing via usage of the user interface. This can be performed either manually or digitally using UI-based testing tools. Sometimes called glass testing or screen testing [W].	• Straightforward step to move from manual testing to automated testing because the manual test scripts can be written as automated UI tests. • Expensive way to automate functional testing (FT), even given record/playback tools. • Tests prove to be very fragile in practice. • Difficult to maintain automated tests because the tests break whenever the user interface evolves.
Workflow/scenario testing. Testing where the focus is on determining how well a solution addresses a specific business workflow or usage scenario. A scenario is described to one or more end users and they are asked to work through that scenario using the solution. This is focused UX testing [W].	• We need to have an understanding of the overall workflow, which typically goes beyond stories and even epics. • See the tradeoffs associated with UX testing.

Figure 19.8. Potential categories of quality requirements.

- Accessibility
- Accuracy
- Availability
- Auditability
- Capacity
- Concurrency
- Consumability
- Customer experience
- Data integrity
- Deployability

- Environment (green)
- Exclusive access/locking
- Historical data tracking
- Internationalization
- Interoperability
- Maintainability
- Operability
- Performance
- Recoverability

- Regulatory
- Reliability
- Reusability
- Scalability
- Security
- Serviceability
- Supportability
- Timeliness
- Traceability
- Usability

Verify Quality of Work

We need to verify that our solution complies with appropriate regulations and organizational guidelines. This is important because this guidance motivates the team to produce better quality work. As you can see in the following table, this can occur manually via reviews and non-solo work strategies or in automated fashion via digital tools.

Options (Ordered)	Trade-Offs
Static analysis. A static analysis tool, sometimes called a static code analysis tool, parses the implementation code/definition without running it to look for potential problems. There are tools to perform static analysis of the user interface, source code, and database schemas [W].	• Provides valuable insight into where quality problems exist within our implementation. • Static analysis tools find most of the problems that would traditionally be found by reviews. • Can find an overwhelming number of problems in the beginning, which is a reflection of the amount of technical debt we face. • Outputs of these tools can be fed into our team dashboard to provide real-time quality information to the team and to whomever is governing us. • Requires us to configure the tool to reflect our organizational development guidelines.
Dynamic analysis. A dynamic analysis tool, sometimes called a dynamic program analysis tool, executes a working program to try to detect problems. There are tools to perform dynamic analysis of the user interface, source code, and database schemas [W].	• Provides valuable insight into potential quality problems with our solution. This includes security, performance, memory leaks, race conditions, and reliability problems. • Can find an overwhelming number of problems in the beginning, which is a reflection of the amount of technical debt we face. • Outputs of these tools can be fed into our team dashboard to provide real-time quality information to the team and to whomever is governing us. • Some dynamic analysis tools, particularly security-oriented ones, are expensive.

279

Non-solo work. This is a collection of collaborative techniques where two or more people work together to perform a task. These techniques include pair programming (two people working at one workstation) [W], mob programming (several people working together at a single workstation) [W], and modeling with others (mob modeling).	• Effectively a continuous review that happens in parallel to the work being performed. • Enables skill and knowledge sharing within the team. • Increases the chance that team members will understand and follow common development conventions. This is particularly true when promiscuous pairing or mobbing occurs.
Definition of Done (DoD). A DoD defines the minimum criteria that a work item must meet before our stakeholders will accept it as completed/done work. The DoD typically addresses levels of testing and required documentation [DoD].	• A DoD increases the trust of stakeholders in the ability of the team to deliver. • A DoD is a simple service level agreement (SLA) that ensures the team produces work that meets the needs of stakeholders. • DoDs become complex with practices such as Continuous Documentation – Following Iteration (see *Produce Potentially Consumable Solution* in Chapter 17) or parallel independent testing (see Choose Testing Strategies above) because some work isn't truly "done" by the end of the iteration.
Informal reviews. A strategy where one or more people provide feedback about an asset. The feedback is often verbal but may be written as well.	• Reviews can find qualitative problems that analysis tools often miss. • Informal reviews can be a valuable education opportunity as they provide opportunities for the team to share and discuss other ways of approaching a problem.
Formal reviews. A structured, and often heavy-weight strategy where one or more people provide feedback about an asset. Feedback is often captured in written form although can be verbal as well.	• Reviews can find qualitative problems that analysis tools often miss. • Supports regulatory compliance needs, particularly in life-critical situations. • Can be expensive and time consuming. • Formal reviews can be used for education purposes but are typically focused on finding potential problems.

Maintain Traceability

Traceability refers to the ability to track (trace) the relationships between a requirement/need, the aspects of our design/architecture that address the requirement, the implementation of the requirement, and the test(s) that validate it. There are several reasons why we should be interested in traceability, including compliance to external regulations and support for impact analysis. As the name implies, impact analysis is the act of determining how a potential change will affect, or impact, the existing solution and supporting artifacts.

Options (Ordered)	Trade-Offs
Generate from tools. Tools such as the Atlassian suite or Microsoft Team Foundation Server (TFS) provide automatic traceability for who, what, when, and where (and optionally why) any change is made to any artifact.	• As accurate as the work captured in the tools. • Traceability is in effect "built into," or is a side effect of, the process. It is effectively free. • May require sophisticated parsing when multiple tools, or instances of the same tool, are used. • This strategy can devolve into manual maintenance (see below) when the focus of creating the references shifts to traceability rather than simply getting the work done.
Generate from test code. When teams have comprehensive test suites the test code effectively contains the traceability information. Detailed requirements (captured as acceptance tests) and similarly your detailed design (captured as unit/developer tests) both invoke the code, therefore you have the heart of traceability.	• We still need a strategy to implement traceability from high-level artifacts such as user stories and architecture models. • Detailed traceability is in effect "built into," or is a side effect of, the process. This aspect of traceability is effectively free as a result. • Requires sophisticated parsing of test code, potentially from multiple sources (e.g., from BDD test tools, from xUnit, …) • Traceability is only as good as your test coverage.
None. The team decides to not maintain any form of traceability at all.	• Zero overhead. • Not regulatory compliant. • Impact analysis must be performed another way, such as through conversations or through making a change to see what breaks.
Maintain manually. The team maintains traceability links between artifacts, often within a separate tool such as a database, a spreadsheet, or traceability-specific tool such as IBM Rational DOORS Next Generation.	• This is a very expensive strategy due to the manual effort to develop and maintain the traceability information. • The resulting traceability information often proves to be inaccurate because the information isn't consistently updated in sync with changes to the artifacts. • Tends to slow development down with the work required to maintain traceability. Basically, the team is "travelling heavy" as Extreme Programming (XP) warns us.

SECTION 4: RELEASING INTO PRODUCTION

The aim of Transition is to successfully release a consumable solution into production or the marketplace. Ideally Transition is a fully automated activity that runs in minutes or hours, rather than a phase that takes days or weeks. The average agile/lean team spends 6 work days on Transition activities, but when you exclude the teams that have fully automated testing and deployment (which we wouldn't do) it's an average of 8.5 days [SoftDev18]. Furthermore, 26% of teams have fully automated regression testing and deployment and 63% perform Transition in one day or less. This section is organized into the following chapters:

- **Chapter 20: Ensure Production Readiness**. Verify that the solution is technically ready to ship and that stakeholders are willing to receive it.
- **Chapter 21: Deploy the Solution**. Deploy the solution into production, and verify that the deployment was successful.

20 ENSURE PRODUCTION READINESS

The aim of the Ensure Deployment Readiness process goal, shown in Figure 20.1, is to determine whether we can safely deploy our solution into production. In many ways this process goal is the embodiment of the *Production Ready* milestone depicted in Figure 20.2 and described in Chapter 6. Remember that Disciplined Agile Delivery (DAD) teams produce consumable solutions, not just "working software." Yes, working software is nice but a consumable (usable + desirable +

Key Point in this Chapter

- The solution/product should be technically ready to ship and the stakeholders should be ready to receive it.

---

functional) solution (software + hardware + documentation + process + organization structure) actually gets the job done. Although our team should have produced a potentially consumable solution all the way through Construction, this is our last chance to ensure the solution is in fact consumable before we deploy it to our stakeholders. This goal is important because it reduces the risks associated with deployment by ensuring that the team is technically ready to ship and that stakeholders are prepared to receive new functionality.

Figure 20.1. The process goal diagram for Ensure Production Readiness.

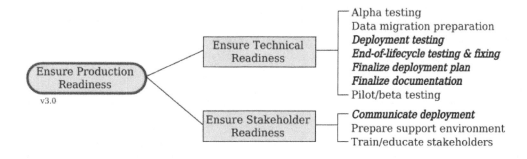

Figure 20.2. The DAD risk-based milestones.

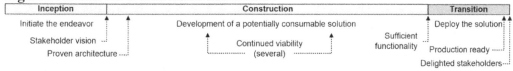

It's important to note that this goal reflects the realities faced by teams that are following the project-based lifecycles: the Scrum-based Agile lifecycle and Kanban-based Lean lifecycle. Teams following these lifecycles tend to release into production every few months (or more) and have not yet completely automated their regression tests nor adopted the continuous integration (CI)/continuous deployment (CD) pipeline required to evolve into one of the two continuous delivery lifecycles. When a team has successfully migrated to a continuous delivery lifecycle they will have either automated the activities encompassed by this goal or alleviated the need for them by taking the low-risk approach of more frequently deploying small changes into production.

When it comes to the cadence of deployments we like to distinguish between three categories:

1. **Irregular deployment**. There is a long time between deployments, often weeks or months or even years. Deployments may be planned, perhaps to meet a fixed delivery date, or may be impromptu.
2. **Regular deployment**. There is a consistent cadence to when we deploy our solution. For example, we could choose to have nightly releases, weekly releases, bi-weekly releases, monthly releases, quarterly releases, and so on.
3. **Continuous deployment**. We deploy our solution, or at least portions of it, many times a day – if something builds successfully in one environment/sandbox then it is automatically deployed to the next environment.

Ensure Technical Readiness

We need to ensure that we are technically ready to ship – that our solution is properly tested, the documentation is up to date, and that our deployment scripts are complete. The following table describes a collection of potential strategies or activities that our team may choose to follow.

Options (Not Ordered)	Trade-Offs
Alpha testing. Put out a limited/early version to a subset of users [W].	• It can be difficult to find end users willing to invest the effort in working with an alpha version of your product who will also actively provide feedback and even work with you to improve it. • If you have the right technical writer on the project, alpha testing is a good task for them. It gives a head start on the user manuals and can provide input for other deliverables. • People involved with alpha testing can be frustrated when functionality that they tested changes dramatically, or is removed, in the final release of the product. • Alpha testing takes time, at least days if not weeks, thereby increasing the length of transition. • Alpha testing can be performed in parallel to Construction if need be.
Data migration preparation. When new functionality is deployed there may be a need to deploy corresponding changes to data sources (these changes are often the result of database refactorings made during Construction). This is also called data conversion.	• Data test tools are often not in place, requiring manual testing in some cases. • Some data migrations are risky in that they are immutable and cannot be backed out. • Potential for significant overhead if traditional data techniques are still in place in the organization. It is possible, and highly desirable, to take an agile approach to data activities (see the *Data Management* process blade [AmblerLines2017]).
Deployment testing. We want to validate that our deployment	• Increases the chance of successful deployment.

286

scripts work as intended by testing them in our pre-production environments. Note that with continuous delivery (CD), or with regular internal releases, your scripts will already be well tested by now.	• Increases the cost and time required for Transition.
End-of-lifecycle testing & fixing. Minimally we need to run our automated regression test suite one more time. Furthermore, if we have a parallel independent test (PIT) effort then we need to wait for that testing to finish. If any serious issues are found, we will need to address/fix them before deployment.	• Ensures that our solution is of sufficient quality. • When user acceptance testing (UAT) and system integration testing (SIT) are left to the end of the lifecycle, instead of performed continuously throughout Construction, the Transition phase can take many weeks. • Takes time, and if serious problems are found can force us to extend or even postpone our deployment date.
Finalize deployment plan. If we have not yet finalized the deployment plan (which should have been developed during Construction) then we need to do so now. Note that with continuous deployment (CD), the plan simply becomes "we deploy upon a successful build."	• Helps us to gain agreement with key stakeholders as to how we're going to deploy. • Reduces risk through identification of the points in the deployment process where we need to make a go/no go decision that we can potentially back out from.
Finalize documentation. Deliverable documentation – user manuals, operations guides, system overviews – are an important part of the overall solution. This documentation must be in sync with what is being delivered, and if it is not yet finished then it needs to be.	• When documentation has been left to the end we only need to write the documentation for the end result, reducing the overall documentation work. • Extends timeline to deploy if documentation has been left late in the lifecycle. • The team may have forgotten critical information by this point.
Pilot/beta testing. We may decide to deploy our solution to a subset of our end users to test our solution via live usage of it. Such testing may take hours, days, or even weeks.	• Reduces risk by limiting the number of people initially affected by a release. • Extends timeline for the overall Transition phase because we need to wait for the pilot/beta test to run.

Ensure Stakeholder Readiness

Just because we are technically prepared to release our solution, that doesn't mean our stakeholders are automatically able to receive the solution, therefore we may have some work to do to get them ready. Remember that our stakeholders are a diverse group of

287

people, including end users, their managers, finance professionals, operations staff, support/help desk engineers, the sustainment team (who may be us), and many more. The point is that we need to do what it takes to ensure that all key stakeholders are ready, not just end users.

The larger the release, or the more complex that it is, the more work we will need to do to ensure that our stakeholders are ready. When we release a "big thing," the riskier that release is, the greater the change for our stakeholders, the more help they will need to learn the new version, and so on. This is why it's important to have very regular releases, say every few weeks or more often, or better yet continuous delivery – the more often we release into production the smaller the actual changes are, which in turn are less risky and require less support to be successful.

Options (Not Ordered)	Trade-Offs
Communicate deployment. We should inform our stakeholders that we are releasing the solution into production. Note that for irregular and long regular releases (quarterly or more) we should have started our communication efforts towards the end of Construction.	• Helps to set accurate expectations with our stakeholders as to what they're going to receive and when. • Works best with active stakeholder participation. • This is typically a non-issue for continuous deployment or very regular (weekly or less) deployments because what is being deployed is small and by now our stakeholders know that new functionality is released constantly.
Prepare support environment. Our support/help desk staff must have updates to their environment (if one exists) deployed either before or at the same time that changes to the production environment are deployed.	• Allows our support engineers to have access to our solution so that they have time to learn about new features before they are required to support end users. • Works best with active participation of the support engineers. • This is typically a non-issue when we have adopted a DevOps "you build it, you run it" strategy.
Train/educate stakeholders. The larger the change being released into production the greater the impact of that change on our stakeholders, therefore the greater their need for training and education (T&E) to understand how to work with what is being deployed. This T&E may be virtual online training, overview videos, face-to-face (F2F) classroom training, written instructions, or combinations thereof.	• Helps stakeholders, particularly end users, to become effective using the solution quicker. • Increases the consumability of, and the chance of success for, your solution. • Requires time and investment to prepare training materials. • Requires time and investment to deliver the training materials.

21 DEPLOY THE SOLUTION

The aim of the Deploy the Solution process goal is to provide options for how to successfully release our solution into production. Many Disciplined Agilists' first reaction to this is "Well, why don't we just completely automate this?" and they're right, we should fully automate deployment. This process goal is important because it captures several strategies for automating deployment, it provides several strategies for releasing our solution into production, it describes what needs to be performed to successfully release into production, and it describes options for how we can ensure our release was in fact successful.

Key Points in this Chapter

- Your end goal should be to automate the entire deployment process, decreasing both the cost and risk of releasing into production.

- Smart teams validate that they've successfully released into production, and better yet strive to determine whether they've delighted their customers.

Figure 21.1. The process goal diagram for Deploy the Solution.

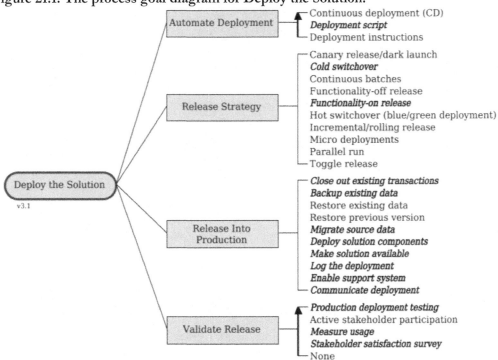

To effectively deploy our solution, we should consider several important questions:

- To what extent will we automate the deployment process?
- What strategy will we follow to release into production (this time)?
- What activities must we perform to release our solution?
- How will we validate that the release was successful?

289

Automate Deployment

From a Disciplined Agile Delivery (DAD) point of view, as well as a DevOps point of view, we want to automate as much of the deployment process as we possibly can. Having said that, it appears that only 26% of agile/lean teams have done so, although another 37% of teams appear to be close in that it takes them less than a day to deploy [SoftDev18]. This reduces the risk and cost of release, therefore making it viable to release more often and thereby increase our ability to react to changing stakeholder needs more effectively. The following table explains several options for the level of automation that we can achieve.

Options (Ordered)	Trade-Offs
Continuous deployment (CD). The solution is automatically deployed through all internal testing environments and into production without human intervention [W].	• Enables teams to rapidly address changing stakeholder needs. • Low risk and low cost because everything is automated. • Requires investment to put the automation infrastructure in place. • By logging information about the deployment we support separation of concerns (SoC), which is required for some regulatory compliance.
Deployment script. The technical aspects of the release process are fully automated and run from a single script (which may in turn invoke other scripts). Someone is required to determine whether it is safe to deploy (see the *Accelerate Value Delivery* process goal of Chapter 19) and then run the deployment script to perform the release. Sometimes this is called "push the deploy button."	• Very close to a CD strategy. • Requires investment to put the automation infrastructure in place. • Low risk but slow due to need for human intervention. • Very often an indication that management hasn't quite adopted a DevOps mindset. • Often justified by the need to support separation of concerns (SoC), but CD accomplishes this more effectively (see above).
Deployment instructions. With this approach there are written instructions describing a collection of steps to manually follow. Very often the steps are to run a series of deployment scripts and then act on the results.	• A brute-force strategy for deploying our solution into production. • Slow, risky, and expensive. • The deployment instructions are often not well tested, and it's only until we try to deploy that we discover problems. • Prevents teams from releasing into production regularly, motivating longer release cadences which thereby reduces opportunity for feedback and overall risk to our team.

Release Strategy

We need to identify what type of release we are performing. Are we releasing to our entire user base or just a subset? Are we running an experiment or is this a full product release? Are we releasing the full solution or a subset of features? Is the functionality turned on or off? Needless to say, we have options to consider as you can see in the table below.

Options (Not Ordered)	Trade-Offs
Canary release/dark launch. Release to a small subset of users. This is sometimes called a pilot test, alpha test, or beta test [W].	• Reduces risk of deployment by limiting potential impact of a mistake. • Provides an opportunity for "live feedback" from actual end users. • Increases overall time to deploy because we need to wait, and then potentially act, upon feedback from the release. • We may require multiple canary releases before we can safely release to our entire end user base. • We need some way to restrict access to a subset of users, often via access control or feature toggles architected into our solution.
Cold switchover. Deploy the solution, or portion thereof, by effectively writing over the current version.	• Easy to automate. • Runs the risk of needing to restore the previous version if this release goes poorly.
Continuous batches. We batch up dozens or even hundreds of small changes and then deploy them as a single group.	• Enables us to support what appears to be a continuous deployment (CD) strategy for developers. • Enables us to target our deployments to defined release windows, often during low-usage periods. • The larger the batch, the greater the chance that changes will collide/conflict with one another. This can be difficult to detect or debug. • Increases the cycle time of your releases.
Functionality-off release. New functionality, which could be very granular, is released into production but the functionality is currently turned off. End users will not have access to this new functionality until it is turned on.	• We safely deploy functionality in small, low-risk "chunks." • We can build up to sophisticated functionality gradually, then toggle it on at once to offer interesting new features to end users. • "Turned off" functionality may have side effects for existing functionality if it isn't truly turned off. Be careful. • We need to have feature toggles, or something similar, architected into our solution (see Chapter 10).
Functionality-on release. New functionality is released into production and is immediately	• Easy to automate. • Runs the risk of needing to restore the previous version, or toggle off the functionality if we can, if

available to end users.	this release goes poorly.
Hot switchover (blue/green deployment). We run two parallel versions of our production environment, one called blue and the other called green (we can call them anything we want). If the current version of the solution is running in blue then we deploy the new version to green and test it appropriately in there. Once it's ready we switchover production from blue (the current version of our solution) to green (the newly installed version).	• Low-risk way to support release into a complex environment. • Very safe as it is easy to back out to last version. • Expensive because it requires two copies of our production environments. However, this can be mitigated if we're deploying into the cloud as we only pay for the additional environment when we need it.
Incremental/rolling release. We release our solution to a few servers, then a few more, and so on until it is deployed across all servers.	• The system remains operational during the release process. • Low risk as it enables us to back out of the release fairly easily, or at least stop and fix things. • Risk of inconsistent business rules running in parallel during the rollout. • Supports international versions as we can release each version when it is available.
Micro deploys. We have many, potentially thousands, of deployments a day. Often used with the functionality-off release strategy.	• We safely deploy functionality in small, low-risk "chunks." • Requires investment to put the automation infrastructure in place. • Supports continuous delivery (CD) lifecycles. • Can be difficult to determine when a specific version of a solution has been released (it's always being released), which can be a problem for some regulatory regimes.
Parallel run. We run both the new version of the solution as well as the previous one simultaneously for a given period of time. Once we're convinced the new version runs properly we turn off the old version.	• Works well in situations where we are doing a direct replacement of an existing legacy system. • Increases cost to deploy because it typically requires dual entry of data by end users. • Requires sufficient production infrastructure to run both versions. • Requires a strategy to resolve any operational differences during the period where both versions are run in parallel.
Toggle release. A release where we turn/toggle a group of functionality on or off. The	• We can build up to sophisticated functionality gradually, then toggle it on at once to offer interesting new features to end users.

functionality would have been previously deployed via one or more function off releases.	• When we have production problems, perhaps because of a failed release or a security attack, we can "back it out" by turning off the misbehaving functionality. • We need to have feature toggles architected into our solution (see Chapter 10).

Release Into Production

There are many activities that we may be required to perform to successfully release our solution into production (as well as into any support, demo, and test environments as appropriate). On average, agile/lean teams release once every 45 calendar days although 30% release at least weekly [SoftDev18]. The following table explains key activities that we may need to perform as part of our deployment effort.

Options (Not Ordered)	Trade-Offs
Close out existing transactions. When a real-time system, or component of it, is updated in production we need to ensure that it is not in the process of processing any transactions to ensure the integrity of the transactions.	• Ensures the integrity of transactions. • Difficult for systems with long-running transactions because we need to wait for them to complete.
Backup existing data. We need to backup our existing data if we can potentially lose that data as the result of deployment.	• Required when we do not have an adequate data regression testing strategy in place. • This is critical for large releases due to the increased chance of defects, particularly with a cold switchover release strategy. • Difficult with real-time or very large amounts of data.
Restore previous data. If we choose to backup our data due to the risks involved with the release we also need to be prepared to restore our data to the previously backed up state.	• See backup existing data. • May not be possible because some data changes cannot be reversed.
Restore previous version. When a release has failed, and when we do not have the ability to toggle it off or address the problem with a patch, then we will need to restore the previously backed up functionality and data.	• Requires us to have previously backed up the functionality and data. • The restore can also fail, particularly when we are taking a cold switchover release strategy.
Migrate source data. We need to apply any data changes, including database refactorings,	• Can take a significant amount of time. • Some data migrations are one-way only and cannot be reversed, and are therefore very risky in

if any, that were implemented since the last release.	practice.
Deploy solution components. We need to deploy the functionality of our solution, or portions thereof.	• Contrary to popular belief, this isn't the only activity required to deploy.
Make solution available. Once the solution, or portion of it that that we're currently targeting, has been fully and successfully deployed we need to make it available to the appropriate users.	• This is the point in time that stakeholders consider the solution to be officially deployed. • Easily implemented with a combination of functionality-off and toggle release strategies (see above).
Log the deployment. We should record what we've deployed, when it happened, and who/what triggered the deployment.	• Provides important insight for the team regarding the deployment. • Supports governance via dashboard technology. • Supports regulatory compliance, in particular by providing proof of separation of concerns (SoC).
Enable support system. Any updates that we make to production should be reflected in our support system (if we have one separate from production).	• This may need to occur before solution deployment to support training of support engineers. • Often an important aspect of your service level agreement (SLA) with customers.
Communicate deployment. We may need to communicate to our stakeholders that we've successfully deployed.	• Important for irregular release environments to help set stakeholder expectations. • Often an important aspect of your service level agreement (SLA) with customers. • Becomes annoying in a CD or very regular release environment. In these cases logging supported by dashboards or a "what's changed" document may be sufficient.

Validate Release

We need to validate that our deployment has been successful. Have we deployed exactly what we thought we deployed and no more? Has our release been made available to the appropriate end users? Are our stakeholders delighted with what they've received? As you see in the following table there are several ways that we can answer these questions.

Options (Ordered)	Trade-Offs
Production deployment testing. We have automated tests that run after we deploy to verify that we have deployed exactly what we thought we would deploy, no more and no	• Ensures that the deployment worked as expected, or detects any problems if not. • Can be difficult in complex operational infrastructures, or when hardware runs autonomously (such as with satellites or military drones).

less.	• Supported by self-testing functionality (see the *Accelerate Value Delivery* goal of Chapter 19).
Active stakeholder participation. Actual end users, or more accurately people whom we believe are using the solution, are contacted directly to determine whether and how they are using the solution.	• We potentially obtain rich and often critical feedback about the solution. • Can be expensive to collect and then analyze the information.
Measure usage. To determine whether our solution is being used successfully we use operational usage data, such as what functionality is being invoked in our solution, the level of sales generated by our solution (in the case of commerce-oriented systems), the amount of information provided, and similar measures.	• Provides (near) real-time insight to the team regarding operational usage of our solution. • Requires instrumentation within the solution, which can affect performance.
Stakeholder satisfaction survey. Do we know what our stakeholders actually think about the new release of our solution?	• It is a skill to create an effective, concise survey that provides useful data. A very useful question is the net promoter score (NPS) one: How likely are you to recommend this new feature to a colleague? (Not likely at all) 0 to 10 (Extremely likely). • Enables us to potentially answer whether we have fulfilled the Delighted Stakeholders milestone of Figure 21.2. • People often perceive surveys as annoying and will often choose to ignore them. • To increase the response rate we can target active users of the new version, people experiencing problems with the system (something we can determine from usage metrics), and people who have responded to surveys in the past. BUT, doing this runs the risk of biasing/skewing the results.
None. We trust that the release was successful.	• Easy to implement. • Production problems may be exacerbated because it takes longer to find them.

295

Figure 21.2. The DAD risk-based milestones.

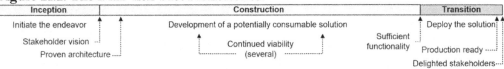

Inception	Construction	Transition
Initiate the endeavor	Development of a potentially consumable solution	Deploy the solution
Stakeholder vision	Continued viability (several)	Sufficient functionality / Production ready
Proven architecture		Delighted stakeholders

296

SECTION 5: SUSTAINING AND ENHANCING YOUR TEAM

The aim of the ongoing process goals is to describe common outcomes that support the team and/or help to make it more effective. This section is organized into the following chapters:

- **Chapter 22: Grow Team Members**. Support people in improving their skills and knowledge.
- **Chapter 23: Coordinate Activities**. Coordinate activities both within the team and with other teams.
- **Chapter 24: Evolve WoW**. Choose and evolve the team's way of working (WoW).
- **Chapter 25: Address Risk**. Identify, assess, and address risks appropriately.
- **Chapter 26: Leverage and Enhance Existing Infrastructure**. Reuse and improve existing assets, including functionality, data, and other artifacts within our organization.
- **Chapter 27: Govern Delivery Team**. Solution delivery teams will be governed, and they deserve to be governed well.

22 GROW TEAM MEMBERS

The Grow Team Members process goal, overviewed in Figure 22.1, captures options for providing opportunities for people to improve. This process goal is highly related to the *People Management* and *Continuous Improvement* process blades [AmblerLines2017] that focus on helping people at the organization level. There are several reasons why this goal is important:

> **Key Points in this Chapter**
> - We need to continually invest in our people, helping them to learn and enhance their skills.
> - Our aim should be to sustain and nurture an awesome team made up of awesome people.

1. **People, and the way we work together, are key to our success**. Remember the agile value "Individuals and interactions over processes and tools?"

2. **Motivated people are effective people**. In *Drive*, Dan Pink argues that autonomy, mastery, and purpose are what motivates people. This process goal focuses on providing opportunities for people to master their craft (the *Develop Common Vision* process goal, see Chapter 13, promotes the idea of teams with purpose and the *Coordinate Activities* process goal, see Chapter 23, enables autonomy).

3. **Solution delivery is a team sport[8]**. Great teams are composed of people who want to work and improve together.

Figure 22.1 The goal diagram for Grow Team Members.

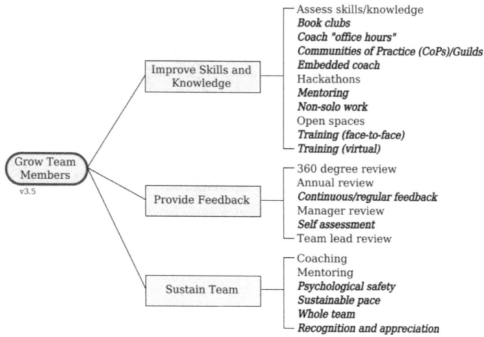

This ongoing process goal describes how we will support our team members in their

---

[8] To paraphrase Alistair Cockburn.

299

personal and professional growth. To be effective, we need to consider three important questions:

- How will we help people improve their skillset?
- How will we provide feedback to team members to help them grow?
- How will we sustain the team over time to enable people to grow?

Improve Skills and Knowledge

This decision point focuses on strategies to provide opportunities to hone our skills and knowledge, to increase our mastery. Figure 22.2 overviews an extension to Noel Burch's Hierarchy of Competence, showing Burch's original four learning levels and an additional fifth level to reflect a self-learning mindset. This hierarchy reflects our learning journey for a given skill or knowledge area – you may be at level 4 (unconscious competence) when it comes to data analysis but level 1 (unconscious incompetence) when it comes to exploratory testing. Not only do we want teams that are cross-functional, as individuals we want to become cross-functional as well. A common strategy in the agile community is to strive to become a "generalizing specialist," someone with one or more specialties (perhaps you love data analysis, user acceptance testing, and R programming) who also has at least a general knowledge of their profession (in this case solution delivery) and the domain that they're working in. A generalizing specialist is the happy medium between being a specialist, someone who knows a lot about a narrow competency, and a generalist, someone who knows a little about a wide range of competencies. Having team members

with a more robust set of skills is a key strategy towards leaning out your team and to eliminate waste (you're less likely create additional artifacts to cater to specialists and less likely to have to wait for them). As you can see in the following table there are many ways that our organization can support us in improving our skills and knowledge.

300

Figure 22.2 The hierarchy of competence.

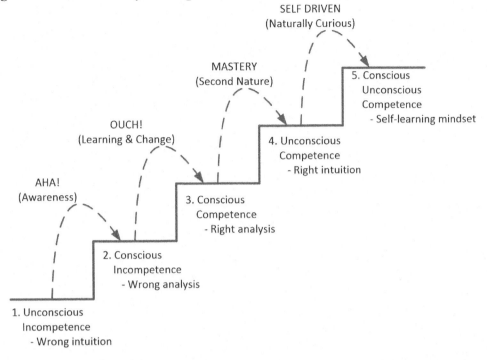

Options (Not Ordered)	Trade-Offs
Assess skills/knowledge. We rank someone, or sometimes self-rank, against a list of skills or knowledge areas.	• Helps to identify competency areas that someone needs to work on. • Enables us to identify someone who would potentially bring new skills into our team. • When people perceive that this information is being used to judge them there is the danger that they will try to game the data to make themselves look better. • Accurate self-ranking can be difficult to achieve. People will often rank themselves generously (particularly when they are at the unconscious incompetence level) or harshly (particularly when they are at the conscious incompetence level). • Requires a description of what each skill is so that we know what we are ranking ourselves on.
Book clubs. A group of people decide to read, and then discuss, a book at the same pace. A common strategy is to read a chapter or two a week and then get together to discuss what we've learned from the material.	• Great way to identify new potential practices or strategies to experiment with. • Motivates people to think through how to apply new ideas in practice. • Helps to build a self-learning mindset. • Requires time to do the reading.

Coach "office hours." A coach makes herself available at specific times so that people can drop in on her to get help with something the coach has expertise in.	<ul><li>Makes it clear when a coach is available to help.</li><li>Enables coaches to expand their reach as it makes their availability predictable.</li><li>Works well for virtual or multi-team coaching.</li><li>Demand for coaching will still vary, with the coach being swamped with requests at time.</li><li>Many people aren't aware what they need coaching in, so are unlikely to reach out for advice in those areas.</li><li>There is a clear cost to coaching but it is hard to measure the benefits.</li><li>It is difficult to find experienced, knowledgeable coaches.</li></ul>
Communities of Practice (CoPs)/Guilds. A CoP/guild is a collection of people who share a craft or profession who have banded together to 'learn' from each other. CoPs form and operate on a volunteer basis, although the CoP Lead may be a budgeted position in some organizations.	<ul><li>Inexpensive way to foster social and collaborative learning.</li><li>Shares practices across teams as they emerge, increasing the rate of organizational improvement.</li><li>Provides people an opportunity to share their expertise, and to be recognized for that expertise.</li><li>CoP involvement takes time away from a person's full-time job.</li><li>Mechanisms are required to capture and share knowledge (one aim of the *Continuous Improvement* process blade [AmblerLines2017]).</li><li>There is a clear cost to CoPs but it can be hard to measure the benefits.</li></ul>
Embedded coach. A coach is embedded on the team, often on a full time basis, to help the team learn and improve their way of working (WoW).	<ul><li>The coach has opportunities to observe people working together, enabling the coach to identify what people need coaching in.</li><li>Helps to keep the team on track in building their agile mindset and applying new techniques.</li><li>There is a clear cost to coaching but it is hard to measure the benefits.</li><li>It is difficult to find experienced, knowledgeable coaches.</li></ul>
Hackathons. A hackathon is an event, the aim of which is to create a functioning solution by the end of the event. Hackathons often develop a solution for a local charity or internal solution focused on supporting our employees. Also known as a hack day, hackfest, or codefest.	<ul><li>Fun way to get something built that we might not have invested in otherwise.</li><li>You can share skills and learnings across work teams.</li><li>Opportunity for people to build relationships with others.</li><li>Opportunity for teams to identify potential future team members that they will potentially work well with.</li><li>Needs to be organized and facilitated.</li></ul>

Mentoring. A more experienced or knowledgeable person helps to guide a less experienced or less knowledgeable person in a certain area of expertise.	• Effective strategy for identifying and growing leaders within our organization. • Opportunity for the mentor to reflect on their own practice, leading to improvement. • Great way to improve our personal network. • Mentors often provide critical insights from outside of our current environment. • It can be difficult to identify mentors (good candidate mentors tend to be in demand). • Mentoring takes time away from experienced people in our organization.
Non-solo work. Two or more people work together to achieve a task. Examples of non-solo work strategies include pair programming, mob programming, and modeling with others.	• Share skills and knowledge between people, enabling people to expand their skillset. • When performed opportunistically it often proves to be the most effective way to accomplish the work. • Can be less expensive way to learn new skills, particularly compared with classroom or even virtual training, as it can be focused on practical issues on a just-in-time (JIT) basis. • Improve the quality of the work because it is effectively being reviewed in progress. • Increase the acceptance of the solution because multiple people were involved. • Progress can be slower because more effort put into doing the work. • Often perceived by management to be inefficient or wasteful.
Open spaces. An open space is a facilitated meeting or multi-day conference where participants focus on a specific task or purpose (such as sharing experiences about applying agile strategies within an organization). Open spaces are participant driven, with the agenda being created at the time by the people attending the event. Also known as open space technology (OST) or an "unconference" [W].	• Share learnings and experiences across teams. • This is a structured meeting requiring a skilled facilitator, preparation time, and post-event wrap-up. • Some people are uncomfortable with the lack of an initial agenda. • Obtain information from a wide range of people, many of whom would never have taken the opportunity to speak up otherwise.
Training (face to face). One or more instructors	• Enables the instructor(s) to observe and guide students in real time.

leads a group of people through learning a specific topic. Also known as classroom training.	• Many topics, particularly mindset, are best taught F2F in a hands-on manner via group work (including games). • A relatively expensive approach that doesn't scale well. • The training needs to be scheduled and advertised in advance. • It can be difficult for people to find sufficient time to attend a training class. • Due to the training being at a specific time, students must adjust their schedule to fit it in. • People may need to travel to attend the training workshop.
Training (virtual). Training is delivered digitally to people. Sometimes this is instructor-led, often to a group of geographically distributed people, although this can also be pre-programmed training where an individual works through it on the computer on their own. Also known as computer-based training (CBT).	• Scales to very large groups of people, to geographically distributed people, and to temporally distributed people. • Lower cost per person when large number of people need to be trained. • Effective for technical skills and updates to existing knowledge. • Individuals can take pre-recorded training on their own schedule. • Virtual training often fails to provide full value because attendees are not truly present. Instead of giving full attention to the course, they're engaged in other work, chats, or responding to email. • Quality of the interaction between the student and the instructor, if any, isn't as robust as FTF.

Provide Feedback

From a technical perspective we like to say that we want to shorten the feedback cycle as much as we possibly can. When providing feedback to people it's a bit more complex than this – we want to provide appropriate feedback when it will be well received by the person in a manner that is effective for them. In other words, it depends. Because it requires skill and experience to provide feedback appropriately, people will very likely need training and coaching in doing so, something our *People Management* efforts [AmblerLines2017] should support. As you can see in the following table there are several options for providing feedback.

Options (Not Ordered)	Trade-Offs
360-degree review. This is a strategy where feedback about someone is gathered from multiple people, including their colleagues, subordinates, managers, and even external sources such as customers or suppliers. Also known as 360-degreee	• Identifies development opportunities for an individual. • Potential for honest feedback from a variety of people. • Can bring people together because it is a shared experience. • Although the feedback should be anonymous, you can often guess where some feedback comes from. • When the feedback is filtered too much it can be inadequate.

304

feedback, a multi-source assessment, or multi-source feedback [W].	• Expensive approach due to the number of people involved and the need for facilitation by People Management professionals. • Potential for people to conspire for or against someone by agreeing to provide similar feedback.
Annual review. The job performance of an employee is documented and evaluated. Also known as a performance review, a performance appraisal, or a career development discussion.	• Provides feedback in a structured manner. • Feedback isn't timely, decreasing its ability to motivate. • This requires dedicated time to perform, and is often run at an already busy time of year. • Tends to lead to angst within people because their annual bonus is often tied to the review results. • Tends to focus on the individual rather than the team, leading to competition amongst team members rather than cooperation.
Continuous/regular feedback. A person is given feedback often.	• Feedback is typically timely and targeted, making it easier to act on. • It requires skill, including knowing how to and when to, deliver the feedback. So you may need training or coaching in this. • Works well with on-the-spot rewards. • Easily forgotten at annual review time (if you're still doing that). • It is easy to forget to provide feedback to someone, or choose to forget because we're uncomfortable doing so.
Manager review. A manager, typically the person that the person being reviewed reports to or the person who is tasked with observing and reviewing them, appraises and documents their performance.	• Feedback is provided by someone outside of the team and as a result may not be as "political" as feedback provided from someone within the team. • A functional manager may not be actively involved with the person they're reviewing, leading to ineffective feedback. • Feedback will likely be irregular. • Typically used for annual reviews. • This may be little more than "busy work" used to justify the retention of the functional manager. • The manager may need training and coaching in how to effectively review people. • Tends to focus on the individual rather than the team, leading to competition amongst team members rather than cooperation.
Self-assessment. Staff members appraise themselves, often following guidance from the *People Management* group.	• Increases accountability and autonomy because it forces people to think about how they perform. • Accurate self-assessment can be difficult to achieve. People will often assess themselves generously (particularly when they are at the unconscious

	incompetence level) or harshly (particularly when they are at the conscious incompetence level). • Requires a description of what the job expectations are so that we know what we are assessing ourselves against. • It is difficult to reflect on issues that you have little awareness of.
Team lead review. The team lead appraises, and often provides feedback to, the members on their team.	• The team lead is more likely than a manager to provide effective feedback because they work closely with them on a daily basis. • Uncomfortable for the team lead to do this as they are also a member of the team. • Can result in undermining the team lead's ability to be a trusted team member because they in effect hold a position of power over the rest of the team. • There is a potential for politics and playing favorites within the team. • Team leads often don't have these skills so will need training and coaching. • Puts the team lead into a position of authority over the other team members, potentially undermining their ability to collaborate effectively with them.

Sustain Team

Organizationally we want to support our teams as best we can, and certainly our teams want to be supported and sustained. As you can see in the following table we have several options potentially sustaining our team...

Options (Not Ordered)	Trade-Offs
Coaching. A coach is responsible for sharing their skills and knowledge with others in a timely and respectful manner.	• Helps individuals or teams to improve their way of working (WoW). • Helps to keep the team on track in building their agile mindset and applying new techniques. • Coaching a team in a new approach often takes longer than you'd hope. • There is a clear cost to coaching but it is hard to measure the benefits. • It is difficult to find experienced, knowledgeable coaches.
Mentoring. A more experienced or knowledgeable person helps to guide a less experienced or less knowledgeable person in a certain area of expertise.	• Effective strategy for identifying and growing leaders within our organization. • Opportunity for the mentor to reflect on their own practice, leading to improvement. • Great way to improve our personal network. • Mentors often provide critical insights from outside of our current environment.

	• It can be difficult to identify mentors (good candidate mentors tend to be in demand). • Mentoring takes time away from experienced people in our organization.
Psychological safety. In psychologically safe teams team members feel accepted and respected. They are safe to share their opinions, to ask questions, to ask for help, and take other interpersonal risks. They are able to show who they truly are without fear of negative consequences [W].	• Increases the possibilities for greater innovation within the team through greater diversity of opinions. • Increases the job satisfaction of people. • Improves the ability of the team to learn from one another. • Decreases the chance that people will hold back ideas or information. • People may require training and coaching to become more open towards others.
Recognition and appreciation. People are acknowledged and praised for their contributions to the team.	• It's very easy to recognize someone's contribution. • Helps team members to gel with the rest of the team. • Helps to communicate team values to everyone. • The behaviors that are publicly recognized and praised will motivate people to continue acting in that way. • When you don't recognize someone for their good work, even if it's unintentional, it may be interpreted by that person that you don't appreciate their efforts.
Sustainable pace. The team works at a pace that it can comfortably sustain while still meeting their goals. The team may have to occasionally put in some "extraordinary effort," but this should be an unusual event [W].	• Protects the team, leading to better morale. • Avoids burning people out, thereby reducing the chance that they will quit. • Often perceived as pushback against a fixed delivery date. • Exposes organizational problems such as unrealistic expectations or quality problems.
Whole team. A team that is cross functional, having a sufficient number of people on the team with the skills and capacity to do the work the team has taken on.	• Reduces dependencies on people outside of the team. • Offers opportunities to streamline our WoW, because we have the requisite skills within the team, thereby increasing team effectiveness. • Doesn't fit well with a functional silo organization structure, complicating existing People Management strategies.

23 COORDINATE ACTIVITIES

The Coordinate Activities process goal, overviewed in Figure 23.1, provides options for coordinating both within a team and with other teams within our organization. There are several reasons why this goal is important:

1. **Support effective collaboration.** It is rare to be completely autonomous because we often need to collaborate with others, hence the need to coordinate with one another. This will help to reduce and hopefully eliminate several sources of waste, particularly wait time and rework.

2. **Support autonomy.** In *Drive*, Dan Pink argues that autonomy, mastery, and purpose are what motivates people. One aim of this process goal is to suggest ways of working that enable both people and teams to work as autonomously as possible, yet still collaborate effectively with others as needed. Note that the *Develop Common Vision* process goal

> **Key Points in this Chapter**
> - Teams have several options for how they will coordinate internally within the team.
> - A team will often need to coordinate their work with other solution delivery teams, within a program (a team of teams), across the organization, and even between physical locations.
> - Within a large organization our team may discover that it needs to coordinate its release schedule with other teams working in parallel.

(Chapter 13) promotes the idea of teams with purpose and the *Grow Team Members* process goal (Chapter 22) provides opportunities for gaining mastery.

3. **Working agreement within the team.** A team's working agreement describes how it will work together as well as with others. An important aspect of our team's working agreement is how we intend to coordinate our activities internally within our team.

4. **Working agreement with other teams.** Similarly, indicating how others may interact with our team is also an important part of our team's working agreement. Having effective coordination strategies in place enables our team to collaborate effectively with others.

309

Figure 23.1. The goal diagram for Coordinate Activities.

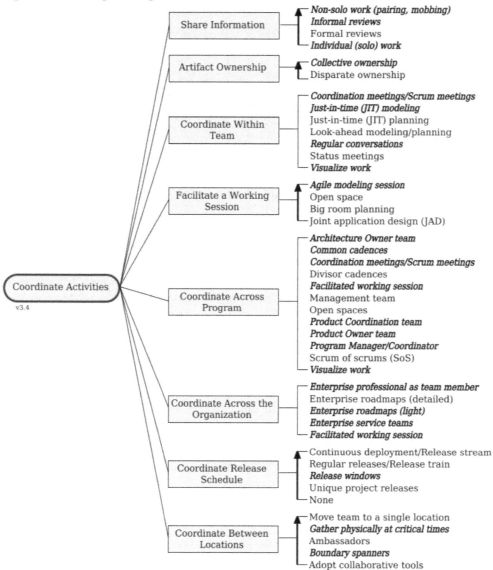

This ongoing process goal describes how we will coordinate our activities both within our team and with other teams within our organization. To be effective, we need to consider several important questions:

- How will we share information within the team?
- Who is allowed to update the artifacts created by the team?
- How will we coordinate within the team?
- How can we facilitate working sessions, potentially with large or diverse groups?
- If we're part of a larger team, how will we coordinate within it?
- How will we work with enterprise teams such as enterprise architects procurement, and finance?
- How will we coordinate our release/deployment with the rest of the organization?
- How will we collaborate with geographically distributed team members?

Share Information

How we share information within the team is key to our success – the more flexible and open we are with sharing information the easier it will be to coordinate our efforts. As you can see in the following table there are several options for doing so.

Options (Ordered)	Trade-Offs
Non-solo work (pairing, mobbing). People work together via practices such as pairing, mob programming [W], and modeling with others. Information is shared continuously as people work together.	• Enables knowledge, skill, and information sharing between team members. • Potential defects/issues found and hopefully addressed at point of injection, leading to higher quality and lower cost of defect removal. • Development can be a bit slower and more expensive than people working alone (although this is often more than made up for by the lower cost of addressing defects).
Informal reviews. Work is reviewed and feedback is provided, often in a simple and straightforward manner. Information is shared via the artifacts reviewed and the conversations during the review.	• Great technique for sharing skills, promoting common values within the team, and for finding potential defects. • May be sufficient for some regulatory compliance situations. • Longer feedback cycle than automated code analysis or non-solo strategies.
Formal reviews. Work is reviewed in a structured manner, often following defined procedures. Information is shared via the artifacts reviewed and the conversations during the review.	• Supports some regulatory compliance requirements. • Long feedback cycle, particularly when compared with non-solo work. • Can require significant planning and documentation overhead. • Can be expensive when many people are involved with the review. • If someone has value to add in a review, they would also have the same value to add via non-solo work.
Individual (solo) work. People work by themselves to complete a task, although may reach out for assistance as appropriate.	• People share information with one another as a matter of course while they interact with one another. • Potential for people to get out of sync with one another without other coordination strategies being applied. • Less skill and knowledge sharing within the team.

311

Artifact Ownership

Our team's rules regarding who is allowed to access, and who is allowed to update, certain artifacts has an effect on how our team will work together. The more flexible our approach to ownership the less effort we will need to put into coordinating the usage and evolution of our artifacts. For example, if you are the only person who is allowed to update our team's data model then everyone else on the team would need to coordinate their updates with you. As you can see in the following table there are two fundamental strategies to artifact ownership.

Options (Ordered)	Trade-Offs
Collective ownership. Everyone on the team may access and update any team artifact. This practice is taken from Extreme Programming [W].	• Knowledge is quickly spread throughout the team. • Lowers the risks associated with losing skills with people leave the team. • Requires people to have the discipline to work with others to update an artifact if their own skills are not sufficient. • Requires adequate CM control (see the *Accelerate Value Delivery* process goal in Chapter 19).
Disparate ownership. Access, and update rights, to certain team artifacts are restricted. For example, only the database administrator (DBA) may update the data model, you are responsible for working with certain parts of the code and a co-worker is responsible for other parts of the code.	• Supports security/access control policies within our organization. • Promotes a separation of concerns (SoC) within the team, something that is required by some regulations. • Promotes specialized skills within team members, increasing their sense of mastery. • Introduces bottlenecks by reducing the number of people able to access a given artifact. • Increases the risk of losing critical knowledge/skills when someone leaves the team.

Coordinate Within Team

Within a team, coordination between individuals occurs in a continuous manner as a by-product of us working together collaboratively. There are three aspects, or perhaps time frames, to consider regarding coordination within a team:

1. **Look-ahead**. Is the team thinking about the future to identify potential problems before they occur so that we may address them and thereby avoid unnecessary waste? This may be something as simple as having roadmaps to work towards, a plan for the current iteration (if you're following an agile lifecycle), leading metrics on our automated dashboard, and visualizing our work to identify potential bottlenecks.
2. **Just-in-time (JIT)**. Team members will naturally coordinate through conversations and non-solo work.
3. **Looking back**. This sort of coordination occurs via status meeting, status reporting, and trailing metrics.

To ensure that we're coordinating effectively across the entire team we may need to adopt one or more explicit practices for doing so. As you can see in the following table there are several strategies available.

Options (Not Ordered)	Trade-Offs
Coordination meetings/Scrum meetings. The team gets together to quickly coordinate what we're doing for the day. These meetings typically take 10-15 minutes. The primary aim is to coordinate although in many ways this is detailed planning. Also called a daily stand-up, a scrum, or a huddle [ScrumGuide].	• Keeps the team on track so that there are no surprises. • Enables the team to eliminate waste of waiting by identifying potential dependencies between the work of team members that day, thereby allowing us to organize accordingly. • Can be run on a regular cadence, for example daily, or on as needed, just-in-time (JIT) basis. • Enables the team to manage change quickly, but this in turn encourages change as well. • People new to self-organization, or more accurately new to being a true team member, see this as a waste of time. • Works well for extroverts – introverts often need coaching and even a bit of prodding by the Team Lead. • Coordination meetings quickly become overhead when performed poorly – our goal is to coordinate the work, not to do the work during the meeting. • Potential to become an opportunity to micro-manage if the team doesn't actively self-organize.
Just-in-time (JIT) modeling. Requirements or design details are explored as needed, often in an impromptu and simple manner. For JIT requirements a team member asks the Product Owner (PO) or one or more stakeholders to explain what they need, and everyone gathers around a whiteboard or similar tool to share their ideas. Also known as model storming, JIT analysis, or JIT design [AgileModeling].	• Enables us to focus on what needs to be built, and on most current needs. • Stakeholder needs are elicited at the last most responsible moment. • Modeling enables people to think through the "big issues" that they face. • Requires easy access to stakeholders or their proxies (such as POs or business analysts).
Just-in-time (JIT) planning. Similar to Iteration/sprint planning, except it is performed as needed and typically for smaller batches of work.	• The team identifies the work to be done and often who will be doing it. • Increased acceptance by the team because it's their plan. • A work item will need to be sufficiently explored, typically via Agile Modeling strategies, before the work to fulfill it may be planned.

Look-ahead modeling/planning. The team considers work items that they will soon be working on, exploring them in sufficient detail so they understand what the work entails. This is sometimes called backlog grooming or backlog refinement [AgileModeling].	• Potential to avoid waste from waiting or poor information sharing because the work item becomes "ready" to be worked on. • Potential to inject waste when you model/plan for work that it dropped or evolved before you get to it.
Regular conversations. Team members speak with each other whenever they need to.	• People coordinate as needed, with whomever is needed. • Conversations are a very effective way to communicate. • Flexible strategy with little overhead. • Requires easy access to other team members, working very well for co-located or near-located teams. • Coordination typically occurs between subsets of team members, making it difficult to get a strategy for the entire team.
Status meetings. The team gathers to share their status, typically discussing what they have recently accomplished.	• Often ineffective without significant discipline, particularly for the purpose of coordination. • Often perceived as a waste of time – the goal of such meetings is often to provide information for a status report, which often proves to be of questionable value. • Lowers morale within the team.
Visualize work. The team visualizes their workflow, and the work they are doing, via a task board or Kanban board (sometimes called a Scrum board). This can be physical using sticky notes on a whiteboard or wall or digital using an agile management tool such as Jira, Jile, or Leankit. These boards are one type of information radiator [Anderson].	• Improves team's ability to coordinate their efforts and to identify potential bottlenecks. • Makes the current work load transparent to stakeholders. • Enables prioritization discussions and scheduling discussions within the team • Makes it clear who has capacity (and who doesn't). • Requires team to keep the board up to date.

Facilitate a Working Session

It is quite common to need to gather either a large or diverse group of people to model or plan together in a face-to-face (F2F) manner. These working sessions will likely need to be long, many hours or even days, and due to the complexity involved require one or more people to facilitate them. Without effective facilitation the working session risks devolving into an unorganized mess. The following table describes several strategies for organizing facilitated working sessions.

314

Options (Ordered)	Trade-Offs
Agile modeling session. Agile modeling sessions can be applied to explore stakeholder needs, architecture strategies, and even design strategies. Key stakeholders and the team gather in a large modeling room that has lots of whiteboard space to work through issue(s) being explored. Several modeling rooms may be required for "breakouts" when large groups of people are involved [AgileModeling].	• Scales to hundreds of people with appropriate facilitation, but works best for groups up to a few dozen. • Organizations new to agile often need to build one or more agile work spaces, and may have organizational challenges doing so. • Modeling enables people to think through the "big issues" that they face. • It is easy to measure the cost, but difficult to measure the value, of doing this. • Often need to fly key people in, and make them available for several days. • Requires facilitation and organization/planning beforehand to run a successful session.
Open space. An open space is a facilitated meeting or multi-day conference where participants focus on a specific task or purpose (such as sharing experiences about applying agile strategies within an organization). Open spaces are participant driven, with the agenda being created at the time by the people attending the event. Also known as open space technology (OST) or an "unconference" [W].	• Share learnings and experiences across teams. • This is a structured meeting requiring a skilled facilitator, preparation time, and post-event wrap-up. • Some people are uncomfortable with the lack of an initial agenda. • Obtain information from a wide range of people, many of whom would never have taken the opportunity to speak up otherwise. • It is easy to measure the cost, but difficult to measure the value, of doing this. • Often need to fly key people in, and make them available for several days. • Requires facilitation and organization/planning beforehand to run a successful session.
Big room planning. Stakeholder needs are explored face-to-face (F2F) via Agile Modeling or other collaborative strategies. Key stakeholders and the team gather in a large modeling room that has lots of whiteboard space to work through the stakeholder needs. Several modeling rooms may be required for	• Scales to hundreds of people with appropriate facilitation, although works best for groups up to a few dozen. • Organizations new to agile often need to build one or more agile work spaces, and may have organizational challenges doing so. • Planning enables people to think through the "big issues" that they face. • It is easy to measure the cost, but difficult to measure the value, of doing this. • Often need to fly key people in, and make them available for several days.

"breakouts" when large groups of people are involved [SAFe].	• Requires facilitation and organization/planning beforehand to run a successful session.
Joint Application Design (JAD) sessions. Formal modeling sessions, led by a skilled facilitator, with defined rules for how people will interact with one another. Can be applied to explore requirements as well (in this case it may be referred to as a Joint Application Requirements (JAR) session instead) [W].	• Scales to dozens of people. • Many people may get their opinions known during the session, enabling a wide range of people to be heard. • Works well in regulatory environments. • Works well in contentious situations where extra effort is required to keep the conversation civil or to avoid someone dominating the conversation. • "Architecture by consensus" often results in a mediocre technical vision. • "Requirements by consensus" often results in a mediocre product vision. • Formal modeling sessions risk devolving into specification focused, instead of communication focused, efforts.

Coordinate Across Program

A program, sometimes called a programme, is a large team that has been organized into a team of teams. Large teams are typically formed to address large, or more accurately complex, problems. As a team grows in size a common strategy is to split it up into a collection of smaller subteams/squads to reduce the coordination overhead required. Ideally each of the subteams are mostly whole, with sufficient people with the required skills to accomplish whatever mission/purpose they have signed up for. Although there are many heuristics for when a team needs to be split, such as Miller's Law (teams should be 7 +/- 2 in size) or the two-pizza rule (if you can't feed the team with two pizzas it's too large), the fact is there are no hard and fast rules – we've seen teams successfully grow to over 25 people with no need to reorganize them into several smaller teams, and we've heard stories of even larger single teams. Having said that, it is common to organize large efforts into a team of teams and when you do, you need to coordinate across the teams somehow. The following table describes several strategies for doing so. Note: This decision point is only applicable to a team of teams.

Options (Not Ordered)	Trade-Offs
Architecture Owner team. The architecture owners (AOs) from each of the subteams work together to guide the development of the architecture for the overall program as you can see in Figure 23.2. The AO team self-organizes and holds working sessions as needed to evolve the architecture for the program. Large programs may have a Chief Architecture Owner	• Share knowledge and vision among architects. • Explicit strategy to evolve the architecture consistently as the subteams learn. • There is a greater need for this early in lifecycle, but the team will always be needed due to the need to evolve the architecture. • Effective way for senior AOs to share their skills and knowledge with junior AOs. • Opportunity to share experiences and coach one another. In some ways this is an AO Community of Practice (CoP)/guild for the program.

(CAO) to lead the AO team.	• The greater the number of teams, the more important this becomes.
Common cadences. The subteams/squads have iterations/sprints that are the same length. For example, in Figure 23.3 we see that subteams B, C, and D have a common cadence of two weeks where they can choose to coordinate their next batch of work given that their previous batch is "done." Note that we can still integrate our work at any point in time, we do not have to restrict ourselves to the end of an iteration.	• Easy to coordinate system integration across teams. • Effective at coordinating medium-sized batches of work across teams. • Subteams are forced to have the same iteration length, and iterations in general, whether it makes sense for them or not. • Difficult when people are assigned to multiple subteams because critical ceremonies/working sessions overlap. • Supports an agile release train (ART) easily (see *Deploy the Solution* in Chapter 21 and *Release Management* [AmblerLines2017])
Coordination meetings/Scrum meetings. The team gets together to quickly coordinate what we're doing for the day. These meetings typically take 10-15 minutes. The primary aim is to coordinate although in many ways this is detailed planning. Also called a daily stand-up, a scrum, or a huddle [ScrumGuide].	• See Coordinate Within Team above.
Divisor cadences. The subteams/squads have iterations/sprints with lengths that are divisors of a larger coordination cadence. For example, in Figure 23.3 subteams A, B, and F have iteration lengths of 1, 2, and 4 weeks respectively which are divisors of 4 weeks. Subteams A, B, and E have iterations of length 1, 2, and 3 respectively and therefore are divisors of 6 weeks. The "divisor number" is important because that is the earliest point that the teams can coordinate their next batch of work given that their previous batch is now "done." Note that we can still integrate our work at any point, not just at "divisor points."	• Provides explicit points in time to coordinate large batches of work. • Provides flexibility to teams to vary their iteration length (or to not have iterations at all). • Increases the cadence for integrating "done" releases, which in turn increases the cycle time to delivery. • Supports an agile release train (ART) (see *Deploy the Solution* in Chapter 21 and *Release Management* [AmblerLines2017]) although with less flexibility than common cadences.
Facilitated working session. Working sessions to explore	• Increases chance the session will produce value. • Requires preparation and follow-up.

317

stakeholder needs, to work through architecture or design strategies, or to plan the next increment of work are often needed on agile teams. When many people are involved, or when there is a potentially contentious issue to work through, these sessions should be facilitated by an outsider (preferably someone with facilitation skills). See the Facilitate a Working Session decision point above for options.	• It can be difficult to find experienced facilitators. • The cost is easily measured but the benefit difficult to measure, making it difficult to justify.
Management team. The program has a team of managers overseeing and guiding the agile/lean subteams.	• Ensures coordination happens, but this is better done by a Product Coordination team or a Program Manager/Coordinator. • Almost always an overhead given that there are Team Leads on the subteams. • Danger of managers injecting busy work into the teams when it becomes clear that there is very little management work required.
Open spaces. An open space is a facilitated meeting or multi-day conference where participants focus on a specific task or purpose (such as sharing experiences about applying agile strategies within an organization). Open spaces are participant driven, with the agenda being created at the time by the people attending the event. Also known as open space technology (OST) or an "unconference" [W].	• See Facilitate a Working Session above.
Product Coordination team. The Team Leads from each subteam work together to drive team coordination efforts as you can see in Figure 23.2. They will self-organize and meet when appropriate to coordinate amongst themselves. A daily scrum of scrums (SoS) is a common approach.	• Decreases the chance that inter-team issues get out of hand. • Provides an opportunity to address People Management issues within the program. • Supporting mechanism for Program Manager/Coordinator. • The greater the number of teams, the more important this becomes. • Opportunity to share experiences between Team Leads and to coach one another. In some ways this is a Team Lead CoP/guild for the program. • Tends to appear when a scrum of scrums (SoS)

	falls apart as a program grows in size.
Product Owner team. The Product Owners (POs) from each subteam work together to manage requirement and work dependencies across subteams as you can see in Figure 23.2. They will self-organize and run working sessions, potentially several a week, to coordinate their efforts. Large programs may have a Chief Product Owner (CPO) to lead the PO team. Similar to LeSS, which has a PO for the overall program and BAs on each subteam.	• Ensures requirements/work is managed effectively across subteams. • Provides an opportunity to reduce risks associated with requirements dependencies. • One more responsibility of POs, who are already very busy. • The greater the number of teams, the more important this becomes. • Opportunity to share experiences between Team Leads and to coach one another. In some ways this is a Product Owner CoP/guild for the program.
Program Manager/Coordinator. A large program will often have someone in a management/coordination role to oversee and guide the entire program. They will typically coordinate the efforts of the Architecture Owner, Product Owner, and Product Coordination teams, manage relationships with vendors (often working with *Procurement* [AmblerLines2017]), and monitor the overall budget and schedule.	• Oversees explicit governance of the program, in particular reporting to leadership. • The larger the program, the greater the need for this role. • Provides explicit Finance governance for the program. This is important given that the cost of a program can be substantial. • Provides explicit vendor management, particularly of service providers, for the program. This is important given the likelihood of using contractors and consultants, and even outsourcing, on large programs.
Scrum of scrums (SoS). Someone from the coordination meeting of a subteam (a scrum) attends the coordination meeting across all teams within the program (the scrum of scrums).	• Straightforward solution for up to 5-6 teams. • Tends to fall apart given the increased need for architecture/technical coordination and requirements/work coordination as a program grows in size.
Visualize work. The team visualizes their workflow, and the work they are doing, via a task board or Kanban board (sometimes called a Scrum board). This can be physical using sticky notes on a whiteboard or wall or digital using an agile tool such as Jira, Leankit, or Jile. These boards are one type of information radiator [Anderson].	• See Coordinate Within Team above

319

Figure 23.2. Coordinating across a program.

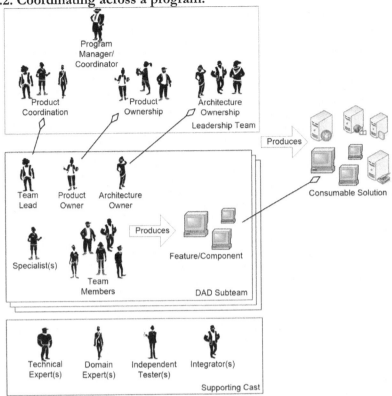

Figure 23.3. Coordinating iteration cadences.

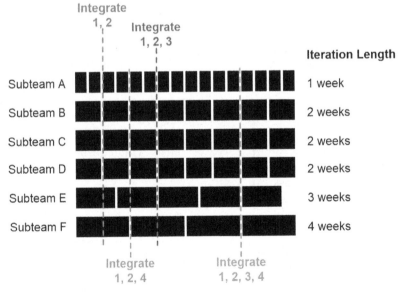

Coordinate Across the Organization

Our team is only one of many teams within our overall organization. When we adopt existing organizational guidance and leverage existing organizational assets, in short when we work in an enterprise aware manner, we operate more effectively – please see the *Align with Enterprise Direction* (Chapter 8) and *Leverage and Enhance Existing Infrastructure* (Chapter 26) process goals. Working in an enterprise aware manner requires us to collaborate with these other teams, and to coordinate our efforts across the enterprise. As you can see in the following table there are several strategies for doing so.

Options (Not Ordered)	Trade-Offs
Enterprise professional as team member. The member of the enterprise team becomes a member of the delivery team. For example, in Figure 23.4 you see that some enterprise architects are also playing the role of Architecture Owner (AO) on delivery teams.	• Great way to share skills and spread knowledge. • Increases the chance that the teams will learn about, and follow, the organizational vision. • When the work requires enterprise expertise or guidance the person is right there. • Requires many people in the enterprise roles. • Teams quickly. become bloated with the extra enterprise people • Doesn't work for all enterprise areas. For example, it is unlikely that a team will require a Finance person on a regular basis.
Enterprise roadmaps (detailed). The organization's vision, often for technical direction or business direction, is captured in detail. These detailed roadmaps typically comprise key diagrams overviewing the vision, detailed descriptions of those diagrams, guiding principles and the thinking behind them, and detailed implementation plans.	• Provides an overview of the vision supported by detailed information. • The more detailed the information the less likely it is to be read or understood. • Roadmaps need to be developed and maintained – the more information it contains the more expensive this becomes. • Roadmaps need to be easily accessible by team members. • Roadmaps need to be something people believe in otherwise they will not be followed. • Supports some regulatory compliance strategies.
Enterprise roadmaps (light). Enterprise roadmaps, often describing our organization's technical vision or our business vision, are captured in a concise manner. These roadmaps typically comprise key diagrams overviewing the vision, principles meant to guide the organization, and often high-level plans and priorities.	• Provides an overview of the vision. • There is a chance that the roadmap(s) will not be read, understood, or even followed. • Roadmaps need to be developed and maintained. • Details are not captured so we need another strategy for teams to get any required info. • Roadmaps need to be easily accessible by team members. • Roadmaps need to be something people believe in otherwise they will not be followed. • May still be regulatory compliant.
Enterprise service teams. The	• Teams can get the help they need, assuming the

enterprise team provides services, often defined through a team working agreement, to other teams. For example, in Figure 23.5 the data management team accepts requests from external teams, self-organizing to fulfill the requests appropriately.	enterprise team has sufficient capacity. • Works well when the enterprise team is minimally staffed. • Typically doesn't support skill sharing with the teams being served. • Potential for low-priority requests to get dropped due to insufficient capacity.
Facilitated working session. Enterprise teams will run modeling and planning sessions occasionally, and sometimes will involve their stakeholders (including members from delivery teams) when doing so. When these sessions become large or diverse they will likely need to be facilitated.	• See Coordinate Across Program above.

Figure 23.4 Enterprise architects as team members.

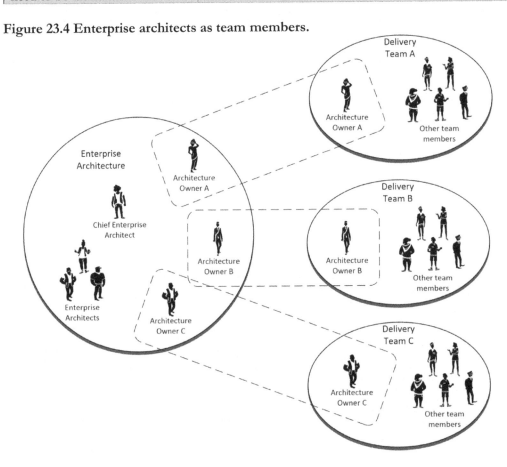

322

Figure 23.5. Data management as an enterprise service team.

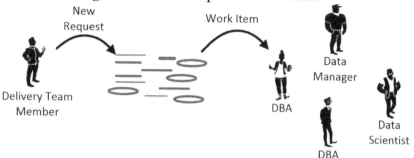

Coordinate Release Schedule

In organizations with multiple solution delivery teams working in parallel, even if it's just a handful of teams let alone hundreds, we will want to coordinate the release schedules of those teams. We do this to reduce the chance of a collision between teams. This decision point presents team-level strategies, as you can see in the following table, whereas the *Release Management* process blade [AmblerLines2017] addresses organization-level concerns.

Options (Ordered)	Trade-Offs
Continuous deployment (CD)/release stream. The solution is automatically deployed through all internal testing environments and into production without human intervention [W].	• Low risk, inexpensive way to deploy into production. • Requires a continuous integration (CI)/continuous deployment (CD) pipeline and by implication sophisticated automated regression testing. • Enables the team to receive continuous feedback from end users. • Enables us to potentially remove our internal demo environment (we can just use production for that). • This is a fundamental practice that enables the team to adopt either the Continuous Delivery: Agile lifecycle or the Continuous Delivery: Lean lifecycle.
Regular releases/release train. The solution is released on a regular schedule – i.e. quarterly, bi-monthly, monthly, bi-weekly – into production [SAFe].	• Release schedule becomes predictable, thereby setting stakeholder expectations and making it easier for external teams to coordinate with our team. • Important step towards a continuous delivery (CD) approach, particularly when the releases are very regular (such as monthly or better). • The cycle time from idea to delivery into production may not be sufficient, particularly with longer release cycles (such as quarterly releases).
Release windows. Release windows, sometimes called release slots, are defined dates and times when teams are allowed to release into production. Similarly, dates and times when teams are	• Sets expectations and enables coordination between potentially disparate teams. • Enables teams to identify slower, low-risk periods for deployment. But, in a 24/7 world there may no longer be slow/low usage periods. • Often insufficient for very large numbers of teams without automation.

323

not allowed to release are sometimes called release blackout periods.	• Scheduling into release windows needs to be coordinated across teams.
Unique project releases. The solution is released into production a single release at a time, with following releases (if any) planned out as separate efforts. Often driven by promises to customer, regulatory needs, or a project mindset.	• This is a very risky way to release because the team will have no experience releasing this solution into production. • Changes identified by end users can be very expensive (on average) to implement, and with a project approach there may not even be budget to do so after the release. • Deployment often includes expensive and slow manual processes. • Appropriate for solutions that are truly one-release propositions, but they are few in practice.
None. There is no coordination of releases across delivery teams.	• Works well for small number of teams, or when there are few dependencies between systems. • Chance of collisions and subsequent finger pointing. • Often results in many emergency production fixes.

Coordinate Between Locations

When our team is geographically distributed we will need to coordinate between locations. We consider a team that is spread across floors within the same building or across different buildings to be geographically distributed, let alone if they are in different cities. There is a very good argument that a team with people working in separate cubicles or offices is also geographically distributed. As you can see in the following table we have several options for coordinating between locations.

Options (Ordered)	Trade-Offs
Move team to a single location. Everyone on the team is moved to a common location, ideally a team work room or at least a common team work area. See *Evolve WoW* (Chapter 24) for strategies to organize physical environments.	• Increased opportunities for effective communication and collaboration. • Fixes the actual problem of people being geographically distributed. • Can create a serious morale problem if people previously counted on being able to work from other locations, such as home. • May be difficult to move away from virtual communication preferences at first, in particular chat and email. Some people may need coaching.
Gather physically at critical times. People come together at a single location, typically to have a working session to work through in important issue such as deciding on a strategy for upcoming work.	• Make critical decisions quickly with a wider range of collaboration. • Builds relationships between people who are working in disparate locations, enabling them to interact more effectively in the future. • Requires planning, facilitation, and follow up. • Some people may not be able to travel. • It is easy to measure the costs but difficult to

324

	measure the benefits, making it hard to justify. • If you're not willing to fund this, and guarantee continued funding over time, our team shouldn't be geographically distributed. • The team will need to leverage collaborative tools when not together.
Ambassadors. An ambassador is someone who travels between locations, working at the location for a period of time before returning to their "home location." In Figure 23.6 there is one person who is an ambassador – perhaps she spends alternating weeks at each location.	• Keeps communication between sites going. • Helps to build relationships between people at disparate sites. • It is hard on the ambassadors and their families. • It is easy to measure the costs but difficult to measure the benefits, making it hard to justify. • Less costly than flying everyone around. • The team will need to leverage collaborative tools when not together.
Boundary spanners. Boundary spanners are responsible for coordinating communication between sites. They look for opportunities to help people at different sites to communicate with one another when needed, working with the boundary spanner at the other site to do so. In Figure 23.6 team members at each location work with their boundary spanner to organize collaboration with people at other sites.	• Improves the chance that people communicate with others at disparate locations. • Once relationships between people are built the need for this lessens but likely doesn't disappear. • Works well with ambassadors (the ambassadors are often boundary spanners as well). • Leverages collaborative tools to facilitate the collaboration.
Adopt collaborative tools. Teams can adopt collaborative tools – such as chat software, videoconferencing, or discussion group software – to interact with one another. In Figure 23.6 you can see that people from each site are interacting as needed with people at other sites.	• Very common strategy that improves communication between sites (compared with sharing documents). • Tends to be a crutch for people when they are near located – people will use chat or email instead of getting up and walking over to have a conversation. • Often enables persistence of information, although it can have too much signal noise compared to purposeful documentation such as roadmaps. • Collaborative tools are not as good as face-to-face.

Figure 23.6. Strategies for coordinating between locations.

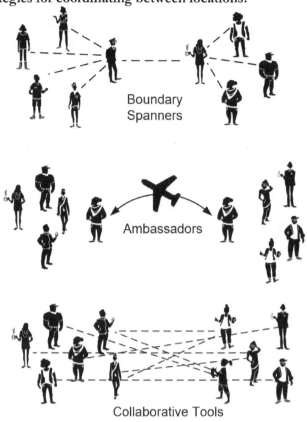

Boundary
Spanners

Ambassadors

Collaborative Tools

24 EVOLVE WAY OF WORKING (WOW)

The Evolve Way of Working (WoW) process goal, overviewed in Figure 24.1, provides options for identifying and evolving how we will work together as a team. This goal is the combination of two former process goals, Form Work Environment and Improve Team Process and Environment, and it is highly related to the *Continuous Improvement* process blade [AmblerLines2017]. The focus of this goal is on the WoW for a team, the focus of Continuous Improvement is to support and enable teams to choose their WoW and to share learnings across the organization. There are several reasons why this goal is important:

> **Key Points in this Chapter**
> - Teams should choose their WoW and then evolve it as their situation evolves and as they learn.
> - The DA toolkit enables teams to take a guided continuous improvement (GCI) approach, increasing their rate of process improvement.
> - Although a team faces a unique situation, they can still apply known strategies and practices – they do not need to invent a new process from scratch.

1. **Every team is unique and faces a unique situation**. We showed in Chapter 2 that because people are unique that teams are therefore also unique. Every team faces a unique configuration of complexity factors including team size, geographic distribution, technical complexity, regulatory compliance, and other issues. The implication is that a team needs to tailor their WoW to address the situation that it faces.

2. **We are constantly learning**. As individuals we learn every day – maybe we learn a new skill, something about the problem we face, something about how our colleagues work, something about our technical or organizational environment, or something else. These learnings will often motivate us to evolve the way that we work.

3. **The other teams we collaborate with are evolving**. Very few agile teams are "whole" in practice – they must collaborate with others to achieve their mission. Because these other teams are evolving their WoW over time the implication is that the way that they interact with us will evolve too, something that we may be able to learn from.

4. **Our environment is constantly evolving**. Our external environment is constantly changing, with our competitors evolving their offerings, the various levels of government introducing new legislation (including regulations that we need to comply with), new and evolving technical offerings in the marketplace, and world events in general. Our internal environment also evolves, with people joining and leaving our organization, our organizational structure evolving, and our IT ecosystem evolving as other teams release their solutions into production. Needless to say, we may need to evolve our WoW to reflect these changes.

5. **The team needs somewhere to work**. With the exception of a few teams where everyone is dispersed and working from home, we will need to provide space for some or all of our team members.

6. **The team needs sufficient tooling**. The team needs access to physical and digital tools so we can do our work.

7. **These strategies are applicable to a wide range of teams, not just solution delivery teams**. We've applied these strategies with leadership teams, marketing

teams, finance teams, enterprise architecture teams, data management teams, and many others. Having said that, the focus of this book is on how solution delivery teams can choose their WoW. Although this process goal applies to all of those teams the rest of the goals within the book may not. Each of these domains (marketing, leadership, …) requires domain-specific advice.

Figure 24.2 provides an overview of how teams typically evolve their WoW over time. When our team is initially formed we need to invest in putting together our initial WoW. This includes identifying the situational context that we face (see Chapter 2), choosing the lifecycle that seems to be a best fit for our situation (see Chapter 6), selecting an initial set of tools to work with, and setting up our physical work environment(s). Because initiating an endeavor/project tends to be very different than executing on the development of a solution, we've found that at the beginning of Inception a team tends to identify the existing process in which we are expected to operate and then tailor our own WoW for Inception. Then, towards the end of Inception when the vision for what we need to accomplish has solidified, our team will likely want to initially tailor our WoW to reflect how we believe we will do that work. Having said this, at any point in time, including during Inception, our team may choose to evolve our WoW based on new learnings (more on this later). Figure 24.1 depicts the process goal diagram for Evolve Way of Working (WoW), and as you can see we have many options available to us.

This ongoing process goal describes how we will improve how we work together and how we'll share potential improvements with others. To be effective, we need to consider several important questions:

- How will we organize our physical work space?
- How will we communicate within the team?
- How will we collaborate within the team?
- What lifecycle will we follow?
- How do we explore an existing process?
- What processes/practices will we initially adopt?
- How will we identify potential improvements?
- How can we reuse existing practices/strategies?
- How will we implement potential improvements within the team?
- How will we capture our WoW?
- How will we share effective practices with others within our organization?
- What digital/software tools will we adopt?

Figure 24.1. The goal diagram for Evolve Way of Working (WoW).

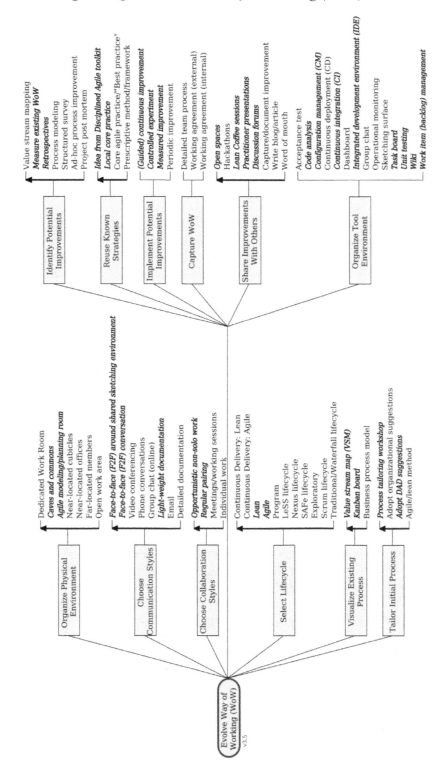

Figure 24.2. Choosing and evolving Your WoW over time.

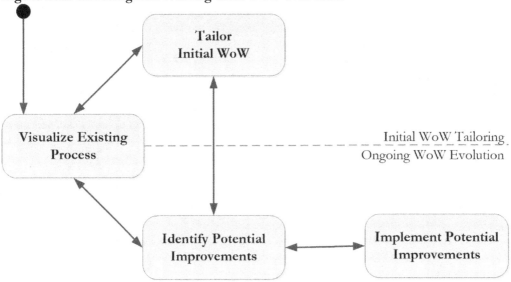

Physical Environment

How we structure our physical work environment is an important contributor to choosing an effective WoW. We will want areas where the team (or subsets thereof) can gather to collaborate and share information and we will want to provide areas where individuals can have some privacy. As an aside, Scott jokingly calls this "terraforming," a concept from science fiction that refers to the strategy of making a planet habitable for humans to thrive there. The following table compares common strategies for organizing our physical work environment.

Options (Ordered)	Trade-Offs
Dedicated work room. A room where the team works together in a co-located manner, often with lots of sketching space (such as whiteboards). Sometimes called a war room or a tiger team room.	• Maximizes close collaboration between team members. • Everyone can see the big visible charts and task board (information radiators) posted in the room. • Shelters from noise distractions outside the team (and reduces disruptions of others by the team). • Can become loud when multiple conversations are going on simultaneously. • The conversations of other team members often prove to be valuable information, not just "noise." • Some consider it claustrophobic. • There is often a lack of whiteboard space (an interior decorating decision). We've seen companies install whiteboards on tracks in front of windows, enabling the team to choose when they want sunlight and when they want board space. • There is a potential for hygiene issues. • There is seldom an opportunity for personalization of individuals' workspaces although great opportunity to do so

	for the team.
	• Some team members may not be comfortable with the lack of privacy, and will likely need to have access to other spaces for private phone calls or work.
	• Teams may be less likely to collaborate effectively with other teams.
Caves and commons. The commons is a dedicated work room or open work area (as above). The caves provide privacy for team members when required [C2Wiki].	• Has all the benefits of a dedicated work room plus the ability for people to find privacy when needed within the "caves." • Can often be difficult to obtain this much space, particularly in organizations new to agile delivery.
Agile Modeling/planning room. A room where there is a lot of sketching space so that people may talk and sketch [AgileModeling].	• Useful for agile modeling sessions, big room planning sessions, and training. • Can be difficult to convince traditional organizations to make the relatively minor investment in properly organizing such a room. Even when the investment is on the order of $5-6000 per person (including furniture) that still proves to be a small amount given the productivity improvement amongst well-paid people.
Near-located cubicles. Most, and often all, team members have their own cubicles on the same floor.	• Team members can personalize their space. More privacy for team members. Team members can still attend the daily coordination meeting. • It is harder to collaborate due to the distance between people. • Team members may forget or neglect updating the physical task board if it is not nearby. • Reduced effectiveness of the physical task board. • It's easier for team members to be distracted by requests of people outside of the team. Critical team members, in particular the Product Owner (PO) and Architecture Owner (AO), should have "office hours" when they ensure they will be in their cubicle. • Success rates of agile teams that are near-located is lower on average than teams that are collocated, even though the distribution of the team is minimal⁹.
Near-located offices. Some, or even all, team members have their own physical offices on the same floor.	• The ability to close the door increases privacy. • Team members tend to use low-collaboration styles of communication such as e-mail. • It's easier for team members to be distracted by requests of people outside of the team. Critical team members, in particular the Product Owner (PO) and Architecture Owner (AO), should have "office hours" when they ensure they

---

⁹ Scott maintains a page sharing the results of all his research at Ambysoft.com/surveys/

331

	• will be in their office. • Consider adopting group chat software so that team members can see when team members are at their desks and be ready for instant answers.
Far-located members. Some, or even all, team members are located farther than an easy walk from each other. Includes teams where we're spread across several floors in the same building, or in separate buildings.	• Possibility for follow-the-sun development around the clock. • Time zone differences can make collaboration very difficult (see the Form Team process goal for discussions around the effects of time zone differences). • Reduces effectiveness of the daily meeting, perhaps even preventing it from happening.
Open work area. A large room or space where multiple teams, or many individuals, work.	• More space than a work room, potentially supporting a very large team. • Better cross-team collaboration and sharing of information compared to office or cubicles. • Can be very loud and distracting because multiple teams, or simply individuals who aren't part of teams, are working in the same space. Note that sound management technologies can help with this issue. • When people surrounding us are not part of our team, their conversations are in effect "noise" that we need to ignore. Conversely, the Conversations of nearby team members often prove to be important information. • Numerous studies have found that open work areas reduce productivity, increase stress, and reduce morale. • Some team members may not be comfortable with the lack of privacy, and will likely need to have access to other spaces for private phone calls or work.

Choose Communication Styles

Media Richness Theory (MRT), overviewed in Figure 24.3 below, informs us about the effectiveness of common communication techniques [W]. We should select the most effective communication style for the situation that we find ourselves in. If someone is nearby, get up and go have a face-to-face (F2F) conversation with them. If they're far away, consider travelling to have a F2F conversation, otherwise have a videoconference (e.g. using Skype or Hangouts) call or a voice call with them if possible. It is particularly important to consider this decision point early in Inception because there are many Inception activities around planning and modeling that require effective communication within the team and with stakeholders.

Figure 24.3. Comparing communication strategies.

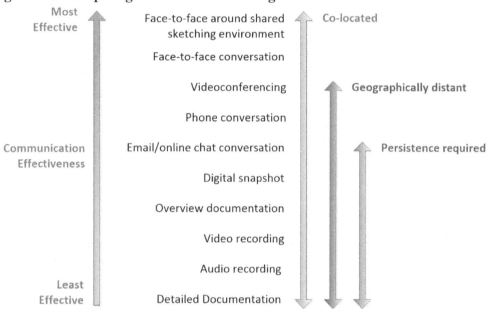

Options (Ordered)	Trade-Offs
Face-to-face (F2F) around shared sketching environment. Two or more people gather around a sketching surface such as a whiteboard or paper.	• Most effective communication option. • Requires people to be in the same location, or at least to travel to the same location. • Doesn't directly support information persistence, although sketches can be easily captured digitally.
Face-to-face (F2F) conversation. Two or more people talk face-to-face.	• Requires people to be in the same location, or at least to travel to the same location. • Doesn't directly support information persistence.
Videoconferencing. People talk and see one another, and	• Very common option when people are geographically distributed.

possibly share their screens, digitally via software such as Skype or Zoom.	• Enables people to see the body language of the people they are interacting with. • Supports persistence of the conversation, although manual transcription can be onerous (luckily some tools now support automated transcription).
Phone conversations. People have voice conversations digitally via phones or Voice-Over Internet Protocol (VOIP) software/devices.	• Common and easy way to have a conversation when people are geographically distributed. • Supports persistence of the conversation, although manual transcription can be onerous (luckily some tools now support automated transcription) .
Group chat (online). Two or more people text chat with one another via chat software such as Slack, Stride, or Messenger.	• Supports persistence of the conversation. • Supports asynchronous communication. • Often provides an excuse for near-located people to not get up and walk over to talk with someone else.
Lightweight documentation. Information is captured as concise, overview or high-level documentation or diagrams. Wikis are often used for this.	• Effective approach to persisting information. • Target audience may not trust, read, or understand the documentation – remember the CRUFT formula (see the *Produce a Potentially Consumable Solution* process goal in Chapter 17) to calculate the effectiveness of documentation. • The documentation needs to be maintained over time, otherwise it gets stale and eventually abandoned.
Email. People share information, and have discussions, via email.	• Supports persistence of the conversation. • Supports asynchronous communication. • Often provides an excuse for near-located people to not get up and walk over to talk with someone else.
Detailed documentation. Information is captured in detailed artifacts, including documents, models, plans, wiki pages, or other formats.	• Least effective means of communication available to us. • In the case of requirement or design specifications, we are often better advised to capture the expected behavior as executable tests and the overview information in concise documentation. • Target audience is very unlikely to trust the documentation and may not even read it. • Unwarranted trust around detailed documentation often leads decision makers to make risky decisions. • The documentation needs to be maintained over time, often an expensive proposition given the level of detail, otherwise it gets stale and eventually abandoned.

Choose Collaboration Styles

The way that we collaborate within our team is key to our success. Where traditional teams tend towards individuals producing artifacts for others, Disciplined Agile teams tend towards the more collaborative end of the spectrum due to the improved opportunities to learn and produce quality outcomes together. The following table compares key collaboration styles that we should consider on our team. Note that a more robust set of strategies for coordinating our work within a team, and for coordinating with other teams, are described in the ongoing process goal *Coordinate Activities* (Chapter 23).

Options (Ordered)	Trade-Offs
Opportunistic non-solo work. Team members follow non-solo practices such as pairing [W], mob programming [W], and modeling with others when appropriate.	• People receive the benefits of non-solo work strategies when it makes the most sense. • Effective way to share skills and knowledge. • Needs to be easy for people to decide to work together in an impromptu manner.
Regular pairing. Team members regularly work in pairs and often follow a "promiscuous pairing" approach where they swap pairs on a regular basis.	• Pairing is good at sharing skills and knowledge between two people. • Promiscuous pairing is very good at quickly spreading knowledge throughout the team. • Long-term pairing, perhaps for several weeks at a time, works well to teach someone a complicated new skill. • Some people don't like pairing. • Sometimes it makes sense for people to work alone. • Eases "onboarding," the act of bringing a new person into the team.
Meetings/working sessions. The team holds planning, modeling, and strategy sessions as needed.	• Effective when critical, high-level ideas or strategies need to be worked through, particularly when the team is in a room with a lot of whiteboard space. • Can be difficult to schedule when people aren't near located.
Individual work. Team members focus on doing "their work" by themselves. Also called solo work.	• Works well when people on the team are fairly specialized and perform focused work as they can apply their expertise and get it done quickly. • Works well for people who like to work on their own. • Results in significant hand-offs between people and the corresponding bureaucracy (such as reviews and traceability matrices) required to make this work. • Very poor at sharing skills between people. • Very poor at sharing knowledge across the team. • Results in significantly slower and more expensive development on average. • Quality tends to decrease the more hand-offs there are.

Select Lifecycle

An important decision that our team needs to make is what lifecycle do we intend to follow? As an agile/lean team we should always strive to learn and improve, and some of the improvements that we make will motivate changes in the lifecycle that we're following. Figure 24.4 compares four of the six DAD lifecycles and overviews improvement paths between them. The Exploratory lifecycle is not shown because it tends to be something you do for a short period of time to explore a new idea, then once that idea has been explored you go back to working via one of the lifecycles shown in the diagram. The Program lifecycle is similarly not shown because it focuses on coordination of a team of teams, each of which is following it's own lifecycle. Chapter 6 describes the lifecycles in detail.

Figure 24.4. Evolving between lifecycles.

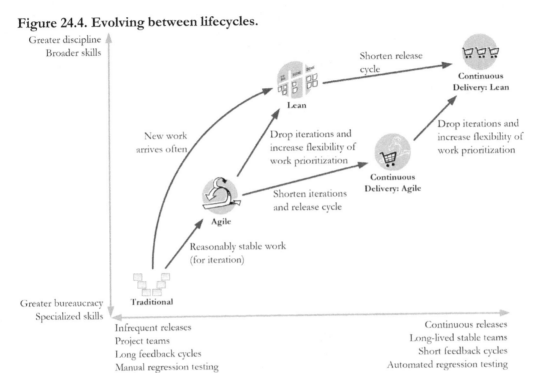

Figure 24.5 shows common paths that we've seen existing traditional teams take at various organizations around the world. The timings that we've indicated reflect what we've seen when teams have received effective coaching from coaches experienced in guided continuous improvement (GCI) – without this your teams are likely to take longer. We've also seen new teams start at the second lifecycle in each of these paths, for example starting with the Agile lifecycle or the Lean lifecycle instead of traditional. The arrows indicate typical times it takes a team to move from one lifecycle to another. These times do not include the length of time that a team was following the previous lifecycle. For example, a team could be following their tailoring of the Agile lifecycle for a year, spend a month transitioning to the Lean lifecycle which they then follow for nine months, then invest a month evolving into Continuous Delivery: Lean.

336

Figure 24.5. Common improvement paths for existing teams following a traditional lifecycle.

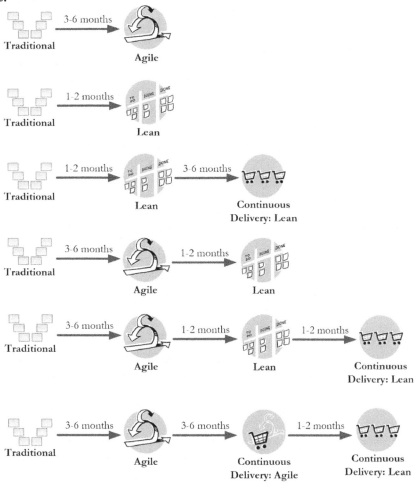

The following table compares several lifecycle options that we should consider, six of which are the DAD lifecycles (see Chapter 6). We have included non-DAD lifecycles to help put them into context.

Options (Ordered)	Trade-Offs
Continuous Delivery: Lean. A Kanban-based lifecycle where the team releases functionality into production, often several times a day, or even more frequently. Long-running, disciplined teams tend to evolve their approach into this lifecycle.	• Very quick feedback cycle, enabling teams to respond to changing stakeholder needs and priorities. • Works well for teams facing constantly changing requirements or new requests for assistance. • Requires significant skill and discipline. • Requires automated testing, integration, and deployment. • Supports very quick time-to-market. • Supports, or more accurately reflects, a #NoProjects strategy.

Continuous Delivery: Agile. A Scrum-based lifecycle with very short iterations/sprints where functionality is released regularly into production at the end of each iteration (often weekly). Long running agile teams tend to evolve into this lifecycle.	• Quick feedback cycle, enabling teams to respond to changing stakeholder needs. • Requires significant skill and discipline. • Requires automated testing, integration, and deployment. • Works well when the work items remain stable for the length of the (short) iteration. • Supports quick time-to-market. • Supports, or more accurately reflects, a #NoProjects strategy. • Appropriate for situations where an application is already in production and new features are delivered every iteration.
Lean. A Kanban-based project lifecycle that explicitly supports the full delivery lifecycle from beginning to end.	• Functionality is released into production when it's ready to go. • Work can be prioritized via a variety of criteria. • Small batches of work lead to quick flow. • Works well for disciplined teams with quickly evolving requirements/priorities. • Often the only viable option for teams who are very resistant to change or who work in environments with low psychological safety. • Lean strategies can be applied to teams following a traditional approach that would like to evolve the WoW via small changes over time. • Requires greater skill and discipline compared to the Agile lifecycle.
Agile. A Scrum-based project lifecycle that explicitly supports the full delivery lifecycle from beginning-to-end.	• Straightforward lifecycle based on Scrum that is easy to learn due to it prescribing the timing of key practices. • Very good starting point for teams new to agile, but can be disruptive for existing teams (so consider Lean lifecycle instead). • Iterations (sprints) motivate teams to build functionality in multi-week batches. • Releases into production are typically a few months apart, leading to longer feedback cycles based on actual usage. • Tends to fall apart when requirements change often (so adopt the Lean lifecycle instead).
Program. A lifecycle that describes how to coordinate a team of teams working on a single solution.	• Provides guardrails for organizing a team of teams, scaling to dozens of subteams/squads. • Each subteam/squad will have it's own WoW, albeit with a consistent way to coordinate between teams (see *Coordinate Activities* in Chapter 23). • Explicitly addresses coordination of people, requirements, and technical issues. • Does not require the subteams to be on the same cadence (e.g. to have the same iteration length), or even to be

	following the same lifecycle.
LeSS lifecycle. Large Scale Scrum, better known as LeSS, is a method for large programs organized as a team of Scrum teams working on a single solution. The lifecycle focuses on the coordination of a team of teams [LeSS].	• Well defined and supported strategy for teams of teams, particularly at the six-to-eight subteam range. • Tends to be prescriptive, requiring significant organizational change to adopt. • When it comes to scaling LeSS focuses on solving the medium-sized team issues but seems to avoid the difficult challenges around geographic distribution, regulatory compliance, and organizational distribution.
Nexus lifecycle. Nexus is a method for large programs organized as a team of Scrum teams. The lifecycle applies Scrum to coordinate a team of Scrum teams [Nexus].	• Familiar with teams already doing Scrum. • Little more than the application of Scrum at the program level. • Far less sophisticated than LeSS, although much simpler than SAFe.
SAFe. A lifecycle for large, multi-team/squad agile programs working on a single product. Although the DA toolkit does not explicitly support this lifecycle, it is possible to tailor DA to appear like SAFe. The lifecycle focuses on how to coordinate a team of teams into an "agile release train" [SAFe].	• Many process decisions are prescribed. This can make this lifecycle easier to adopt in the short term but less flexible in the long term. • Oriented towards large programs of 50-250 people, organized into a team of teams. • Requires skilled, experienced agilists because it is geared for large teams, which is inherently more complex than small teams. • Where a Scrum-based approach is a small batch system of bi-weekly deliveries, SAFe is a large batch system, typically resulting in deliveries approximately every three months (although they do say to develop at a common cadence but release on demand). From a lean perspective this is both a source of large planning and coordination waste, and results in infrequent delivery of value.
Exploratory. An experimentation-oriented lifecycle based on Lean Startup to determine the true market value of an idea. The proven and market-tested result is known as a minimal viable product (MVP) [Ries].	• Quick and inexpensive way to run business experiments. • Low-risk approach to validating potential new business strategies or potentially significant product features. • Requires a way to target a subset of our (potential) user base. • Appropriate for the exploration of a new product or service offering for the marketplace where there is a high risk of misunderstanding the needs of potential end users. • Often not applicable in regulatory compliance situations. • Often perceived as a strategy for start-up companies only, yet can be applied within established enterprises easily enough.

339

Scrum lifecycle. A partial lifecycle focused on Construction where software is developed incrementally in short time boxes call Sprints. This lifecycle is not explicitly supported by DAD although it is a part of the two Agile lifecycles [ScrumGuide].	• The lifecycle is focused on Construction, leaving the rest of the delivery lifecycle up to you. • Our recommendation is that if you want to do Scrum then adopt DAD's Agile lifecycle instead and avoid all the work required to figure out the rest of the lifecycle.
Traditional/waterfall lifecycle. Software is built in a serial manner through a series of functional phases (i.e. Requirements, Architecture, Design, Programming, Testing, Deployment). This lifecycle is not explicitly supported by DAD, although the DA Manifesto (see Chapter 2) explicitly addresses the fact that many organizations will have traditional teams working in parallel with more modern agile/lean teams via its 15th principle.	• Comfortable approach for experienced IT professionals who have not yet transitioned to an agile or lean way of working. • Appropriate for low-risk projects where the requirements are stable and the problem has a well-known solution. For example, upgrading the workstations of a large number of users or migrating an existing system to a new platform. • Time-to-market tends to be slow. • Lean strategies can be applied to traditional teams, including Guided Lean Change as described in Chapter 1. • Tends to be very high-risk in practice due to long feedback cycles and delivery of a solution only at the end of the lifecycle. • Associated risks are often overlooked by management due to a façade of predictability and control provided by the paperwork produced.

340

Visualize Existing Process

An existing team should understand it's current WoW so that it can identify potential waste and inefficiencies. The following table compares common strategies for exploring and communicating an existing process.

Options (Ordered)	Trade-Offs
Value stream map. Depicts processes, the time spent performing them, the time taken between them, and the level of quality resulting from processes. Used to explore the effectiveness of existing processes and to propose new ways of working [MartinOsterling].	• The value stream map (VSM) begins and ends with the customer, providing insight into the customer experience. • Describe an existing process in a graphical manner, capturing critical information around timing and quality. • Enables the team to understand their complete process so that they can explore potential improvements to the overall flow (see the DA principle Optimize Flow in Chapter 2). • Captures the process for a specific scenario, several VSMs may be required to explore the overall process. • Analysis of the timing information can be used to pinpoint areas in a process where significant waste occurs and to estimate potential lead and cycle times for your process. • Enables teams to have honest, and sometimes uncomfortable, discussions about how effective an existing process actually is. • Particularly useful when there is disagreement within the team as to where their process-related problems are, or when they aren't aware that there are problems. • Suitable when the focus of the team is on improving the process flow. • Requires someone with sufficient modeling experience to facilitate the creation of the VSM.
Kanban board. All work items are visually shown in one of the columns on a task board. A Kanban board may be either manual (e.g. stickies on a whiteboard) or digital [Anderson].	• Enables the team to visualize their process and the current work in progress. • Provides transparency to the team and its stakeholders regarding the work currently in progress, who is doing that work, and the current status of that work • Physical boards require wall space, which can be hard to come by in some organizations. • Digital boards often need to be integrated with other digital tools, such as defect management or status reporting tools, adding complexity to our tool strategy. • The glue of inexpensive stickies is often weak, or over time the glue weakens, requiring other strategies such as magnets to keep the stickies from falling off the board.
Business process model. Used to depict the activities and the logical flow between them within a process.	• Useful to understand current and future state business processes. • Can be useful for understanding hand-offs, responsibilities, delays and other valuable information about the process being explored.

Could be done in freeform format or with a notation such as Business Process Modeling Notation (BPMN) [W].	• If the diagrams become too formal their creation and maintenance can become expensive and time consuming. • Some modeling notations, particularly BPMN, can be overly complex and difficult for business stakeholders to work with.

Tailor Initial Process

From the very beginning of the Agile movement agile teams were told to own their own process, an important part of what we call choosing your WoW in Disciplined Agile. Choosing our WoW means that as a team we decide how we're going to work together to achieve the outcomes we've agreed to. An important part of this is to tailor DAD to reflect the situation that we face, something that is particularly crucial when our team is new. The following table compares several common options for how we can initially tailor DAD (note that we'll evolve our approach later as we learn).

Options (Ordered)	Trade-Offs
Process tailoring workshop. A facilitated session where the team works through the DAD goal diagrams to identify how they intend to work together.	• Great way to find out how well people actually understand the individual strategies that the team intends to adopt. • The team comes to a working agreement about how we believe we will work together, making roles and responsibilities much clearer and potentially avoiding misunderstandings later in the lifecycle. • Can be seen as "process overhead" by developers who just want to get on with things. • Sessions can be several hours long, so it's better to organize the workshop into two: one early in Inception for Inception work and one later during Inception for Construction and Transition.
Adopt organizational suggestions. Some organizations choose to define pre-configured versions of DAD for common scenarios faced by their teams.	• Great starting point for tailoring our team process because the common work has been addressed. • We will still need to do a bit of tailoring because every team is unique. • Effective way for organizations to share common strategies across teams, particularly around governance. • Danger that an organization will overly constrain teams by inflicting the "one repeatable standard approach." • Potential that teams will skip tuning their process because the "standard" option is close enough.
Adopt DAD suggestions. The DAD goal diagrams have highlighted suggestions that are geared for teams new to agile that are	• Very similar to having an organizational suggestion/standard, without sharing of common organization-specific strategies. • If our team isn't small, at least near located, and taking on a straightforward problem then at least some of the suggestions will not be appropriate for the team.

342

small, co- or near-located, and taking on a straightforward problem. It's effectively a combination of strategies from Scrum, Extreme Programming (XP), Agile Modeling, and a bit of Unified Process (UP).	• Even when the team is in this "simple" situation the suggestions may still not be completely right for the team (although most of them will be).
Agile/lean method. Adopt an existing method, such as Scrum or SAFe, out of the box (OOTB).	• Very comfortable for people who have invested a few days to become "certified masters" or "certified professionals" in that method. • One size does not fit all; we'll have a lot of tailoring to do with very little advice from that method beyond "our team can figure it out as it goes." • Risk that we choose an inappropriate method, or have one chosen for us. • Very expensive and slow approach under the guise of a simple and quick process solution.

Identify Potential Improvements

On an ongoing basis our team should strive to reflect on our experiences, to learn from them, and to identify potential ways to improve our WoW. The Theory of Constraints (ToC) [W] suggests that we should look for things constraining our WoW and then do what we can to reduce or remove them. There are potential people-oriented constraints such as lack of skills or misaligned mental model, process-oriented constraints such as ineffective organizational policies or bureaucratic procedures, and tooling-oriented constraints such as insufficient automation or an inadequate workspace. As you can see in the following table we have several options for identifying potential improvements.

Options (Ordered)	Trade-Offs
Value stream mapping. This is a lean-management method for analyzing the current state and designing a future state for a process. It is done with the customer of that process being the start and end point of the map [MartinOsterling].	• Reveals potential waste in an existing process and the levels of quality delivered by that process. This can be very disconcerting for people who believe in the existing approach. • Requires a bit of skill to facilitate the creation of value stream maps (VSMs). • The mathematical calculations required to determine levels of efficiency and quality delivered are straightforward and can be (and often need to be) easily supported using a spreadsheet. • The focus often becomes streamlining an existing process, which definitely has its place. But we still need to question whether the process, or portions thereof, is the "right"

	approach.
Measure existing WoW. The team's current WoW is measured so as to better understand it. Potential metrics to consider include lead time, cycle time, throughput, work in progress (WIP), incidents, colleague engagement, and net promoter score (NPS) [W].	• Better data enables teams to make better decisions. • Requires the team to invest time to put the measurements in place. • Requires the team to understand how to use the measures to inform their improvement efforts. • See *Govern Delivery Team* (Chapter 27) for a discussion of options for metrics gathering and reporting.
Retrospectives. A reflection technique where a team looks back at how they have worked to identify potential opportunities for improvement. Retrospectives are often performed on a regular basis throughout the lifecycle [Kerth].	• Effective strategy for getting a group of people to reflect on the way that they work. • Retrospectives enable us to identify potential improvements, but if we don't act on them then we're wasting our time. • By holding retrospectives throughout the lifecycle, particularly on a just-in-time (JIT) basis when we experience a problem, we reduce the feedback cycle between experiencing a problem and (hopefully) resolving it.
Process modeling. A process model depicts a process, either the current of future state of it, in terms of workflows and activities. There are many notations to choose from, including Business Process Modeling Notation (BPMN), UML Activity Diagram, Data Flow Diagram, Flowchart, and more.	• Typically easier to understand than a VSM, see above, but also less effective as they typically don't focus on efficiency nor quality. • Some notations, particularly BPMN and UML, prove to be overly complex for non-modelers, although it is possible to get value from only using a subset of the notation.
Structured survey. The team sends out a survey asking to indicate the strengths and weaknesses of our current WoW to gain insight into potential improvement opportunities.	• Surveys are a good way to quickly get information from a range of people. • Offers the opportunity for people to provide feedback anonymously (if the survey is built that way). • It is a skill to develop a survey that results in valuable findings without injecting significant bias into the results. • There is "survey fatigue" amongst most people, making it difficult to get a good response rate.
Ad-hoc process improvement. The team considers ideas whenever something comes to mind.	• Rarely happens, or at least ideas are rarely acted on. • It is better to have an impromptu, just-in-time (JIT) retrospective.
Project post mortem. A reflection technique where, at the end of a project, the team identifies what	• Once the project is over people are rarely motivated to change their WoW because the team has very likely been disbanded or is about

344

went well and what didn't go well.	to be.
	• Writing a "lessons learned" document can be cathartic if the team has had a bad experience.
	• The "lessons learned" coming out of a post-mortem are rarely acted upon, implying they are little more than "lessons indicated."
	• Often little more than process compliance.

Reuse Known Strategies

As this book readily shows, there are hundreds if not thousands of practices and strategies that our team can potential adopt and tailor for our situation. In other words, we should consider and then experiment with known strategies whenever we possibly can. The following table shows that we have several options for doing so and Figure 24.6 provides insight into their effectiveness.

Figure 24.6. Comparing the options.

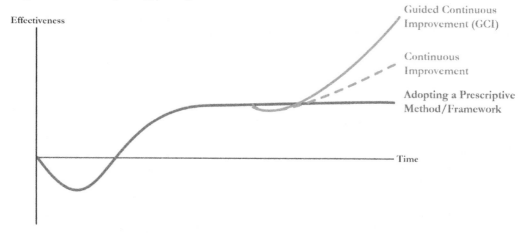

Options (Ordered)	Trade-Offs
Idea from Disciplined Agile (DA) toolkit. The team leverages the DA toolkit, perhaps via this book or through a supporting tool, to identify potential strategies to consider adopting. We call this guided continuous improvement (GCI).	• When we recognize that we are suffering from a problem, or that we want to potentially improve an aspect of our WoW, we can look it up in the DA knowledgebase to discover what options we have available to us to experiment with. • Improvement occurs as small changes, ideally minimal viable changes (MVCs) [LeanChange2], which reduce risk and enables us to focus. • We can leverage agnostic learnings from the thousands of teams that have come before us, even though our team is in a unique situation – we don't have to start from scratch when choosing our WoW. • As you see in Figure 24.6 this approach tends to have a steeper productivity curve because the

345

	team is making better, guided decisions regarding which strategies to consider adopting. • We will still need to experiment with the potential improvement to see how well it works for us in the situation that we face, even though the trade-offs associated with the strategies and practices captured in DA are indicated • When the options for a decision point are ordered, such as with this one, we can clearly see which potential options are likely to be more (or less) effective than what we're currently doing[10].
Local core practice. Our team considers potential improvements that we've heard about from other teams, perhaps via our *Continuous Improvement* efforts at the organizational level [AmblerLines2017] or via common process assets (see *Leverage and Enhance Existing Infrastructure* in Chapter 26). This is an example of a continuous improvement strategy, as shown in Figure 24.6.	• Improvement occurs as small changes, ideally minimal viable changes (MVCs) [LeanChange2], which reduce risk and enables us to focus. • There is a greater chance that a strategy that worked well for another team may work well for us because they've at least discovered how to overcome any organizational challenges associated with the strategy. • We still need to experiment with the strategy to discover how well it works for us. • The other team may not have been aware of better strategies to address their situation (perhaps they're not aware of DA yet).
Core agile practice/"Best practice." The team adopts industry or organizational "best practices" that have often been identified/selected by our organization. See the *Leverage and Enhance Existing Infrastructure* process goal (Chapter 26). This is an example of a continuous improvement strategy, as shown in Figure 24.6.	• Improvement occurs as small changes, ideally minimal viable changes (MVCs) [LeanChange2], which reduce risk and enables us to focus. • There is the potential to increase the consistency across some aspects of the WoW for individual teams, making it easier for teams to share learnings and to collaborate with other teams. • There is no such thing as a "best practice" – all practices are contextual in nature, working well in some situations and very poorly in others. Just because someone else thinks a practice is "best" for us doesn't mean it actually is. • We still need to experiment with the strategy to discover how well it works for us. • "Best practices" are often the excuse that bureaucrats use to inflict common processes on teams to make it easier for them, regardless of the negative impact those practices have on the teams.
Prescriptive	• Gives the team a defined WoW.

---

[10] DA is arguably a maturity model in that respect.

346

method/framework. The team chooses to adopt a defined method such as Scrum, DSDM, or SAFe.	• Can result in significant dysfunction, or require significant organizational change, if there is a misfit between the context of the team and the context addressed by the method/framework. • Improvement occurs as a large change (Scrum) or very large change (DSDM, SAFe), offering the potential to address a large number of problems at once but also increasing the chance that the improvements will not be adopted effectively due to the greater complexity of the change. • Often requires significant training and coaching. • Although team productivity does tend to improve over time, it often plateaus when the team hits the limit of the advice of the method or framework as you see in Figure 24.6. As Ivar Jacobson observes, you end up in "method prison" [Prison]. • For continued improvement this strategy needs to be combined with one of the above.

Implement Potential Improvements

It isn't enough to simply identify a potential improvement, we also need to implement them. As you can see in the following table we have several options for doing so.

Options (Not Ordered)	Trade-Offs
(Guided) continuous improvement. Our team will strive to improve on a regular basis. Improvement through a series of small, incremental changes is called "kaizen" [W]. This approach is considered continuous improvement (CI) when the team identifies potential improvements without the aid of a toolkit such as DA, and guided continuous improvement (GCI) when it does.	• Increases the chance that the team will in fact improve their WoW. • A continuous approach tends to be less risky than a periodic approach because the changes identified are often smaller and easier to implement. • Teams improve their WoW at a steady pace. • Requires team members to regularly reflect on how they work together. • Supports the development of a learning organization. • Easier said than done – improvement activities are easy to push off into the future in favor of more pressing needs (such as delivering new business functionality).
Controlled experiment. The team explicitly tries out a potential improvement for a short period of time to determine how well it can work within our environment. The process for doing this is shown	• Low-risk and inexpensive way to determine whether a potential improvement actually works for our team in the situation that we face. • We are likely to discover what aspects of the improvement work well, if any, for us and what aspects don't work well. This insight will enable us to effectively tailor the strategy to our situation.

in Figure 24.7 and it can be used with both a guided and non-guided continuous improvement strategy. This is also called a validated learning approach [W].	• Even when an experiment "fails" the team still learns what doesn't work for them. This helps us to refocus on something that might work. • It supports (and requires) critical thinking by team members to assess the effectiveness of a technique. • Experiments need to be given sufficient time to run, and this can vary. • Some organizations don't like the word "experiment" because of the perception that experiments don't always succeed. Get over it. • Need to measure the results of the experiment.
Measured improvement. After adopting a new improvement the team measures their effectiveness at applying it in practice.	• Solid way for a team to determine if a potential change was actually beneficial. • The team needs to know what is important to them, adopting a technique such as Outcomes and Key Results (OKRs) or Goal Question Metric (GQM) [W]. Jonathan Smart promotes the slogan "better value sooner safer happier" for desired outcomes for agile/lean teams. • We may not have baseline data against which to compare that is applicable to the potential improvement. We can still start measuring now, but it may take us longer to determine the effectiveness of a potential improvement. • Can be hard to tease out the effects of a single change from the metrics – you'll need to make a judgement call, albeit an informed one. • Works well with the other strategies. • Many organizations want to compare themselves against other, similar organizations or against the industry in general. But it is very rare for organizations to share their metrics with others, and rarer still to find organizations measuring themselves in a similar way to yours. • Management may desire to start comparing teams with one another, motivating the teams to either stop measuring or to manipulate their numbers so that they look good.
Periodic improvement. Our team will strive to improve our WoW periodically, perhaps once a quarter or at the beginning of a project.	• When many potential improvements are adopted by a team in a large batch it is difficult to determine the effects of a single improvement. • Process improvement becomes an effort because the team rarely tries to do it, so we never build up improvement skills within the team and as a result we likely do it poorly. • Riskier when changes are adopted as large batches.

Figure 24.7. Running experiments to evolve our WoW.

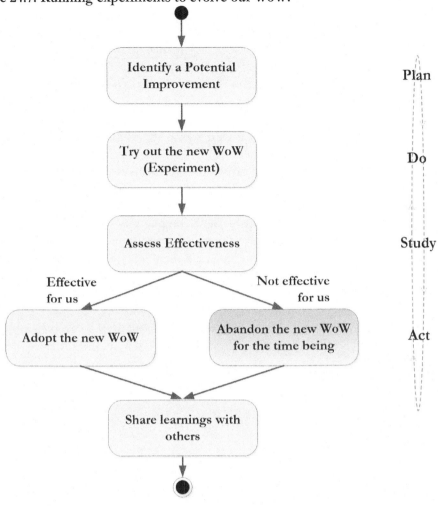

Capture WoW

In a recent study Google found that having structure and clarity (around our WoW) was one of five factors for successful teams within Google [Google]. We may decide, or be required for regulatory compliance, to document the team's WoW. The regular agile documentation advice naturally applies to this: document only if that's our best option, be concise, only write what we intend to maintain over time, and work closely with the audience of the documentation so that we understand their true needs. As you can see in the following table we have several options for doing so.

Options (Not Ordered)	Trade-Offs
Detailed team process. The team's WoW will be captured in detail, perhaps in a Wiki or in a document, often linking to even greater detail elsewhere on the web	<ul><li>Makes it clear how the team intends to work together.</li><li>Supports regulatory compliance regulations around process definition.</li><li>Like other forms of documentation, process documentation suffers from all of the issues around</li></ul>

or within our organization's knowledgebase.	CRUFT (see the *Produce a Potentially Consumable Solution* process goal in Chapter 17) and the ineffectiveness of documentation for communicating information. • Often onerous in practice, particularly when the process documentation is maintained manually. • A process definition tool, particularly one that natively supports DA, can help a team to maintain their process definition over time.
Working agreement (internal). This is a short document describing the principles or rules that team members are expected to follow when collaborating within the team.	• Makes it clear within the team how people will work together. • Many working agreements call out the roles and responsibilities of people on the team, making it clear who is responsible for what. • This may be a simple way to support regulatory compliance requirements around process definition. • The working agreement will need to evolve over time to reflect the evolution of the team's WoW.
Working agreement (external). This is a short document describing how other teams can interact with, or collaborate with, our team. It may indicate times the team is available, how to contact the team, or what artifacts are needed for given services that the team provides. Also known as a team interface or service level agreement (SLA).	• Makes it clear to people external to the team what it does and how to interact with it. • The working agreement will need to evolve over time as the team evolves its WoW and as the needs of the team's customers evolve.

Share Improvements With Others

Our team should be willing and eager to share our learnings with others, and of course to learn from others as well. Although this is the focus of the *Continuous Improvement* process blade [AmblerLines2017], there are several important practices at the team level that we're likely to adopt (as you can see in the following table).

Options (Ordered)	Trade-Offs
Open spaces. An open space is a facilitated meeting or multi-day conference where participants focus on a specific task or purpose (such as sharing experiences about applying agile strategies within an organization).	• Share learnings and experiences across teams. • This is a structured meeting requiring a skilled facilitator, preparation time, and post-event wrap-up. • Some people are uncomfortable with the lack of an initial agenda. • Obtain information from a wide range of people, many of whom would never have taken the opportunity to speak up otherwise.

Open spaces are participant driven, with the agenda being created at the time by the people attending. Also known as open space technology (OST) or an "unconference" [W].	
Hackathons. A hackathon is an event, the aim of which is to create a functioning solution by the end of the event. Hackathons often develop a solution for a local charity or internal solution focused on supporting our employees. Also known as a hack day, hackfest, or codefest [W].	• Fun way to get something built that we might not have invested in otherwise. • You can share skills and learnings across work teams. • Opportunity for people to build relationships with others. • Opportunity for teams to identify potential future team members that they will potentially work well with. • Needs to be organized and facilitated.
Lean Coffee sessions. Lean coffee is a structured, agenda-less meeting where people gather, build an agenda, and then have a discussion.	• Easy way to share learnings with other. • Requires someone to facilitate the session, but that's very easy. • Can be evolved into a "Lean Beer" session after work. • Extroverts often dominate the discussions, although a good facilitator will draw out introverts.
Practitioner presentation. Someone decides to share a learning or experience by presenting it to others. This presentation may be to just the team or may be to a wider audience.	• Easy way to share experiences and learnings with others. • Presentations can take a lot of preparation effort. • Presentations will often open up dialogs between people who normally may never interact with one another. • Presentations can often be one-way communication from the presenter to the audience. • Presentations can often become a bottleneck to sharing due to the need to arrange the presentation. • Introverts will rarely take the opportunity to present.
Discussion forums. People interact within internal (to our organization) discussion forums using software such as Slack or Discourse.	• Discussion forums will likely need to be supported by members of a community of excellence (CoE) who are focused on the forum topic. • Discussion forums are a great way to support the learning efforts of members of a community of practice (CoP)/guild that is focused on that topic. • Discussions tend to repeat, which is a reflection of where the people are in their learning process. • We will likely want to capture important points outside of the discussions, perhaps in process documentation, a

	blog, or an article.
Capture/document improvement. We capture our improvement in our process documentation, typically captured in a Wiki or word processor, and share that with others (perhaps via an artifact repository such as Microsoft SharePoint).	• Supports regulatory compliance regulations around process definition. • Likely difficult for other teams to find and read. • Like other forms of documentation, process documentation suffers from all of the issues around CRUFT (see the *Produce a Potentially Consumable Solution* process goal in Chapter 17) and the ineffectiveness of documentation for communicating information. • This is often seen as an overhead. Keep it concise, ask yourself if you're ever going to refer to this information again.
Write blog/article. We write a blog or article, posting it either internally within our organization or better yet externally on the web, so that others may read it.	• Form of documentation, albeit a focused one, potentially suffering from all the issues around CRUFT. • Likely easy for others to find it. • Blogs and articles rarely describe the context of an improvement (although that is something you could choose to do). • Typically not considered "proper" process documentation by regulatory auditors.
Word of mouth. We tell others about the improvement that we've made, either verbally or through digital means.	• Effective way to communicate the improvement at the time. • The improvement isn't persisted for the long term.

Organize Tool Environment

What tools, either physical or digital, will the team use? We want to get started on tool setup during Inception, but we should expect to evolve our strategy over time as we learn more about what we need and what the various tools do for us (and to us). It is important to recognize, however, that installing new tools does not make us agile. In the traditional world some people could get away with just learning how to use a tool to perform a task because that was their entire job. On agile teams we work in a flexible, collaborative, and often sophisticated manner. Process and tools are important, but people and the way we work together is far more important. The following table overviews common categories of tools.

Options (Not Ordered)	Tradeoffs
Acceptance test. Acceptance test tools capture and run user-level tests.	• Validates detailed requirements. • Enables us to take a test-driven, executable specifications, approach to requirements. • Forces us to think through detailed requirement logic. • Requires the person(s) capturing requirements to use a test tool rather than a documentation tool. • Acceptance tests can be difficult for stakeholders to read (at least at first).

Code analysis. There are two categories for this type of tool: static analysis tools that examine the source code and dynamic analysis tools that examine running software [W].	• Static code analysis tools can implement clear-box-level validation of code. • Dynamic analysis tools can implement black-box-level validation of code. • Automates grunge work of code reviews, enabling teams to focus on higher-level quality issues and education during such reviews.
Configuration management. Stores and tracks changes to artifacts, including source code, models, pictures, documents, data, and many others [CM].	• Enables teams to manage their assets effectively. • Foundation for continuous integration (CI). • Requires team to establish a CM strategy. What assets will be put under CM control and what is our branching strategy (see the *Accelerate Value Delivery* goal in Chapter 19)?
Continuous deployment (CD). Automatically deploys assets – such as working builds, image files, and data – from one environment to another [W].	• Enables teams to deploy more often and more consistently, thereby reducing deployment risk. • Reduces the cost of deployment, in some cases making it effectively free. • Requires investment in deployment infrastructure, often called a "CI/CD pipeline." • Requires investment in training and team process improvement, particularly around continuous integration (CI) and automated regression testing.
Continuous integration (CI). When something is checked into CM control, the CI tool automatically rebuilds the solution by recompiling, running regression test suite(s), and running code analysis tools [W].	• Automates the grunt work involved with building our solution. • CI is a fundamental technical practice for agile teams. • Requires investment in setting up tooling and the development of automated regression tests. • Requires investment in training and team process improvement, particularly around adoption of agile quality practices and automated regression testing.
Dashboard. Displays reports and critical information as configured by the team, in real-time. Uses data warehousing (DW) and business intelligence (BI) technologies to process data generated by the tools used by the team.	• Provides the team with real-time information about the status of their work. • Provides transparency to people outside of the team, enabling the monitoring aspects of governance and (hopefully) fact-based discussions. • Automates the generation of what used to be in (often fictional) project status reports, freeing management to focus on value-added activities. • Requires people using the dashboards to understand what information the various report widgets convey.
Integrated development environment (IDE). The programming and	• Fundamental development tool for software developers that combines a tailorable suite of programming, testing, and even visualization tooling.

testing tools used by team members.	
Group chat. Enables two or more people to send text messages (and often files) between each other.	• Enables discussions between team members that are geographically or temporally distributed. • Risk that it motivates people to not have face-to-face (F2F) conversations.
Operational monitoring. Tools that track end-user usage of a solution. Sometimes called crash analytics tools.	• Enables crash analytics, particularly important for exploring potential issues. • Provides real-time, operational intelligence to developers to help them identify what functionality is being used. • Supports Exploratory lifecycle and experimentation practices such as canary testing and split (A/B) testing. • Requires architectural scaffolding for event logging. • Potential for performance degradation due to logging.
Sketching surface. Somewhere that people can draw, such as a whiteboard, chalkboard, or paper.	• An inclusive strategy that enables effective communication between people and potentially active stakeholder participation. • Can be a valuable information radiator, particularly when the sketches are agile models such as architecture diagrams, screen design sketches, or business rules. • We can capture the information digitally if we need to.
Task board. A physical place where the team manages their work, typically a whiteboard or wall with sticky notes on it. Often called a Scrum board or Kanban board. See work item management below.	• A simple, inclusive tool that enables planning and coordination discussions. • Requires people to be physically present. • A physical task that illustrates development flow, is a good place for teams to start, before introducing tools and virtual boards. • Sticky notes will often fall off the board (so use little magnets).
Unit testing. Enables team members to write detailed tests, often using the xUnit framework.	• Enables test-first programming strategies. • Enables granular automated regression testing. • Requires both "test thinking" and development skills.
Wiki. A simple, Web-based documentation tool that supports multi-user editing.	• Straightforward, collaborative documentation tool. • Wiki pages can go stale over time and sometimes need to be pruned. Similarly the organization structure of the wiki will need to evolve too.
Work item (backlog) management. Software-based task board tool. Often called agile management tools, a Scrum board, Kanban board, or task board.	• Enables distributed planning and coordination. • May be required for regulatory compliance. • Requires more effort than a physical task board (see above).

25 ADDRESS RISK

Disciplined Agile Delivery (DAD) has several risk mitigation strategies built in:

1. **The Address Risk process goal**. Originally DAD had two risk-focused process goals, this one and *Identify Initial Risks*, but due to the significant overlap between the two we decided to simplify the framework by combining them into a single process goal.

2. **Support for a risk-value lifecycle**. DAD promotes a risk-value lifecycle approach where we recommend that risk be considered when prioritizing work in addition to stakeholder value – many agile methods focus just on value to their detriment. Figure 25.1 summarizes the risk-value profile for a DAD team, showing how DAD teams address a lot of risk very early in the lifecycle via addressing the *Stakeholder Vision* and *Proven Architecture* milestones (see Chapter 6). Figure 25.2 compares the risk profile/burndown of a typical DAD team with that of a typical Scrum team (which only takes a value-driven lifecycle) and a typical traditional team that pushes a lot of risk to the very end of the lifecycle.

3. **Support for ordered ways of working (WoW)**. As you've seen throughout the book, within each process goal diagram many of the decision points have ordered option/choice lists. This makes the lower-risk ways of working explicit because the more effective options tend to be towards the top of the lists.

Figure 25.1. The risk-value profile of a DAD team.

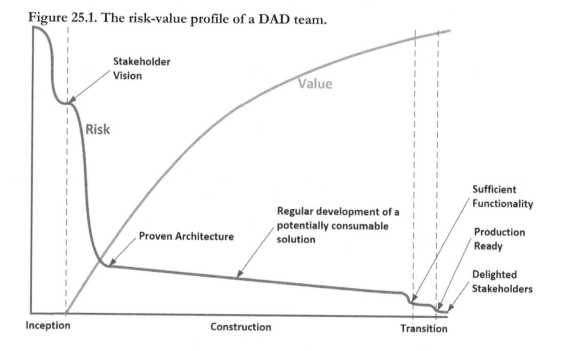

355

Figure 25.2. Comparing the risk burndowns of typical DAD, Scrum, and traditional teams.

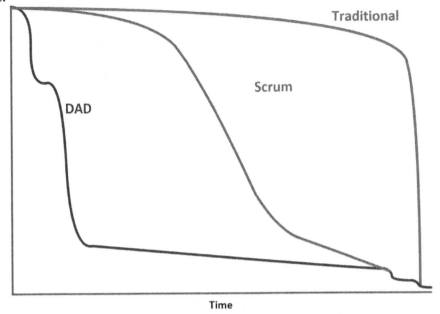

The Address Risk process goal, overviewed in Figure 25.3, provides options for how we will approach risk within our team. Although the project management community prefers the term "manage risk" rather than "address risk," not surprisingly, we find that the word manage comes with too much baggage – managing risk leaves the door open to needless bureaucracy, whereas addressing risk motivates us to focus on dealing with the challenges that we face. There are several reasons why the Address Risk goal is important:

1. **We face many risks.** Many risks are addressed within the team, but some risks we'll need help from outside the team to address. Disciplined teams make risks transparent, making it easier for them to garner the help they need.

2. **Understanding the level of risk is a critical decision factor for moving forward.** Two of the questions that we should ask at the Stakeholder Vision milestone is whether the team understands the risks that it faces and if so, does it have a viable strategy to respond to them? Similarly, any go-forward decision made during Construction should take the current level of risk faced by the team into account.

3. **Reducing risk increases our chance of success.** 'Nuff said.

4. **It's usually better to deal with risks early (in other words, shift risk mitigation left).** Risks tend to grow (but not always). If a risk proves to be a problem, it's better to know that early when we still have time and budget to fix it, or if the risk proves insurmountable, it's better to cancel or go in a different direction and thereby not waste time and money.

Figure 25.3. The goal diagram for Address Risk.

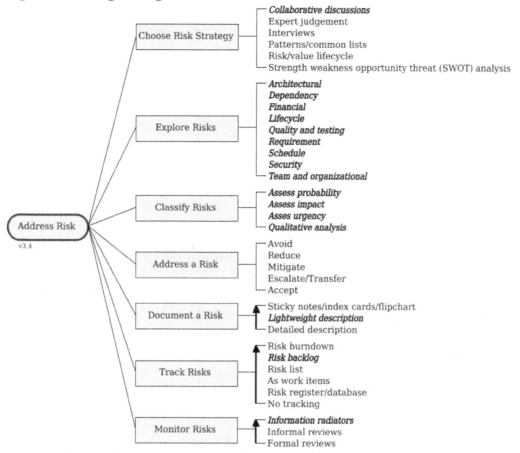

To address risk effectively, we need to consider several important questions:

- How will we identify risks?
- What type of risks will we consider?
- How will we classify/prioritize the risks?
- How will we respond to risks?
- How detailed will the risk descriptions be?
- How will we manage identified risks?
- How will we monitor risks on an ongoing basis?

Choose Risk Strategy

Part of the "discipline" in DAD is to explicitly identify and manage risks early and continuously throughout the release. The following table compares several strategies for doing so. The strategies can and should be combined.

Options (Not Ordered)	Trade-Offs
Collaborative discussions. The team, and often key stakeholders, openly discuss potential risks and their impacts.	• We obtain a wide range of opinions about the risks that we face. • The discussion needs to be facilitated, otherwise we run the risk of strong personalities dominating the discussion. • People may not be willing to publicly discuss some risks, particularly those that are people-oriented.
Expert judgment. The team seeks out the opinion of someone with deep experience in the domain that we're working in.	• A quick way to identify risks. • We may not have access to such experts, or we may not recognize that such expertise is available to us. • Inexperienced teams may choose to ignore risks identified by experts in the false belief that it's different this time or because they become overwhelmed with the nature of what they face.
Interviews. Someone from the team, often the Team Lead or Product Owner, interviews stakeholders to identify what they believe to be risks.	• Potential to have private discussions about risks that people may not be willing to discuss openly. • Potential to miss risks when not discussed as a group, because each individual may only understand a part of the overall risk, and the overall risk doesn't become apparent until we piece it together.
Patterns/common lists. A checklist of common risks, or risk categories, faced by IT delivery teams.	• Reusing existing risks increases likelihood reoccurring risks from past endeavors are not missed. • New types of risk may be missed because they are not included in the list.
Risk/value lifecycle. The team actively addresses risk early in the lifecycle, and may choose to develop risky functionality early so as to prove the architecture with working code.	• Increases the team's chance of success. • Enables the team to address risky items when they still have the most time and money available to do so. • If the team discovers a risk cannot be addressed, they can pivot or cancel the endeavor before they've spent too much effort on it. • Risky functionality tends to be more complex in nature, and can be difficult for a newly formed team to address when they are still learning how to work together.
Strength weakness opportunity threat (SWOT) analysis. A brainstorming technique to identify potential risks [W].	• Can take more time, but it is more rigorous in exploring potential risks. • Goes beyond risk identification, particularly in the identification of opportunities, which can drive interesting scope discussions. • Useful for assessing risks in competitive situations. • Useful in collaborative group discussions.

Explore Risks

Understanding what we need to explore in our discussions about risks is also important. The traditional thinking around RAID (Risk, Assumptions, Issues, and Dependencies) provides important insight for agilists, assuming we can keep things light [W]. Furthermore, the context of our situation is an important source of risk – for example, architectural risks are born in technical complexity and requirements risks in domain complexity. Thinking about the different types of risks can help ensure that important risks are not missed. The following table describes common risk types that we should consider [PMI].

Options (Not Ordered)	Trade-offs
Architectural. What technical risks, or long-term platform risks, do we face? Teams facing significant technical complexity are likely to face architectural risk.	• We want to ensure that we know the chosen technologies will work together as we expect in our environment, that our team understands how to work with the chosen technologies, and that any reusable assets we've chosen to work with are viable. • Potential for significant cost and delay if architectural problems are found late in the lifecycle. • Technical debt in existing legacy assets introduces architectural risk that can be very difficult to address. • We will want to work with our Enterprise Architects, if available, to explore these risks. • Architecture risk is often mitigated via the *Prove Architecture Early* process goal in Construction (Chapter 15), architectural spikes during Inception or Construction, and proof-of-concept (PoCs) mini-projects.
Dependency. Do we have dependencies on deliveries from other teams or organizations? Do they have dependencies on us? Teams facing significant technical complexity, domain complexity, or organizational distribution are likely to face dependency risk.	• When there are any changes in schedule, scope of functionality delivered, or quality of what is delivered, they will have a potentially negative impact on the dependent teams. This could impact schedule, cost, and even ability to deliver for those teams. • Dependency risk is mitigated by DAD teams via scheduling in the *Plan the Release* process goal (Chapter 11) and through continuous monitoring of those dependencies and adjusting the plan accordingly throughout Construction via the *Produce a Potentially Consumable Solution* process goal (Chapter 17).
Financial. Will we spend the investment in the team wisely?	• We want to ensure that we have sufficient funding to deliver the solution. • If funding is cut back or even cut completely, at least with a Disciplined Agile approach we've been delivering a potentially consumable solution that could be deployed into production if our stakeholders request that. • Financial risk is often mitigated via the *Secure Funding* process goal (Chapter 14), by updating our release plan and estimate throughout the lifecycle, and by providing transparency to our stakeholders.

Lifecycle. Have we chosen the appropriate lifecycle for our initiative?	• Each lifecycle has its strengths and weaknesses, even a traditional lifecycle (which isn't supported by DA, but we recognize that some teams will still choose to work this way). Our team should choose the best lifecycle given our skill set and the situation we face. • Many organizations choose to inflict a single lifecycle on all teams, often to simplify their governance, training, and other support strategies. This increases the chance that teams will waste effort making it appear that they're following the process. It also decreases the chance that our organization's agile transformation efforts will succeed because people will become convinced that agile isn't right for them, when the real problem is that one process size doesn't fit all. • A long release lifecycle increases the chance that we will build the wrong thing or miss the market. • We mitigate lifecycle risk on DAD teams via having several lifecycles (Agile, Lean, Continuous Delivery: Agile, Continuous Delivery: Lean, and Exploratory, and Program) to choose from. Chapter 6 explains these lifecycles, their trade-offs, and provides advice for when to choose each one. A consistent set of milestones across lifecycles enables senior management to govern effectively.
Quality and testing. Will our solution meet or exceed the functional and quality requirements set out for it? Teams facing technical or domain complexity are likely to face these sorts of risks.	• We want to ensure that our solution will meet the functional requirements, or fulfills the outcomes, of our stakeholders. We want to at least meet if not exceed their expectations so we delight them. • We want to ensure that our solution will meet quality requirements related to issues like performance, scalability, usability, and availability. • Potential to lose market share if quality is poor. • We will want to work with our Enterprise Architects, Data Managers, User Experience (UX) experts, and others to identify potential quality risks. • Quality risk is mitigated on DAD teams through explicit requirements exploration via the process goals *Explore Scope* (Chapter 9) and *Produce a Potentially Consumable Solution* (Chapter 17), through the process goal *Address Changing Stakeholder Needs* (Chapter 16), and through explicit support for testing via the *Develop Test Strategy* (Chapter 12) and *Accelerate Value Delivery* (Chapter 19) process goals.
Requirement. Do we sufficiently understand the requirements? Teams facing significant domain	• Although agilists embrace change that doesn't mean that all of our stakeholders do. We need to get the "stability" of the requirements to a point where our primary stakeholders are comfortable with the amount of

complexity are likely to face requirements risks.	potential change they will experience (or, to be more accurate, inject into the effort). • Reducing the feedback cycle by building the solution incrementally will enable us to both identify and reduce requirements risk early. • Early in the lifecycle we may be setting expectations about scope, schedule, and cost that will evolve as our understanding of the requirements evolve, and that may be seen as a risk by some stakeholders. • When requirements are very uncertain, our team can reduce risk by adopting the Exploratory lifecycle (Chapter 6) to identify what customers really want. In other situations it may be sufficient to identify the high-level requirements early via the *Explore Scope* process goal (Chapter 9) and then allow the details to evolve via the *Address Changing Stakeholder Needs* process goal (Chapter 16).
Schedule. Will we be able to deliver in a timely manner? The greater the complexity faced by a team, the greater the chance of schedule risk.	• We want to ensure that we are able to deliver the right business value at the right time to the right people. • In project-based cultures there is a risk that a desire to be "on schedule" is misinterpreted as delivering in a timely manner – don't let artificial deadlines motivate the team to make unwise decisions. • Schedule risk is mitigated in DAD through initial release planning during Inception to set initial expectations, having regular go-forward decisions throughout Construction, and through updating the release plan throughout Construction.
Security. How can our solution be misused to harm our customers, staff, or organization?	• We want to ensure that we understand the potential threats, from both people inside our organization and from outside of it, to our solution. • Potential for significant loss, both monetary and image, if security risks are not addressed. • We will want to work with our organization's security engineers, if available, to explore these risks. • Security risk is mitigated in DAD by identifying security requirements early in the lifecycle, by addressing those requirements in both our architectural strategy and testing strategy, and by including security engineers as stakeholders and potentially as technical experts within the team.
Team and organizational. What people-oriented risks do we face? Large teams or teams that are either geographically or	• We want to ensure that our team has sufficient skills, resources, and authority to fulfill our team's mission. • In the case of a new team, there is a risk that we may not work well together at first. • The existing organization culture and structure may add to the risks faced by the team.

organizationally distributed are likely to face these kinds of risk.	• We will want to work with key decision makers within our organization to identify and mitigate these risks. • Team and organizational risks are addressed via the *Form Team* process goal (Chapter 7), the *Grow Team Members* process goal (Chapter 22), and through DAD's people first philosophy, which promotes collaboration, humility, and respect.

Classify Risks

Classifying risks helps to prioritize them, which informs us about which ones to focus on. The following table identifies several strategies, which can be combined, for classifying risks [PMI]. Note that there may be an organizational standard in place for risk classification, likely driven by a desire for rolling up risks to the enterprise level (see the process goal *Align With Enterprise Direction* in Chapter 8). If so, we need to be aware of this.

Options (Not Ordered)	Trade-Offs
Assess probability. What is the likelihood of the risk occurring?	• Important input into assessing the urgency of a risk (see below). • Can be difficult to assess the probability of a risk that we know little about, or one that has many contributing factors. • Groups of people can downplay risks, so it's important for someone to question any group decisions.
Assess impact. What will happen if the risk does occur?	• Important input into assessing the urgency of a risk (see below). • Many risks are qualitative in nature, but their impact can still be assessed quantitatively (see below). • Some risks are "creeping risks" that start small and grow over time – they can be difficult to identify at first and you become inured to them over time until they become large and difficult (if not impossible) to address. • Risks that appear to be low-impact at the team level can have a huge impact at the enterprise level if they occur across teams.
Assess urgency. How important do we consider this risk?	• One way to easily calculate this is urgency = probability X impact. • The urgency is an important driver of whether, and if so when, we will address a risk. • Because urgency is qualitative there is the opportunity for people to either overestimate or underestimate it given their priorities. The implication is that we want several people collaborating together to determine urgency.
Qualitative analysis. How could this risk impact qualitative issues such	• Some risks are hard to quantify and are more subjective in nature. Some risks are "infinite risks" that are difficult to quantify but can also completely nullify our work (such as persistent technical debt problems in our data or code).

as customer trust, our public image, or staff morale (to name a few)?	• Some risks may have several potential impacts – i.e. There is X% chance of impact A, Y% change of impact B, and Z% of impact C. • Qualitative risks should still be quantified, but must be done so in a consistent manner.

Address a Risk

It isn't enough to identify potential risks, we also want to address them in some way [PMI]. Our advice is that risks should be addressed at the most responsible moment for doing so – Although this is often earlier (avoid risk or "shift left") rather than later, it still requires a judgement call on the part of the team. As you can see in the following table we have several options for doing so.

Options (Ordered)	Trade-Offs
Avoid. We steer our efforts so that the risk doesn't occur. For example, we might not use a specific technology or not implement certain functionality.	• Very often a risk disappears given time, so avoiding it now may allow for this to happen. • Our risk profile remains the same. • Some risks grow over time, so avoiding a risk now may make it even worse if it does occur. • We may make decisions that hurt us in the long run.
Reduce. We work to lessen the impact of the risk, but not fully remove it, if/when it does occur.	• The risk is understood and the potential impact of it is now acceptable to our stakeholders. • Reduces the risk profile of our endeavor. • This risk has not completely disappeared. • Requires investment to reduce the risk, which could have been spent on new functionality.
Mitigate. We work to remove (fully reduce) the risk.	• Reduces the risk profile of our endeavor. • Requires investment to mitigate the risk, which could have been spent on new functionality.
Escalate/transfer. We ask someone else to address the risk. This is escalation when it is senior leadership and transfer when it is another group.	• The risk is transferred to people with the ability to address it properly. • The risk profile of our endeavor had not changed until the risk is actually mitigated/reduced.
Accept. We decide to take on the impact of the risk if/when it occurs. This can be passive ("We'll deal with it if it occurs") or active ("Let's come up with a plan to put into action if the risk is realized")	• The risk is understood and the potential impact of it is acceptable to our stakeholders. • Our risk profile remains the same. • We will need to monitor the risk even though we have accepted it.

Document a Risk

Traditional risk management can be overly rigorous in its descriptions, response strategies, and tracking. We want to keep the documentation as concise as we possibly can. Note that regulatory compliance may require that we provide proof that we have a risk management strategy in place, thereby requiring some sort of documentation for that proof.

Options (Ordered)	Trade-Offs
Sticky notes/index cards. A risk is captured on paper and managed on a wall. The stickies/cards are typically organized as a prioritized stack, with the high-risk items at the top and the lowest risk at the bottom.	• A simple, inclusive approach to documenting risks. • We may still need to report risks to management as part of our IT governance strategy. • Regulatory compliance can be achieved by taking a picture of our risk list on a regular basis and putting the picture under configuration management (CM) control.
Lightweight description. A brief overview of each risk, perhaps with an indication of the potential impact and probability, is captured. This is typically done digitally via a spreadsheet, wiki, or agile management tool (such as Jira, Jile, or LeanKit).	• A straightforward strategy that works well. • Viable in organizations new to agile that are used to traditional, heavier forms of capturing risks. • Regulatory compliance is achieved in most cases with this strategy (remember to verify this by reading the regulations ourselves).
Detailed description. A detailed write-up of each individual risk is captured and maintained.	• A heavy-weight, time-consuming process. • Often applied in situations where audits or formal risk reviews are likely. • Life-critical regulations may require more detailed risk descriptions, response strategies, and contingency plans. • Traditional approaches around risk documentation include taking either a RAID (Risks, Assumptions, Issues, and Dependencies) or a SWOT (Strengths, Weaknesses, Opportunities, and Threats) based approach.

Track Risks

How are our identified risks going to be tracked? The following table compares strategies for capturing and then maintaining documented risks.

Options (Ordered)	Trade-Offs
Risk burndown. A chart that shows the trend in the risk score for the team. The risk score is the quantitative total of	• Enables us to explicitly show how our risk profile is trending over time. • Risk scores (as a scalar value) are not comparable across teams. Risk trends, the change in the risk score over time, are comparable across teams (although using metrics to

probability × impact. An example is shown in Figure 25.4.	compare teams tends to be a risky strategy in practice). • Provides important governance insight to senior management.
Risk backlog. Risks are put into a backlog and prioritized like other work.	• Teams that are familiar with managing their work in backlogs, or better yet work item lists or work item pools, will find this to be a straightforward strategy. • Works particularly well when risks are monitored as an information radiator (see below). • When the risk backlog is part of the normal work management strategy (such as a product backlog or work item pool), we will need to ensure that risks are prominent so that they will be addressed properly.
Risk list. Risks are maintained in a list, typically in a spreadsheet (placed under CM control) or a Wiki page. An example of a risk list is shown in Figure 25.5 [PMI].	• Simple strategy that benefits from the math and reporting functionality of spreadsheets. • Risk lists, when not maintained as an information radiator (see below), tend to be forgotten and unused by the team. • Meets most regulatory requirements.
As work items. Risks, and by implication the work required to mitigate each risk, are managed as work items in our work item list/pool.	• Simple and straightforward approach that works well for risks that can be mitigated quickly. • Some risks require a significant amount of work to address, which would need to be captured as several work items. • With a manual work item management strategy, risks are often captured using a specific color of sticky. With a digital strategy, a risk work item type will need to be created and supporting risk reports or dashboard widgets.
Risk register/database. A specialized tool for tracking risks is adopted. Risk registers are often maintained at the organizational level outside of the team so that enterprise-level risk may be managed [PMI].	• Useful when needing to report risks across teams, assuming the other teams are using the same tooling in roughly the same way. • Often seen as a management burden by agile teams because it is outside of their work environment. • Risk registers, even when displayed as an information radiator, tend to get forgotten and are unused by the team. • Very likely to meet strict regulatory requirements, particularly in life-critical situations.
No tracking. Although we discuss risks as a team we choose not to keep track of them.	• Applicable for very low-risk situations. • Many potential risks will be forgotten until the point that they occur. • Risks are typically ignored until they become a problem for the team and are often expensive to address.

365

Figure 25.4. An example risk burndown chart.

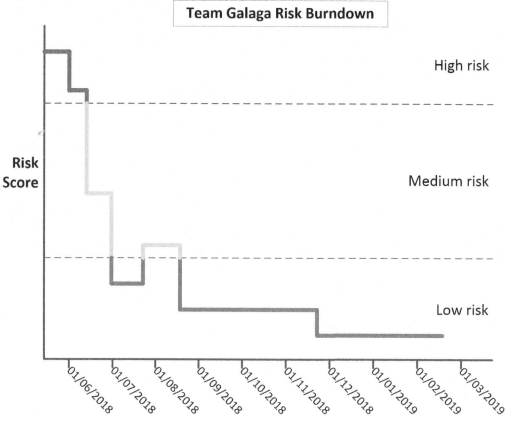

Figure 25.5. A risk list captured via a spreadsheet.

Risk	Probability (1-10)	Impact (1-10)	Magnitude
If the team has insufficient access to key stakeholders we will not understand their real needs	8	10	80
If the security framework is not available on or before June 15 our schedule will slip	4	10	40
If the the continuous connection to Head Office for inventory management is sufficiently fault tolerant the solution will not be sufficiently responsive	7	5	35
If we do not have 3 second response time or better on credit transactions the solution will not be sufficiently responsive	6	4	24

Monitor Risks

We need to monitor risk over time and work to mitigate the risks appropriately [PMI]. The following table compares common strategies for monitoring risks.

Options (Not Ordered)	Trade-Offs
Information Radiators. Risks are displayed publicly, either physically on a team wall or digitally on a team dashboard. Also known as "big visible charts."	• Because the risks are "in our face," it increases the chance that people will understand and address the risks. • The team's risk management efforts are transparent to the team and to stakeholders.
Informal reviews. The team reviews the current risks, updating them accordingly. Informal risk reviews are often incorporated in iteration reviews.	• Ensures that we explicitly manage our risks. • The cadence of the informal reviews must reflect the amount of risk faced by the team – the more risk, the more we want to review where we are in addressing them. • Often perceived as "yet another meeting" by the team, particularly when the reviews are run separately from other sessions such as coordination meetings or iteration reviews.
Audit/formal reviews. An outside auditor periodically works with the team to assess their current risk response strategy.	• Can inject schedule delay, or last-minute scrambling to meet a review date, into the efforts of the team. • Can motivate creation of overly comprehensive risk documentation in the fear that we may fail a review. • May be required in complex or regulatory situations where risks need to be reviewed by enterprise authorities and shared between teams and other stakeholders.

26 LEVERAGE AND ENHANCE EXISTING INFRASTRUCTURE

The Leverage and Enhance Existing Infrastructure process goal, overviewed in Figure 26.1, provides options for reusing and hopefully improving existing assets within our organization. These assets may include guidance, functionality, data, and even process related materials. This process goal is related to the *Improve Quality* process goal (see Chapter 18) which focuses on strategies to pay down technical debt in such assets and the *Reuse Engineering* process blade [AmblerLines2017] which focuses on the reuse of existing assets.

> **Key Points in this Chapter**
> - Greater levels of reuse lead to lower costs, quicker time to market, and higher levels of quality.
> - Reuse is hard. Really hard.
> - Paying down technical debt is critical to your organization's long-term success.

There are several reasons why this goal is important:

1. **A lot of good work has occurred before us**. There is a wide range of assets within our organization that our team can leverage. Sometimes we will discover that we need to first evolve the existing asset so that it meets our needs, which often proves faster and less expensive than building it from scratch.

2. **We can reduce overall technical debt**. The unfortunate reality is that many organizations struggle under significant technical debt loads – poor quality code, poor quality data, and a lack of automated regression tests are all too common. By choosing to reuse existing assets, and investing in paying down some of the technical debt that we run into when doing so, we'll slowly dig our way out of the technical debt trap that we find ourselves in.

3. **We can provide greater value quicker**. Increased reuse enables us to focus on implementing new functionality to delight our customers instead of just reinventing what we're already offering them. By paying down technical debt we increase the underlying quality of the infrastructure upon which we're building, enabling us to deliver new functionality faster over time.

Figure 26.1. The goal diagram for Leverage and Enhance Existing Infrastructure.

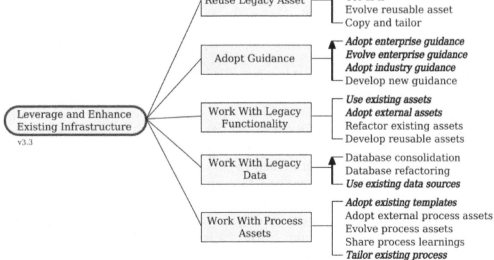

369

This ongoing process goal describes how we will ensure that our team will take advantage of, and hopefully improve, our existing organizational assets. To be effective, we need to consider several important questions:

- How are we going to reuse an asset?
- What guidelines should we adopt and follow?
- What technical assets, such as services and legacy systems, can we reuse?
- What existing data sources can we access?
- What practices and procedures can we adopt?

Reuse Legacy Asset

When it comes to reuse, there are several important principles to keep in mind. First, you need to make a tailoring decision when you "reuse" something. Will you work with the asset as is, configure it, refactor it to pay down any technical debt that you have found, or evolve it to meet your full needs? These options range from zero tailoring to significant tailoring, and the more you tailor an asset the more likely it is that it would be better for you to not try to reuse it at all. Second, reused assets will need to evolve over time, implying that we may need to bring those changes into our solution. This is great if there is an automated regression test suite in place for the asset (if appropriate) and our team regularly releases into production. It's not great if we're taking a project-based approach and we don't currently have plans for future releases. Third, building something to be reusable is hard. Having said all of these things, we are still firm believers in reuse in the proper context. You can see in the following table that there are several options for reusing legacy assets.

Options (Ordered)	Trade-Offs
Configure asset. The asset is reused without modification to the code, but configuration information is modified to tailor the asset's behavior.	<ul><li>Increases the quality of our solution (reusable assets are usually very high quality).</li><li>Reduces overall technical debt within our organization.</li><li>Better time to market for our team because we can focus on achieving the unique aspects of the outcomes that we've committed to.</li><li>We may be able to get help from our organization's reuse engineering team (see the *Reuse Engineering* process blade [AmblerLines2017]).</li><li>Provides greater flexibility than a non-configurable asset.</li><li>Requires greater investment in the development of the asset to make it configurable.</li><li>Not everything we need may be configurable. We may need to submit new functionality to the owner, or work with them to get the functionality that we need.</li><li>We need to invest the time to learn how to configure the asset.</li></ul>
Use as is. The asset is reused without any modification. Examples include invoking an	<ul><li>Increases the quality of our solution (reusable assets are usually very high quality).</li><li>Reduces overall technical debt within our organization.</li><li>Better time to market for our team because we can focus on achieving the unique aspects of the outcomes that we've committed to.</li></ul>

370

existing service or working with a commercial code library.	• We may be able to get help from our organization's reuse engineering team (see the *Reuse Engineering* process blade [AmblerLines2017]). • The asset may not provide all the functionality we need. We may need to submit new functionality to the owner, or work with them to get the functionality that we need.
Evolve reusable asset. The asset is evolved to meet the needs of the team, and the changes are made available to other users of the asset.	• We can ensure that the reusable asset meets our needs. • It may take a lot of effort to negotiate and then work with the owner of the asset to evolve it. • The changes that we need may not be of interest to others, and may be rejected by the asset owner. • It can be expensive and difficult to develop reusable assets, requiring sophisticated engineering skills that we may not have on our team. • The new or evolved feature(s) are not reusable until they've been reused, implying we risk overbuilding an asset in the name of potential reusability. • We should get help from our organization's reuse engineering team (see the *Reuse Engineering* process blade [AmblerLines2017]).
Copy and tailor. The asset is copied and the team evolves the copy to meet their needs.	• A quick and easy approach, at least in the short term. • We get what we want. • If we need to make a lot of changes to the asset we may have been better off developing that functionality from scratch. • There is a potential to miss out on future changes of the original asset, or we may need to perform a potentially expensive refit to accept the new version. • Increases the overall technical debt in our organization because multiple copies of the same asset exist.

Adopt Guidance

An easy way to improve the quality of our work is to adopt and then follow, where appropriate, commonly accepted guidance (see the *Improve Quality* process goal of Chapter 18 for other strategies) – effective guidance is an enabling constraint that provides guardrails for teams. Another benefit of adopting common guidance is that it is a great way to share learnings across the organization. The topic of guidance may address a specific technology (i.e. MongoDB), a programming language (e.g. Java or Python), a platform (e.g. Linux or MQSeries), or even an activity (e.g. security or user experience (UX)). Examples of potential guidance include coding standards, user interface (UI) guidelines, security guidelines, data standards, and many more.

Our experience is that the best guidance comes from proven practice tempered with the insights of people with experience in that topic. Figure 26.2 captures the lifecycle of the development and evolution of guidance. The need for guidance often starts with a team. They're working with a topic where the organization doesn't have existing guidance and they recognize the need for it. Sometimes an enterprise team may be waiting for a delivery team to run into the need for the guidance, and may have even gotten a bit ahead of things and have begun working on what they believe to be appropriate guidance. Either way, the enterprise team and the delivery team collaborate to develop guidance that is appropriate for the situation at hand. This strategy helps to ensure that the practical considerations of the team is addressed, that the guidance is developed on a just-in-time (JIT) basis, and that long-term enterprise concerns are also taken into account. In Figure 26.2 you see that Team A and Enterprise Team work together to develop and then apply the initial draft of the guidance. The appropriate enterprise team is determined by the topic. For example, data guidance is typically the responsibility of the data management team, technical guidance the responsibility of the architecture team, security standards the responsibility of the security team, and so on. Once the guidance is shown to be effective in practice, the responsibility for it is taken over by the enterprise team. You can also see in Figure 26.2 that the enterprise team provides the guidance to other delivery teams, in this case Team B and Team C. Evolution of the guidance occurs over time, with the enterprise team working closely with delivery teams to do so (which Team C is doing in Figure 26.2).

Figure 26.2. Collaborative development and support of guidance.

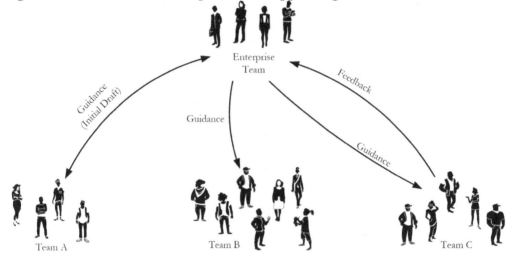

As you can see in the following table we have several options for adopting guidance within our team. In all cases our advice is to keep the guidance light weight, easy to read and understand, easy to access (maintaining it in a Wiki works well), and most importantly practical.

Options (Ordered)	Trade-Offs
Adopt enterprise guidance. Our organization has recommended guidelines that teams are expected to adopt. Enterprise guidance is often based on industry guidance that is adapted to the organization (hopefully with slight modifications).	• Common guidance across teams increases the chance that team members coming from existing teams will know it. • Enterprise guidance is likely to be proven to work within our organization. • Following enterprise guidance decreases the chance that we'll inject technical debt based on inconsistent work. • The team will need to familiarize itself with the guidance.

372

	• Enterprise guidance needs to be supported and evolved over time, otherwise it goes stale and will be ignored.
Evolve enterprise guidance. When existing enterprise guidance doesn't perfectly fit our situation, or when the topic of the guidance has evolved, our team should work with the enterprise team responsible for the guidance to evolve it.	• We will have guidance that fits with our situation. • Easier than developing our own from scratch. • Our team will need to invest the time to work with the enterprise group responsible for the guidance to evolve it to meet our needs.
Adopt industry guidance. Many platforms, languages, and technologies have recognized guidelines for their effective usage.	• The guidance has been proven to work in other organizations. • The source of a topic likely knows it best and will produce better guidance. • External parties have taken on the cost of developing and maintaining the guidance. • New hires are more likely to know the industry guidance than something we created in house. • It is better to first try to adopt existing enterprise guidance, then if that doesn't exist work with the appropriate enterprise team to adopt industry guidance. • Industry guidance is a good starting point, although we may need to modify for our unique situation. • The industry guidance may not be evolved in a timely manner, or updates to the industry guidance may be difficult to bring into our modified version.
Develop new guidance. When no guidance exists for a given topic our team may find that it needs to develop the initial draft of the guidance, often collaborating with an enterprise team to do so.	• We are able to develop guidance that exactly meets our needs. • This requires a lot of work and should be seen as a strategy of last resort. • We will need to maintain the guidance over time. • We may not have the expertise on the team to develop effective guidance (although we may believe we do). • Other teams may follow a different strategy, leading to collaboration and integration problems later and thereby increasing technical debt.

Work With Legacy Functionality

In many organizations there is a significant amount of functionality available to reuse. This functionality may include web services, microservices, frameworks, domain components, platforms, code libraries, and many other technologies. Disciplined Agilists will reuse these existing assets whenever they can, and more importantly they will pay down technical debt that they run into so that the functionality becomes a true organizational asset. Greater reuse and the investment in quality enables us to increase our overall consistency of service and potentially enables DevOps through promoting a common infrastructure. You can see in the following table that there are several options for working with legacy functionality.

Options (Not Ordered)	Trade-Offs
Use existing assets. Use the existing asset as is.	• This is a straightforward strategy requiring minimal effort by the team. • We will need to invest the time to understand the asset, which is best done by working closely with the enterprise team (see *Coordinate Activities* in Chapter 23). • Our solution will now have a dependency on the asset. • Promotes greater consistency across solutions.
Adopt external assets. The team downloads (in the case of open source), purchases (in the case of commercial products), or obtains access to (for cloud-based services) assets that are currently external to our organization for use in building their solution.	• This is often faster and cheaper than building the asset. • We will need to work with the enterprise groups to ensure it's on the roadmap (or at least not prohibited by the roadmap). • We may not be able to find an external asset that is a perfect fit, requiring us to evolve it. The more we need to modify it, the less the benefit of reusing the asset. • Our solution will now have a dependency on the asset. • There is a potential for unexpected costs in the future. • There may be negative impact in the future if the asset provider changes direction or abandons the asset.
Refactor existing assets. The team improves the quality of an existing asset while using it in building their solution. See the *Improve Quality* process goal (Chapter 18).	• Pays down organizational technical debt. • Decreases the risk of using the asset due to increased quality. • Requires investment of time and money.
Develop reusable assets. The team develops something with the intent of making it available for others to reuse. See the *Reuse Engineering* process blade [AmblerLines2017] for strategies to develop reusable assets.	• We will develop a high-quality asset that works well for us. • Requires skill and significant investment in quality and design. • It is very hard to predict what others will want and this strategy often leads to a "reuseless asset" that nobody else is interested in. It is usually better to wait until another teams needs it and then do the work to harvest, rework, and then reintegrate the asset.

374

Work with Legacy Data

Our organization likely has many data sources that we can potentially reuse. In particular, we should always strive to work with the "source of record" (SoR) for any given data to work with the "official" values. If we instead choose to create yet another data source we are effectively increasing the technical data debt within our organization. Yes, working with existing legacy sources can be frustrating at times, particularly when the owners of those databases work in a less-than-agile manner (see AgileData.org for agile strategies for data professionals). Because Disciplined Agilists are Enterprise Aware we understand that it's for the good of our organization that we strive to leverage and enhance existing data sources whenever possible. The following table describes several options for doing so.

Options (Ordered)	Trade-Offs
Database consolidation. We refactor existing databases to move critical data into a smaller number of SoRs while simultaneously refactoring our solutions to work with the SoRs.	• Pays down data-oriented technical debt. • Increases data consistency and quality across solutions. • Makes data warehousing easier due to few data sources to work with. • Requires investment and often significant effort. • Must be thoroughly tested, requiring automated regression tests that don't (yet) exist.
Database refactoring. We apply refactorings, small changes to the design that improve without changing its semantics in a practical manner, to fix any problems before we use the data source in a solution [DBRefactoring].	• Pays down data-oriented technical debt. • Higher quality data sources means our code can be simpler as we won't need to code around data quality problems any more. • Requires skill and tooling infrastructure (many options now exist). • We will require an automated regression test suite for the database if we are to safely refactor it.
Use existing data sources. The team uses the existing data source(s) as is.	• We do not need to do the work to create and then maintain a new data source. • Appropriate when the data source is high-quality or the SoR. Otherwise should be considered for refactoring or consolidation. • Any data quality problems are addressed within our source code, thereby increasing technical debt.

Work with Process Assets

Just because our team finds itself in a unique situation, that doesn't imply that we need to develop our own process from scratch (as this book should make readily clear). We can and should reuse existing process assets, particularly when we are working in a regulatory environment where we are required to have a defined process to follow (and proof of doing so). We should also help to evolve these assets as we learn and improve so that others can benefit from our experiences. As you can see in the following table we have several options for working with our organization's process assets. For greater detail see the *Evolve Your Way of Working (WoW)* process goal (Chapter 24).

375

Options (Not Ordered)	Trade-Offs
Adopt existing templates. The team chooses to apply existing artifact templates, typically for documentation. See the process goal *Improve Quality* (Chapter 18) for a discussion of templates.	• Increases consistency of artifacts across teams. • Concise templates tend to lead to focused documentation albeit with "free form" sections for the unique parts. • Comprehensive templates tend to lead to low-quality documentation.
Adopt external process assets. The team adopts existing process advice (practices, strategies, even entire methods) from external sources.	• The process/method might not be a very good fit for our actual situation. • You may not be able to find external people experienced in that process asset. • Even when it is a good fit for us, the process/method will still require some tailoring. • The trade-offs that you're making may not be explicitly described (unlike with DA).
Evolve process assets. The team updates existing process assets, including external ones, to reflect potential improvements. See the *Continuous Improvement* process blade [AmblerLines2017] for detailed advice.	• Increases the process fit with the rest of the organization. • Enables the team to share learnings with others. • Requires investment of time and effort. • Changes to the existing assets need to be coordinated across teams, often something a Community of Practice (CoP)/guild does.
Share process learnings. The team shares their potential improvements with others. See the *Continuous Improvement* process blade [AmblerLines2017] for detailed advice.	• Increases overall organizational effectiveness. • Requires investment of time and effort. • Requires venues/opportunities for the team to share, such as lunch-and-learns, internal discussion forums, or open spaces.
Tailor existing process. The team tailors existing process assets to meet the needs of the situation that we actually face.	• Increases the process fit with our situation. • Requires skill and expertise (so get certified in DA to get that). • Requires the team to have somewhere to publish then maintain our process, such as a Wiki or internal web site.

376

27 GOVERN DELIVERY TEAM

The Govern Delivery Team process goal, overviewed in Figure 27.1, provides options for governing agile and lean delivery teams. Governance establishes chains of responsibility, authority and communication in support of the overall enterprise's goals and strategy. It also establishes measurements, policies, standards and control mechanisms to enable people to carry out their roles and responsibilities effectively. You do this by balancing risk versus return on investment (ROI), setting in place effective processes and practices, defining the direction and goals for a team, and defining the roles that people play within a team.

Key Points in this Chapter
• Agile/lean teams will be governed by your organizational leadership, and they deserve to be governed well.
• Effective governance is about motivating people to "do the right thing" and then enabling them to do so.
• Ineffective governance is about enforcing consistency or process or deliverables across teams.

The Govern Delivery Team process goal is supported by both the *IT Governance* and the *Control* process blades [AmblerLines2017]. There are several reasons why this goal is important:

1. **We are going to be governed**. Many in the agile community believe that governance is a swear word, likely because they've had negative experiences when traditional governance strategies [COBIT] were applied to agile teams. Although we understand this attitude we find it to be counterproductive because someone is going to govern our teams, like it or not. Someone will govern the finances, they will govern the quality, and they will govern what we produce – just to name a few issues.

2. **We deserve to be governed well**. Our team is made up of intellectual workers, people who are smart and skilled at their jobs. They respond well to leadership, to deciding for themselves what to do and not very well to management, or being told what to do. As a result effective governance is based on motivation and enablement, not command and control.

3. **Governance is context sensitive**. The way a team is governed is situational. A traditional waterfall team is governed in a very different way than an agile project team, which in turn is governed in a different way than a team following the Continuous Delivery: Lean lifecycle. Teams that are less experienced or facing significant risk will require more governance than those that are not.

4. **Our team is part of a larger organization, and we need to leverage that**. Our organization is a complex adaptive system (CAS), a collection of teams working together in an adaptable and constantly changing manner. And we've been doing this for a very long time, in some cases decades and even centuries. We have a wealth of experience, skills, intellectual property, and physical assets available to us that we can use in new ways to delight our customers. The point is that we don't need to work on our own, and in fact we likely can't given the complexity that we face, and we certainly don't need to build everything from scratch.

5. **Effective governance enables collaboration**. Given that our organization is a CAS, the leaders who are governing us must focus on helping our teams to be successful. This includes ensuring that we have the resources we require to accomplish our mission and to ensuring that we're collaborating effectively with the

other teams whom we need help from.

6. **We have responsibilities to external stakeholders**. Our team has stakeholders to whom we are beholden, and one aspect of governance is to ensure that our team meets their needs. These stakeholders include auditors who need to ensure that we're compliant to any appropriate regulations or internal processes, legal professionals who help us to address appropriate legal issues, and company shareholders (citizens when we work for a government agency or non-profit) whom we effectively work for.

Figure 27.1. The goal diagram for Govern Delivery Team.

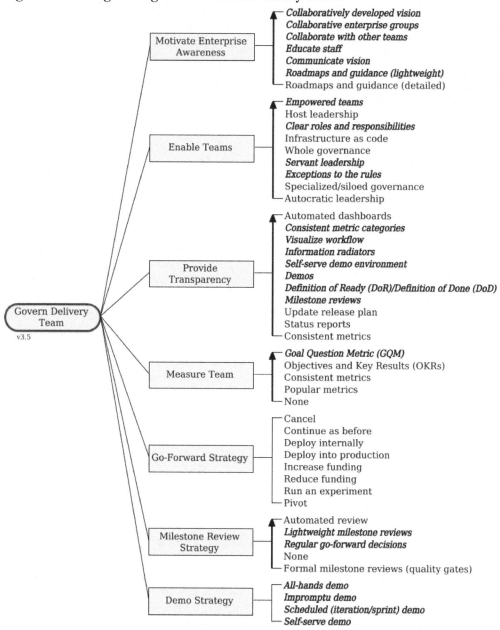

The potential scope of governance is depicted in Figure 27.2. Our focus in the process goal is on Delivery/Development governance, but as you can imagine the other governance categories have an effect on it. For example, solution delivery teams will still be governed in their use of data, guided by user experience (UX) standards, funded in accordance to Finance guidelines, while fulfilling roles supported by People (Management) governance.

Figure 27.2. The scope of governance.

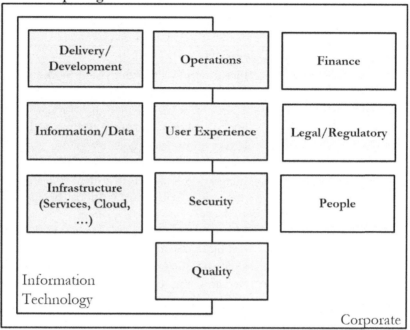

Throughout this chapter we use several terms that we want to define now:
- **Leadership (n)**. People within our organization, often senior management, who are leaders.
- **Enterprise groups**. Teams responsible for information technology (IT) or enterprise-level activities such as enterprise architects, finance, security, and procurement [AmblerLines2017].
- **Enterprise professionals**. People such as enterprise architects, finance professionals, security engineers, and procurement specialists.

This ongoing process goal describes how we will ensure that our team is successful. To be effective, we need to consider several important questions:
- How can leadership motivate staff to be enterprise aware?
- How can leadership enable teams to follow their vision?
- How will we provide visibility to our stakeholders?
- How will we measure our effectiveness as a team?
- How will we regularly determine how we will move forward as a team, if at all?
- How will we run reviews, if at all?
- How will we run demonstrations?

Motivate Enterprise Awareness

An important aspect of effective governance is to help teams understand and then work in an enterprise aware manner. Enterprise awareness is one of the seven principles of the Disciplined Agile (DA) toolkit, see Chapter 2, and it refers to the concept that people should strive to do what is right for the organization, not just what is convenient for them. In other words, to understand and work towards the "big picture." For this to work in practice, people need to understand what that big picture is and why it's important, we need to motivate them to be enterprise aware. As you can see in the following table there are several options for doing so.

Options (Ordered)	Trade-Offs
Collaboratively developed vision. The "governed" are actively involved with the development and evolution of our organization's vision.	• Increased buy in to the vision by the people meant to follow it. • There's a greater chance the vision will be realistic due to a wider range of people involved. • It takes time and effort, and more of it due to the greater number of people involved.
Collaborative enterprise groups. Enterprise groups collaboratively work with teams. Part of this collaboration is to help the team achieve its mission and another part is to educate and coach the team in the skills and knowledge of the enterprise-level topic.	• Increases the chance that delivery teams will follow the vision, reuse organizational assets, and follow guidance. • Requires the enterprise groups to be sufficiently flexible to work with a range of teams, each of which has their own way of working (WoW). • Requires the enterprise group to be sufficiently staffed.
Collaborate with other teams. Our team is only one of many within the organization and we often need to collaborate with other teams to achieve the outcomes that we want.	• Other teams can help our team to achieve the outcomes that we're aiming for more effectively than if we worked alone. • Interacting with other teams provides opportunities to learn about their viewpoint and priorities, helping us to understand the bigger picture. • The other teams may not be willing, or able, to work in an agile manner and may need help to do so. • Collaboration with other teams may introduce bottlenecks in our workflow that will need to be addressed.
Educate staff. Our organization must educate, train, and coach staff members in enterprise-level concerns such as security, our business vision, our technical vision, and many other critical issues.	• Increased knowledge within a team increases the chance that people will act in an enterprise aware manner. • The more knowledge and skills within a team, the less support the team will need from enterprise groups. • Enables the team to optimize the overall workflow because they have a better understanding of the

	• overall strategy. • Requires ongoing investment.
Communicate vision. Leadership must consistently communicate their vision, and the reasons behind the vision, to the rest of the organization.	• Increases the chance that people will understand the organization's direction and priorities. • Requires ongoing effort due to the need to reinforce the (evolving) vision. • Requires several communication channels due to differences in learning preferences. • No guarantee that everyone will listen.
Roadmaps and guidance (lightweight). Our organization's business and technical roadmaps, as well as guidance in enterprise issues such as security, data, operational excellence, user experience (UX), and many more topics is captured in a concise and easily consumable manner.	• Provides guardrails, also called "enabling constraints," for teams. • Increased probability that people will read the artifacts compared with detailed artifacts. • The details won't be there, requiring another strategy (such as collaborative enterprise groups), to get the details to teams. • Investment is required to keep the artifacts up to date.
Roadmaps and guidance (detailed). Our organization's roadmaps and enterprise guidance is captured in detail and made accessible to the appropriate audiences for it.	• Provides explicit guardrails for teams. • Detailed information is available to anyone who requires it, anytime and anywhere it's needed. • Detailed documentation is the least effective means available to communicate information, and people are less likely to trust it. • Significant investment required to keep the artifacts up to date.

Enable Teams

Agile team members are human, and being human their natural tendency is to do the easiest thing possible. The implication is that for things that we want to have happen we should enable the teams to do those things, to make them easy to do. Effective governance strategies focus on making it as easy as possible for people to follow the organization's vision and painful not to. As you can see in the following table we have several options for doing so.

Options (Ordered)	Trade-Offs
Empowered teams. The team has the authority and resources that it requires to fulfill its mission.	• Teams will still require some guidance/guardrails. • Provides flexibility to the team to do what is best for the context that they face. • Requires organizational leadership to trust the teams. • Can be disconcerting, at first, for command-and-control (C&C) leaders.
Host leadership. A host is someone who receives and	• Provides the flexibility for teams to choose their way of working (WoW) while providing the support and

381

entertains guests. Sometimes they act as a hero, planning and organizing things. Sometimes they act as a servant, encouraging, providing space, and joining in [Host].	guidance they need. • Requires skills and resources to be the hero when need be. • Coaching is often required to help leaders evolve away from a C&C mindset.
Clear roles and responsibilities. The roles – such as Team Lead, Team Member, Product Owner, and Architecture Owner – and their responsibilities are defined and accepted by the team. This information is often captured, or at least referenced, in the team's working agreement.	• Provides clarity regarding decision making authority. • Can dramatically reduce "politics," both within a team and with external groups. • Requires everyone to agree to the roles and responsibilities (R&R), in particular leadership roles. • Agile R&R tends to be empowering, which is threatening to C&C managers.
Infrastructure as code. Common monitoring, measurement, and reporting functionality is automated. This may include code and data analysis tooling to monitor quality, logging functionality to record important events such as builds and deployments, and automated dashboards [Kim].	• Guidance can be checked automatically using open source or commercial tooling. • Makes it easier for teams to follow the organizational guidance because it's automated. • Supports evidence required for regulatory compliance. • Supports greater transparency and accuracy of information, thereby improving decision making.
Whole governance. The governance body, sometimes called a governance team or control tribe, is whole in that it contains people with sufficient skills and expertise so that between them they can govern all aspects of solution delivery. These aspects may include security, data, finance, quality, user experience (UX) and more. See Figure 27.2 for potential governance aspects.	• Single point of governance direction, increasing clarity for the team. • Streamlines overall governance because it is addressed in a holistic manner. • Easier to ensure regulatory compliance due to consistent guidance from a single source. • Requires greater knowledge, generally, from the governance body.
Servant leadership. A servant leader shares power, putting the needs of the people that they lead first, helping them to develop and to perform [W].	• Can be very effective at helping teams to streamline their work. • Enables teams to focus on their mission and not on organizational politics or resourcing challenges. • Servant leaders need the authority, or at least the right connections, to actually help.

382

	• Many C&C managers struggle with this at first. • Requires skill and experience. Many Scrum Masters struggle with this because they don't have the authority or connections required.
Exceptions to the rules. Teams are allowed to deviate from the accepted guidance but are asked to justify why they need to do so.	• Can be easily abused if teams are not required to justify the exception or if management requires onerous justification. • Works well when used sparingly – if there are good reasons to support many exceptions that's an indication that the guidance needs to evolve to handle the current situation. • Enables teams to have reasonable flexibility and remove guard rails when they aren't needed or appropriate.
Specialized/siloed governance. There are several governing bodies applicable to a team, each of which is specialized in one or more aspects (security, data, UX, …) that need to be governed. See Figure 27.2 for potential governance aspects.	• Enables our organization to ensure that specialized areas/topics are addressed. • Multiple-points of governance lead to overlap, inconsistency, and significant waste for the teams. • Often leads to many specialized "quality gates" or reviews. • Ensuring regulatory compliance can be difficult due to inconsistent interpretations by each silo. • Significant governance burden on the teams.
Autocratic leadership. Autocratic leaders tell people what to do, they often dictate the time and cost allowed to do it and may even dictate how people are to do their work.	• Comfortable for existing C&C managers. • Intellectual workers generally don't like to be told what to do and will often ignore autocrats and instead do what they feel is right. • Likelihood that the team will create artifacts solely to be compliant, increasing waste. • Can kill motivation of team members, because autocratic decisions reduce people's autonomy, thereby reducing overall productivity.

Provide Transparency

Transparency enables governance. When our team provides transparency about what we're doing and how we doing it then people outside of our team, including our organizational leadership, can make better decisions due to having more accurate information. This has a positive side effect of putting them in a better position to work with us effectively and actually help us in practice! Similarly, when we have transparency into what other groups are doing we can make better-informed decisions that will lead to better collaboration with them. As you can see in the following table we have several options for providing greater transparency.

Options (Ordered)	Trade-Offs
Automated dashboards. Team dashboards that use business	• This enables both the team and our stakeholders to monitor the team's progress in a continuous real-

intelligence (BI) technology to display real-time measures generated by the use of development tools and the ongoing use of the solution in production. Also known as development intelligence (DI).	time manner. • Our team can tailor the dashboard to provide insight into what we currently hope to improve. • The information displayed on the dashboards is accurate because it is automatically generated as a side effect of tool usage. • This approach is effectively free after the initial cost of setting up the dashboard technology.
Consistent metric categories. Teams are asked to report measures in a common set of categories such as quality, staff morale, and time to market. The team is required to provide sufficient insight in each category, but is free to take the appropriate measures (for them) in that category. See Figure 27.3 for an example of metrics in three different categories for three different teams.	• Provides flexibility for teams yet enables monitoring against organizational goals. • It is possible to compare teams, which can be dangerous, based on their scores or better yet trends in a given category. • It is still possible to suggest a common set of metrics in a given category, although teams should be allowed to opt out if they can justify why that metric doesn't apply.
Visualize workflow. The team visualizes their workflow via a task board or Kanban board (sometimes called a Scrum board). This can be physical using sticky notes on a whiteboard or wall or digital using an agile management tool such as Jira, Jile, or Trello. These boards are one type of information radiator [Anderson].	• Improves team's ability to coordinate their efforts and to identify potential bottlenecks. • Makes the current work load transparent to stakeholders. • Enables prioritization discussions and scheduling discussions within the team • Makes it clear who has capacity (and who doesn't). • Requires team to keep the board up to date.
Information radiators. Critical team information – such as architecture diagrams, requirements artifacts, and task boards – are displayed in a publicly accessible manner. Information radiators are often physical, such as sketches on whiteboards, but can be digital as well (for example, our team's automated dashboard and task board can be displayed on monitors on the wall of the	• Increases visibility of critical information within the team. • Increases visibility to stakeholders, assuming they can access the information radiators. • Increases stakeholder's trust in the team. • Requires physical wall space or access to digital tooling (such as automated dashboards). • Physical radiators don't work well when some team members are geographically distributed. • It is difficult to hide "bad news" or other unpleasant information.

team's work room) [CockburnAgile].	
Self-serve demo environment. Our team regularly deploys the current working version of our solution into an environment where our stakeholders can access it and work with it at any time.	• Increases opportunities for stakeholder feedback. • Increases stakeholder's trust in the team. • Good way to develop our continuous deployment (CD) strategy, reducing our overall deployment risk when doing so into production. • Requires initial creation of the environment plus ongoing update into the environment.
Demos. We demonstrate the current version of our solution to a subset of our stakeholders. See the decision point Demo Strategy below for greater detail.	• Increases opportunities for feedback from stakeholders. • Increases stakeholder's trust in the team. • Provides stakeholders with concrete transparency (many software development artifacts are too abstract or too detailed for them to work with). • Requires investment of time and effort to organize, run, and then act on the results. • Demoing is a skill which may require coaching and even training. • An unexpected bug during a demo can be problematic, particularly in low trust environments.
Definition of Ready (DoR)/Definition of Done (DoD). Our DoR defines the minimum criteria that a work item must meet before our team will work on it. Similarly the DoD defines the minimum criteria that a work item must meet before our stakeholders will accept it as completed/done work [Rubin].	• A DoR can help avoid delay from having to wait for a work item to be better described, and decreases the chance of rework due to fuzzy requirements. • A DoR is a "quality gate" which protects the team from poorly formed work items. • A DoD is a simple service level agreement (SLA) that ensures the team produces work that meets the needs of stakeholders. • A DoD increases the trust of stakeholders in the ability of the team to deliver. • DoRs can be difficult to meet when Product Owners are new to the job or are overwhelmed with work (the implication is that the team will need to help them). • DoRs can be an excuse for POs to produce artifacts instead of sitting down with the team and having a conversation. • DoDs become complex with practices such as Continuous Documentation – Following Iteration (see *Produce Potentially Consumable Solution* in Chapter 17) or parallel independent testing (see *Accelerate Value Delivery* in Chapter 19) because some work isn't truly "done" by the end of the iteration.

Milestone reviews. We hold an explicit review at important, risk-based milestones in the lifecycle. See the Milestone Review Strategy decision point for details.	• See the tradeoffs associated with the various techniques described by the *Milestone Review Strategy* decision point.
Update release plan. Throughout our endeavor we update the release plan, either the projected delivery date or cost (often both), whenever new knowledge informs us that the schedule/cost has shifted.	• Sets expectations around schedule and cost. • Can be disconcerting early in lifecycle when the numbers may be evolving significantly, particularly when stakeholders are not used to that level of transparency. • Typically better to present ranged plans (via ranged burn up/burn down charts perhaps) than point-specific projections, but only if stakeholders are used to dealing with projections presented that way.
Status reports. The team produces a status report, often the Team Lead will do this, to summarize the current state of the endeavor and what has happened since the last status report.	• Often works of fiction because the status reports are hand-crafted and thus contain whatever information the creator(s) decide to capture. • Requires time and effort to develop the report. • Team status often improves due to management massaging the information, sometimes referred to as green shifting, as it moves up the hierarchy. • Organizations with cultures that do not promote psychology safety will motivate teams to avoid sharing unpleasant, yet incredibly important, information in their status reports.
Consistent metrics. Teams are asked to report on specific measures - such as Production incidents, cycle time, or velocity – so that stakeholders are provided with a consistent view into each team.	• Enables leadership to measure teams consistently. • The metrics aren't meaningful in every situation, therefore their collection is a waste (often resulting in inaccurate information anyway) when they aren't appropriate. • Leadership will miss key information that is applicable to the team if it isn't asked for. • Metrics collection is perceived as a waste by the team in these situations, and we typically forgo important intelligence that would enable us to improve.

Figure 27.3. Metrics gathered by three different teams across a consistent set of categories.

	Quality	Time to Market	Stakeholder Satisfaction
Data Warehouse	• Production incidents • Automated test coverage • Ratio of data to errors • Number of empty values • Data transform error rates	• Cycle time • Lead time • Data time to value	• Net promoter score (NPS) • Reports run • Time in warehouse
Mobile Development	• Production incidents • Automated test coverage • Cyclomatic complexity	• Cycle time • Lead time	• Net promoter score (NPS) • Session length • User retention • Time in app • Lifetime value
Package Implementation	• Production incidents • Automated test coverage • UAT issues	• Schedule variance	• Net promoter score (NPS) • Production incidents • UAT issues

Measure Team

Metrics should be used by a team to provide insights into how they work and provide visibility to senior leadership to govern the team effectively. When done right metrics will lead to better decisions which in turn lead to better outcomes. When done wrong your measurement strategy will increase the bureaucracy faced by the team, will be a drag on their productivity, and will provide inaccurate information to whoever is trying to govern the team. There are several measurement strategies overviewed in the following table. Here are several heuristics to consider when deciding on your approach to measuring your team:

- **Start with outcomes**. The metrics you gather should provide insights into whether we are achieving the outcomes (goals, objectives) that we desire.
- **There is no "one way" to measure**. Every team is unique, you need to work through your measurement strategy to get it right.
- **Every metric has strengths and weaknesses**. We're going to need to collect several metrics to provide sufficiently robust insight.
- **Use metrics to motivate, not to compare**. Whenever leadership applies metrics to compare people or teams, even if it's to reward them, the likelihood that the metrics will be gamed increases.

387

- **You get what you measure.** The way that a team is measured will change its behavior, although perhaps not in the way that you had hoped for.
- **Teams use metrics to self-organize.** Metrics provide insights to teams that indicate potential issues or opportunities that they may want to address.
- **Measure outcomes at the team level.** Start by identifying the outcomes or goals that you want to achieve, such as improving quality or time to market, and then collect metrics that will provide insight into whether you are achieving those outcomes.
- **Each team needs a unique set of metrics.** Every team is unique, facing a unique context and therefore will need to collect metrics that are appropriate to them.
- **Measure to improve.** Our team should use metrics to help us identify where we need to improve – we should be competing against ourselves, not others.
- **Have common metric categories across teams.** Leadership can motivate achievement of organizational goals through metrics categories (see Figure 27.3 for an example).
- **Trust but verify.** Leadership should trust their people to do the right thing, but use metrics to monitor what is happening so as to identify teams that potentially need assistance.
- **Don't manage to the metrics.** Metrics provide insights, but if leadership wants to know what is actually happening then they need to go and talk with the team.
- **Automate wherever possible.** This reduces the cost and accuracy of the metrics, and can enable real-time monitoring by the team.
- **Prefer trends over scalars.** The change in value of a metric over time will provide insight into whether something is improving (or not), which is likely the outcome you're trying to achieve.
- **Prefer leading over trailing metrics.** A leading metric provides insight into what is happening, or better yet what is likely to happen, whereas a trailing metric indicates what has happened. Leading metrics provide insights that enable us to make decisions that could affect future outcomes.
- **Prefer pull over push.** Metrics should be available whenever people want them, often via an automated dashboard, to provide insights when decisions need to be made.

Options (Ordered)	Trade-Offs
Goal Question Metric (GQM). The team identifies the goals (outcomes) they are trying to achieve, the questions they need to answer to determine if they are achieving their goals, and then metrics they can gather to provide insight into the questions [W].	<ul><li>Enables teams to identify the metrics that will provide insights to them given the context that they face.</li><li>GQM can and should be applied in a very agile manner.</li><li>Tends to be easier to adopt than OKRs (see below) as the middle step of identifying questions makes GQM more concrete.</li><li>GQM has been adopted in a very heavyweight manner in some organizations, so some practitioners may be leery of adopting this strategy.</li><li>Can be applied at the organization, team, and personal levels.</li><li>Stakeholders can be frustrated because of a lack of</li></ul>

	consistency across teams (so ask teams to take a consistent metric category approach).
Objectives and Key Results (OKRs). Desired objectives (outcomes) drive the identification of measurable key results [W].	• Enables teams to identify the metrics that will provide insights to them given the context that they face. • Many teams find OKRs to be too abstract and as a result mis-execute on its application. • Can be applied at the organization, team, and personal levels. • Stakeholders can be frustrated because of a lack of consistency across teams (so ask teams to take a consistent metric category approach).
Consistent metrics. Teams are asked to report on specific measures - such as Production incidents, cycle time, or velocity – so that stakeholders are provided with a consistent view into each team.	• Enables leadership to measure teams consistently. • The metrics aren't meaningful in every situation, therefore their collection is a waste (often resulting in inaccurate information anyway) when they aren't appropriate. • Leadership will miss key information that is applicable to the team if it isn't asked for. • Metrics collection is perceived as a waste by the team in these situations, and we typically forgo important intelligence that would enable us to improve.
Popular metrics. Our team adopts metrics based on how commonly they are applied elsewhere, perhaps adopting metrics prescribed by a method, whatever our tools provide by default, or based on a "top 10 agile metrics" article.	• Quick way to get some measures in place. • The metrics aren't meaningful in every situation, therefore their collection is a waste (often resulting in inaccurate information anyway) when they aren't appropriate. • The team is very likely going to miss important insights when the choice of metrics isn't driven by outcomes.
None. The team decides to not collect any measures at all.	• The team avoids the overhead to put the metrics in place. • May work well in small organizations where leadership can monitor the team in other ways such as attending daily coordination meetings. • The team is essentially "flying blind" because they don't have any metrics to provide insights. • Often results in leadership asking the team to put together a regular (weekly) status report manually to get the insight they require to monitor and guide the team.

Go-Forward Strategy

On a regular basis our solution delivery team should make what is known as a "go-forward decision" during Construction – do we continue on as we have been, do we go in a different direction, or do we do something else? In teams following one of the agile lifecycles this typically occurs at the end of an iteration, whereas teams following a lean lifecycle will make this decision on an as needed basis. As you can see in the following table there are several options to consider when making a go-forward decision.

Options (Not Ordered)	Trade-Offs
Cancel. The stakeholders decide to stop investing in the endeavor.	• Cancelling some efforts is a reflection that you're taking on some risks, which in competitive situations is something you typically want to do. A very low cancellation rate may be an indication that you're not being aggressive enough. • May be politically difficult in some organizations to cancel an effort. • Typically an option for project-based efforts. However, in most cases it is far better to keep the team together and pivot in a different direction.
Continue as before. The stakeholders decide to continue funding the team.	• Reflects the fact the team is doing a good job. • Easy decision to make, so could be an indication there's a need for an explicit Continued Viability review if it has been a long time between releases.
Deploy internally. The stakeholders decide to have the solution deployed internally into an environment that is not production (such as testing or demo environments).	• Opportunity to get feedback from stakeholders. • Opportunity to learn how to deploy, thereby reducing risk, and better yet to automate deployment to a greater extent.
Deploy into production. The stakeholders decide to have the team ship the working solution into production.	• Opportunity to get feedback from actual end users. • Opportunity to learn how to deploy into production (hopefully you've had internal deployment experience before this).
Increase funding. The stakeholders decide to increase their investment in the team/product.	• Enables a team to increase or improve their output. • Enables our organization to invest in teams that provide good value. • Assumes that the team can use more funding, this may not always be the (immediate) case.
Reduce funding. The stakeholders decide to decrease their investment in the team/product.	• Enables our organization to decrease investments in teams struggling to provide good value. • Sends a clear signal to a team that they need to improve without resorting to cancelation. • May result in someone(s) needing to leave the team, so a

	strategy to help them find appropriate work somewhere else may be needed. We will need to work with our *People Management* [AmblerLines2017] team for this.
Run an experiment. The stakeholders decide to run an experiment, perhaps an A/B test or the release of a minimal viable product (MVP). This is effectively a decision to apply the Exploratory lifecycle (see Chapter 6).	• Reduces risk by gaining feedback in a relatively safe environment. • Opportunity to learn, and thereby improve. • Some organizations are uncomfortable with the idea of experimentation because some experiments "fail." Get over it.
Pivot. The stakeholders decide to continue investing in the team but to have the team go in a different direction [Ries].	• Keeps funding for an effective team even though they are doing work that isn't providing the value they originally hoped for. • Politically safe way to move away from an ineffective strategy, particularly compared with Cancel as it avoids stigma of a project failure.

Milestone Review Strategy

As you learned in Chapter 6 the Disciplined Agile Delivery (DAD) lifecycles have a collection of risk-based milestones. These milestones are overviewed in Figure 27.4, they are described in the following table, and are an effective means for our team to provide transparency to our stakeholders. An important aspect of these milestones is that they are applied consistently, where appropriate, across all of the DAD lifecycles. This has the advantage of enabling teams to choose their way of working (WoW), including an appropriate lifecycle, while enabling leadership to govern them in a consistent manner. In other words, senior management doesn't have to enforce the same process on all teams to support their governance efforts.

Figure 27.4. The DAD milestones.

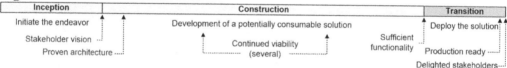

Milestone	Fundamental Question Asked	Risks Addressed
Stakeholder vision	Do we have agreement around the direction that we're going?	• Ensure that the stakeholders agree with the strategy, schedule, and finances associated with the endeavor. • Ensure that the team agrees to the strategy for moving forward. • Ensure that everyone understands their role and responsibilities.
Proven Architecture	Have we shown that our strategy	• Ensure that the technical strategy works in the organizational ecosystem while still meeting the

	works within our operational infrastructure?	key quality requirements for it. • Reduce stakeholder concern regarding the ability of the team to fulfill the vision for the solution.
Continued viability	Does this endeavor still make sense?	• Ensures that a team is still on track even though it has been several months since their last release into production. • Show that the Product Owner, who should be leading stakeholders through a go-forward decision on a regular basis, is actually doing so in practice. This is effectively an explicit go-forward decision point for a long-running project.
Sufficient functionality	Do we have a minimal marketable release (MMR)?	• Ensure that the team has produced a solution with sufficient functionality, the value of which exceeds the cost of deployment into production. • Ensure that the solution is released into production as soon as the sufficient functionality point is reached.
Production ready	Are we ready to ship our solution into production?	• Ensure that the solution is technically ready to be shipped, including being adequately tested and documented. • Ensure that stakeholders are ready to receive the solution. • Ensure that the people responsible for operating and supporting the solution, which may be the delivery team itself, is ready to do so.
Delighted stakeholders	Have we delighted our stakeholders with the current release of our solution?	• Identify any potential issues with the solution so that they may be swiftly addressed.

When people initially hear "milestone review" they often think that it has to be heavy and formal. As you can see in the following table there are several options for holding milestone reviews.

Options (Ordered)	Trade-Offs
Automated review. Some of the risks that milestone reviews would look for in the past effectively disappear as the result of increased automation of the delivery pipeline, including automated regression tests, code/schema analysis tools, continuous integration (CI) and continuous deployment (CD).	• Decreases cost and overhead. • Increases consistency of reviews. • Supports separation of concerns (SoC), or separation of duties (SoD), of some regulations (e.g. PCI-DSS). • Effective automation increases workflow of a team. • Not everything can be automated, but a lot can, enabling teams to focus on adding value.

Many risks can be automatically checked for via application of data analytics or artificial intelligence (AI) against data generated by the team's tools. All of these techniques are aspects of "infrastructure as code."	• Requires investment and ongoing evolution.
Lightweight milestone reviews. The review is very informal, with minimal documentation produced to support it. The review may even be as simple as an impromptu meeting with key stakeholders [COBIT].	• Very likely supports our regulatory compliance requirements, but work with our internal auditors to verify this (we may need to educate them in DA fundamentals first). • Provides transparency to stakeholders and obtains feedback from them. • Low cost compared to formal reviews. • Less stressful for the team, easier to accomplish, compared to formal reviews. • Still requires time and effort to perform, albeit much less than formal reviews.
Regular go-forward decision. A very informal review, where someone representing the stakeholders determines how the team will continue onwards, if at all. Likely options are described by Go-Forward Decision earlier. This review is typically held by agile teams as part of their iteration wrap-up or by lean teams in an impromptu manner.	• Provides an ongoing, near continuous viability check on the team to ensure that we're going in the right direction. • Increases the team's transparency to stakeholders. • The person making the decision, often the Product Owner, needs to have the discipline to dispassionately make this decision. • Requires stakeholders to be responsible for steering the team.
None. A review isn't held.	• Effectively free. • Doesn't support regulatory compliance. • We will still need to provide transparency. • Still need to address the risks associated with the milestones via other means.
Formal milestone reviews (quality gates). A review meeting is planned for in advance, (optionally) facilitated, results of the review documented, and any action items are followed through on. Formal milestone reviews are sometimes used to validate comprehensive documents or critical artifacts [COBIT].	• Supports regulatory compliance needs, even life-critical regulations. • Expensive and stressful for the team. • Often not very effective as it relies on very good, diligent reviewers. • Difficult to properly review large artifacts (most people don't want to read that much material). • Time consuming and often reduces team morale.

Demo Strategy

Demonstrations, colloquially called demos, of the current version of our solution are a great way to both gain feedback from our stakeholders and to provide transparency to them. Note that we described the general tradeoffs with demos earlier in the section describing the Provide Transparency decision point. There are several approaches to holding demos, as you can see in the following table.

Options (Not Ordered)	Trade-Offs
All-hands demo. A demo where a very wide range, potentially all, stakeholders are invited to attend.	• Can be used to verify that the team is addressing the full range of stakeholder needs (and how well the PO represents the stakeholders). • Successful demos can reduce any fears stakeholders may have with our team. • Failed demos can undermine trust in our team. • Great way to get feedback from a wide range of people. • Many stakeholders do not have the time to attend, so you may need to record.
Impromptu demo. A demo held on an as needed, just-in-time (JIT) basis. Typically performed for a small group of stakeholders.	• Satisfies as-needed requests by key stakeholders. • Can get out of hand if done too often. • Many requests to demo may be a sign that you need regularly scheduled demos.
Scheduled (iteration/sprint) demo. A regularly scheduled demo, typically at the end of an iteration, that is targeted to a specific group of stakeholders.	• Sets expectations regarding when upcoming demos will occur. This enables stakeholders to attend as they can schedule around it. • Sets a regular feedback and transparency cadence with stakeholders.
Self-serve demo. Stakeholders are provided access to an internal demo version of our solution that they may work with at their leisure.	• Enables stakeholders to work with the current version of the system whenever they want. • Requires an environment where people can safely work with the solution that doesn't affect production (particularly data). • Stakeholders need to be informed where it is and need to understand that it's not the production system. • Not a substitute for other forms of demos, but complementary to them.

SECTION 6: PARTING THOUGHTS AND BACK MATTER

This section is organized into the following chapters:
- **Chapter 28: Disciplined Success.**
- **Appendix A – Disciplined Agile Certification.**
- **References**
- **Abbreviations**
- **Index**
- **About the Authors**

28 DISCIPLINED SUCCESS

If you have read the entire book up to this point, congratulations. We appreciate that we have covered a lot of ground. When we wrote our first book on DAD in 2012, we ended up with a book of more than 500 pages, after having cut 200 pages of content. As we set out to write this book as its replacement and removing materials related to agile "basics", we had a goal of making it smaller, and yet still ended up with over 400 pages. Yes, there is a lot to DAD. But as Scott likes to say, "it is what it is." Some people have called DAD "complicated" and have been reluctant to make the investment to learn these strategies. This is unfortunate, as the inconvenient truth is that effective delivery of IT solutions has never been simple and will never be – DAD simply holds up a mirror to the inherent complexity that we face as software professionals in enterprise-class settings. DAD is a very robust toolkit that addresses the challenges you face in all aspects of delivering your solutions.

If you are doing Agile, you are already using DAD

Scrum is a subset of two of DAD's lifecycles. So if you are just doing Scrum you are by definition doing DAD. However, if Scrum is all that you are referencing, you are likely not aware of some things you should be thinking about, or not using some supplemental practices to help you be most effective. In our experience, if you are struggling to be effective with agile, it may be that either you aren't aware of strategies to help you, or are being given advice by inexperienced, unknowledgeable, or purist agile coaches.

DAD is Agile for the Enterprise

Unfortunately our industry is full of "thought leaders" that believe that their way, often because it is all that they understand, is the one true way. DAD is based upon empirical observations from a vast array of industries, organizations, and all types of initiatives, both project and product based, large and small. DAD's inherent flexibility and adaptability is one of the reasons it is such a useful toolkit. DAD *just makes sense* because it favors:
1. Pragmatic *over* purist approaches
2. Context-driven decisions *over* one-size-fits-all
3. Choice of strategies *over* prescriptive approaches

If you are a "Scrum shop" you very likely are missing some great opportunities to optimize your way of working. Scrum is actually a phenomenally bad lifecycle to use in many situations in most organizations which is why we have a choice of other lifecycle approaches in DAD. If you rely solely on Scrum, or a Scrum-based scaling framework such as SAFe, Nexus, or LeSS, we recommend you expand your toolkit with DAD to expose more suitable approaches and practices.

Learn Faster to Succeed Earlier

Agile is fond of the phrase "fail fast", meaning that the quicker we fail and learn from our mistakes, the quicker we get to what we need. Our view is that by referencing proven context-based strategies, we fail less and succeed earlier. In our daily work we are continually making decisions, which is why we call DA a process decision toolkit. In fact, if you have thought that the diverging arrows in Disciplined Agile's logo look like a decision tree, you would be right. Without referencing the toolkit to help with decision making, sometimes we either forget things we need to consider, or make poor decisions on those we do. DAD surfaces decision points for discussion, making the implicit, explicit. For instance, when beginning an initiative in Inception and referring to the "Develop Test Strategy" goal diagram, it is like a coach tapping you on the shoulder and asking "How will we test this thing? What environments do we need, where will we get the data, what tools, how much is automated versus manual, test-first or test-after?" By surfacing these critical decisions for explicit consideration by your team, we reduce the risk of forgetting things, and increase your chance of choosing a strategy that works well for you. We call this guided continuous improvement (GCI).

Use This Book!

Keep this book handy. In practice, we regularly reference goal diagrams in our coaching to point out why certain practices are less effective than others in certain situations, and what alternatives we should consider. Take this book to your retrospectives, and if your team is struggling with effectively meeting a DAD goal, review what options and tools you can experiment with to remedy the situation. If you are a coach, this book should make you more effective with helping teams to understand the choices and the tradeoffs that they have available to them.

Invest in Certification to Retain your New Knowledge

We are sure that you have learned about new techniques in this book that will make you a better agile practitioner, increasing your chances of success on your initiatives. The key is to not let these new ideas fade from memory. We encourage you to cement this new knowledge by studying the content to prepare and take the certification tests. The tests are difficult but passing them results in a worthwhile and credible certification truly worthy of updating your LinkedIn profile. Companies that we have worked with have observed that their teams that have made the investment in learning and certification make better decisions and are thus more effective than teams that don't understand their options and tradeoffs. Better decisions lead to better outcomes.

Make the investment in learning this material and proving it through certification. You will be a better agilist, and those around you will notice.

Please Get Involved

We also suggest that you participate in the Disciplined Agile community. New ideas and practices emerge from the community and are continually incorporated into DA. Let's learn from each other as we all seek to continue to learn and master our craft.

Mark & Scott, December 2018

APPENDIX A – DISCIPLINED AGILE CERTIFICATION

The Disciplined Agile certification strategy is based on the martial arts concept of Shu-Ha-Ri, where Shu is beginner level, Ha is intermediate level, and Ri is expert level. It takes several years of experience and learning, not several days of workshops, for someone to move between levels.

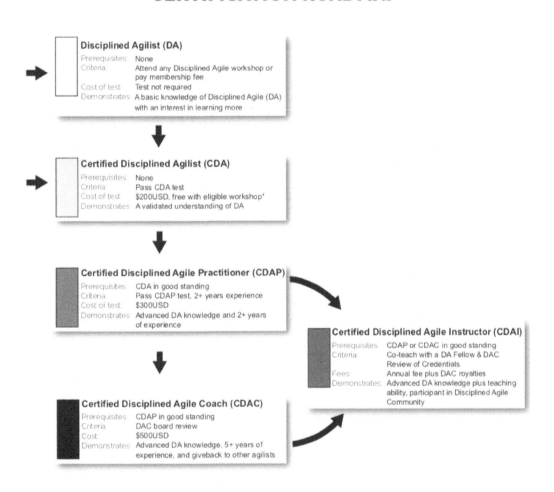

CERTIFICATION ROADMAP

Disciplined Agilist (DA)
- Prerequisites: None
- Criteria: Attend any Disciplined Agile workshop or pay membership fee
- Cost of test: Test not required
- Demonstrates: A basic knowledge of Disciplined Agile (DA) with an interest in learning more

Certified Disciplined Agilist (CDA)
- Prerequisites: None
- Criteria: Pass CDA test
- Cost of test: $200USD, free with eligible workshop*
- Demonstrates: A validated understanding of DA

Certified Disciplined Agile Practitioner (CDAP)
- Prerequisites: CDA in good standing
- Criteria: Pass CDAP test, 2+ years experience
- Cost of test: $300USD
- Demonstrates: Advanced DA knowledge and 2+ years of experience

Certified Disciplined Agile Instructor (CDAI)
- Prerequisites: CDAP or CDAC in good standing
- Criteria: Co-teach with a DA Fellow & DAC Review of Credentials
- Fees: Annual fee plus DAC royalties
- Demonstrates: Advanced DA knowledge plus teaching ability, participant in Disciplined Agile Community

Certified Disciplined Agile Coach (CDAC)
- Prerequisites: CDAP in good standing
- Criteria: DAC board review
- Cost: $500USD
- Demonstrates: Advanced DA knowledge, 5+ years of experience, and giveback to other agilists

*Eligible courses are indicated on course curriculum.

There are five designations in the program:
1. **Disciplined Agilist (DA) – Shu level, "white belt."** This designation indicates a basic knowledge of Disciplined Agile and an interest in learning more.
2. **Certified Disciplined Agilist (CDA) – Shu level, "yellow belt."** This designation indicates a validated understanding of Disciplined Agile because they have passed the comprehensive CDA test.
3. **Certified Disciplined Agile Practitioner (CDAP) – Ha level, "green belt."** This designation indicates a validated understanding of Disciplined Agile because they have passed the CDAP test and has at least two years of verified agile experience.
4. **Certified Disciplined Agile Coach (CDAC) – Ri level, "black belt."** This designation indicates a validated understanding of Disciplined Agile, at least five years of Agile experience, and the person must already be sharing knowledge via strategies such as coaching, teaching, writing, or mentoring.
5. **Certified Disciplined Agile Instructor (CDAI) – Ri level, "blue belt."** This designation indicates that the person has the ability to teach Disciplined Agile workshops. Anyone with a CDAI must also be at least a CDAP or CDAC in good standing.

Why Disciplined Agile Certification?

For individuals, there are several benefits:
1. **Increase your knowledge**. Disciplined Agile certification requires you to have a comprehensive understanding of Disciplined Agile Delivery, which in turn describes how all aspects of agile principles and practices fit together in an enterprise-class environment.
2. **Improve your employability**. Disciplined Agile certification indicates to employers that you're dedicated to improving your knowledge and skills, a clear sign of professionalism.
3. **Advance your career**. Disciplined Agile certification can help you gain that new position or role as the result of your increased knowledge base and desire to improve.

For organizations, there are several benefits:
1. **It is meaningful**. Disciplined Agile certification has to be earned. It is an indication that your people have a comprehensive understanding of enterprise-class development, and not just cargo cult agile.
2. **It forms the basis of measurable skills assessment**. Because the certifications build upon each other you can use them as a measure of how well agile skills and knowledge are spreading through your organization.
3. **It is trustworthy**. Because Disciplined Agile certification is externally managed it is difficult for teams to game the numbers, unlike the self-assessment approach that is becoming all too common.

In summary, we believe that there is value in certification for both individual IT practitioners and for organizations.

The Principles Behind Disciplined Agile Certification

The following principles drove the development of this certification program:

1. **Certifications must provide value.** First and foremost, a certification must provide value to the person being certified. This value comes from learning new and valuable strategies during the process of earning the certification as well as greater employability resulting from the certification. Of course there are always limits.

2. **Certifications must be earned.** The effort required to earn the certification must be commensurate with the value provided. For example, it is easy to earn and become a Certified Disciplined Agilist because this is an indication that someone has basic knowledge of Disciplined Agile and wishes to learn more. A Certified Disciplined Agile Practitioner is harder to earn because it is an indication of both knowledge and experience. It is very difficult to earn and become a Certified Disciplined Agile Coach because it's an indication of expertise and competence.

3. **Certifications must be respectable.** We believe that the Disciplined Agile certifications are respectable for several reasons. First, the fact that you have to do some work to earn them is a welcome difference from other agile certifications. Second, we're aligning with other respectable certification programmes and are requesting participation in one or more of those programmes as part of the Practitioner and Coach certifications.

4. **Certifications must be focused.** The focus of this programme is on disciplined agile approaches to IT solution delivery. Disciplined agile certifications are an indication of knowledge and experience in disciplined agile methods.

5. **Certification is part of your learning process.** Disciplined professionals view certification as part of their learning process. Learning is not an event but instead an ongoing effort. The implication is that once you have earned your certification you must continue working to keep your skills up to date.

6. **Certified professionals have a responsibility to share knowledge.** Not only have we adopted the concept of earning belts from martial arts we have also adopted the mindset that people have a responsibility to help teach and nurture people with lower belts to learn new skills and knowledge. The act of teaching and sharing information often leads one to a greater understanding and appreciation of the topic, and thus helps the teacher as well as the student to learn.

How to Learn More

You can find out more about the certification process at DisciplinedAgileConsortium.org.

REFERENCES

[Adkins] *Coaching Agile Teams: A Companion for ScrumMasters, Agile Coaches, and Project Managers in Transition.* Lyssa Adkins, 2010, Addison Wesley.

[AgileContracts] *Agile Contracts Home Page.* AgileContracts.org

[AgileData] *Agile Data Home Page.* AgileData.org

[AgileDocumentation] *Agile/Lean Documentation: Strategies for Agile Software Development.* AgileModeling.com/essays/agileDocumentation.htm

[AmblerLines2012] *Disciplined Agile Delivery: A Practitioner's Guide to Agile Software Delivery in the Enterprise.* Scott Ambler and Mark Lines, 2012, IBM Press.

[AmblerLines2017] *An Executive's Guide to Disciplined Agile: Winning the Race to Business Agility.* Scott Ambler and Mark Lines, 2017, Disciplined Agile Consortium.

[Anderson] *Kanban: Successful Evolutionary Change for Your Technology Business.* David J. Anderson, 2010, Blue Hole Press.

[AoS2016]. *2016 Agility at Scale Survey Results.* Ambysoft.com/surveys/agileAtScale2016.html

[Appelo2010] *Management 3.0: Leading Agile Developers, Developing Agile Leaders.* Jurgen Appelo, 2010, Addison-Wesley Professional.

[Appelo2016] *Managing for Happiness: Games, Tools, and Practices to Motivate Any Team.* Jurgen Appelo, 2016, Wiley.

[APIFirst] *API-First Home Page.* Api-first.com

[Argyris] *Double Loop Learning in Organizations.* Chris Argyris, Harvard Business Review, September 1977, hbr.org/1977/09/double-loop-learning-in-organizations

[Beck] *Extreme Programming Explained: Embrace Change (2nd Edition).* Kent Beck and Cynthia Andres, 2004, Addison Wesley Publishing.

[BeyondManifesto]. *Beyond Agile Manifesto.* BeyondAgileManifesto.org

[Brooks] *The Mythical Man-Month, 25th Anniversary Edition.* Frederick P. Brooks Jr., 1995, Addison-Wesley.

[BRUF] *Examining the "Big Requirements Up Front (BRUF) Approach".* AgileModeling.com/essays/examiningBRUF.htm

[BurnUp] *Burn up vs burn down chart.* ClariosTechnology.com/productivity/blog/burnupvsburndownchart

[C2Wiki] *C2 Wiki.* wiki.c2.com

[CapabilityMap] *A Guide to the Business Architecture Book of Knowledge.* BusinessArchitectureGuild.org/page/BIZBOKLandingpage

[ChaosReport] *Standish Group Chaos Report.* StandishGroup.com/outline

[CM] *Configuration Management Best Practices: Practical Methods that Work in the Real World.* Bob Aiello and Leslie Sachs, 2010, Addison Wesley Professional.

[CMMI] *The Disciplined Agile Framework: A Pragmatic Approach to Agile Maturity.* DisciplinedAgileConsortium.org/resources/Whitepapers/DA-CMMI-Crosstalk-201607.pdf

[COBIT] *COBIT 5 Home Page.* isaca.org/COBIT/pages/default.aspx

[CockburnAgile] *Agile Software Development: The Cooperative Game 2nd Edition.* Alistair Cockburn, 2006, Addison Wesley.

403

[CockburnHeart] *Heart of Agile Home Page.* HeartOfAgile.com/

[Communication] *Communication on Agile Software Development Teams.* AgileModeling.com/essays/communication.htm

[Cohn] *Agile Estimating and Planning.* Mike Cohn, 2005, Addison Wesley.

[Covey] *The 7 Habits of Highly Effective People: Powerful Lessons in Personal Change 25th Anniversary Edition.* Stephen R. Covey 2013, Simon & Schuster

[Cynefin] *A Leader's Framework for Decision Making.* David J. Snowden and Mary E. Boone, Harvard Business Review, November 2007, hbr.org/2007/11/a-leaders-framework-for-decision-making

[DABlog] *Disciplined Agile Delivery Home Page.* DisciplinedAgileDelivery.com

[DAC] *Disciplined Agile Consortium Home Page.* DisciplinedAgileConsortium.org

[DADRoles] *Roles on DAD Teams.* http://DisciplinedAgileDelivery.com/roles-on-dad-teams/

[DAMA] *DAMA Guide to the Data Management Body of Knowledge.* Technicspub.com/dmbok/

[DAManifesto] *Disciplined Agile Manifesto.* DisciplinedAgileDelivery.com/disciplinedagilemanifesto/

[DBRefactoring] *Refactoring Databases: Evolutionary Database Design.* Scott W. Ambler and Pramod J. Sadalage, 2006, Addison Wesley.

[DDD]. *Domain Driven Design: Tackling Complexity in the Heart of Software.* Eric Evans, 2003. Addison Wesley Professional.

[DeMarco] *Slack: Getting Past Burnout, Busywork, and the Myth of Total Efficiency.* Tom DeMarco, 2002, Crown Business.

[Deming] *The New Economics for Industry, Government, Education.* W. Edwards Deming, 2002, MIT Press.

[DevSecOps] *The DevSecOps Manifesto.* DevSecOps.org

[Essence] *Software Engineering Essentialized.* Ivar Jacobson, Harold "Bud" Lawson, Pan-Wei Ng, Paul E. McMahon, and Michael Goedicke. Addison Wesley.

[Estimation] *3 Powerful Estimation Techniques for Agile Teams.* David Green, SitePoint.com/3-powerful-estimation-techniques-for-agile-teams/

[ExecutableSpecs] *Specification by Example: How Successful Teams Deliver the Right Software.* Gojko Adzic, 2011, Manning Press.

[EventStorming]. *Introducing Event Storming.* Alberto Brandolini. ziobrando.blogspot.com/2013/11/introducing-event-storming.html

[Fowler] *The State of Agile Software in 2018.* Martin Fowler, MartinFowler.com/articles/agile-aus-2018.html

[Gagnon] A retrospective on years of process tailoring workshops. Daniel Gagnon, 2018, DisciplinedAgileDelivery.com/a-retrospective-on-years-of-process-tailoring-workshops/

[GenSpec] Generalizing Specialists: Improving Your IT Career Skills. AgileModeling.com/essays/generalizingSpecialists.htm

[Gilb] *Competitive Engineering: A Handbook For Systems Engineering, Requirements Engineering, and Software Engineering Using Planguage.* Tom Gilb, 2005, Butterworth-Heinemann.

[Goals] *Process Goals.* DisciplinedAgileDelivery.com/process-goals/

[Google] *Five Keys to a Successful Google Team*. Julia Rozovsky. https://rework.withgoogle.com/blog/five-keys-to-a-successful-google-team/

[GregoryCrispin] *Agile Testing: A Practical Guide For Testers and Agile Teams*. Janet Gregory and Lisa Crispin, 2009, Addison Wesley.

[Highsmith] *Agile Software Development Ecosystems*. Jim Highsmith, 2002, Addison Wesley.

[HopeFraser] *Beyond Budgeting: How Managers Can Break Free From the Annual Performance Trap*. Jeremy Hope and Robin Fraser, 2003, Harvard Business Press.

[Host] *The Host Leadership Community*. HostLeadership.com

[ImpactMap] *The Impact Mapping Site*. ImpactMapping.org

[ITGovernance] *IT Governance*. DisciplinedAgileDelivery.com/agility-at-scale/it-governance/

[Kim]. *DevOps Cookbook*. RealGeneKim.me/devops-cookbook/

[Kerievsky] *Modern Agile*. ModernAgile.org/

[Kerth] *Project Retrospectives: A Handbook for Team Reviews*. Norm Kerth, 2001, Dorset House.

[Kruchten] *The Rational Unified Process: An Introduction 3rd Edition*. Philippe Kruchten, 2003, Addison Wesley Professional.

[LargeTeams] *Large Agile Teams*. DisciplinedAgileDelivery.com/agility-at-scale/large-agile-teams/

[LeanChange1] *The Lean Change Method: Managing Agile Organizational Transformation Using Kanban, Kotter, and Lean Startup Thinking*. Jeff Anderson, 2013, Createspace.

[LeanChange2] *Lean Change Management Home Page*. LeanChange.org

[LeanEnterprise] *Lean Enterprise: How High Performance Organizations Innovate at Scale*. Jez Humble, Joanne Molesky, and Barry O'Reilly, 2015, O'Reilly Media, Inc.

[LeSS] *The LeSS Framework*. LeSS.works

[Lifecycles] *Full Agile Delivery Lifecycles*. DisciplinedAgileDelivery.com/lifecycle/

[LinesAmbler2018] *Introduction to Disciplined Agile Delivery 2nd Edition: A Small Agile Team's Journey from Scrum to Disciplined DevOps*. Mark Lines and Scott Ambler, 2018, Disciplined Agile Consortium.

[Manifesto] *The Agile Manifesto*. AgileManifesto.org

[Marick] *Agile Testing Directions: Tests and Examples*. Exampler.com/old-blog/2003/08/22/#agile-testing-project-2

[MarketingManifesto] *Agile Marketing Manifesto Home Page*. AgileMarketingManifesto.org/

[MartinOsterling] *Value Stream Mapping: How to Visualize Work and Align Leadership for Organizational Transformation*. Karen Martin, and Mike Osterling, 2015, McGraw Hill.

[NoEstimates] *The #NoEstimates debate: An unbiased look at the origins, arguments, and thought leaders behind the movement*. TechBeacon.com/noestimates-debate-unbiased-look-origins-arguments-thought-leaders-behind-movement

[NoProjects] *#NoProjects – A Culture of Continuous Value*. Evan Leybourn & Shane Hastie, 2018, C4Media.

[Nexus] *The Nexus Guide*. Scrum.org/resources/nexus-guide

[ObjectPrimer] *The Object Primer 3rd Edition: Agile Model Driven Development with UML 2*. Scott Ambler, 2004, Cambridge University Press.

405

[Patton] *User Story Mapping: Discover the Whole Story, Get the Product Right.* Jeff Patton, 2014, O'Reilly Media.

[Pink] *Drive: The Surprising Truth About What Motivates Us.* Daniel H. Pink, 2011, Riverhead Books.

[PIT] *Parallel Independent Testing.* DisciplinedAgileDelivery.com/independent-testing/

[PMI] *A Guide to the Project Management Body of Knowledge: PMBoK Guide 6th Edition.* pmi.org/pmbok-guide-standards

[Poppendieck] *The Lean Mindset: Ask the Right Questions.* Mary and Tom Poppendieck, 2013, Addison Wesley Professional.

[Powers] *Powers' Definition of the Agile Mindset.* AdventuresWithAgile.com/consultancy/powers-definition-agile-mind-set/

[Prince] *Prince2.* Axelos.com/best-practice-solutions/prince2

[Prison] *Tear Down the Method Prisons! Set Free the Practices!* Jacobson, I. & Stimson, R. ACM Queue, January/February 2019.

[RaceCar] *The Race Car Metaphor.* DisciplinedAgileDelivery.com/the-agile-tractor-engine-analogy/

[Ranged] *Ranged Burndown Charts.* DisciplinedAgileDelivery.com/ranged-burndown-charts/

[Refactoring] *Refactoring: Improving the Design of Existing Code 2nd Edition.* Martin Fowler, 2018, Addison Wesley.

[Reifer] *Quantitative Analysis of Agile Methods Study (2017): Twelve Major Findings.* Donald J. Reifer, InfoQ.com/articles/reifer-agile-study-2017

[Reinertsen] *The Principles of Product Development Flow: Second Generation Lean Product Development.* Donald G. Reinertsen, 2012, Celeritis Publishing.

[Resources]. *The Disciplined Agile Resources Page.* DisciplinedAgileConsortium.org/Disciplined-Agile-Resources

[Reuse] *Reuse Engineering.* DisciplinedAgileDelivery.com/agility-at-scale/reuse-engineering/ [Ries] *The Lean Startup: How Today's Entrepreneurs Use Continuous Innovation to Create Radically Successful Businesses.* Eric Ries, 2011, Crown Business.

[RightsResponsibilities] *Team Member Rights and Responsibilities.* DisciplinedAgileDelivery.com/people/rights-and-responsibilities/

[Rubin] *Essential Scrum: A Practical Guide to the Most Popular Process.* Ken Rubin, 2012, Addison Wesley Professional.

[Rugged] *The Rugged Manifesto.* RuggedSoftware.org

[SAFe] *SAFe 4.5 Distilled: Applying the Scaled Agile Framework for Lean Enterprises (2nd Edition).* Richard Knaster and Dean Leffingwell, 2018, Addison Wesley Professional.

[SchwaberBeedle] *Agile Software Development with SCRUM.* Ken Schwaber and Mike Beedle, 2001, Pearson.

[ScrumGuide] *The Scrum Guide.* Jeff Sutherland and Ken Schwaber, 2018, Scrum.org/resources/scrum-guide

[SDCF] *Scaling Agile: The Software Development Context Framework.* DisciplinedAgileDelivery.com/sdcf/

[SenseRespond] *Sense & Respond: How Successful Organizations Listen to Customers and Create New Products Continuously.* Jeff Gothelf and Josh Seiden, 2017, Harvard Business Review Press

[Sheridan] *Joy, Inc.: How We Built a Workplace People Love*. Richard Sheridan, 2014, Portfolio Publishing.

[SoftDev18] *2018 Software Development Survey Results*. Ambysoft.com/surveys/softwareDevelopment2018.html

[Sutherland] *Scrum: The Art of Doing Twice the Work in Half the Time*. Jeff Sutherland and J.J. Sutherland, 2014, Currency.

[Tailoring] *Process Tailoring Workshops*. DisciplinedAgileDelivery.com/process/process-tailoring-workshops/

[Target] *Target Customers' Card Data Said to be at Risk After Store Thefts*. csoonline.com/article/2134248/data-protection/target-customers--39--card-data-said-to-be-at-risk-after-store-thefts.html

[TechDebt] *11 Strategies for Dealing with Technical Debt*. DisciplinedAgileDelivery.com/technical-debt/

[Tuckman] *Tuckman's Stages of Group Development*. en.wikipedia.org/wiki/Tuckman%27s_stages_of_group_development

[ValueProposition] *Value Proposition Design: How to Create Products and Services Customers Want*. Osterwalder, A., Pigneur, Y., Bernarda, G., Smith, A., 2014, John Wiley & Sons.

[W] *Wikipedia*. Wikipedia.org

ACRONYMS AND ABBREVIATIONS

AD	Agile Data
AI	Artificial Intelligence
AIC	Agile Industrial Complex
AM	Agile Modeling
AO	Architecture Owner
BDD	Behavior Driven Development
BA	Business Analyst
BI	Business Intelligence
BDUF	Big Design Up Front
BMUF	Big Modeling Up Front
BoK	Body of Knowledge or Book of Knowledge
BRUF	Big Requirements Up Front
BSA	Business System Analyst
C&C	Command and Control
CapEx	Capital Expense
CAS	Complex Adaptive System
CCB	Change Control Board
CD	Continuous Deployment
CDA	Certified Disciplined Agilist
CDAC	Certified Disciplined Agile Coach
CDAI	Certified Disciplined Agile Instructor
CDAP	Certified Disciplined Agile Practitioner
CI	Continuous Integration –or– Continuous Improvement
CM	Configuration Management
CMMI	Capability Maturity Model Integration
COBIT	Control Objectives for Information and Related Technologies
CoE	Center of Expertise/Excellence
CoP	Community of Practice
CRUFT	Correct Read Understood Followed Trusted
DA	Disciplined Agile
DAE	Disciplined Agile Enterprise
DAIT	Disciplined Agile Information Technology
DAMA	Data Management Association
DevOps	Development-Operations
DW	Data Warehouse
EA	Enterprise Architect or Enterprise Architecture
F2F	Face to face
FASB	Financial Accounting Standards Board
FTE	Full Time Employee
GCI	Guided Continuous Improvement
GQM	Goal Question Metric
HR	Human Resources
IDE	Integrated Development Environment
JBGE	Just Barely Good Enough
KM	Knowledge Management
KPI	Key Performance Indicator

IASA	International Association of Software Architects
ISO	International Organization for Standardization
IT	Information Technology
ITIL	Information Technology Infrastructure Library
IR4	Industrial Revolution 4.0
LoB	Line of Business
MMF	Minimal Marketable Feature
MMP	Minimal Marketable Product
MMR	Minimal Marketable Release
MTBD	Mean Time Between Deployments
MVC	Minimal Viable Change
MRT	Media Richness Theory
MVP	Minimal Viable Product
NFR	Non-Functional Requirement
NPS	Net Promoter Score
OKR	Objectives and Key Results
OODA	Observe Orient Decide Act
OpEx	Operating Expense
Ops	Operations
OST	Open Space Technology
PSCA	Plan Do Check Act
PDSA	Plan Do Study Act
PI	Program Increment
PM	Project Manager
PMI	Project Management Institute
PMO	Project Management Office
PO	Product Owner
PMI	Project Management Institute
QoS	Quality of Service
ROI	Return On Investment
RUP	Rational Unified Process
SAFe	Scaled Agile Framework
SDLC	System/Software/Solution Delivery Lifecycle
SEMAT	Software Engineering Method and Theory
SIT	System Integration Test(ing)
SLA	Service Level Agreement
SoC	Separation of Concerns
SoD	Separation of Duties
SoR	Source of Record
SRS	Software Requirements Specification
TFS	Team Foundation Server
TDD	Test Driven Development
ToC	Theory of Constraints
UAT	User Acceptance Test(ing)
UX	User Experience
V&V	Verification and Validation
VSM	Value Stream Map(ping)
WIP	Work in Progress
XP	Extreme Programming

INDEX

ABOUT THE AUTHORS

Scott W. Ambler is the Chief Scientist at Disciplined Agile, Inc. He leads the evolution of the DA toolkit and working with organizations around the world to help them improve their way of working. Scott provides training, coaching, and mentoring in disciplined agile and lean strategies at both the team and organization level. Scott is the co-creator, along with Mark Lines, of the Disciplined Agile (DA) toolkit and founder of the *Agile Modeling (AM)*, *Agile Data (AD)*, and *Enterprise Unified Process (EUP)* methodologies. He is the (co-)author of several books, including *Disciplined Agile Delivery*, *Refactoring Databases*, *Agile Modeling*, *Agile Database Techniques*, *The Object Primer 3rd Edition*, and *The Enterprise Unified Process*. Scott blogs about DAD at DisciplinedAgileDelivery.com and you can follow him on Twitter via @scottwambler.

Mark Lines is Managing Partner at Disciplined Agile, Inc. and a Disciplined Agile Fellow. He is an Enterprise Agile Coach and co-creator of the DA toolkit. Mark is co-author with Scott Ambler of several books on Disciplined Agile. For over twenty years Mark has helped clients around the world transform from traditional to lean and agile enterprises. He is a frequent keynote speaker at industry conferences and blogs about DAD at DisciplinedAgileDelivery.com. Mark's services include enterprise and team assessments, coaching, workshops, and training. You can follow him on Twitter via @mark_lines

If you would like Scott or Mark to speak for your event or organization, please send a request via the contact form at Disciplined-Agile.com

55593990R00241

Made in the USA
Columbia, SC
16 April 2019